IN MEMORI,

To the memory of Eva Løvbugt Helgetun, the lovely 14-year-old Lutheran Norwegian girl who was gang raped in Trondheim in May 2011 by "three young males of foreign origin" who were never caught. Even with the love and support of her family and friends, Eva began suffering from post-rape depression. Less than a month later, she committed suicide.

DUAL DEDICATION

First, to my father and my grandfather who both survived Nazi concentration camps and were refugees in Europe after World War II. They lost everything yet expected nothing. It never occurred to either of them to be anything but *eternally grateful* to the countries and people that helped them along the way.

Next, to the brave men, women, teens, and children of Europe who are dealing with a massive influx, *not of their making,* of migrants from far-off foreign lands being championed by peculiar politicians, dedicated special interest groups, the old-fashioned-controlled-media, and its controllers. Like the unwitting victims of a home invasion, many Europeans are in a complete state of disbelief. *What's happening? This can't be happening. It will soon stop. They won't hurt us if we do what they ask. Surely, we can reason with them. Everything will soon be back to normal. How did this happen?*

Godspeed and best wishes.

CONTENTS

FOREBODINGS 1

A SERIOUS WARNING UP FRONT ABOUT RACISTS, HATERS, XENOPHOBES, AND OTHER TOOLS OF THE TRADE 8

CRITICAL THINKING & WHAT I'M BEING TOLD ISN'T WHAT I'M SEEING 12

INTRODUCTION 19

ALL EUROPEAN UNION COUNTRIES ARE BOUND BY MIGRANT QUOTAS... WELL, ALL *EXCEPT* FOR ENGLAND, IRELAND AND DENMARK 23

HEY, LET'S JUMP THIS TRAIN TO AUSTRIA, AND WHILE WE'RE AT IT, MAYBE WE SHOULD RAPE THE INFIDEL... 25

JE SUIS CHARLIE *vs.* JE SUIS DAN PARK 29

SEX, BIG LIES, AND VIDEOTAPE 33

LEARNING FROM THE EXPERIENCES OF LEBANON 39

HOW UNEMPLOYMENT FIGURES ARE HIJACKED 43

GET THIS THROUGH YOUR THICK SKULL, YOU'RE A WOMAN, THEREFORE UNCLEAN, AND I'M NOT SHAKING HANDS WITH YOU! 45

THAT INCONVENIENT TRUTH ABOUT GAY RIGHTS, *OR NOT* 49

A QUICK PREVIEW OF SWEDEN - WHERE THEY HAVE BEEN EXPERIMENTING WITH MULTI-CULTURALISM FOR A LONG, LONG TIME. AND THEN A FEW MOMENTS IN NORWAY 56

NO-GO ZONES & BODY ARMOR FOR AMBULANCE PERSONNEL 74

WHEN GERMAN POLICE THROW IN THE TOWEL... 78

CHILD SOLDIERS 81

CHILD BRIDES & POLYGAMY 84

A LOOK AT THE COUNTRIES AND INDEPENDENT STATES OF EUROPE 88

(1) ALBANIA 90

(2) ANDORRA 93

(3) ARMENIA 94

(4) AUSTRIA 96

(5) AZERBAIJAN 102

(6) BELARUS 104

(7) BELGIUM 106

(8) BOSNIA AND HERZEGOVINA 117

(9) BULGARIA 118

(10) CROATIA 122

(11) CYPRUS 127

(12) CZECH REPUBLIC 130

(13) DENMARK 133

(14) ESTONIA 138

(15) FINLAND 142

(16) FRANCE 154

(17) GEORGIA 173

(18) GERMANY 175

(19) GREECE 215

(20) HUNGARY & MEDIA SPIN 228

(21) ICELAND 246

(22) IRELAND 249

(23) ITALY 252

(24) KAZAKHSTAN 263

(25) KOSOVO 265

(26) LATVIA 267

(27) LIECHTENSTEIN 270

(28) LITHUANIA 271

(29) LUXEMBOURG 272

(30) MACEDONIA 277

(31) MALTA 280

(32) MOLDOVA 284

(33) MONACO 285

(34) MONTENEGRO 286

(35) NETHERLANDS	288
(36) NORWAY	293
(37) POLAND	299
(38) PORTUGAL	305
(39) ROMANIA	308
(40) RUSSIA	311
(41) SAN MARINO	314
(42) SERBIA	315
(43) SLOVAKIA	322
(44) SLOVENIA	326
(45) SPAIN	329
(46) SWEDEN	338
(47) SWITZERLAND	416
(48) TURKEY	425
(49) UKRAINE	437
(50) UNITED KINGDOM	441
(51) VATICAN CITY / HOLY SEE	482
THE GULF COUNTRIES	484
HOW WILL THIS "CRISIS" AFFECT THE UNITED STATES?	485
2016. NEW YEAR. SAME OLD STORY	501

FOREBODINGS

"The situation is very, very serious. ... if we do not deliver some immediate and concrete actions on the ground, in the next few days and weeks, I do believe that the European Union, and Europe as a whole, will start to fall apart."

Miro Cerar
Prime Minister of Slovenia

"Sweden is falling apart..."

Göran Persson
Former Swedish Prime Minister (1996-2006)

"It's one step closer to the end of the European Union. The dream of multiculturalism is over."

Jaak Madison
Youngest Member of Parliament, Estonia

"We must control our borders and prevent migrant workers, infiltrators, or generators of terror."

Benjamin Netanyahu
Prime Minister of Israel

"Everything which is now taking place before our eyes threatens to have explosive consequences for the whole of Europe, and is now causing alarm throughout the world… there are millions more intending to set out for Europe, driven by economic motives."

"For us today, what is at stake is Europe, the lifestyle of European citizens, European values, the survival or disappearance of European nations, and more precisely formulated, their transformation beyond recognition. Today, the question is not merely in what kind of a Europe we would like to live, but whether everything we understand as Europe will exist at all."

"No one raised the question of whether the essence of the matter is more about our existence, our cultural identity and our way of life. I do not know for certain what is actually happening, and I do not want to blame anyone; but the suspicion arises that none of this is happening by chance. I am not brave enough to publicly talk about this as a certainty; the suspicion inevitably emerges, however, that there is some kind of master plan behind this."

Viktor Orban
Prime Minister of Hungary

"We have a problem… all deny… nobody say that we have a big problem… but this will give a bad result in the future… If we can unite in Europe, we will be able to combat the Islamization of society. In Norway, there is now a requirement that these Islamists have a prayer room in every school. Their ambition has no limits, but they say they are moderate."

Walid al-Kubaisi
Norwegian writer & film producer
Iraqi Muslim immigrant to Norway

"We need an integration law. We are a liberal and free country. If we give up the foundations of our liberality, we will wake up in a different country."

Julia Klöckner
German Politician

"Why should we provide them with jobs? I'm sick of the bleeding hearts, including politicians. Jobs would settle them here, they'll make babies, and that offer will only result in hundreds of thousands more coming over here."

Eli Yishai
Interior Minister of Israel

"I think most people feel that we cannot maintain a system where perhaps 190,000 people will arrive every year – *in the long run, our system will collapse.*

Margot Wallström
Foreign Minister of Sweden

"Attempts to export a problem that certain countries have themselves created without the input of other members cannot be called solidarity."

Beata Szydlo
Prime Minister of Poland

"People should not be put in opinion straightjackets and should be able to think differently."

Miloš Zeman
President of the Czech Republic

"...we should not look at the flaws of so-called foreign Swedes as a problem. Instead it is we, the white majority, which is so numerous. We have to understand that *we* are the problem, and that we must change *our* ways."

Mona Sahlin
Former leader Sweden's Social Democrats commenting on the *Four Shades of White* report compiled by the Swedish Social Democratic Youth

"Our nation cannot be so overly sensitive in defending other cultures that we stop protecting our own."

Beth Van Duyne
Mayor of Irving, Texas

"Most people think we're only talking about something that will be a problem in 50 years, but we're already seeing part of the problem. If current (birth) numbers hold, every new generation of Spaniards will be 40% smaller than the previous one."

Alejandro Macarrón Larumbe
Author "The Demographic Suicide of Spain

"It is a crazy idea for someone to let refugees into their own country, not defend their borders and say, now I will distribute them among you, who did not want to let anyone in."

Viktor Orban
Prime Minister of Hungary

"... to believe that not a single citizen warrior is among the refugees, is naive. France shows that in matters of security, we cannot make any more compromises."

Markus Söder
Finance Minister of Bavaria

"We have stood up for our values; of freedom of the press, of freedom of democracy, freedom of religion and freedom of expression. Freedom does not mean being free *of* something, but to be free *to do* something."

Angela Merkel
Chancellor of Germany

"I used to think that Merkel was some sort of strong leader. What Merkel has done in Europe is insane."

Donald Trump
American Billionaire & US Presidential Candidate

"If Europe opens its gates, soon millions will come through, and while living among us, will start exercising their own customs, including beheading."

Lech Walesa
Nobel Peace Prize (1983)
President of Poland (1990-1995)

"In the wake of the horrific attacks in Paris, effective immediately, I am directing all state agencies to suspend the resettlement of additional Syrian refugees in the state of Indiana pending assurances from the federal government that proper security measures have been achieved. Indiana has a long tradition of opening our arms and homes to refugees from around the world but, as governor, my first responsibility is to ensure the safety and security of all Hoosiers. Unless and until the state of Indiana receives assurances that proper security measures are in place, this policy will remain in full force and effect."

Mike Pence
Governor of Indiana, USA
November 16, 2015

"Illegal immigration is crisis for our country. It is an open door for drugs, criminals, and potential terrorists to enter our country. It is straining our economy, adding costs to our judicial, healthcare, and education systems."

Tim Murphy
US Congressman

"Europe has not yet learned how to be multicultural. And I think we are going to be part of the throes of that transformation, which must take place. Europe is not going to be the monolithic societies that they once were in the last century. Jews are going to be at the center of that. It's a huge transformation for Europe to make. They are now going into a multicultural mode, and Jews will be resented because of our leading role. But without that leading role, and without that transformation, Europe will not survive."

Barbara Lerner Spectre
Founding Director of Paideia European Institute for Jewish Studies in Sweden

"We have 50 million Muslims in Europe. There are signs that Allah will grant Islam victory in Europe — without swords, without guns, without conquests ... [they will] turn it into a Muslim continent within a few decades... Europe is in a predicament, and so is America. They should agree to become Islamic in the course of time, or else declare war on the Muslims."

Muammar Gaddafi
Leader of Libya (1969-2011)
April 10, 2006 on Al-Jazeera

"The Sweden we knew just a few years ago is now a mere fairy tale. The result is extreme. The rest is silence...self-righteous Swedes, treacherously lulled into a social democratic dystopia of control and political correctness."

Mikael Jalving
Author, Historian, Journalist
Absolut Sverige

"Every month at least 200 churches or places of worship are attacked. Every day, in every region of our planet, we register new cases of systematic violence and persecution against Christians. No other religious community is faced with such hatred, violence and aggression as is the Christian community."

Antonio Tajani
European Parliament Vice-President
December 1, 2015

"In countries where people have to flee their homes because of persecution and violence, political solutions must be found, peace and tolerance restored, so that refugees can return home. In my experience, going home is the deepest wish of most refugees."

Angelina Jolie
American actor and humanitarian
BBC News, 4/8/2004

"... Germany now is somewhere at the edge of anarchy and sliding towards civil war, or to become a banana republic without any government."

Hansjoerg Mueller
German Politician, 2015 Alternative for Germany Party

A SERIOUS WARNING UP FRONT ABOUT RACISTS, HATERS, XENOPHOBES, AND OTHER TOOLS OF THE TRADE

> "The only thing more frustrating than slanderers is those foolish enough to listen to them."
>
> — Criss Jami

Racists, haters, xenophobes, and others with similar prejudices have no place here.

When we set out to investigate what was going on behind the scenes and on the ground during this refugee crisis in Europe, we ran into many roadblocks on official avenues. Undeterred, we took the roads less traveled – side streets and byways – to compile this report of events. Thus, we feel we ended up with something far more valuable than the same old "company line."

The old-fashioned-controlled-media
Our references to the "old-fashioned-controlled-media" refer to the statistically impossible similarities and blatant biases held by so many *allegedly* independent "major news sources." To bastardize the words of the Founding Fathers, the "truths" the

old-fashioned-controlled-media hold are not self-evident – they border more on propaganda and groupthink.

It seems more and more obvious that there is one main *fountain of spin*, and all the major media players drink heavily from it. If today's traditional news sources were anything more than craftily scripted, highly censored, and clearly controlled entertainment vehicles, we wouldn't refer to them as the "old-fashioned-controlled-media."

But the days of Walter Cronkite are gone. *Long gone.*

Silencing debate
Further, during the course of our investigation, we found that many people from all walks of life and from a multitude of demographic backgrounds asked questions about immigration, multi-culturalism, and the "refugee" crisis.

As a reward for their questions and thoughts, many have been labeled, often by the old-fashioned-controlled-media, with a variety of intentionally destructive nicknames such as:

- Racist
- Xenophobe
- Anti-immigrant
- Self-hating black
- Hater
- Pro-white
- White-supremacist
- Neo-Nazi
- Nationalist
- Sell-out
- Klan supporter
- Ethnophobe
- Refuge denier
- Fascist
- Extremist
- Intolerant
- Patriot
- Enemy of the state
- Truther
- Right-winger
- Prepper
- Conspiracy theorist
- Tinfoil-hatter
- Clown

Charming right? For asking questions and doing some critical thinking and reasoning. *Think about that.*

It appears that media outlets and others are using these *tools of the trade*, these very serious accusatory terms, almost indiscriminately, *and often with little or no evidence*, to sway public opinion, to push agendas, and to silence viewpoints from people that don't please them.

No proof and no truth required. What is everyone so scared of?

Think about it.

Shutting people up
It seems that if someone says something irrefutable or thought-provoking, just label them a "racist" and you can marginalize or neutralize them quickly. Think 1950s and the term "Communist," "Commie," or even "Pinko." *Better Dead than Red.* Same kind of stigma and effect, except redesigned for a new age.

Even in Sweden, the one-time posterchild for "freedom of expression," members of the media, in 2013, assisted by a security flaw on a popular internet discussion board, "obtained" the identities of 40,000 Swedes, many of whom had anonymously (or at least they *thought* they were anonymous) posted web comments that the media then deemed "hateful" and proceeded to label the authors as "racists."

These comments, which had so infuriated the media, included references calling refugees:
- invading forces
- rabble
- locust swarms
- enrichers
- cave people
- opportunists

The comments were hardly as hideous as one might have been led to believe by the media's resulting witch hunt. In fact, quite a few of the same terms were used by EU prime ministers, heads of state, and others. Yet in Sweden, "politically correct" is an obsession worthy of demonic possession and nothing less.

By the time the "outing" and very public national "shaming" of the authors was over, people had resigned from positions, lost work, were fired from jobs, and apparently one even committed suicide.

Over expressing their opinions and thoughts.
http://www.thelocal.se/20131212/millions-of-disqus-comments-leaked-to-swedish-group

Think about it
In fairness to the many sides of this "refugee crisis," please restrain from forming attitudes until you finish the book. We further encourage you to do your own research. Most importantly, give yourself an honest chance to form an unadulterated opinion, free from the influences of the old-fashioned-controlled-media.

We know it's hard, maybe harder than a 12-step-program, but as is the case with that program, it so worth it to have your mind back again. We guarantee it.

Further, without free discourse, without honest debate, *free of repercussions brought on by unpopular ideas, new perspectives, or independent opinions*, what can any people hope to end up with save scripted group think and slavery of the mind?

Seriously. Silence debate and you kill thinking.

Unfortunately, as fewer people actively *think for themselves*, it seems easier and easier to tell them *what* to think, and *how* to think it.

Which leads us to *critical thinking*.

CRITICAL THINKING & WHAT I'M BEING TOLD ISN'T WHAT I'M SEEING

"Freedom of the press is limited to those who own one."

— A.J. Liebling

Think back to the days of the Soviets. You might very well have found yourself on a bread line along with hundreds of fellow hungry souls passing the time by reading a third-hand dog-eared copy of the official newspaper telling you how the economy was booming and how things were so much better. *Nyet*, you'd say as you experienced a serious disconnect.

Similarly, as we delve into the "refugee crisis," once you know what to look for, it's hard *not* to see and experience a serious disconnect. On one side you will have what you are *being shown* and *allowed* to read and hear in the old-fashioned-controlled-media – the bulk of which will look, sound, and feel *very* similar and familiar.

On the other hand, often diametrically opposed to what you've been shown and told to think, will be actual events, eye witness accounts, independent and/or amateur video evidence of what happened.

For the record, since we started delving into the European refugee crisis, we have seen countless examples of ostensibly intentional media spin. It is a miracle that anyone can see through the densely crafted smoke screen. Surprisingly, there are quite a few shining lights courageously telling the truth and appealing to reason. Not surprisingly, many of them have been labeled and marginalized.

Interestingly, to date, we have not found the old-fashioned-controlled-media refer to anyone who stood up for their country or homeland or protected their border against illegal activity as a hero, or patriot, good Samaritan, or good anything. Not once.

We don't have the space to delve fully into the mechanics of propaganda and opinion manipulation, but we do touch upon some of "it" in the chapter on "Hungary & Media Spin." It's well worth the read, especially since we go through quite a few very specific examples of how stories were intentionally slanted.

Warning – once you get the gist of it, you'll never be able to hear, watch, or read another traditional news story the same way again. Ever. Whatever the case, critical thinking is fascinating stuff. Which is what brought us here.

How "we" got here
We authors (*no, it's probably not schizophrenia, we'll explain the "we" in a moment*) were happily consuming major media versions of the European refugee crisis for literally years until, quite independently, we ran into an internet story, or blogpost, or video that didn't match the "official" version one bit. Intrigued, we dug further. The more we dug, the more we unearthed stuff that didn't match the "approved" version of events we were reading off the newsstands and watching on television.

So in 2011 we started, informally, to try and outdo each other in the search for real unadulterated events. We took "official" stories from the old-fashioned-controlled-media and scoured the internet for what "really happened." And we found that many times, the two versions couldn't be more different. In 2013, we started compiling our research into a book. By 2014, we had well over several thousand pages. And by 2015, we pared it down, and rewrote it to ensure it was as relevant and as timely as we could make it – which became a seemingly never-ending editing process. Ultimately, we went ahead and published, knowing more stuff would be coming out every minute.

The goal is to tell it like it is on behalf of *true* refugees
As authors, we committed to getting this story out there. Period. We knew that proponents of the "official version of events" would likely try and make "the story" about anything but the truth. And marginalize the message. And distract people with silliness. And anything else to misdirect the spotlight. So we chose one of us to represent all of us – under the penname *Col. Walter T. Richmond* – in the spirit of "Je Suis Charlie" and freedom of the press and to "tell it like it is" on behalf of the many refugees that are *truly refugees* and equally aghast at the mayhem being caused by certain people.

When the offices of French satirical magazine *Charlie Hebdo* were shot up, leaders from most European nations flocked to Paris to walk in solidarity for "Free Speech" and "Freedom of Expression." The big story centered on an affront to liberty, not about each individual satirist killed. Similarly, with this book, the big story is about a mega-crisis, and not about us. In line with that, we wrote the final version with a one-author voice. And we self-published to avoid editors and others who could potentially cut important sections or sugarcoat things to make them more palatable.

We put all our resources together to approach this European refugee crisis with as even a hand as possible, flavored with our considerable life experiences which may include, but are not limited to European historical studies, archeology, business operations analysis, financial and legal services, marine biology, law enforcement, journalism, media and advertising, military, disaster, and emergency services. Our backgrounds could span the continents and our religious persuasions, if we have any, could cover the major ones.

Some may place significance on the fact that among us are direct descendants of survivors of Nazi concentration camps. They were our fathers, uncles, cousins, and grandparents. And they weren't "survivors" who escaped to other lands *before* trouble started. No, they were actually incarcerated, and can be found on the official rolls of prisoners at camps including Auschwitz. This has given us a unique and very personal connection to the plight of true "refugees."

Writing style
Our writing style is rather conversational. Like a chat between friends. Maybe it's the way we feel most comfortable relaying information. And since we aren't compiling an academic tome, you'll see that we shattered, trounced, and ignored a whole volume of "good grammar" rules and writing style guides in the last few sentences alone. Get used to it. We'll be doing a lot more. Sorry, all you style guides. Regrets, Strunk & White.

And, when we start sentences with "and," and when we mix the terms *migrants* with *refugees* with *immigrants* with *wanderers*, get over it. Look past the mere words to get to the big picture. When we say they *swarmed* or *invaded* or *overwhelmed* an area, it probably simply reflects what we saw as we reviewed hundreds of hours of video. Or it could also be our military, or emergency services, or disaster relief, or law enforcement training or street experiences kicking in.

Sources, citations, citings, and sightings
In the old days, our publishers would have insisted that we provide numbered citations and list the sources at the bottom of pages, at the end of chapters, or at the back of the book.

That was then. This is now.

We decided to provide available links to every one of our sources as close as possible to the actual content. If you are reading this as an e-book, chances are you'll be able to link directly to the source documents via an internet connection (at your own risk, of course, since all links are third party sites and we can't and don't guarantee safety, appropriateness of content, or anything else related to those links.).

We felt it important to provide as many links as we could so that you would be able to do your own research, see, view, and often hear things for yourself, confirm what we're reporting, and make up your own mind.

Another warning
While we're at it, this is *not* a book about what "could happen" if everyone behaved. We won't be revealing a grand plan to solve all ills, nor will we be overanalyzing people's actions. Nay. We are reporting on, relaying, and commenting on what we discovered. This book records, to the best of our abilities, what we found to be "happening," not what we were imagining or hoping.

If you require your news heavily cleansed, sugarcoated, or redacted to make you feel all warm and safe and happy, this book is definitely *not* for you –please return this book now for a refund. No hard feelings.

Source checking *Then & Now*
As to the actual content we investigated, we tried to double and triple check stories and sources like the old fashioned journalists some of us still try to be. In the golden age of reporting, sources were checked so many times, your brain started to hurt – and so did the sources' heads, if they didn't get super insulted at some point.

These days, major media outlets seem to pump out content with little if any corroboration, as is witnessed by the massive amount of pure fiction that regularly floods the presses. From imagined military escapades to pretend weapons of mass destruction, from self-drawn symbols of hatred to other preposterous claims, the old-fashioned-controlled-media routinely blames its steady stream of snafus on a lack of time to check facts or no budget to hire fact checkers or whatever is convenient – which all adds up to a bunch of slick professional entertainers mindlessly reading teleprompters and rushing from deadline to deadline without having to think or analyze anything deeper than the next deadline. Although major media outlets seem to be encouraging more and more reporters to blurt out their "opinions," the opinions frequently sound scripted, and are quite often "textbook party line."

> *Q: What do you call a reporter that blurts out an honest opinion that doesn't mesh with the party line?*
> *A: Unemployed...*

At times we've used italics to signify thoughts. Other times we've used italics to break up sections. And we may have also occasionally stressed poignant points within quotes by using italics to help us highlight points.

As we already mentioned, we tried to place most website sources near the sections to which they are related. Instead of having to search through indexes and citations and footnotes, following tiny numbers only to lose your place or disrupt your attention, we reasoned that you could immediately confirm our sources and do your own probing if you so wished. And we also ended up rewriting entire sections as new material came to light. Things are developing so fast that we fully expect that revisions will be constantly required – and therefore everything we wrote is subject to revision, change, and additional fine-tuning as more truths and trends are revealed.

One of the most challenging yet possibly most rewarding endeavors we undertook was to check source materials at their native sources. We spent a large amount of time reading and translating accounts and stories in their many native European languages. While we may have missed some nuances and misunderstood some vernacular expressions, we wanted to be as close to original sources as possible.

We endeavored to ensure accuracy, but will not be held responsible for any errors, omissions, inaccuracies, et cetera. Hey, mistakes happen. However, should you notice corrections, including anything big we missed, or examples we didn't find, especially new content we need to consider for inclusion in future editions, we would be grateful if you would let us know at HastaLaVistaEurope@outlook.com

The Golden Rule
Finally, we believe that every people on this Earth have a right to live free, in peace and harmony, in their own space, pursuing their own cultures, following whatever customs and traditions they fancy, so long as they harm none. To each his own. Live and let live.

Do unto others as you would have them do to you.

Peace.

INTRODUCTION

> "In a time of universal deceit,
> telling the truth is a revolutionary act."
>
> — George Orwell

Europe is doomed.

Make no mistake about it. We are all watching the end of an era. An era when you used to be able to take a jaunt to London to enjoy the local British experience. And vacation in Paris to immerse yourself in French culture. Stay on the Greek Island of Lesvos and stroll on its glistening beaches and enjoy its medieval architecture. Tour Hungary to experience legendary centuries-old European hospitality. And end up in beautiful Dresden, Germany, home to the Kings of Saxony, and one of the ancient centers of culture, education, and finance in Europe.

Used to be able to.

Well, technically, you still can. But the experience is so vastly different that you may be as shocked as you are dismayed.

For instance, the area around Dresden's main train station is now a cesspool of crime. It is the area's main hub for business travel and tourists. Newspapers reported in 2015 that the theft and drug crime wave there was "obviously alarming" and that there is a "climate of fear" just like in similar areas of Berlin, Hamburg, and Frankfurt.

The reporters who went down to Dresden to look things over for themselves said that what they saw made them "shudder."

Shudder? Seeing is believing.

"Desperate businesses, intimidated employees, shocked passersby – criminals dealing their drugs for all to see. This creates a climate of fear - and must be countered swiftly." The reporters said that, "It *cannot be* that a gang of young men can lay claim to an entire area to operate their illegal business."
https://mopo24.de/nachrichten/dresden-hbf-drogen-dealer-razzia-6255

But they did, and do.

Police say the perpetrators are primarily African migrants "from Tunisia, Algeria, and Morocco." These thieves, drug dealers, pickpockets, and other criminals saunter and swagger around with impunity. They attack shopkeepers and pedestrians alike. Police confirmed that stolen property is brazenly offered for sale and that sales "no longer take place in secret but in public."
http://www.bild.de/regional/dresden/drogenhandel/wiener-platz-ist-gauner-platz-41803202.bild.html

Police can't keep up
In the meanwhile, overwhelmed police continued to make many "mass arrests" in the area, but to no avail. The problem was simple. The criminal gangs had become very "tricky" using highly sophisticated drug trafficking methods including lookouts, orders by cellphone, and keeping the actual drugs at arm's length. Case in point – a recent police raid in Dresden

involving dozens of suspects who were searched, only yielded *two* drug arrests. The police reported that this is because the gangs are using the "ant trade." They keep very little amounts of physical drugs on themselves so there is rarely any evidence.
http://www.bild.de/regional/dresden/drogenhandel/dealer-vom-wiener-platz-41819802.bild.html

Hidden facts
Currently, the old fashioned media, the controlled media, the politically correct but morally twisted media, is working overtime to sell its steadily shrinking audience a slanted and biased view of the migrant crisis facing Europe today.

The old-fashioned-controlled-media is supported in its work of creating and spreading propaganda by a variety of players, from pundits to politicians who support whatever plot is personally lucrative, from duped charities to well-meaning do-gooders, and from hopelessly optimistic "nice" people to devious opportunists.

Further, these groups will stumble over each other in an attempt to deny that there is a crisis brewing. They'll prepare excuses for the outrageous misbehavior of the migrants. And they'll work overtime coming up with justifications for any variety of criminal activity the migrants engage in.

The first, and most telling bit of media spin is labeling all of the migrants as "refugees." If only that were true. But it is not. Traditional refugees seek refuge from immediate life-threatening dangers. Natural disasters. Wars. Famine.

But, by their own admission, many of these "refugees" invading Europe are seeking a better quality of life that they envision based on something different, almost aspirational. Maybe it's the vivid pictures of European wealth that the old-fashioned-controlled-media has been painting for years. Throw in some lavish Western sitcoms, some European late night adult television, sprinkle in a generous sampling of Hollywood movies, and the migrants know exactly what they are expecting.

I'm here, so how much do I get?
These refugees have also brought along with them a very healthy sense of entitlement. As one charming migrant stated during an interview, "The salary for refugees decreased..." so he was traveling to another part of Europe that had a better migrant "salary."

You heard that right... But we bet you didn't hear it from the major media.
https://youtu.be/EmqbtyfQ3f8

Or how about the refugees who were enraged and indignant that the Swedish relief workers assisting them didn't provide enough bed lamps, television sets, or washing machines?
https://youtu.be/kGWi8Qyy1CM

Seriously, now, are these refugees like the refugees my grandfather accompanied after living through Auschwitz?

In *Hasta la Vista Europe!*, you'll find no excuses or justifications. No explanations or apologies. No academic theories on why anything is happening, or what to do about it. Just the facts as we found them or uncovered them or saw them for ourselves, and that you can read and see for yourselves as well.

Before we look at the 51 countries and independent states that make up Europe, let's take a look at some happenings that should spark some serious questions about the current "refugee crisis" and what is really going on.

ALL EUROPEAN UNION COUNTRIES ARE BOUND BY MIGRANT QUOTAS... WELL, ALL *EXCEPT* FOR ENGLAND, IRELAND AND DENMARK

> "All animals are equal, but some animals are more equal than others."
>
> — George Orwell

In September 2015, The New York Times reported that in a migrant distribution plan, based on a complex formula and approved* by European Union ministers, 11 EU countries had met the quota, and 14 countries would need to take in more migrants. *Well, actually, the Czech Republic, Hungary, Romania and Slovakia all voted against the scheme.*

Germany, Netherlands, Belgium, Sweden, Austria, Bulgaria, Cyprus, Malta, Italy, Greece, and Hungary would "meet" their imposed quotas.

France, Spain, Poland, Romania, Portugal, Czech Republic, Finland, Slovakia, Croatia, Lithuania, Slovenia, Estonia, Latvia, and Luxembourg would "fail to meet" the imposed quotas and would have to fill up on more migrants to be in compliance.

This caused many disagreements. For example, Poland said that if it tried really hard, it could *possibly* handle 2,000 more migrants. Yet the EU called for Poland to take in 600% more – close to 12,000.

You can pay a "fee" to be left alone for a year
If the idea of thousands of extra migrants attaching themselves to your nation's resources scares you, just pay the EU about .002% of your GDP and they'll leave you alone for a year.

In Poland's case, that would be about 10 million euros.
http://www.nytimes.com/interactive/2015/09/04/world/europe/europe-refugee-distribution.html

Get-Out-of-Jail-Free Cards
Did you notice that Denmark, Ireland, and England (UK) are conspicuously missing from any of the lists? Why is that?

Apparently the migrant strategy was amended by the European Commission, after legal concerns, so that Denmark, Ireland, and England (UK) would "not be required to take part in any quota scheme for housing migrants..." Seems that according to EU law, the EU can't legally force Ireland or England to join in the migrant scheme, and Denmark has a "blanket 'opt-out.'"

Bottom line is, these three select countries have the luxury of participating at their own discretion *and* on their own terms.

It's nice to have special privileges.
http://www.independent.ie/irish-news/ireland-can-optout-of-housing-migrants-under-eu-quota-plan-31218301.html

HEY, LET'S JUMP THIS TRAIN TO AUSTRIA, AND WHILE WE'RE AT IT, MAYBE WE SHOULD RAPE THE INFIDEL...

"Anything is better than lies and deceit!"

— Leo Tolstoy

Following is the powerful and shocking story of a young European woman who allegedly decided to take a trip to Vienna from Budapest, in September 2015.

Could this story be fake? Anything is possible on the internet, but we saw no reason to doubt this account, which was publically posted by a European news agency and featured a lengthy video interview of this woman's personal eyewitness testimony.

Nothing could have prepared the young woman for the scene that met her at the train station in Budapest. According to her story, instead of the orderly, almost machine-like precision that is the Budapest rail system, great roving masses of people, smelly, unwashed, and loud, moved about. As she tried to enter the station, they blocked her way. Then they began shouting insults at her in Arabic and tried to steal her luggage.

She didn't know it yet, but she was about to be on one of the now world famous "refugee trains" that was overrun by migrants trying to leave Hungary for the economic bounty of Germany – and the train was about to become the poster child for, and a symbol of, the "refugee crisis." We all saw the clips and heard the sound bites - tired, maltreated, beleaguered, "refugees" trying desperately to save their lives, crowding onto a train to escape the unimaginable horrors of having to mill about in Hungary.

At least that was the story the old-fashioned-controlled-media was spinning. And it almost worked, save for one thing – this European woman, who might have gone along with this official propaganda, said she is fluent in Arabic and knows the Quran by heart, having lived in Arabic countries for half a decade. As noted in her video, had she not understood Arabic, she may very well have had a different opinion of the events that she saw unfold.

Based on an interview she gave in September 2015, the woman said that as she waited in the station for the train, migrants were relieving themselves wherever they found themselves. They had no shame. There were huge piles of trash everywhere and no one seemed to be able to speak anything but Arabic. Migrant women were shouting as they were hit by other migrants. Children were screaming.

As people passed by, the migrants would lash out with obscenities and grab at their luggage. A far cry from the old-fashioned-controlled-media's picture of fleeing families, the young lady reported that 90% of the migrants she saw that day were healthy men between the ages of 18 and 45.

This will not be the first, nor the last time we hear and see evidence from the street-level that the "refugees" are mostly young fighting-age males.

The young lady was upset that she witnessed men grab random children and use them as "shields" as they pushed forward toward the train. As a ticketed passenger, the young woman took her seat on her assigned train car, along with five other ticketed passengers. The rest of the car was empty. Suddenly, there was screaming, windows began cracking, and like "a black cloud," masses of fighting migrants poured into the train.

According to the woman, as they settled down, the migrants began calmly talking to each other in Arabic, wondering if they should rob the ticketed passengers, calling them "infidels."

The young lady listened in horror as the migrants turned their attention to her and casually began discussing raping her. She said the migrants discussed her clothes, and felt her European style proved she wasn't dressed like a proper woman, and thus she was bad – making her fair game for their desires.

As you continue to read this book, watch for this theme that native women from European countries can be mistreated with impunity. Will you be surprised how many times it surfaces?

When the train stopped and announcements were made saying it wasn't going any further, the young lady and the other four ticketed passengers started battling their way past the migrant masses to exit the train. Per the young woman, at first the migrants blocked the exit while they discussed, in Arabic, taking the young lady and her fellow passengers "hostage."

The young woman said she felt that the train station was "completely under siege," as she allegedly watched migrants who stormed around, throwing the provided relief baskets including bread, apples and biscuits onto the floor, trampling the food as they shouted, "Money.. give us money!" The migrants were shoving and grabbing at people's luggage and other valuables. Based on her eyewitness experience, the young woman concluded that these migrants were in search of "European welfare."

She concluded the interview with a stark and honest assessment: "Aside from hatred, absolute ill-will, they have nothing to give European people... So before we protect these people, I suggest we learn the Arabic language so we can understand and see that while these people are smiling at us, they are spitting at us behind our backs. I saw this with my own eyes."

Was this an honest appraisal? A straightforward account from a real eyewitness? We have been given no reason to feel it was anything but what it was purported to be –a young lady's disturbing migrant experience.

Thank you for the brave warning!

Sadly, *no one* will listen….
https://youtu.be/VjbqJeAyjSM

As the migrants exited the same train in Austria, oblivious Austrians cheered and applauded their arrival, completely unaware of what the young European lady had heard and seen. Volunteers greeted the migrants with food and warm smiles. Children ran to greet them and hug them.

Little did *they* know… but now *you* do.
https://youtu.be/647eKqsFYMs

JE SUIS CHARLIE *vs.* JE SUIS DAN PARK

> "If we don't believe in freedom of expression for people we despise, we don't believe in it at all."
>
> — Noam Chomsky

On the 7th of January 2015, two Muslim militants attacked the offices of a French newspaper, *Charlie Hebdo* known for its parodies. In apparent retribution for anti-Islamic content and, cartoons, and satires, the murderous pair began executing *Charlie Hebdo* staff as they shouted, "Allahu Akbar!"

According to witnesses, as the killers fled the scene they yelled something along the lines of "We have avenged the Prophet Muhammad. We have killed Charlie Hebdo!" The reference most likely referred to the fact that the *Charlie Hebdo* newspaper had often lampooned, made fun of, insulted, and depicted the Prophet Muhammad in ways that many devout Muslims felt was vile and blasphemous.

In the aftermath of the bloodbath, a dozen people lay dead including *Charlie Hebdo* staffers and two police officers. Almost a dozen more people were wounded. Another 5 people were murdered in a related attack at a kosher supermarket. Supporters of free speech adopted the slogan, "Je suis Charlie"

(I am Charlie), as a sign of solidarity with freedom of expression.

Although US President Barack Hussein Obama was not available that weekend, many of the world's heads of state and leaders turned out to show solidarity on Sunday January 11, 2015. More than 40 world leaders joined millions of people who marched (and if they were crammed in too tight, milled about) the streets of Paris in support of free speech, freedom of self-expression, freedom of the press, and resistance to intimidation and threats.
http://kdvr.com/2015/01/07/charlie-hebdo-satirical-magazine-is-no-stranger-to-controversy/
http://www.lemonde.fr/societe/live/2015/01/07/en-direct-des-coups-de-feu-au-siege-de-charlie-hebdo_4550635_3224.html

Elite show up to show support for freedom of expression
Among the dignitaries and world leaders avowing their undying support for freedom of speech, press, and expression were Benjamin Netanyahu (Israel), Mahmoud Abbas (Palestine), François Hollande (France), Angela Merkel (Germany), David Cameron (UK) Jean-Claude Juncker (European Commission), Sergey Lavrov (Russia), Ahmet Davutoglu (Turkey), King Abdullah II and Queen Rania (Jordan), Petro Poroshenko (Ukraine), Sameh Shukry (Egypt), and Swedish Prime Minister – Stefan Löfven.

And therein lies the irony.

While he was marching purportedly in support of the freedom of expression and in support of a newspaper that had printed repulsive cartoons depicting both the Prophet Muhammad and Jesus in the most abominable ways (including but certainly not the least of which were Muhammad lusting after a goat and Jesus having anal sex), in Prime Minister Stefan Löfven's Sweden a street artist, Dan Park, who created satirical posters was found guilty of "offending African and Roma (formerly *'Gypsy')*" people. In 2014, A Malmö court sent Park to jail for half a year and fined him 60,000 kronor. The art gallery owner who displayed the artwork was also found guilty and sentenced, but his sentence was suspended and he ended up paying "only" a fine. Commentators called the sentencing reminiscent of old draconian Soviet and Communist Chinese control techniques.

After serving his prison sentence, Park was out again plastering the streets with his politically charged posters. In October 2015, concerned and alert civilian *wanna-be* thought police in Sweden turned Park in and the real police investigated. While the real police found no grounds upon which to arrest Park, he and his supporters were fined for hanging up posters all over the place.

Ok, we can see that. You don't want stuff attached to every billboard and lamp post and bus stop in town. But what was Park parodying this time?

In one poster parody of a "Refugees Welcome" sign which traditionally features a man, a woman, and a child (even though 70-80% of the refugees are young males), Dan Park went one step further and recreated the emblem as a "Terrorist Welcome" sign with a man carrying a grenade launcher, a woman carrying an assault rifle, and a child in a suicide bomb belt.

Life imitates art, n'est pas?

In the meanwhile, clearly Prime Minister Stefan Löfven is a man torn apart. On one hand he makes a highly publicized and grandiose showing in support of a newspaper that has depicted vile, crass, and sacrilegious "satirical" anti-Jesus and anti-Muhammad content you really *can't* imagine, and on the other hand he sits idly by as a street artist in his own country serves jail time for "satirical" posters. Obviously, Prime Minister Löfven can't belong to both sides concurrently. So was he dishonest when he supported Charlie, or was he duplicitous when he ignored Park?

Either way, could he be a proponent of freedom of expression?
http://www.dr.dk/nyheder/kultur/kunst/hornsleth-og-trykkefrihedsselskabet-viser-kun-skrabet-dan-park-udstilling
http://www.thelocal.se/20140821/swedish-artist-jailed-for-race-hate-pictures

Nowadays, Sweden seems to be wired very differently. As reported by Sweden's Local,
> "In international law, expressed by the European Convention on Fundamental Human Rights and interpreted by the European Court of Human Rights in cases such as Jersild v. Denmark (1994), Gündüz v. Turkey (2003), Erbakan v. Turkey (2006), shows that it is 'of essential importance to combat racial discrimination in all its forms and expressions.'
>
> The court also establishes that 'on principle it can be **justified for some democratic states to punish and even prevent all forms of expression which spread, call, advocate or justify hatred based on intolerance.'"**

We can only guess that somewhere in Prime Minister Löfven's head, depicting Jesus Christ having anal sex, or lampooning the Prophet Muhammad lusting after a goat was worthy of his traveling to a far-off country to make a very public display of support for such "freedom of expression" and that such expressions didn't "spread, call, advocate or justify hatred based on intolerance."

But the creations of a local Swede satirist were just too much!

Aha.
http://www.thelocal.se/20111101/37092

SEX, BIG LIES, AND VIDEOTAPE

> "It's discouraging to think how *many* people are shocked by honesty and how *few* by deceit."
>
> — Noël Coward

Let's start at the end... VIDEOTAPE. Frankly, without millions of hours of independent video posted on the internet by brave individuals, all we would have is the created version of utopia and sanitized events spun by the old-fashioned-controlled-media. Unfortunately, we'll get to the sickening and depraved SEX crimes a bit later.

Which brings us to the middle – the **BIG LIES**.

The number one BIG LIE that the old-fashioned-controlled-media is trying so desperately to sell us is that these "migrants" or "illegal aliens" or "foreign invaders" are really just "refugees." *Some analysts have said that this is akin to calling home invaders "asylum seekers"...*

And if you dare to deviate from the approved script, if you express an opinion based on what you see with your own eyes that isn't up to snuff, you will instantly be labeled a variety of terrible things like xenophobe, racist, nationalist, prejudiced, a neo-Nazi fascist, and possibly even, *gasp,* a democrat. Luckily, after the first several labelings, you won't even notice the sting.

The next BIG LIE, is that mixing these migrants into the European countries will somehow magically make those countries so much better. (Spoiler alert – based on the empirical evidence of the last few years, there is no basis for this provocative claim.)

Rainbows just won't be beautiful rainbows if they aren't rainbows anymore…
Well, that is correct. But the next BIG LIE follows along on the coattails of this universal TRUTH – that "a rainbow is made beautiful by its many distinct and separate colors." And that certainly is TRUE!

The BIG LIE is that instead of keeping the colors distinct and vibrant, that somehow *if the colors are all mixed together into a stew*, that the beauty of the rainbow will be enhanced.

Wrong. It will be destroyed. Ask any school kid who has painted with water colors and they will tell you the truth – if you don't clean your brush, pretty soon everything looks grey. The fact is that if you obliterate the individuality of the colors, your beautiful rainbow is no longer. Sorry, it's just the way it is.

More lies
Some other BIG LIES that the old-fashioned-controlled-media is trying very hard to package and sell, with NO supporting evidence, include:
- Since all people are human, they all *must* have similar peaceful goals
- People of different religious backgrounds show great tolerance towards each other, respect each other's beliefs, and work to ensure that everyone is allowed to believe, or not to believe, in anything they choose

- Local populations are responsible to welcome, house, feed, and entertain any migrants that decide to show up at their doorsteps
- If you don't open your doors and support all migrants gleefully, at a minimum you're an anti-foreigner, but you're probably a hostile neo-racist
- There is something fundamentally wrong with you if you wish to preserve *your* culture, *your* customs, and *your* way of life
- There is something fundamentally wrong with you if, speaking about migrants, you don't protect *their* culture, *their* customs, and *their* way of life
- Multi-culturalism means everyone will join into one cohesive happy family celebrating each other's differences and accepting each other's points of view
- Refugees simply want to be safe – they are running for their lives and would die if they didn't flee
- Refugees are grateful for the safe haven provided to them for free
- Refugees will respect your local customs, dress codes, follow your laws, as they "live and let live"
- Refugees see all women as equals and are respectful to European women, even when they aren't wearing burkas
- Taking in refugees always pays off in the long run and makes a country so much better

And dozens of equally hopeful, naïve, preposterous, or patently dangerous notions being fronted as "truths." People are people, and to try and fit everyone into one box just won't work.

Among the *most dangerous* lies that the old-fashioned-controlled-media is trying desperately to sell us is that the poor refugees are "all pitiable fleeing families with little children."

Which is just not true.

Hiding in plain sight

As you will see, upwards of 70-80% of the "refugees" are reportedly actually young fighting-age males. *When you really take the time to look at enough videos and photos, and study the majority of the people, in the background, and foreground, you will see a preponderance of young men.* Yet, the old-fashioned-controlled-media stumbles over itself in order to portray a completely different reality that is a *fairytale*.

In the news you will almost exclusively see photos and clips of children with their families served up to you. To get those few snippets, the old-fashioned-controlled-media must really have to search hard, since it is not uncommon for witnesses to describe migrants to be made up of 90%, or more, young men.

Imagine the enormous effort you need to invest in order to get that one perfect "family with child" shot.

But when you're busy creating an "alternate reality" in the minds of viewers, every little bit of subtle messaging goes a long way. Especially if it is repeated ad nauseam.

Hmmm. Like the fake "Weapons of Mass Destruction" lie that triggered the Iraq war.

Think about it.
http://www.theguardian.com/world/2011/feb/15/defector-admits-wmd-lies-iraq-war

You know all those cute pictures of your family, and your friends, and your dog on your phone? The migrants are just like us, and have photo collections, just like us...
Hungary's public broadcasting station aired several reports in October 2015 investigating content found on cell phones left behind at Hungary's border by migrants. More than a thousand photographs and seemingly endless video content centered around violence, jihadists cutting off people's heads with swords and other beheadings, dead bodies, terrorist training

exercises, combat videos, mutilated bodies, dead soldiers, all sorts of weapons, torture, knives and daggers, and well, you get the picture. Much of the content was so graphic and disturbing that the reporter said it couldn't be aired, ever.

Just like the photos and videos on your phone, right?

Think about it.
https://youtu.be/6f992PM2qiY
https://youtu.be/silF8UT4mTE

Weasel clauses

Possibly nervous that the *jig was up* and that sustaining the "refugees from war" lie was going to be impossible, the old-fashioned-controlled-media started making a subtle but very noticeable (to those alert members of the public) shift, and adding some version of "and/or escaping economic oppression" hedge to their narrative.

For instance, the finally discredited "refugee families fleeing war" became "people" fleeing to "escape poverty *or* armed conflicts." The simple addition of "or" in that sentence means that even if 0% of the migrants were fleeing war, the sentence was still technically true if people are seeking a better economic future, and who isn't?

Huge difference. Seriously. Think about it.

And then throw in what you *now know*, and *will see* ad nauseam going forward, about the make-up of the migrants – 70-80+% young males of fighting-age...

Think huge. Think "weapons of mass destruction" to "no weapons found" huge...

We predict that with typical insolence, and an ingrained inability to apologize for misdirecting viewers, the old-fashioned-controlled-media will now begin making the stories and narratives about the "poor oppressed masses looking to better themselves." Less mention of war and more about economic hardships and dangerous circumstances. But there will likely be zero retractions about the volumes of misinformation already accepted as truth by most media consumers.

Think "global warming" to "climate change" huge.

Think about it.
http://en.mehrnews.com/news/110888/Serbia-expects-arrival-of-nearly-7-000-refugees

Before we look at refugee-related events in each of the European countries, let's take a look at some interrelated and very relevant but *inconvenient* truths surrounding the crisis.

Each will serve as another small view into the much bigger picture from a window out of which you have *never* been allowed to gaze. Until now.

LEARNING FROM THE EXPERIENCES OF LEBANON

"We learn from history that we learn nothing from history."

— George Bernard Shaw

Lebanon wasn't exactly a booming economic paradise before the Syrian refugee crisis. This ancient Semitic nation's populace was just over half Muslim and a bit less than half Christian, and both religions' holidays were peacefully and respectfully celebrated. Lebanon was known for its beautiful ocean front beaches on the Mediterranean, and half dozen ski resorts, the largest being Mzaar which included massive ski lifts amidst Roman temple ruins.

As the Lebanese Board of Tourism put it, "aficionados can ski from sun-washed peaks, enjoying breathtaking views of the Mediterranean in the morning – and then swim in the sea the same afternoon." That was *then*.

The Switzerland of the Middle East
According to MiddleEastOnline, "Arab and other foreign tourists have still not returned to Lebanon in real numbers since last year's (2006) military conflict with Israel." To try and reinvigorate the ski slope business, a daring lingerie show was

held in Beirut in 2007 in support of the "Switzerland of the Middle East." Then, some few short years later, the Syrian refugee crisis put an end to the old "Switzerland of the Middle East." Between 2011-2013, Lebanon lost almost 1,000,000 tourists, and 66% of its own population is now "poor." That's devastating!
http://www.middle-east-online.com/english/?id=20012

According to the United Nations, Lebanon, a country of just over 4 million citizens, has taken in over 1.5 million refugees from neighboring Syria. Almost 25% of all of the people living in Lebanon are refugees. And all with *no formal camps* or shelters.
http://www.unhcr.org/pages/49e486676.html

Years back, the UN and Lebanon had set up formal camps for the half million Palestinian refugees that now reside in Lebanon, some for over 60 years. But the Lebanese learned the hard way that if you provide permanent shelters, the refugees will be encouraged to settle in permanently. And that's not part of the plan. Or at least it wasn't the intent. Lebanon's Minister of Education added that they are currently schooling at least 140,000 refugee children, and they plan on schooling around 500,000 refugee children in the not so distant future.

So what is the real toll on Lebanon and its citizens? From 2009-2012, Lebanon's annual GDP growth rate dropped from 8.5% to 1.4%. Shattering.
http://www.independent.co.uk/voices/refugee-crisis-lebanon-is-doing-its-bit-to-help-its-neighbour-syria-10509469.html

Partners in deprivation
In a report on the implications of the Syrian refugee crisis on Lebanon, since Lebanon started providing refuge to the refugees in 2011,
- Lebanese citizens have become "partners in deprivation"
- The labor force has grown by 50%

- Unemployment has doubled
- New public infrastructure costs were close to $600 million in 2014 alone
- Additional electric costs and education costs are in the hundreds and hundreds of millions of dollars

How about crime? Does anything specific stand out?

Well, yes.

Since the Syrian refugees were offered sanctuary in 2011,
- "Small crimes" have shot up over 60%
- Lebanese prisons are overcrowded
- More than 25% of the prisoners are Syrians

http://www.sciences-po.usj.edu.lb/pdf/The%20Syrian%20Crisis%20%20its%20Implications%20on%20Lebanon%20-%20Khalil%20Gebara.pdf

So we know that the country of Lebanon has taken in over a million refugees. But the old fashioned media never asks, *how's that worked out for you?*

They should have asked the Lebanese Social Affairs Minister, Derbas. He knows only too well. Derbas said Lebanon's infrastructure, which was projected to last 15 years, has been so worn out and damaged by overuse by refugees, that it will have to be completely rebuilt in less than two years.

He also said that Lebanon is suffering enormous economic losses since refugees are using up natural resources, as well as an enormous amount of electricity, without any ability to pay for anything they consume. And the already beleaguered people of Lebanon are stuck paying the bill for their new guests.

http://news.yahoo.com/syria-crisis-cost-lebanon-20-bn-says-minister-165712453.html

More really bad news – another reported 500,000 tourists have cancelled plans to visit Lebanon, creating even more economic hardship and losses for the Lebanese people.

Think about it.

A little too little
In January 2015, Lebanon finally tried to implement controls over the vast influx of Syrians entering their country. New initiatives in Lebanon called for limiting the number of Syrian refugees allowed into Lebanon while "addressing the rising security concerns."

The Lebanese also planned to *aid their own citizens* while they are helping refugees so that everyone would benefit from humanitarian efforts, not only the refugees.

Sounds like a fair approach. Helping your own family *while* you still help strangers. How long will it take for the old-fashioned-controlled-media to uncover "racism" in that methodology?

Nostradamus Lives
In September 2015, a very concerned Lebanese Minister of Education, Elias Bousaab, warned British Prime Minister David Cameron that 2% of the migrants were *radicals* looking to cause havoc – "terror."

He said most had and *would continue to enter* via Turkey into Greece.

He was sooo right....

Was anyone listening?
http://www.dailymail.co.uk/news/article-3234458/Two-100-Syrian-migrants-ISIS-fighters-PM-warned-Lebanese-minister-tells-Cameron-extremist-group-sending-jihadists-cover-attack-West.html

HOW UNEMPLOYMENT FIGURES ARE HIJACKED

"If you tell the truth, you don't have to remember anything."

— Mark Twain

Beginning in 2011, EU agencies that analyze and report on unemployment statistics haven't been permitted to count as unemployed *those unemployed people* participating in job schemes funded by the government or training programs. Even though these hapless souls are very much unemployed, they "aren't." Well, they *aren't* according to the EU statisticians.

We are most concerned with youth unemployment rates since 70-80%+ of the migrants streaming into Europe are young males.

Where will they work?

With June 2015 youth unemployment rates averaging over 20% (ranging from 7% in Germany to almost 54% in Greece), if the established and often native locals are unemployed in large numbers, and struggling to get by, where will the newly arriving migrants find legal work? If they can't find work, what will they do? And since we don't want to put words in their mouths, and force them to do anything they don't want to do, what if they decide they simply don't want to find work? What will they do then?

Think about it.

Figures don't lie, but liars figure
Sadly, mathematicians will tell you that with no universal formula for determining true unemployment rates, accomplished finaglers can make a set of statistics support a wide variety of conclusions and opinions. Further, there is an extreme bias among politicians and authorities who all want the numbers to be as *low* as possible. To that end, to make the overall results look better, they carve out whole segments of unemployed people who aren't working and can't find work.

The results are called "tightly focused," since they only include very narrowly defined groups and paint a far rosier picture than what truly is happening on the streets. As to how exactly the manipulations are done, we'll look at some specific examples in the chapter on Portugal.

At any rate, it's about to get really bad.

With hundreds of thousands of young males showing up in Europe, exactly where will they work? And what exactly will they do to occupy their time if they can't find work like so many of their "fellow" youths?
http://www.dw.com/en/dodgy-stats-understate-portugals-unemployment-rate/a-18414326
http://ec.europa.eu/eurostat/statistics-explained/index.php/File:Youth_unemployment_rates,_EU-28_and_EA-19,_seasonally_adjusted,_January_2000_-_September_2015.png

GET THIS THROUGH YOUR THICK SKULL, YOU'RE A WOMAN, THEREFORE UNCLEAN, AND I'M NOT SHAKING HANDS WITH YOU!

"Our religion has defined a position for women: motherhood."

— Recep Tayyip Erdogan
President of Turkey
2014 speech at Women's Justice Conference

In September 2015, German politician Julia Klöckner was visiting a refugee camp in Rhineland-Palatinate. She thought she was helping. When she went to shake the hand of the local imam, he refused to shake her hand because she is a woman.

The experience so repulsed Klöckner that she wanted Germany to pass a mandatory integration law so all migrants get on the program from day one, or find their fortunes elsewhere. Klöckner said "The people who want to stay here must, from day one, accept and learn that in this country religions coexist peacefully and we cannot use force to resolve conflicts."

All true, but how terribly unwelcoming on Klöckner's part...

Klöckner also expressed grave concern for the future of integration, citing the example of male Muslims refusing to speak to female schoolteachers about their children. "When fathers say that they do not talk with their children's (female) teachers, you have to ask them how they imagine their future in Germany," said Klöckner.

Good question.

The answer is, they probably don't care what you think. And not just because you're a woman. At the rate Germany is loading up with refugees, "their future in Germany" is that they will soon be able to simply vote you out of office in certain areas.

But thanks for the welfare checks, in the meanwhile.
http://www.focus.de/politik/deutschland/imam-verweigerte-handschlag-kloeckner-fordert-gesetz-zur-integrationspflicht-fuer-fluechtlinge_id_4965163.html

This attitude towards women is not new, but now it can be rather rewarding financially
The case goes something like this... In 2013, in Sweden, a Muslim migrant man is offered an internship with the *Integration Division* (the irony will soon be deafening) at the municipality of Trollhättan. Some would say he was lucky to be working since Sweden's unemployment rate stinks and by October 2015 would be over 15% in good old Trollhättan.

Anyway, back to our fun-loving integrated intern.

So Mr. Intern shows up at his new office and is introduced to his new supervisor. All fine so far, ja? Well, except his supervisor is a woman. Strike 1.

Here comes strike 2. It's a curve ball, so watch out. The female supervisor greets the man and welcomes him by trying to shake his hand. *Really bad move.* How incredibly insensitive and racist! For a woman to offer her hand in a handshake! How awful! And soon to be a very costly mistake.

The man recoiled and "he refused to shake her hand, explaining his religion forbade him from shaking hands with women unless he washed his hands directly afterwards."

The supervisor allegedly mentioned that there was hand sanitizer in the office he was welcome to use if that would help, but that the office couldn't really have an intern that wouldn't shake hands with everyone equally. Strike 3.

Mr. Intern screamed "discrimination!" and filed charges.

In the end, he got bought off. Trollhättan decided to throw him a wad of cash instead of spending months in court defending their actions.

A municipal spokesperson was quoted saying, "By law, a person who feels they've been disadvantaged because of their religion has a right to damages. We made a mistake, we took responsibility for it, and the person was compensated."

Think about it and let that sink in. It hurts, right?

What a stark contrast to the recent case in the United States where Kentucky State County Clerk Kim Davis spent 6 days in jail for not issuing marriage licenses to homosexual couples based on her faith and religious beliefs.

The US District Court judge who chose to imprison Ms. Davis instead of simply fining her, said, "Our form of government will not survive unless we, as a society, agree to respect the US Supreme Court's decisions, regardless of our personal opinions. Davis is certainly free to disagree with the Court's opinion, as many Americans likely do, but that does not excuse her from complying with it. To hold otherwise would set a dangerous precedent."

Imagine if Ms. Davis had been a Muslim working in Sweden. She likely would have been enriched rather than jailed. Also, the judge might have had a rude awakening if he tried to favor secular law and turn his back on her rights to her religious beliefs and practices.

In the meantime, I'm headed for Trollhättan, Sweden to get an internship. Once I'm settled, I'll mention that my religion (*The New Church of Sloth*) forbids me from actually doing any real work, anytime. *Where's the big screen for my video games?* Oh, so you racists can't use an intern that doesn't actually do work? Ok, ok, so how much are you going to pay me off so I go away?

You know, there's a precedent now...
http://www.thelocal.se/20130520/48008
http://www.thelocal.se/jobs/article/50756
http://www.latimes.com/nation/la-na-will-she-or-not-kim-davis-20150914-story.html

THAT INCONVENIENT TRUTH ABOUT GAY RIGHTS, *OR NOT*

> "It (homosexuality) does not augur well in building the very foundations of society - stability, family relationships. And it is something we would certainly not, in any form, encourage the community to be involved in."
>
> — Sir Iqbal Sacranie
> *Knighted* by Queen Elizabeth II in 2005
> Founding Secretary General of the Muslim Council of Britain

Chancellor Merkel talks a big game when it comes to welcoming migrants and painting grandiose visions of assimilation and peaceful coexistence. Yet, even a cursory search of the internet and university library resources quickly revealed a huge chink in Merkel's armor. While Germany protects the rights of lesbian, gay, bisexual, and transgender people, and Ms. Merkel has said that discrimination on the basis of sexual orientation won't be tolerated, many of the people she has *and is* inviting to take up residence in her country may hold *very* contradictory views.

But instead of guessing or putting words in people's mouths, let's hear it from them directly.

A Muslim caller to a popular British radio talk show in 2015 laid it out. She said, "My religion is very clear what happens to gay people, you know what it says about gay people. I don't know what the exact punishment in the Koran is, but it is the death penalty. I believe the Koran is the word of God."
http://www.mirror.co.uk/news/uk-news/listen-muslim-woman-telling-radio-6692687

Sharia law
Sharia law is Islamic law. It is often the basis for the legal code in most Muslim countries and covers all aspects of life including religious obligations, personal conduct, manner of dress and appearance, daily routines, family relations, marriage and divorce, and even financial interactions and inheritance. Sharia law stems from the Quran and the teachings of the Prophet Muhammad.

A proponent of Sharia law being implemented worldwide, Dr. Muzammil Siddiqi (*Harvard University PhD., in charge of UCLA religious studies, past president of the Islamic Society of North America, author, radio talk show host, invited by a US President to lead interfaith prayer services at the National Cathedral and at Ground Zero*) wrote:

> "Homosexuality is a moral disorder. It is a moral disease, a sin and corruption... No person is born homosexual, just like no one is born a thief, a liar or murderer. People acquire these evil habits due to a lack of proper guidance and education. There are many reasons why it is forbidden in Islam. Homosexuality is dangerous for the health of the individuals and for the society. It is a main cause of one of the most harmful and fatal diseases. It is disgraceful for both men and women. It degrades a person. Islam teaches that men should be men and women should be women. Homosexuality deprives a man of his manhood and a woman of her womanhood. It is the most un-natural way of life. Homosexuality leads to the destruction of family life."

These are very strong and direct statements from a highly respected academic and thought leader (when's the last time *you* led a prayer service at Ground Zero at the personal request of a US President?). He tells it like he believes it. And we have no reason to believe that he is anything but sincere and true to his faith and beliefs. And we suspect that he does speak for many many Muslims around the world.

In an interview in the San Francisco Chronicle, Dr. Siddiqi told the reporter, "I ask those people to repent, turn to God and take Islam seriously. Being gay and Muslim is a contradiction in terms. Islam is totally against homosexuality. It's clear in the Koran and in the sayings of the prophet Mohammed." While Dr. Siddiqi didn't suggest that violence should be aimed at gays, he did support the laws in nations where homosexuality was punishable by death.

Again, we have no reason to believe that these views are anything but his sincere beliefs.
http://www.islamandafrica.com/islam_homosexuality.html
http://www.islamopediaonline.org/fatwa/dr-siddiqi-north-american-fiqh-council-responds-question-what-islamic-manner-talking-about-hom

Stoning gays to death
Quite a few of the migrants hail from countries that take their views on homosexuality very seriously. As in literally *stoning-to-death* seriously. According to the Washington Post (2-24-14) the ten countries where homosexuality was punishable by death were:

- Yemen
- Iran
- Iraq
- Mauritania
- Nigeria
- Qatar
- Saudi Arabia
- Somalia
- Sudan
- United Arab Emirates

So, how do you integrate hundreds of thousands of refugees who may firmly believe that your EU anti-discrimination laws protecting homosexuality are merely secular verbiage while their faith and religious beliefs leave little to the imagination?

And how about the many thousands of migrants that come from countries where they grew up *knowing* that homosexuality was such an abomination, such a "heinous crime," that it was punishable by death? And death by stoning, no less?

Of course, we may be concerned for no reason whatsoever.

Maybe someone in the EU has already prepared a mandatory "new citizens assimilation" class designed to integrate people that may hold unchallengeable beliefs that will not mesh with the nation's beliefs or laws. *Surprise!* If anyone has thought that far ahead, we haven't found them. And if the assimilation program exists, we'd love to see the class material and especially the instructor's handbook.

And we'd really like to see the Pass/Fail results from the final exams.
https://www.washingtonpost.com/news/worldviews/wp/2014/02/24/here-are-the-10-countries-where-homosexuality-may-be-punished-by-death/

Racist gay pride parade
In a very twisted bit of irony, when Pride Järva, a gay pride parade, was organized in Sweden for the summer 2015, and routed to go through some highly Muslim areas of Stockholm, the government-supported Swedish Federation for Lesbian, Gay, Bisexual and Transgender Rights (RFSL) denounced the organizers of the gay pride parade as "pure racist" and "xenophobic" provocateurs since the parade route included a walk through a predominantly Muslim neighborhood.

Yes, yes, one group of gay activists was attacking another group of gay activists and calling them "racists" because that group was planning to march through a Muslim part of Stockholm. You read it right. No need to go back.

Far from making any Islamophobic comments, instead, one organizer responded, "The same laws of assembly and expression should apply everywhere, regardless of the area or population."

True, but soooo naïve. Trying to hold on to old European ideas in the new European whirlwind is maddening indeed.

The gay pride parade went off without much trouble, but one alleged police officer who worked the parade route reported engaging in conversations with "young people" who held strong and inflexible *beliefs* that being gay was "disgusting," "unnatural," "spreads diseases," and many more similar convictions.

The only reported disruption to the actual gay pride parade itself was when a group of *gay anti-parade protestors* showed up and heckled the official *gay pride participants* calling them "racists." As they had no permits, the gay anti-parade activists were quickly dispersed by police.

Clear signals from local youths
At the end of the parade, participants and supporters gathered in a park and celebrated. It was reported that several neighborhood "youths" passed by and shouted anti-gay hate speech. Later, it was reported that there had been multiple assaults near a subway station, where local neighborhood youths had beaten up some gay people. As police investigated, neighborhood youths continued to shout homophobic slogans at the gay participants and tried to intimidate them.

One police officer noted that the *anti-gay* views held by some people were identical in spirit to *anti-migrant* views held by others – and that the key to changing such beliefs would be to "calmly and respectfully" explain to these prejudiced people the error in their "insulting and illogical values."

Sounds like a plan, officer dude. Since it was your idea, you go first. Probably you should write out your best arguments and points so you don't forget them as you're pelted with stones by the youths. And to get the best instant feedback, maybe go to a NO-GO zone and use it as a testing ground. And let us know how that goes for you. Us? Oh, we'll be in the squad room brewing coffee and catching up on reports.

And what exactly is a Swedish NO-GO zone? It will be explained in the upcoming chapter named "NO-GO ZONES & BODY ARMOR FOR AMBULANCE PERSONNEL."

To the naïve go the boils…
http://www.blazingcatfur.ca/2015/07/21/sweden-democrats-plan-gay-pride-parade-through-muslim-areas-leftists-and-gay-rights-groups-decry-the-parade-as-racist/
https://www.facebook.com/events/1607616332820322/
http://www.independent.co.uk/news-19-4/sweden-right-wingers-plan-lgbt-march-through-stockholms-muslim-majority-neighbourhoods-10415932.html
http://www.csnaz.com/pride-jarva-and-hate-crimes-in-husby/

All the commotion will soon be moot after everyone is vaccinated against the homosexuality "virus"
Has Big Pharma finally lost their minds? An anti-homosexuality vaccine? Well, no. In October 2015, P4 Swedish Radio ran a story about a Muslim imam in Sweden teaching that when raising children it is essential that parents insure that their children have good immune systems to protect them from the viruses in the Swedish community such as homosexuality.

Homosexuality is a virus?

And, you guessed it, no outcry from the old-fashioned-controlled-media or the political correctness police.
http://sverigesradio.se/sida/artikel.aspx?programid=128&artikel=6267837

Must be stoned
On January 10, 2016, according to police reports from Dortmund, a group of North African teens attacked two transgender women. The teens originally approached the women to "get friendly" but upon realizing that the women were transgender, the boys insulted and harassed them, attacked them, and ripped at their hair and breasts.

Then the women were "tossed around" as the North African teens threw stones at them. Dortmund police responded and arrested the three boys.

According to the police report, the suspects said that "such people (transvestites) must be stoned."
http://www.presseportal.de/blaulicht/pm/4971/3222010

In the meanwhile, regardless of what side of the fence you fall on, it appears that, no matter how you spin it, no matter how deep you bury your head in the sand, and no matter what you desperately wish for, Europe is headed for a BIG change.

And the LGBT community, which has fought for, gained, and enjoyed many basic human rights under the *old* European regime, may be in for a *very* rude (or worse) awakening.

A QUICK PREVIEW OF SWEDEN - WHERE THEY HAVE BEEN EXPERIMENTING WITH MULTI-CULTURALISM FOR A LONG, LONG TIME. AND THEN A FEW MOMENTS IN NORWAY

> "Sweden has been naïve... I was dismayed that we have people (Muslim Swedes) who sympathize with and want to fight for these evil powers (ISIS)."
>
> — Stefan Löfven
> Prime Minister of Sweden

Forget the great Swedish Empire and the Vikings and the highly advanced culture that existed in 3,000 BC. Forget Swedish notables such as Saint Bridget (among Europe's patron saints), Alfred Nobel (Nobel Prize founder), and Dag Hammarskjöld (quiet diplomacy).

Sweden, the largest of the Scandinavian countries, has been taking in "refugees" for a long time...

It started many years ago. In the aftermath of the violent American race riots, Swedish Prime Minister Tage Erlander addressed Sweden's Parliament in 1965 saying,

"We Swedes live in a so infinitely happier situation. The population in our country is homogeneous, not just according to race but also in many other aspects."

One could say that the Prime Minister was happy that his nation's homogenous population enjoyed a wonderfully peaceful existence compared to the unrest in America.
http://www.frontpagemag.com/fpm/137565/taking-sweden-back-ingrid-carlqvist
http://www.thelocal.se/20151119/swedish-pm-country-naive-about-terror-threat

Only a few years later, in 1968, a motion from the Rightist Party to the Parliament, on page 149 said "The disappearance of a culture is always a loss, no matter how small or large the group is which supports the culture in question. Therefore, it seems important to us that Sweden, besides the application of a proper immigration policy for the country, also feel responsibility for the organized minorities and offer their cultures opportunity for continued existence and further development on Swedish ground."

Great humanitarian plan, but it seems the only "group" whose culture the Swedish Parliament neglected to preserve and protect was that of the native Swedes. More on that soon.

Re-creating Sweden
Then, in 1975, the Parliament decided to "recreate" Sweden *officially* as a multicultural state. The general thought was that the immigrants would bring and cultivate the best of their own cultures and values and experiences, *share* these with Sweden, all the while *assimilating* into Swedish society – one big happy extended family.

Plan in hand, the Swedes went all out.

By 2010, over 14% of the population of Sweden was reported to be foreign-born, the majority being non-Europeans. In fact, in 2013-2014, the top 3 fastest growing foreigner groups in Sweden were from the Middle East and Africa (Syria, Eritrea, and Somalia).

In mid-2013, it was reported that those seeking asylum in Sweden were being offered furnished new homes and a typical family could expect to receive an additional $2,500 in monthly cash to spend anyway they desired, all from the generous Swedish welfare system.

Attracted by such generosity, by January 2015, over 21% of the population had foreign backgrounds.
http://www.scb.se/Statistik/BE/BE0101/2012A01x/be0101_Fodelseland_och_ursprungsland.xls
http://www.thelocal.se/20150115/a-portrait-of-sweden-in-ten-statistics

This orchestrated demographic shift didn't just happen in the large cities either. In 2014, the small 65,000 person town of Sodertalje (outside Stockholm), became a majority Syrian and Iraqi town. Within a few years, native Swedes were the new minority, but without any of the many protections and privileges afforded minorities. And many of the immigrants had no intention of embracing Sweden and assimilating. Why bother to learn new languages, new ways, and follow new rules when you don't really have to do any of that to get your housing, your welfare checks, or your other benefits?

As the International Business Times reported, "The lack of assimilation has driven a wedge between native Swedes and the immigrants living in Sodertalje, and the influx of nonworking immigrants has meanwhile stretched social services and increased pressures on schools, housing and health care."

From an assimilation standpoint, a native Swede said, "the immigrants are more likely to embed themselves with the culture and language they know, eroding the likelihood of them integrating into Swedish culture or even bothering to learn the language."

We can afford all this altruism, *right?*
Worse yet, the native Swede noted that, "Sweden's basic approach to granting asylum has been that refugees would eventually become taxpaying residents. But industrial decline means that job opportunities have diminished."

> *Translation:* A huge piece of the plan where immigrants eventually *put in* instead of *take out* has evaporated.

That's huge. Think about it.
http://www.ibtimes.com/syrian-iraqi-refugees-are-half-population-swedish-city-1619232

One pundit asked, "how much more would Swedes have if they didn't have to support an enormous group of non-contributing guests?"

As far as EU analysts are concerned, the Muslim population will reach 40% of the total population in Sweden by 2030. And Swedish economic experts estimate that *at least 70-80% of welfare payments in Sweden go to Muslims.* That was based on 2010 figures in a 2011 study. The situation has only worsened.

So the answer is, "No one really knows." But we can only wonder what plan "B" is.
https://affes.wordpress.com/2011/07/16/ekonomiskt-bistand-i-24-kommuner/#more-4144

When in doubt, throw the native Swedes out!
Economically, the grand plan seems to be deathly flawed. Money is tight and getting tighter. Which brings up the next natural concern – place. Or more accurately, space. Where are you housing all your new guests?

In 2012, a report showed that Sweden had so overstretched in trying to accommodate refugees that certain towns had started evicting retired Swedes from housing projects and apartments to make room for newly arrived migrants for which the town governments would get lucrative state aid. When asked by a journalist to comment about the housing shenanigans that favored immigrants over native Swedes, a local politician said, "You must have racists there, godam nazi pig."

Not surprisingly, the media sided with the towns and politicians, so the victims were left out to dry. In incident after incident, the retired, "pensioners," the elderly, the infirm, almost exclusively native Swedes, were being moved out of their housing to make way for the immigrants.

Oh, and it's so much worse than you can guess. Imagine you lived through two (2) world wars, and survived! I bet you'd think that the worst was behind you, far far behind you, right? Well, unless of course, a town in Sweden was spending so much money on refugees that they needed to cut some corners...

In a bit of cruel and twisted irony, around 2012 it was reported that in the city of Oskarshamn, a 103-year-old Swedish woman was evicted from her senior housing, along with 4 other Swedish pensioners in their 90s, so the local city government could "save money." You guessed it – Oskarshamn has been spending big bucks on housing for refugees.

I mean, how do politicians sleep at night?
https://youtu.be/7pLB1sAPfgA
http://avpixlat.info/2012/07/04/kommunen-ska-spara-103-ariga-anna-vraks-fran-aldreboendet/

Open season on retirees
In Munkedal, in August 2015, some 400 retired Swedes were ousted from their senior hall, where they previously enjoyed activities such as meetings, dances, parties, movies, and the

like, so that an entrepreneur could turn their space into a lucrative (for himself) haven for refugees.

Ironically, adding insult to injury, these native Swedes will be among the taxpayers footing the bill for this refugee housing project.

It will be a cash cow – as one politician put it, "It's an income for the municipality to get new citizens." Translation: the town will get a chunk of change for each refugee they take in. Unfortunately, after two years, those payoffs end. And the grand scheme collapses *unless* the immigrants are employed, paying taxes, and have their own apartments by then – a complete fantasy if the current trends and statistics hold true. http://swedishsurveyor.com/2015/05/28/swedish-pensioners-evicted-so-as-to-make-room-for-asylum-seekers/

Fine. So maybe the economic part of the plan is warped, but surely that whole part about "offering immigrant cultures the opportunity for continued existence and further development on Swedish ground" has got to be doing well, right?

Let's see how it has affected native Swedes.

Scared to offend non-Swedes, Sweden has gone to extraordinary levels to be as welcoming and thoughtful as possible to the foreigners arriving to its lands. Actually, "extraordinary" may be too tame a term.

No Displaying Swedish Flags, Unless You're Burning Them!
Who can forget when authorities banned the wearing of the Swedish flag? What? The old-fashioned-controlled-media didn't highlight that story? I bet not. Here's what happened.

It was picture day at an elementary school in Karlshamn, Sweden, in 2007. Some kids wanted to be photographed wearing their favorite national soccer team shirts with a Swedish flag on them. Soccer. Sports. Flags. Team spirit. Cool?

Oh no, no, no, you little racists!

The school principal forbid children to show up to be photographed wearing *any* clothes depicting the Swedish flag as he was frightened people looking that the photos might think that the clothes were "a political demonstration."

The principal was quickly ridiculed but he wouldn't change his ruling, saying that if the children wore Swedish flags, they would risk *ruining their reputations* and become known as the *"the racists from Karlshamn."*

Seriously?

Using this simpleton's definition, the Olympics must be the world's *most* racist events. All those uniforms with flags...
http://www.thelocal.se/20070905/8401

Swedish flag, national anthem, and other Nazi symbols
Also in 2007, a 13-year-old boy showed up to his school in Kuriren wearing a sweater featuring the Swedish flag on the front and an excerpt of the Swedish national anthem on the back. *Horror of horrors!*

The boy's panicked teacher told him to take it off, or wear it inside out. When the confused boy refused, he was summarily thrown out of his classroom.

Quick! Shield those impressionable young eyes from the ghastly sight of a kid wearing a sweater with the nation's flag on it!

The principal of the school called the boy's mother and said that if the boy should *ever* wear the sweater again, he would not participate in classes and would sit in a separate room.

Clearly the American Revolution would NEVER have happened in today's Sweden...

The poor mother, who must have been hoping this was all some sick joke, wanted clarification that school officials had sent her son home for wearing a sweater with the country's flag on it. The all too serious principal explained yes, and that the school had policies against such potential Nazi displays.

Nazi??! Long before the Hogan's Heroes TV sitcom about Nazis and POWs, there used to be a time right after World War II in the Bronx, when you were losing an argument with someone who was running circles around you, that you could regain a bit of ground by blurting out "Nazi." It didn't make up for the lack of substance to your position, but it pretty much silenced further argument.

Yes, the principal reportedly told the mother that the sweater could be perceived as hate speech promoting "Nazis."

A Swedish flag on a sweater promotes Nazis?

The young boy now was in the position of defending himself, to profess unequivocally that he was *not* a Nazi, and that he was just a kid who got a sweater because he thought it looked really neat. He had been excited to wear his country's flag, but his enthusiasm had been harshly extinguished.

In the meanwhile, the deputy principal of the school warned that the "school has a policy against clothing that can be perceived as offensive." The nation's flag is offensive? *Offensive??*

Think about that one.
http://www.kuriren.nu/nyheter/flaggan-portad-i-skolan-1459555.aspx

Maybe there is something in the water

More definitive proof that stupidity can be spread by casual contact came in 2014 at a school in Halmstad, when students received a memo from the principal stating that the display of the Swedish flag would not be tolerated *except* on a few official calendar flag days. Again, the flag of Sweden had become potentially "offensive against ethnic groups."

When the school banned the Swedish flag, it stated that displaying it could very well be considered a *hate crime*, and that wearing it in yearbook photos would be considered unacceptable "political expressions" of nationalism.

The school claimed it was necessary to ban the national flag in order to keep students from offending certain people, and to keep them from committing a "hate speech" crime. The official memo prohibiting the Swedish flag, reminded students that their "school photos must obviously be free of national symbols and weapons."

Seriously? As serious as a hate crime, apparently.

There is definitely something in the water
In the meanwhile, only a year prior, at the same school, the Culture Department in collaboration with the *National Public Art Council* commissioned 20 graffiti artists to cover 180 square meters of student lockers with their artwork. Included was the work of an artist that specialized in female genitalia.

And she didn't disappoint.

A large part of her mural features the lower extremities of a woman, her spread legs clad in fishnet pantyhose, and her open vagina featured prominently.

Oh so seriously...

Citing the importance of freedom of expression, and its power to move boundaries, the school authorities and their supporters vehemently defended this graphic symbol claiming that art is meant to generate debate.

One defender said, "It is good that art affects and even upsets. It is a part of art's mission."
http://nyheteridag.se/nu-forbjuds-skolelever-att-anvanda-svenska-flaggan/
http://www.halmstad.se/upplevagora/2013/nationelltmediafokuspasondrumsskolansgraffitikonst.10245.html

So art and freedom of expression are vital, and if art causes debates, or even upsets people, well that is fine since that's part of art's mission. Especially a huge vagina.

But wearing the nation's flag is a hate crime? *Seriously?*

Smiles make everything better
Had the leadership at the Halmstad school only had the guts to get some advice from the leadership at the school in Nykoping, things may have *never* gotten so far.

Didn't hear about Nykoping? The strong and courageous leadership there fought for, and won, the right to prominently display at their middle school a symbol they deemed inspiring and wondrous.

Swedish flag? National anthem? An elk? Not even close.

At some point, the middle school (for 13- to 15-year-olds) at Nykoping commissioned and paid for artwork from that same graffiti artist, who specializes in vaginas and ovaries, and she created an enormous mural of a woman's spread legs, clad in fishnet stockings and featuring her gaping open "smiling" vagina.

Seriously? Oh. So. Seriously.

What were they thinking?? Just because the other school got away with it, we'll make ours bigger and better?

Well, yes and yes.

While a few brave politicians and parents protested and tried to have the gaping smiling vagina mural removed in 2014, saying that the "art" was inappropriate for 13-year-old pupils to have to look at daily, the school would have none of it. No one was going to tell them what they could and could not display for all to see!

It wasn't a cursed wretched Swedish flag after all…

The school's unwavering headteacher staunchly defended the mural and the graffiti artist, saying "I see many *pedagogic* advantages to having her art in the school."

> "Pedagogic" has *bad* written all over it (and it sounds bad, too… Peda? Gog? Ick?) but it just means "educational" – as in the headteacher thinks that a mural of a woman's spread legs, clad in fishnet stockings and featuring her gaping open "smiling" vagina at a middle school is somehow "educational."

Forget that most of the students at that school are younger than the sexual age of consent in Sweden. Why not sex them up early?

A local politician added, "Should we censor this just because it depicts female genitalia? Maybe the students think this is a really cool thing, that they have a school who dares!"

Dares what? To be absurd?

Back to the matter at hand. Did you notice the contrast?

Enormous porn art at schools for youngsters = ok.
Attracts immediate support for the "art" from authorities and others.

Swedish flag on a shirt = hate speech.
Attracts immediate condemnation, from many directions, with severe penalties thrown in.

Now why is that ? Think about it.
http://nyheteridag.se/nu-forbjuds-skolelever-att-anvanda-svenska-flaggan/
http://www.bbc.com/culture/story/20140124-is-this-what-you-think-it-is

As will often be the case as we proceed, we're not close to finished. Not by a long shot.

Obviously the national anthem is offensive
At the 2015 graduation of the Ljungby high school class, the headteacher forbid the display or waving of Swedish flags, or any other flags at this truly international school. He also forbid the singing of a version of the national anthem explaining, "We do not want anyone to feel offended on this joyous day."

International flags and the national anthem would offend graduating students? Seriously?

One brave politician opined. "Is it any wonder that more and more (people) trust in the SD (Sweden Democrat party), when our own national anthem and flag are taboo?! When can we be proud of Sweden without being afraid of being called racists and creating debates?"

Interesting point, but it may be way too late.
http://www.thelocal.se/20150610/multicultural-flag-ban-at-student-graduation

Burn baby burn!
In the meanwhile, some have said that *burning Swedish flags* has become the rage – from virtually no incidents to a new tradition and national past time amongst migrants.

On the 6th of June in 2014, Sweden's official flag day, a group calling itself 365-movement encouraged people to "hunt down" Swedish flags, burn them, and post pictures of the roasts. The group called the Swedish flag, "the ultimate symbol of the nation state, the racist construction that sets up the boundaries between people."

In support of the idea, about 100 people gathered at Malmö's People's Park to burn Swedish flags. Police took away some people for "disturbing public order" but dared not to arrest anyone.

In June 2015, an editorial in Borås Tidning, one of Sweden's oldest newspapers, stated that simply flying "a Swedish flag on the balcony is usually regarded as a signal of xenophobia," the dislike of foreigners or racial intolerance.

So native Swedes are committing hate crimes by wearing or displaying Swedish flags, but others burn them with impunity.

Think about it.
http://www.expressen.se/kvallsposten/flaggor-brandes-pa-nationaldagen-i-Malmö/
http://samtiden.nu/3190/flagga-stolt/
http://www.bt.se/ledare/en-langtan-efter-gemenskap/

What about the police? Aren't the police trying to maintain law and order? It can't be that bad, right?

Cops keep out!
In 2012, a news crew interviewed a young male Muslim gang member who controlled the entrance and exit to his gang's part of town. When asked by the reporter about the police, the migrant said that the police don't dare come around and pointed to a huge graffiti warning to police that said, "Those who kill police go to paradise."

Well that pretty much says it all.

Hey, coppers, you've been warned. *Now scram!*
https://youtu.be/JTAH86qg4l8

Crime statistics tell an unpopular story
Speaking of law enforcement, apart from hate crimes based on displaying Swedish flags, what else is going on? Well, car thefts are down 68% since 2004. But house burglaries are up 17%

since 2003. And with some 1.4 million crimes reported in Sweden in 2013, if you're in a room with a dozen people, chances are that about 1½ of them either committed a crime or were victims of crime.

Or something like that.
http://www.thelocal.se/20150115/a-portrait-of-sweden-in-ten-statistics

According to the Swedish National Council for Crime Prevention, in 1950, the time from which the stats were initially tracked, there were 2,784 crimes per 100,000 people in Sweden. In 1975, the year that the multiculturalism plan was launched, the number went to 9,221 crimes per 100,000 people. By 2014, Sweden saw that initial base number jump more than 500% to 14,890 crimes per 100,000 people.

Anyone need those dots connected?
http://www.bra.se/bra/bra-in-english/home/crime-and-statistics/crime-statistics.html

And the crimes aren't just against property.

According to a 2013 Swedish Public Radio report highlighted by LiveLeak.com, "Muslims raped over 300 Swedish children and 700 women in first 7 months of 2013. In the first seven months of 2013, over 1,000 Swedish women reported being raped by Muslim immigrants in the capital city of Stockholm. Over 300 of those were under the age of 15. The number of rapes is up 16% so far this year compared to 2012 numbers. A large proportion of the increase include rape of young [pre-teen] girls."

As you will see in the chapter on Sweden, this is just the tip of an enormous and ugly iceberg.
www.liveleak.com/view?i=de1_1394099792#X3bky83JAm4IGEbd.99
http://sverigesradio.se/sida/artikel.aspx?programid=103&artikel=5612131

Well, the Swedish results are very disturbing. Out of curiosity, how about neighboring Norway?

Shock of all shocks, Norway has similar experiences
In 2013, four Muslim immigrants, ages 15-18, gang raped, multiple times, a 12-year-old Swedish girl on a school playground in Namsos, Norway. All four confessed, but defended the rapes, claiming the aggravated assault on the preteen girl had been consensual.

So are they doing hard time? Locked away for a long long time?

Nope.

Unbelievable as it seems, in the spirit of multiculturalism and tolerance, the prosecutor, Kaja Strandjord, only asked for a punishment of *community service.*

Further, the Namdalingen Court found that 12-year-old had "voluntarily participated" in gang sex. Ultimately, the four rapists paid fines, and three of the rapists got community service.

To add insult to injury, *one of the rapists was also found to have raped yet another minor girl, and was fined again.*

And in a stranger twist, during the trial it was uncovered that the youngest of the confessed rapists might have been younger than previously thought, *so he was acquitted purely based on his extremely young age during the time he had actually participated in the gang rape.*

He still paid a fine, though.

http://fyret.nu/
https://shariaunveiled.wordpress.com/2013/10/14/norway-four-muslims-gang-rape-a-12-year-old-girl-and-only-receive-a-fine-and-community-service/

It has been going on for a long long time
Just look at Norway's capital city, Oslo. In 2010, the Oslo Police Department, issued a report detailing that *all* (100%) of the sexual assaults involving rape over the preceding 5 year period

where the rapist could be identified were committed by "non-western" (immigrant) males. Virtually all the victims were ethnic Norwegians.

One of the Norwegian women that had been raped stated that her assailant, a Pakistani asylum seeker, told her that because of his religion he had "the right to do exactly as he wanted to a woman... since women do not have rights or opinions, he was in charge."
https://youtu.be/rPNO2BVT1NM

A 2012 television report noted that the prospects for native Norwegians appeared bleak. Scared Norwegian women had reportedly begun to die their blonde hair black, and only traveled in larger groups. After all, many of the resident and regularly arriving asylum seekers have stated that they have no respect for European women.

Norwegian therapist Kristin Spitznogle revealed in a broadcast interview that the rape problem is mostly Muslim men raping non-Muslim women. She added that the Muslim men see women who don't wear the Muslim head covering as fair game for rape, and as "the Norwegian whores," clarifying that when she says "whores" she is "really just referring to their own words – this is what they (migrant men) told the journalists."

Spitznogle also stated that the left wingers in Norway have been blaming the victims of rape for getting raped, "because the whole notion that Islamic culture is dangerous to women is very politically incorrect here."

So for fear of political correctness (what exactly is political correctness? I mean, with so many politicians ending up in jail, what is so correct about politics?), rape victims get blamed so as not to offend the Muslim attackers. Seriously?

Sit and be quiet while we have our way

According to *Alarm! Thoughts About a Culture in Crisis* author Hanne Herland, "not all values from Islamic countries or culture are excellent to bring in to the European society, and I think that many times the Norwegians fear to speak about that, in fear of being called a racist."

So, Norwegians sit in fear of expressing their thoughts while migrants rape and pillage with impunity.

Luckily, Iraqi Muslim, former refugee and legal immigrant to Norway (in 1981), and a well-respected Norwegian writer and film producer, Walid al-Kubaisi, had no such concerns.

He warned of impending doom, saying in various places and at various times:

> "We in Norway have an extreme naivety based on something called "snillisme" in Norwegian culture that gives us hope that the Islamists will change. I believe that the history of the Brotherhood shows the opposite. They do not change... They also talked about... world domination."

> "I believe (there is) a double discourse: There is one for the Western public and another that they don't talk about. When they speak Arabic among themselves, these ambitions (world domination) pop up."

> "If we can unite in Europe, we will be able to combat the Islamization of society. In Norway, there is now a requirement that these Islamists have a prayer room in every school. Their ambition has no limits, but they say they are moderate."

"Most of the areas where the Muslim is the majority, the Norwegian feels that they are not in their country, that they're not in Norway. They feel like (they're in) a Muslim country."

"We have a problem...all deny... nobody says that we have a big problem... but this will give a bad result in the future..."

It did.

So why wouldn't it continue to deliver bad results? And what can the EU learn from all of these practical experiences?
https://youtu.be/xoiCYwoJKrE
http://www.clarionproject.org/analysis/walid-al-kubaisi-muslim-brotherhoods-two-faced-discourse

NO-GO ZONES & BODY ARMOR FOR AMBULANCE PERSONNEL

> "Every society gets the kind of criminal it deserves. What is equally true is that every community gets the kind of law enforcement it insists on."
>
> — Robert Kennedy

Is it *really* all that bad? Aren't you just highlighting a few rogue dandelions on what is otherwise a beautiful pristine lawn?

You be the judge.

In late October 2014, Svenska Dagbladet media reported that there were 55 "NO-GO" zones in Sweden. According to the media outlet, "The number of residential areas in Sweden where the **police cannot maintain law and order** now totals 55."

The National Criminal Intelligence Section has identified the geographical areas where "local criminal networks are considered to have a major negative impact on the environment. There are areas where showdowns among criminals can result in gunfire on the streets, where the

residents do not dare to testify and where the police are not welcome."
http://www.svd.se/55-no-go-zoner-i-sverige-minner-om-parallellsamhallen_4051399

By the way, the politically correct term for no-go zones is "exclusion zones." But "no-go" sounds so much better.

Troubles began with routine and often violent attacks on firefighters, ambulance crews, and postal workers entering those areas. When those public servants began requesting police escorts, the police found themselves under attack as well. The migrant gangs that control these NO-GO zones continuously send clear messages to Swedish police – *back off or else.* The gangs have tried to blind officers with lasers, they have stoned their cruisers, blown up court houses, torched and destroyed police vehicles, have shot hand rockets and fireworks at police cars, and have followed police officers to their homes after work.

The 55 NO-GO zones include many differing areas in Sweden from parts of Stockholm to Gothengurg to Landskrona. Landskrona was where a gang of more than 50 thugs cornered 2 police officers. Things looked mighty grim. Worse yet, the officers frantic calls for help *forthwith* were *officially ignored* by a police commander who didn't want to "upset" the migrants and "escalate things"...
http://www.expressen.se/gt/har-beskjuts-polisen-med-raketer-av-gang/
http://dailycaller.com/2014/11/02/swedish-police-release-extensive-report-detailing-control-of-55-no-go-zones-by-muslim-criminal-gangs/

I can assure you, dear reader, that those of us with law enforcement backgrounds or experience just got sick.

To put it in perspective for the civilians out there, imagine calling the '911 emergency' number and being told "Sorry, we can't help you, it may offend or upset your attackers."

It could have ended really really badly had one of the officers not recognized a few residents he knew, and the residents were able to convince the thugs to let the officers leave alive.

As you probably guessed, these NO-GO areas are almost exclusively populated by non-Swedes. By the way, it is important to know that most of the migrant residents are not thought to be criminals – they are simply living in dread, and therefore routinely refuse to cooperate with police for fear of the various ethnic gangs that control the streets.

In the meanwhile, the police are talking about various plans to try and regain control of these dangerous areas.

Good luck with that.
https://polisen.se/Aktuellt/Rapporter-och-publikationer/Rapporter/Publicerat---Nationellt/Ovriga-rapporterutredningar/Kriminella-natverk-med-stor-paverkan-i-lokalsamhallet/
http://fof.se/tidning/2015/5/artikel/darfor-okar-de-kriminella-gangens-makt

Bulletproof vests on the ambulance

The Chairman of the Ambulance Association in Sweden in late 2014 said that they were requesting riot helmets, body armor, bulletproof vests, leg guards, and gas masks for ambulance personnel due to the marked increase in violent incidents.

Insisting on the necessity for these drastic measures, the Chairman added, "For those exposed to enemy fire or knife attacks, this is reality."

He pointed to the multiple incidents of ambulance crews being targeted for violence and also shot at.
http://mobil.svd.se/nyheter/ambulansfacket-kraver-skyddsutrustning_svd-4094045

Open season on police, too

Violent and dangerous attacks against police have become so commonplace that some Swedish police departments are starting to install shatterproof glass on their patrol cars.

Ever since migrant protesters started throwing large heavy stones at the police during the 2013 Husby migrant riots, local police report being pelted with stones and bricks weekly. Many officers have been injured.

We can attest based on street-patrol experience that even small stones and pieces of brick can be very dangerous, if not deadly.

In one incident, a violent gang of migrant boys dropped boulders from a bridge and hit a police bus, shattering the windshield, sending glass flying everywhere. While amazingly no one was blinded, one police officer had glass splinters lodged in his mouth.

Unfortunately, most patrol areas have yet to install the new shatterproof windshields and police officers are concerned about their safety as anti-police violence continues to grow.
http://www.svt.se/nyheter/regionalt/stockholm/nya-super-rutor-ska-skydda-polisen-fran-stenkastande-gang

Well, Sweden certainly is in trouble. But surely the German police have it all figured out, ja?

WHEN GERMAN POLICE THROW IN THE TOWEL...

> "We have freedom to demonstrate in Germany, but there is no place for incitement and insulting people who come to us from other countries."
>
> — Angela Merkel
> Chancellor of Germany

Towards the end of 2014, German news giant DieWelt ran a story about a report from the Office of Criminal Investigation that said that police in Hamburg were overwhelmed by a crime wave being orchestrated by mostly young African migrants. DieWelt said that the report showed the "helplessness of the police officers" to stem the rising crime rate.

The situation back then was bleak. It has only worsened.

Hamburg free-for-all
Back in 2014, reportedly over 1,000 unaccompanied migrant minors (usually ages 14-17) from Africa were roaming the streets of Hamburg and engaging in all types of illegal activity.

DieWelt mentioned a recent criminal break-in where the 3 burglars were 12, 13, and 15 years old, and pointed out that to encounter such very young criminals is "no longer a rarity" and they are "almost always refugees who have come without their parents or guardians to Hamburg."

Here are some additional highlights from the official report:
- "Even the slightest controversy can quickly lead to aggressive offensive and defensive behavior. The young people involved come together in groups, support each other and or to fight each other..."
- "The young people quickly dominated pickpocketing and robbery. They frequently burglarize homes and vehicles, but these crimes may often be listed as trespassing or vandalism because the youngsters were just looking for a place to sleep. Shoplifting for obtaining food is commonplace. When they are arrested, they resist and assault [police officers]. The youths have no respect for state institutions."
- "The young people are often irreverent, and exhibit a marked lack of respect for local values and norms when dealing with other people."
- "The behavior of highly delinquent young people towards police officers can be characterized as aggressive, disrespectful and condescending. They are making it clear that they are indifferent to the police..."

Unfortunately, the state chairman of the German Police Union said he fears Hamburg will "experience a significant increase in crimes by the group" of young African migrants. Worse, due to the young ages of the children committing the serious crimes, German authorities are reluctant to deport them.

Fast forward to July 2015. Hamburg police were trying to make Hamburg safe again for tourists. Unfortunately, you already know what they were facing.

This time, police attempted to put a dent in pickpocketing. There were 20,000 incidents by the end of 2014. That's over 50 crimes a day. Every day. 365 days a year. And, no surprise, the trend is up, up, up.

Seems thieves were targeting people in crowded locations such as train stations, department stores, or at major events. Victims would be pushed or punched or asked for directions and then "relieved" of cell phones and cash.

The head of Federal Police inspection Hamburg said that 90% of the suspects were foreigners, mainly from North Africa and Southeast Europe. After a 5 week effort, police had caught 78 perpetrators. Nice police work but sadly only a drop in the bucket.

You will likely recall this chapter when you read the disturbing story at the end of the book about the shocking Hamburg New Year's Eve 2016 mayhem.

As far as making Hamburg safe again for tourists, after New Year's Eve 2016, we're not betting too many knowledgeable people will be choosing to stroll around the city any time soon.
http://www.welt.de/regionales/hamburg/article134823100/Polizei-kapituliert-vor-kriminellen-Fluechtlingskindern.html
http://www.ndr.de/nachrichten/hamburg/Offensive-gegen-Taschendiebe-Erste-Erfolge,taschendiebe112.html

CHILD SOLDIERS

> Childhood should be carefree, playing in the sun; not living a nightmare in the darkness of the soul."
>
> — Dave Pelzer,

In 2008, the United States criminalized the use of children as soldiers under the newly enacted *Child Soldiers Prevention Act*. According to Human Rights Watch,

> "The Act makes it a federal crime to recruit knowingly or to use soldiers under the age of 15 and permits the United States to prosecute any individual on US soil for the offense, even if the children were recruited or served as soldiers outside the United States. The law imposes penalties of up to 20 years, or up to life in prison if their action resulted in the child's death. It also allows the United States to deport or deny entry to individuals who have knowingly recruited children as soldiers."

Sen. Richard Durbin, the Democrat from Illinois, introduced the legislation and issued a statement saying:

> "The United States must not be a safe haven for those who exploit children as soldiers. Period. The use of children as

combatants is one of the most despicable human rights violations in the world today and affects the lives of hundreds of thousands of boys and girls who are used as combatants, porters, human mine detectors and sex slaves. The power to prosecute and punish those who violate the law will send a clear signal that the US will in no way tolerate this abhorrent practice."

At the time, at least 27 countries had used, or were known to be using children as soldiers or militants, some as young as 10 or younger, to assist in their warring efforts. Between 2001 and 2007 these included:

- **Afghanistan**
- **Angola**
- Burma
- **Burundi**
- **Central African Republic**
- **Chad**
- Colombia
- **Cote d'Ivoire**
- **Democratic Republic of Congo**
- **Guinea**
- India
- Indonesia
- **Iran**
- **Iraq**
- **Liberia**
- **Occupied Palestinian Territories**
- Nepal
- Philippines
- **Republic of Congo**
- **Rwanda**
- **Sierra Leone**
- **Somalia**
- Sri Lanka
- **Sudan**
- Thailand
- **Uganda**
- Yemen

The highlighted (**bold**) countries are also nations (or areas) from which many of today's refugees in the European refugee crisis are emanating. Forbes Magazine reported that some 300,000 children soldiers were taking part in conflicts all over the world.

So when you see "young fighting-age males" streaming in from countries notorious for cultivating children soldiers, do you wonder? Are you at all concerned, *just a little bit,* about children trained in the use of military weapons, deadly fighting techniques, and taught to settle conflicts by killing the enemy?

Is anyone screening for child soldiers?

Think about it.

Recently, US President Barrack Hussein Obama said he felt it was in the best national interest of the United States to make special specific allowances for Chad, Libya, Central African Republic, South Sudan, Yemen, Rwanda, Somalia, and the Democratic Republic of the Congo. So, President Obama signed various "Presidential Determinations" that removed some or all of the restrictions on US arms trade and other dealings with those countries, even though they use children as soldiers.

Seriously?
https://www.hrw.org/news/2008/10/03/united-states-president-bush-signs-law-child-soldiers
http://www.state.gov/documents/organization/135981.pdf
https://www.whitehouse.gov/the-press-office/2012/09/28/presidential-memorandum-presidential-determination-respect-child-soldier
http://www.forbes.com/sites/realspin/2012/12/09/for-child-soldiers-every-day-is-a-living-nightmare/
https://www.whitehouse.gov/the-press-office/2014/09/30/presidential-memorandum-determination-respect-child-soldiers-prevention-

CHILD BRIDES & POLYGAMY

Way Too Young to Wed

International child advocacy group *Save the Children* issued a report "Too Young to Wed" that shows child marriage has more than doubled in Syrian refugee communities.

> "Data collected by UNICEF shows a quarter of all Syrian refugee marriages registered in Jordan now involve a girl under the age of 18." Some are as young as 13. The report also shows that about half the girls "are being forced to marry men *at least* 10 years older than they are."

As you can guess, the physical and psychological damages to little girls are many.
https://www.savethechildren.org.uk/sites/default/files/images/Too_Young_to_Wed.pdf

We'll be forced to revisit this sickening topic later on, in the chapter on the Netherlands, where girls as young as 12 are being legally "reunited" with their aging husbands. Crazy but true.

Now let's look at polygamy.

Three may be company, but four is a nice income stream
Polygamy is illegal in Germany. But that doesn't stop many Muslim migrants from having multiple wives according to a special report aired on April 29, 2013, by German news giant RTL.

The RTL broadcast revealed that in the Berlin-Neukölln area, which is more than half Muslim, one third of the Muslim men are "married" to multiple wives.

They featured the mayor of Berlin-Neukölln stating "Polygamy is a fact. It is practiced," and that he has warned about this for a long time. He said that often school teachers are the ones who casually discover that a child has a second or third mother.

One young Muslim male, whose father had two wives, defended the practice saying, "Yes, most men have several wives, that's completely normal with us. I mean, among Muslims it's completely normal these days... of course, one can do it in Germany too."

So what's the big deal?

Polygamy was traditionally reserved for wealthy Muslims (twice, thrice, or quadruple the family size means a lot more expenses), not to mention the reported average 25,000 euros for a Turkish-Arabic wedding, plus another 10,000 euros for jewelry. Big ticket stuff. So how do migrants of modest means hope to foot the initial bill and then the added ongoing family expenses? Relax. In today's Germany, you really don't have much to worry about.

What was that? No worries? Where's the extra cash coming from? Oh, don't tell me...

RTL reported that in Germany, one man can only be married to one woman, and the marriage is registered with the government. Muslims are married in religious ceremonies performed by imams. There is no central registry for Islamic marriages so it is *virtually impossible* for German authorities to detect or confirm Islamic marriages. And with 80+ mosques to choose from in Berlin alone, if you planned it properly, you could easily get married a handful of times without arousing much suspicion.

And that is the root of the problem.

Here is how RTL showed the "fraud at the taxpayer's expense" works. The ultra-generous German "Job Centre" provides social welfare assistance to people in need. Knowing this, a Muslim man in Germany would reach out to a local woman he fancies, or maybe invite a woman to come over from, say, Syria, to marry him and help extend his family. After a few dress rehearsals on how to answer questions regarding welfare needs, it's off to the Job Centre to apply for welfare.

It's quite the cottage industry
A counsellor revealed to RTL that he's never seen a migrant woman have to work since these secret second and third wives get welfare payments each month to help with rent and living expenses from the Job Centre. And since they are coached to say they are *single mothers with children, and that they don't know who the father is*, they qualify for and get even bigger welfare checks.

A serious win-win for the man who now is pulling in loads of extra cash monthly for each of his wives posing as *"single-mother-no-idea-who-fathered-my-children"* welfare recipients. And since we already know that Islamic marriages aren't centrally recorded, it is really hard to stop the shenanigans or get caught. Case workers reported their hands "are tied" and they "cannot really do research."

Seriously, is this the same country that makes luxury sports cars and precision tools?

RTL questioned staffers at the Job Centre and determined that the widespread fraud is "an open secret." One unidentified staffer said while he agreed that it was fraud, "but I'm not allowed to say it like that."

Not allowed? Not allowed to call fraud *against taxpayers* fraud?

Luckily, the press relations woman at the Job Centre cleared up all the confusion. She explained it to RTL this way, "I believe these cultural differences are very sensitive, we are a very tolerant country... Germany is very sensitive, very tolerant."

Very tolerant indeed! Or, probably more accurately, *very tolerant to a fault!*

The *multi-wife-cash-machine* practice was widespread in 2013, and was growing. With so many hundreds of thousands of new migrants arriving in Germany, being a wedding planner may mean job security for decades to come.
https://youtu.be/zTIjbiIiUuI

Well, if the last few chapters didn't raise some serious doubts or hoist more than a few red flags about the whole refugee crisis, a quick look at what has been going on in each of the 51 countries and independent states that make up modern Europe might help solidify the deal.

Hang on tight, this won't be pretty.

A LOOK AT THE COUNTRIES AND INDEPENDENT STATES OF EUROPE

"Let us keep our minds open by all means, as long as that means keeping our sense of perspective and seeking an understanding of the forces which mold the world. *But don't keep your minds so open that your brains fall out!* There are still things in this world which are true and things which are false; acts which are right and acts which are wrong, even if there are statesmen who hide their designs under the cloak of high-sounding phrases."

— Walter Kotschnig
US Deputy Assistant Secretary of State
Smith College Speech 1940

In the following chapters, we will look at each of the 51 countries and independent states that make up Europe today. We'll try to touch on what we've found, what we haven't found, and anything else that may have struck a chord.

Sometimes we'll include a brief history of the country and throw in some interesting facts, sometimes not.

When we use some version of our signature tagline, "Think about it," don't assume we agree or disagree with the content. We simply are asking you to "think about it" and form *your own opinion* based on facts and your own research.

As to the many website links, we provide those as citations and references. We don't endorse them, we don't necessarily agree with them, or support them. We don't know if, NOR DO WE GUARANTEE, that the links are safe, or active, or trustworthy, or aren't malicious, or whatever.

Again, follow any and all links at your own risk.

> Here's something else we noticed. *Articles and videos have been disappearing.* Seriously.

Since we started doing our thousands and thousands of hours of research and investigation, we saw web content, articles, and videos containing less than flattering views of migrants that would mysteriously disappear. Sometimes the content simply no longer existed. Sometimes a notice was posted saying the content had violated copyright laws, had been removed, or was no longer available. Occasionally, we'd find another copy that someone had made and reposted. Many times not. Therefore, we tried to provide a summary of what we saw and heard for each source cited – so should the source video or content be "disappeared" in the future, for any reason, the description would have a chance to live on.

(1) ALBANIA

Named by the New York Times as one of the top four global tourist destinations in 2014, Albania is suffering from its own refugee problems. A steady influx of Kosovo refugees fleeing war have been pouring into Albania for years.

In September 2015, Edi Rama, the Prime Minister of Albania, was quoted in Italy's Corriere Della Sera as saying "Albania is a small country and it is difficult for us to give advice. We have not been confronted with such a challenge because they (migrants) prefer to go north towards Germany... But when we hear about walls... against refugees, we think about 1999 when we received half a million Albanians from Kosovo... If we were able to accommodate them, surely Europe can do it [now]."
http://www.balkaninsight.com/en/article/albania-would-welcome-refugees-premier-says-09-16-2015

Also in September 2015, the International Business Times indicated that Albania had agreed to accept 75,000 Syrian refugees from the EU. That's a huge commitment for a country that has a total population of just under 3 million people.
http://www.ibtimes.com/syrian-refugee-crisis-albania-says-it-will-take-75000-seeking-asylum-2105030

There are no examples we could find of migrants residing in Albania lashing out.

Curiously, as Albania was agreeing to *accept* tens of thousands of refugees, Albanians themselves were *fleeing* Albania in droves. On the road is where we noticed a few examples of *Albanian* immigrants in Europe getting into trouble.

For instance, in September 2015, an 18-year-old Albanian man and an 80-year-old Pakistani man were waiting for lunch to be served at a shelter in Germany. The Albanian man reportedly grew impatient, jumped a barrier, pushed his way to the front of the food line, and got and ate food. A while later, the Pakistani man caught up to him and called him out on his line cutting. The Albanian hit the Pakistani in the face and fighting ensued, culminating in 300 Albanians and Pakistanis rioting, throwing benches, flinging steel rods, swinging clubs, and using pepper spray.

Only a month later, in October 2015, it was revealed that Albanian gangs at the Hamburg refugee shelter in Germany were apparently charging non-Albanian migrants to use the showers. This resulted in a violent fight between Albanian, Afghan, and Syrian migrants, and involved knives, metal bars, and a possible gun, with one volunteer aid worker among the five people injured.
http://www.express.co.uk/news/world/610421/Migrant-crisis-mass-brawl-Germany-refugees-charge-shower

In May 2015, Albanian asylum seeker applications submitted to Germany were in first place, outnumbering asylum seekers from Syria. But without any proof of actual persecution, virtually none of the Albanian refugees were being approved.

In fact, so many Albanians were setting out specifically for Germany to seek their fortunes, that the German government took out ads in late June 2015 in popular Albanian newspapers with the headline "**No economic asylum in Germany**."

The ad further explained the legal requirements to be considered for asylum and warned that

- "Germany rejects, on principle, asylum applications submitted for economic reasons."
- "Looking for work, poverty, or illness are not acceptable as reasons to claim asylum."
- "Do not give up your livelihood in your current place of residence and ruin your children's future! After you return to Albania, your situation will be even more difficult."

Were the ads effective? Not so much. By September 2015, Albanians were now the *second* largest group of asylum seekers applying to Germany after Syrians.
http://www.tagesspiegel.de/politik/anzeigenkampagne-in-albanien-warnung-vor-wirtschaftsasyl-in-deutschland/11968368.html

But still no examples of migrants misbehaving *in* Albania.

(2) ANDORRA

The principality of Andorra is home to about 85,000 people and lies between France and Spain. It is not an EU member. Some 10 million tourists had visited Andorra annually, especially for its skiing, providing for about 80% of its total GDP. Recent economic downturns have cut into the tourist industry and the government has instituted some austerity measures. As far as we could tell, Andorra is not currently being affected by the refugee crisis.
https://www.cia.gov/library/publications/the-world-factbook/geos/an.html

(3) ARMENIA

Thousands of refugees have taken up living in Armenia, a country of only 3,000,000 residents. Over 15,000 of the migrants are ethnic Armenians who had been living in Syria. Many others are Syrians. The United Nations has programs that provide new arrivals with equipment to start businesses in their fields. But the "good life" for migrants isn't guaranteed.

In a scenario that will soon sound all too familiar, unfortunately, Armenia is still suffering from terrible poverty levels affecting its own people. It has yet to get back on its own feet economically, after participating in a major war. It is so bad that Armenia has sent hundreds of thousands of its own citizens to other countries in search of work. It's a recipe for disaster as the Armenian government is increasingly seen as pro-migrant, and anti its own citizens.
http://www.al-monitor.com/pulse/originals/2015/07/syrians-displaced-armenia-origin-situation.html#
http://www.aljazeera.com/indepth/features/2015/04/syrians-armenia-refugee-story-150412132753714.html

The stats prove how ridiculous this system is – as of December 2014, the United Nations reported that just about 18,000 of the world's refugees *originated from* Armenia, while just about

18,000 refugees were *residing in* Armenia. As many people seem to flee Armenia as settle there...
http://www.unhcr.org/cgi-bin/texis/vtx/page?page=49e48d126&submit=GO

Most of the first person video evidence surrounding the migrant situation in Armenia centered on poor housing conditions in a country whose economy is faltering. From what we could see, the story really is that for Armenia to be doing *anything* for migrants is quite amazing based on its own financial instability.
https://youtu.be/HmnWhMDWu7s

A late June 2015 protest in Armenia, where police were accused of using excessive force and water cannons to disperse the crowds, focused on increases in electrical rates, and poverty in Armenia. The protesters were a mix of people all upset about deteriorating economic conditions.

But, as far as refugees in Armenia causing havoc, if there were instances, we didn't find them.
https://www.youtube.com/watch?v=BBXQ4ih_NS4

(4) AUSTRIA

Who could forget the horror of the human smuggling truck, abandoned in Austria, filled with the dead bodies of 71 asylum seekers discovered in August 2015. Most of the dead were males. A shocked world condemned the opportunists that provided the lethal transportation services.
https://youtu.be/CtBHcrbbxps

September 2015 saw Johanna Mikl-Leitner, Austria's Minister of Internal Affairs point out that migrants that got to Croatia or Slovenia had, in fact, reached "safe countries." As such, the migrants had to stay put and seek asylum there. Based on the evidence that these so-called asylum seekers rarely apply for asylum in Croatia or Slovenia, Ms. Mikl-Leitner suspected that this behavior "suggests they are not looking for safety but are choosing the most economically attractive countries."

Well, yes. Of course. And we'll repeat this insight in the Croatian and Slovenian sections again.

Ms. Mikl-Leitner promised that "if refugees arriving from Slovenia and Croatia to Austria seek asylum, we will return them to Croatia and Slovenia."

Maybe that will send a message to economic opportunists.

Or maybe they'll just claim to be Syrians and better rehearse their "stories" to stack the odds for asylum success.
http://www.b92.net/eng/news/region.php?yyyy=2015&mm=09&dd=24&nav_id=95551

In a most deceptive media spin sound bite, Voice of America reported on September 22, 2015, that the Austrian town of Bad Radkersburg was the "new hot spot for refugees fleeing war and persecution."

As Ms. Mikl-Leitner stated earlier, these migrants had already reached safe countries, like Croatia and Slovenia, so they were no longer "refugees fleeing war and persecution." Instead, they were **economic opportunists**, moving through perfectly safe countries to get to the richer wealthier areas they desired.

And what's not to love about Austria? Voice of America said the arriving migrants received, food, drinks, new clothes, and shelter. Nice gig if you can get it.
http://www.voanews.com/media/video/2973504.html

None of this is all that new, however.

In November 2013, some of the 52,000 refugees living in Austria at the time, demonstrated about their "horrible" living conditions and "demanded their rights."

One Pakistani migrant, sporting a fashionable new jacket with a $500+ Canon digital camera hanging around his neck, whined about overcrowding, sleeping and eating quarters, and toilets.

Well-meaning Austrians supporting the "rights of refugees" made strange comments about how the European Union needs to *do more*. No one mentioned any of the countries in the Middle East, and what part of the burden they should shoulder. Guess it's a European thing.
https://youtu.be/wFLM-X_GWUg

In 2013, a refugee in Vienna sporting a "refugee Protest Camp Vienne" t-shirt, demanded that Austria provide better housing, jobs, and no deportation to unsafe countries. This young man equated his shelter with a "prison," saying that 20-25 people in a room means "the situation is very bad." His authority? Well, this charming fella knew that the Austrian shelter was identical to a "prison" because of his personal prison record.

That's right. Seems this serial prisoner served prison time in "Pakistan, and *a lot of other*…. and in Kashmir" (see video marker 0:52-0:56).

Too bad he caught himself just as he was about to reveal where "a lot of other places" that he was incarcerated were. Man, that would have been interesting viewing. What a character. Oh well.

Then he said "the staff is very very bad… They're not treat like human being… nobody knows when he will get an interview appointment, when he will get the result, after one year? After one month? After five years? After six years?"

So, he and his fellow migrants showed up in Austria, and were really upset no one was in a hurry to decide whether or not to accept them. The food and supplies and shelter kept coming, but that wasn't enough. Towards the end of the interview, he summed up his frustration with the slow asylum approval process with the following gem, "They *can't* trust us."

Interesting that the title of the video is "They *don't* trust us," not "They *can't* trust us" which is what the young man said at video marker 3:07. To misquote the man is akin to a court reporter "correcting" witness testimony to suit their fancy… Very different spin, from "they *don't want to* be trusting humans," to the possibly more accurate quote, "we're *not trustworthy*…" Let the media spinning begin.
https://youtu.be/e7zlELjHH04

Wait a minute! How about us locals?

Way back in 2011, Austrians realized that they were being edged out of their jobs by the swarms of migrants filling their country. Thousands of young Austrians held a massive protest in Vienna against high unemployment and job insecurity. On the other hand, migrants felt they were being *blocked* from working by Austrians, whom they felt should allow them to take jobs.

Experienced knowledge workers were calling for larger and stronger unions to combat the so-called "black economy" made up of "many thousands of undocumented workers" taking jobs away from citizens.

Sound familiar?

In the meanwhile, migrants blamed lingering "Austrian racism" as the cause of their economic troubles and that this Austrian "racism" restricted the ability of migrants to grab a piece of the Austrian golden fleece for themselves.

Really? Reminds me of the story of the home invader who demands better food from the victimized family. I'd love to see how far that attitude gets you in my old hometown of Detroit...
https://youtu.be/_u99DjJ3VZc

Finally in a most touching scene reported by a leading news organization, thousands and thousands of refugees in early September 2015, arrived in Austria. Like anxious tourists, they were seen weighing the advantages of Germany vs. Sweden, trying to decide where they will be *better off economically*.

The reporter mentioned that on the previous day, only 40 of the migrants opted to stay in Austria, since Germany was seen as the land of gold and riches. Then the train pulled away and off the migrants went, arriving next in Germany, amidst cheering and great joy. Oh to be young, male, and a migrant!
https://youtu.be/txdKyT2tscU

They come bearing gifts
In an article titled "Leprosy cases in Salzburg asylum-camp," Austria's largest newspaper, Kronen Zeitung reported on September 18, 2015 that doctors at the Salzberg refugee camp were indeed dealing with leprosy. The doctors thought that the leprosy hadn't spread to others, but the concern was that diseases can spread quickly in unsanitary and crowded conditions.

It was rumored that the authorities had tried to hide the news of leprosy, and had even denied it initially.

Gee, why would they do that? Especially when everything is going so well?
http://www.krone.at/Nachrichten/.-Story-473366

In a Vienna refugee shelter, authorities confirmed that at least 3 cases of dysentery had been diagnosed by mid-October 2015. The official spin was that with some 130,000 migrants flowing through Vienna at that time, only 3 cases was a tiny number.

Rejoice!

By the way, there are two kinds of dysentery and together both kinds are responsible for about 600,000-750,000 deaths annually. If properly diagnosed and treated in a timely manner, people suffering from dysentery will often recover within 2-4 weeks. If not, it isn't pretty.
http://www.krone.at/Wien/Wien_Faelle_von_Ruhr_in_Fluechtlingsheimen-Drei_Diagnosen-Story-474924
http://www.who.int/mediacentre/factsheets/fs330/en/
http://www.infoplease.com/cig/dangerous-diseases-epidemics/epidemic-dysentery.html

Powder Keg Hamburg
On October 16, 2015, the Hamburger Abendblatt newspaper, an article detailed the dire situation in Hamburg's biggest refugee village. "Frustration, violence, arson" were among the many challenges faced by stressed employees who were calling

for help. Allegedly, at least 100 migrants were diseased, and the mood at the 3,300 person shelter was "highly explosive." In fact, the director of the refugee shelter reported being threatened by a chair-wielding asylum seeker after which he emailed, "we are sitting on a powder keg here. We think soon it will explode... we can't handle this burden anymore."
http://www.abendblatt.de/hamburg/altona/article206292615/Dramatische-Zustaende-in-Hamburgs-groesstem-Fluechtlingsdorf.html#

In the meanwhile, worried Austrians were stocking up with shotguns and firearms. There are an estimated 900,000 firearms in Austrian homes and apparently concerned women are pushing the new sales to record levels – police reported that 70,000 guns were bought by Austrians in the first 10 months of 2015.

The media credits the enormous "numbers of refugees, coupled with a fear of break-ins as a result" for the uptick in gun sales. In fact, shotguns were allegedly already virtually sold out nationwide before the end of 2015.

A sociologist opined, "Many see danger in these foreigners among them. But this fear is unfounded."

We certainly hope he is right. Surely there must be a preponderance of decent people among the refugees. But after you complete this book, you may think the sociologist was either a paid propagandist, or a complete loon.
http://www.dailymail.co.uk/news/article-3291978/Shotguns-virtually-sold-Austria-citizens-rush-buy-arms-amid-fears-massive-influx-migrants-dealers-claim.html

(5) AZERBAIJAN

The Republic of Azerbaijan used to be a part of the Soviet Union, and has been inhabited by people since the Stone Age. With its ancient art, interesting architecture, and lively folk dances and music, Azerbaijan has an almost 100% literacy rate and a robust internet business sector. It also is rich with various natural resources, from oil and gas to gold and titanium. And its experience with refugees seems to have been rather "smooth."

Dag Sigurdson, representative of the Office of the UN High Commissioner for Refugees (UNHCR) in Azerbaijan, speaking about the "refugee crisis" in September 2015 made some points worth analyzing.

Sigurdson thought Azerbaijan could show the European Union how to properly handle refugees stating that, "for example, the government of Azerbaijan granted citizenship (with full equal rights) to all the refugees that came from Armenia in 1998 together with 50,000 Meskhetian Turks that had been drawn out of Central Asia." Sigurdson said this was "an example of how things should be done."

Continuing, Sigurdson then said migrant assimilation in Azerbaijan was successful since the new citizens "stayed for a while and they have integrated, and they are part of the society, refugees are resources... they are members of the parliament, they are professors in the universities, they are judges and lawyers, they are not refugees, they are seen as a kind of, uh, somebody..."

Which begs the question – isn't Azerbaijan's success in part due to the fact that the majority of the refugees whom they accepted were from surrounding areas with generally similar backgrounds, experiences, and religions? Azerbaijan certainly wasn't assimilating people of dramatically differing cultures and beliefs, say, for instance, purple-colored rock-worshipping anarchists who only ate three legged crows while attacking Azerbaijani values...

Sigurdson also repeatedly claimed that the crisis is "mainly a refugee crisis" since "people have been "living in camps in neighboring countries" around Syria, such as Lebanon, Turkey, Jordan, and Iraq, and these people "have lived under difficult circumstances," and although "everybody has been trying to help, but over time, they have exhausted their resources and they have exhausted their possibilities of having a life in this temporary situation and they have moved on..."

Translation: the migrants have literally eaten their hosts out of house and home. Now that the cupboards are bare, they are on to their next host.

And exactly how will that work out?
https://www.youtube.com/watch?v=-zTJo6582hE

As far as migrant violence in Azerbaijan against Azerbaijanis, we didn't find any examples on the internet. Maybe it was because the former refugees were too busy truly assimilating into their new culture and were spending their time building careers and futures for themselves as Azerbaijanis.

What a concept.

(6) BELARUS

Now independent, and originally settled many centuries ago by ancient Slavs, Belarus, and its famous capital, Minsk, had been annexed by Russia in the late 18th century. It still shows signs of heavy Russian influence and its primary religion is Eastern Orthodoxy.

Compared to the international average of 5%, Belarus has a high 25% average acceptance rate when approving asylum seekers. Since 1997, about a thousand people, the majority from Afghanistan, have gained refugee status in Belarus.

So why isn't Belarus being overrun by refugees?

In August 2015, Belarus Digest reported that Belarus is not an attractive destination for migrants since in Belarus the "public authorities are under no obligation to provide refugees with housing, a means of subsistence, or even language courses."

Hmmm. No shelter. No money. No interest…

Could any of this explain why only 63 Syrians applied for asylum in Belarus in 2013?

In the meanwhile, over 100,000 Ukrainians arrived in Belarus over the 12 month period, ending in August 2015. Since there is no "official war" in the Ukraine, and Ukraine is not persecuting them, these migrants don't qualify for "refugee status." But their sheer numbers are adding up, increasing the total Belarus population numbers by 1%.

This influx of foreigners has strained Belarus's already depressed economy. Apparently, most Ukrainian migrants are willing to take jobs for "a salary several times lower than what a Belarusian would find acceptable. This makes it even harder for Belarusians who have lost their jobs due to economic recession to regain footing." Reportedly, many of the Ukrainians "have settled in rural areas," and most found work in "agriculture, construction, or commerce."

While there is no video evidence we could find of migrant crimes against native Belarusians, about 200 Ukrainians allegedly involved in criminal activity were deported in 2014.

In 2015, police in Belarus reported that crimes amongst Ukrainian migrants had gone up 30%. Some examples cited included Ukrainians walking across streets when lights were red and drinking beer in public. The police also reported several fights between Ukrainian individuals during heated political discussions. Well, yeah.

To us, it sounds like there really isn't much of a migrant crisis story in Belarus.

Yet.
http://belarusdigest.com/story/migrants-eastern-ukraine-put-pressure-belarus-22949
http://belarusdigest.com/story/belarus-produces-more-refugees-it-saves-18408

(7) BELGIUM

Legendary Belgium is a kingdom with a monarch, centuries of rich history, and just over 10 million inhabitants. Per square kilometer, it has more castles than any other country. Its capital, Brussels, features many impressive and significant architectural structures including the Royal Palace, which is far bigger than England's Buckingham Palace. Brussels is also the official capital of the European Union, and it is where NATO has its headquarters.

They make great chocolate, too.

Recently, well dressed, well-spoken migrants at an emergency shelter in Belgium complained during an interview that the food they are being served *for free* is "not good." One migrant rated the food as "medium" because he felt that the quality just wasn't there.

If a career in international mooching doesn't work out for them, maybe they could become food critics for local papers.

But it's not all fun and games.
https://youtu.be/Q_XHkgScOSY
http://www.monarchie.be/palace-and-heritage/palace-brussels

Back in 2012, according to CBNews, the most common baby name in Brussels, the capital of Belgium, was "Mohammed" for 4 years in a row. The Muslim community in Belgium predicted that they would be the majority by 2030. They were already 25% of the population of Brussels. In nearby Antwerp, over 40% of the children in the school system were already Muslim. Sharia law was being promoted by Muslims in Belgium and enforced in Muslim neighborhoods. This included, according to CBNews, "amputation for theft, stoning for adultery, and death to homosexuals."

There was reportedly a call for the end to democracy, which was seen as the opposite of Islam. A woman activist who posed in a bikini received death threats from Muslims while her father was called a "pimp." Other girls wearing bikinis were attacked. Jewish and Christian symbols were vandalized.

As the report ended, a Belgium man said he was sad to say that Belgium would soon be a foreign Muslim state. A Muslim migrant agreed.
https://youtu.be/ZDKk15KcqNk

In August 2015, at a Florennes refugee center, a group of Iraqis were allegedly harassing two Afghan minors that ended in a violent fight. Police had to be called in, two arrests were made and a half dozen people were hospitalized. Theo Francken, Belgian State Secretary for Asylum Policy and Migration, said at a press conference that Belgium "can't tolerate behavior like this."

Well, that showed them. Surely they will get along now.

But things were just getting started.
http://deredactie.be/cm/vrtnieuws.english/videozone_ENG/1.2463878

Barely two months later, in October 2015, the Florennes shelter erupted in violence, yet again. This time, a massive riot between Iraqi and Afghan migrants ended in at least 10 arrests and 10 people wounded. Initially, 30 police officers showed up for the *first* phase of the riot, and were able to settle things down. But only a few hours later, the migrants were at it again. This time, federal police had to be called in to assist the overwhelmed local police.

Reportedly, beyond the physical violence, there was also considerable property damage as migrants used pipes, baseball bats, and other weapons to break windows, doors, tables, and other things at their own shelter.

We suppose that in a few days, migrants will complain about broken windows, faulty doors, and a lack of useable tables at their "newly remodeled" shelter.

And we're betting they're just getting started.
http://deredactie.be/cm/vrtnieuws/binnenland/1.2463630
http://nieuws.vtm.be/binnenland/161626-massale-vechtpartij-opvangcentrum

More disturbing crime stats

In 2012, a detailed article on migrants and rape - *Hidden violence is silent rape: sexual and gender-based violence in refugees, asylum seekers and undocumented migrants in Belgium and the Netherlands* - was published by the Taylor and Francis group. In the report, 166 migrants (132 in Belgium) described 389 acts of sexual and gender-based violence that was either committed on them or that they knew occurred to someone close to them since arriving in Europe.

The results were disturbing.

About 70% of the victims were females, and about a third of the victims were males. The perpetrators were 75% male, most over the age of 30, with only about 20 women who were perpetrators. A majority of the perpetrators were migrants, usually the ex-partners, family, friends, acquaintances, and neighbors of the migrant victim.

Shockingly, about 20% of the sexual violence involved multiple rapes and even gang rapes. This was *migrant-on-migrant* crime, in the shelters and communities where they lived.

The report stated that "the bulk of the sexual violence cases consisted of rape with multiple (rapes) and gang rape appearing to be common practice."

Common practice? **COMMON PRACTICE??** That was the conclusion in 2011 when the report was first compiled.

So are we to similarly conclude that the many horrific instances of migrants raping, *and gang raping*, girls and women in their host countries nowadays was in line with what they did to each other in their migrant communities?

And no one threw a fit? No one in the old-fashioned-controlled-media investigated this travesty and revealed some of these dark truths behind the "refugee crisis." Seriously?

All we were shown were photos of poor suffering families with tired sad children – while 70-80% of the migrants, mostly young males of fighting-age, swarmed around the cameras, and were ignored by photographers and networks seeking to only reveal what bolstered their one-sided-cobbled-together-agenda-driven fantasy. Oh, but I digress....

Think about it.
http://www.tandfonline.com/doi/abs/10.1080/13691058.2012.671961

In familiar scenes repeated daily across Europe, many native residents are trying hard to be "good people."

Embracing the wonder
As the Rev. Hallanan, rector of the Episcopal Church in Waterloo, Belgium, noted, "Diversity is a wonderful thing for people everywhere. If God made people who are different from us, we should get to know them and share in them and rejoice. Who knows what wonders people will work in Europe and in

our midst, through these people who come and bring us a different perspective?"

The Rev. Sunny Hallanan, volunteered at a "refugee" camp in Maximilien Park in Brussels and befriended migrants from Syria, Iraq, and Afghanistan. The good Reverend may have even chatted it up with some of the young men we'll hear from in a moment.
http://episcopaldigitalnetwork.com/ens/2015/10/13/what-if-it-were-you-responding-to-the-refugee-crisis-in-belgium/

Some migrants tell it like it is
The improvised shelter camp was cleared out in October 2015 as local Belgian families offered to host the remaining refugees. And just like that, gone were the overflowing trash bins, the wretched and reeking toilets, and the tents.

What's really going on is a bit of a mystery though.

An aid worker remarked that curiously, far from masses of fleeing young families with babies in tow, the bulk of the camp inhabitants had been young single men, many from Iraq.

The Wall Street Journal Europe edition reported a story that offered fascinating insight into the minds of several migrants.

The heroes of this story were two brothers claiming to be from Iraq. One loves soccer, the other loves America. They "fled" the horrors of Iraq by taking an airline flight from Baghdad to Turkey.

Airplanes are always a great way to "flee." Onboard restrooms, puke bags, little pillows and blankets, and beverage carts really make the journey that much more tolerable.

Making their way from Turkey to Greece, they later walked to Macedonia where they encountered their first dose of alleged "police brutality."

Police brutality incident number 1
As the duo illegally tried to enter Macedonia, police allegedly lashed out with sticks and shot at their feet. Luckily, the brothers were unscathed and ended up sneaking through Serbia. But the run in with cops trying to protect their nation's borders had left an impression.

Warning. The upcoming "police brutality" incident number 2 happened in Hungary and isn't for the faint of heart.

Police brutality incident number 2
The Iraqi brothers were victims of what the Wall Street Journal called "police brutality" in Hungary as the brothers said police "forced us to give our fingerprints. All ten fingers!"

What an outrage! You illegally sneak into a country, and the police have the audacity to fingerprint you? All 10 fingers? ALL 10! Wow, this second act of police brutality is one for the books! What is this world coming to?

Seriously?

Anyway, after touring Vienna, Austria, and Hamburg, Germany, which the Iraqis didn't find suitable for their needs, they stopped off in Belgium. One brother made it a point to say the Belgian police weren't "helpful." Still not having found what they were looking for, the duo were headed for Finland.

Ah, Finland. Their "dream country." That's where the brothers told the reporter that they soon hope to bring their parents and other siblings. The Wall Street Journal also reported that during the several weeks that the Iraqi brothers had been "fleeing," their journey had cost the two of them about $11,000 in cash so far.

So far??!! Seriously now, how many people have $11,000+ in cash just lying around?
http://blogs.wsj.com/brussels/2015/09/04/from-baghdad-to-a-park-in-brussels-some-migrant-tales/

There's always one
Back to Theo Francken, Belgian State Secretary for Asylum Policy and Migration.

In April 2015, Francken stirred up a bit of a controversy when he warned that migrants from Africa, who try to sneak through Serbia to get to Belgium, should not try and seek asylum in Belgium, since the minute they set foot in Serbia, they had reached a safe, free, democratic country. Pretty direct.

In August 2015, Francken revealed that "just 5 or 6 countries account for over 80 per cent of the total number of people coming in, with Germany making the biggest effort. This situation is not a sustainable one." Chancellor Merkel, are you awake?

In September 2015, with 4,000-5,000 migrants seeking Belgium asylum monthly, Francken said Belgium might consider border controls. *You think?*

In October 2015, Francken told state broadcaster Radio 1 that "many of these people pay 10,000 euros to get here. It's naive to say they have not 50 euros for a hotel room. It's a caricature to see them as completely penniless." A reasonable statement from an experienced insider.

Of course, whenever you tell the truth, the loons fly in. And quickly.

A hired propagandist for an "organization working with asylum seekers," rebutted, "It's not about whether they still have some cash left, it's *about whether the government has made sufficient resources available to support the people* who are here."

Seriously?

Don't ask migrants to contribute to their own upkeep, especially if they have the funds? Instead, put the burden on the taxpayers and lay the blame on the government?

Think about it.
http://deredactie.be/cm/vrtnieuws.english/News/1.2423305
http://uk.reuters.com/article/2015/08/04/uk-belgium-asylum-idUKKCN0Q91M020150804

Don't cross the migrants
The migrants are doing their part to keep local authorities on their toes. In August 2015, police in Belgium arrested a Muslim migrant. In reviewing his cell phone, they discovered that the migrant had a whole series of wonderful family photos, close-ups, and intimate stills. *Charming right?* Well it might have been except the photos weren't of the migrant's family... They were clandestine photographs of some police officers, their families, and even their children.

Innocent photography, right?

The terrified police department, realizing that some of their officers and their families, were very possibly being targeted for something unpleasant or even deadly, immediately placed the potential targets under special protection.

But besides a few little annoyances, all is well. Except if you were on *that* train.
http://www.dhnet.be/actu/belgique/panique-a-la-police-des-enqueteurs-places-sous-protection-speciale-55de067435708aa437c2fb01

Another choo-choo to hell
Surely you heard this one. It was late August 2015 and a high-speed train was careening to Paris with hundreds of passengers enjoying the ride. The train stopped in Belgium to pick up passengers, including a Muslim male who is the son of a Moroccan immigrant to Europe, as well as a Moroccan citizen. Shortly after the Belgium station stop, the Moroccan went into a toilet, loaded a rifle, and emerged shooting at passengers.

Miraculously, although there were serious injuries, there were no fatalities. The five travelers who stopped the rampage immediately jumped into action. One tried to tackle the attacker but fell. The next grabbed the rifle but the attacker shot him in the back with a handgun. Then three American tourists jumped the attacker, disarming and subduing him.

Oh, and it turns out, this Moroccan allegedly might also be connected to a group in Belgium that police suspect had been planning to kidnap and video-broadcast themselves beheading a prominent Belgian law enforcement official. They were also thought to be planning the capture of a Belgian police station and the execution of a large group of police officers. Luckily, Belgian police had thwarted their plans but this particular group member apparently slipped through their fingers. Until the train incident.

In the meanwhile, in late August 2015, a Belgian politician lamented that Syrian refugees are being threatened by "radicalized local Muslim youths" who see the migrant Syrians as cowards that didn't fight alongside their brethren in Syria. The politician added that without additional funding, he couldn't guarantee the safety of the Syrians in his community, let alone any new arrivals seeking asylum. And so it grows.

Think about it.
http://www.cnn.com/2015/08/21/europe/france-train-shooting/
http://newsmonkey.be/article/53090

If we all say the same thing...
In August 2015, about half of the 5,600 asylum seekers who submitted applications in Belgium were Iraqis, many telling suspiciously similar stories. So suspicious, that Theo Francken, Belgian State Secretary for Asylum Policy and Migration, decided to suspend all requests from Iraqis from Baghdad until his office could figure out what was going on with the "security situation" in Iraq.

Francken also announced plans to buy social media ads in an attempt to dissuade other Iraqis from trying to seek asylum in Belgium. Apparently, social media is a useful tool for economic opportunists seeking to find their pot of gold.
http://blogs.wsj.com/brussels/2015/09/29/as-belgium-turns-to-facebook-to-deter-iraqis-more-arrive-daily/

We visit with Theo Francken one last time
For the record, we believe Francken really has one of the world's most thankless jobs. No matter what he does, he gets criticized by one group or another.

And to add insult to injury, for all his efforts and hard work, Francken received a nasty death threat, via email, in mid-August 2015. Seems someone emailed him that with all the unemployment in Belgium, to give money to migrants was just too much. The writer then went on to wish he could "place a grenade" in Francken's mouth.

You really can't please everyone.
http://brusselstimes.com/belgium/3888/death-threat-theo-francken-files-complaint

In late October 2015, Foreign Affairs magazine reported that Belgium was "the top European country of origin" for foreign fighters – that is men that travel to Syria and/or Iraq to support and fight for Islam. "Belgium saw 440 Belgian residents leave for Sunni militant organizations in Iraq and Syria in 2015."

Anyone else see the potential problems with a system like this? Where are your loyalties? Are you a resident, or something else? And when you return, how exactly do you assimilate back into peaceful society?
https://www.foreignaffairs.com/articles/syria/2015-10-25/foreign-fighters-financing
http://icsr.info/2015/01/foreign-fighter-total-syriairaq-now-exceeds-20000-surpasses-afghanistan-conflict-1980s/

Youngsters on the train
On January 10, 2016 a group of three Syrian refugee boys (12 and 13 years of age) decided to board a train going from Brussels to Tournai.

What to do to pass the time? Read a book? Play charades? Maybe a game of cards or hang-man? Hmmm...

You just know this won't end well.

Instead, the three Syrian refugee children decided to try and rape some girls.

The trio singled out a 22-year-old young lady, surrounded her, and then "threw themselves" at her. The girl "was in a state of shock" as the youngsters proceeded to sexually assault her. Some other passengers heard the girl's screams and "alerted train staff and the police arrived to catch them."

Yet, since this is the *new* Europe, police let the youngsters go after chatting with them since reportedly the police decided not "to make a big deal of it."

Guess if it happened to one of their daughters, they may have felt differently... But not making a big deal of migrant violence is in vogue in Europe right now...

Then, another two young ladies came forward and reported also being sexually assaulted on the same train. And the police were forced to reopen the case. Police are now trying to determine if the 3 separate sexual assaults on the same train were committed by the 3 Syrian boys they initially caught or if more migrants were involved.

Note to self. Stay off the trains!
http://www.express.co.uk/news/world/635022/Sexual-assaults-refugees-migrants-Belgium

(8) BOSNIA AND HERZEGOVINA

After declaring independence from Yugoslavia, Bosnia found itself at war from 1992-1995. The fighting involved Serbs and Croats with many reported war crimes and atrocities including genocide. Reports showed at least 100,000 casualties, military and civilian, and millions of refugees.

Some say Bosnia has yet to recover. About "100,000 Bosnians are still refugees in their own country," according to EuroNews. There is a widespread belief that Bosnia is still in dire straits and is failing its own citizens, let alone assisting migrants.

In June 2015, UN statistics showed 6,805 refugees and 11 asylum seekers *residing* in Bosnia. At the same time, 19,628 people *left* Bosnia as refugees, and 6,284 *left* as asylum seekers.

As far as recent migrant unrest or violence against Bosnians in Bosnia related to the current refugee crisis, we found no videos or stories.
http://www.balkaninsight.com/en/article/bosnia-mulls-action-in-case-of-refugees-influx-08-25-2015
http://www.unhcr.org/pages/49e48d766.html
http://www.euronews.com/2015/07/11/nowhere-to-call-home-in-bosnia-the-bitter-legacy-of-the-balkan-wars/

(9) BULGARIA

The European Union's poorest country, Bulgaria is reportedly listed in an Arabic language refugee handbook as the "top country to avoid" if you are an asylum seeker. Bulgaria also seems to be the most "labeled" or "smeared" of the EU nations. Targeted by various special interest groups, Bulgaria has been called everything from xenophobic and racist, to intolerant, and prejudiced, and chock full of unpunished hate crimes.

In a country where the average monthly salary is around $400, many Bulgarians are forced to seek work elsewhere in Europe. Health care is simply too expensive for most, and social services are far and few between. The unexpected, and unplanned-for influx of migrants is only exacerbating things.

In late 2013, PBS reported that conditions for Syrian refugees in Bulgaria were dire. Overcrowding, poor facilities, and a lack of dependable utilities plagued the migrants. And their dreams of living the "good life" weren't matching up with reality.

One Syrian refugee put it this way, "coming here, it's different, *not what we think* or what *we have dreamed* or something like that. *That's a big problem for us*, but what we can do? We are in here now."

In 2014, after some 15,000 Syrians showed up in Bulgaria, Bulgaria tried to stop accepting refugees. Bulgaria beefed up its border patrols, and attempted to keep the refugees in Turkey. Authorities were heavy handed. But the migrants kept coming.

It got so bad that in September 2015 the Orthodox Church of Bulgaria said on its website,
> "We help refugees who have already arrived in our motherland, but the government must absolutely not let more refugees in.. This is a wave that looks like an invasion.." The troubles in the countries of the refugees "must be resolved by those who created them and the Bulgarian people must not pay the price by disappearing."

http://www.aljazeera.com/indepth/features/2015/03/hate-attacks-bulgaria-invisible-crime-150302060433067.html
http://www.middleeasteye.net/news/dont-let-muslim-refugees-says-bulgarias-orthodox-church-1024482681

Young men and their cool selfies
A big wakeup call happened in September 2015. According to Bulgarian NOVA TV, Bulgarian police arrested 5 young men carrying cell phones with photographs of decapitated people, terrorist group promotional videos, and jihadist prayers. When the suspicious group was originally stopped by Bulgarian border patrol officers, the men tried to bribe their way out of trouble with a "wad of dollars."
http://israelamerica.blogspot.com/2015/09/islamic-state-jihadis-caught-crossing.html

But none of this should be surprising.

In January 2015, the Turkish government stated that at least 3,000 "refugees" residing in Turkey were connected to radical militant groups. And remember the warning issued by the Turkish National Intelligence Agency (MIT) in February 2015? If not, it's probably because no one in the old-fashioned-controlled-media paid it much attention. According to MIT in a written memo to police, about 3,000 members of ISIL from Syria and Iraq planned to enter Turkey on their way to Europe.

MIT reported that some group leaders were already in safe houses in Turkey. The memo also detailed that "some Syrian and Palestinian citizens – aged between 17-25 – have entered Turkey undercover as refugees and are planning to travel to Europe through *Bulgaria* in order to attack anti-ISIL coalition member countries."
http://www.hurriyetdailynews.com/intelligence-isil-could-hit-embassies-in-turkey.aspx?pageID=238&nID=78545&NewsCatID=359

In February 2015, RT News ran a story with a similar theme. Apparently, one influential militant revealed plans that "revolve around posing as illegal immigrants, to then start an all-out attack on southern Europe by seeding chaos and bloodshed."

The militant is quoted as saying, "We will conquer Rome, by Allah's permission," during a video showing the beheading of 21 Egyptian Christians. It was the same video that reportedly prompted Egypt's bombing of key targets in Libya.
https://www.rt.com/news/233335-isis-islamic-libya-europe/

Turning a deaf ear to credible warnings, again
Further, in May 2015, a government advisor to Libya warned that militants were among the 60,000 "refugees" that boated from Libya to Italy in the first 5 months of 2015. The advisor warned that European police would be unable to determine who is a refugee and who is a militant.

Similarly, the Egyptian Ambassador to the UK warned of "boats full of terrorists." Other "experts" chimed in and claimed that since you could never really tell for sure who was a real refugee, and who was a militant pretending to be a real refugee, it would be hard to prove that militants were among the boatloads of mostly young men...
http://www.ibtimes.co.uk/isis-militants-are-being-smuggled-europe-migrant-boats-libyan-government-adviser-1501692

Terrifying. Especially as you watch thousands of young men overrunning Europe's borders without identification verification or background checks.

Could any of this explain why Bulgaria is nervous about migrants? And less than welcoming? Think about it.

By mid-October 2015, things turned even more deadly as a young male Afghan (25) died while hiding under a bridge near Sredets. He, and about 50 other Afghans, had stolen into Bulgaria from Turkey and were apparently sneaking through when they were spotted.

The group of trespassers apparently tried to evade arrest. When a border guard fired what he said were some warning shots, one bullet allegedly ricocheted and hit the Afghan man, and he died on the way to the hospital.
http://www.independent.co.uk/news/world/europe/refugee-crisis-afghans-shooting-is-grim-landmark-as-eu-hardens-its-heart-against-refugees-a6697441.html

(10) CROATIA

In an all too familiar scenario, Croatia is being vilified for "not doing enough" and for trying to protect its country and borders.

> *It's like being angry at a person for being unable to lift 225 pounds before looking to see that the person only weighs 110 pounds to begin with...*

So what's the short story on Croatia?

A small country, Croatia is home to about 4 million people. Economically struggling, Croatia is barely making ends meet for its own citizens. As for refugees and economic migrants, Croatia has been taking in maybe 1- 1 ½ thousand annually. In the meanwhile, many native Croats are in dire straits and with an unemployment rate of about 45% for 18- to 30-year-olds, many must leave Croatia to find work.

Let's throw in a load of live landmines still buried in the ground, a remnant of the Balkan wars. After the wars, over the years, hundreds of people have been killed and many hundreds more have been maimed. Not a country you want to go storming through without a working knowledge of the safe routes around the minefields, literally.

Suddenly, in September 2015, over the course of just two days, 13,300 refugees stormed Croatia. Complete overload.

Croatian Prime Minister Zoran Milanović announced that Croatia would give safe passage to "refugees" into Europe. Instead of following EU rules and registering and accommodating these hoards, Milanović cleverly structured his aid in terms of "passage," saying, "They will be able to pass through Croatia..." He added, "We cannot register and accommodate these people any longer. They will get food, water and medical help, and then they can move on. The European Union must know that Croatia will not become a migrant hotspot."
https://www.youtube.com/watch?v=MpJ6eMLQ2Cs

Well, maybe not a "migrant hotspot," but mayhem ensued.

After Hungary began using force to protect itself from alien invaders, including tear gas and water cannons, Croatia suddenly became the route of choice for the masses.

The resulting chaos was really no surprise, except to the politically asleep...

Here are just a few examples.

In a scene repeated in Europe time and time again, migrants lost patience when the infrastructure of their host country wasn't up to their lofty expectations. In 2015, Croatian police were attacked by angry groups of rock and brick throwing "asylum seekers" who were furious that they were stranded at a train station.
http://www.presstv.ir/Detail/2015/09/18/429784/Croatian-PM-Zagreb-cannot-control-influx-of-refugees

In September 2015, surrounded by riot police, disgusted migrants staged a sit-in at a hotel, in Croatia's capital, and had this to say about Croatia's terrible treatment of them –

"Croatia is not good"... the monthly cash amount given freely to each migrant is too little ....."eat every day, eat spaghetti and macaroni, same thing, not good"

And the interview ended with the fed-up migrant saying, "Me go to Germany, because Germany very good." We're guessing dozens of Croats would have volunteered to drive this upset and disappointed fellow the whole way.
https://youtu.be/712kr7SKLCs

Around the same time, hundreds and hundreds of "refugees" ran amok in the streets of Croatia, destroying property and throwing concrete, missiles, pipes, rocks, and anything else they could find. They quickly overwhelmed several police officers who were woefully unprepared to deal with the unrest.

At one point, you can hear several refugees screaming repeatedly for "money" as they attack authorities, and each other, in what really looks like a prison yard gang melee.
https://youtu.be/NhJlZNz4L98

In September 2015, in Tovarnik, a Croatian border town, thousands of angry and crazed refugees swarmed and pushed and rioted as they expressed anger that they had to wait in long lines for free bus transportation to the border crossing up north. If you look closely, the vast majority are young men. And yes, the refugees attacked police, who were overwhelmed.
https://youtu.be/kJkwGWa-aqE

Again in September 2015, at a Croatian border crossing, thousands of screaming and rioting refugees overwhelmed the police and broke through the border, running, screaming, hooting, laughing, as they illegally swarmed Croatia's border.
https://youtu.be/r9PHxNQnJPM

And yet again in September 2015, refugees in Croatia boarded trains headed for Austria and Slovenia. Well, at least that's what the old-fashioned-controlled-media would have you believe. Actually, the migrants got really angry about having to wait in lines, and to wait for trains in an orderly fashion. In a scene repeated time and time again all over Europe, as the train pulled in, mayhem erupted.

Does one enter the train through the doors like a normal passenger? Why bother when you can climb through windows?

In a scene from some sort of zombie apocalypse flick, instead of waiting their turn, hundreds of refugees swarmed the arriving train, and literally climbed like insects into half open windows.
https://youtu.be/B_LvFj0aO3Q

Upon finding out that Hungary wasn't accepting them, refugees rampaged through Croatia on their way to a new destination, Serbia. The swarm quickly overwhelmed Croatian police and Croatian security forces. The migrants rioted through towns and fields, destroyed property, stole, and defecated in the streets. When busses were provided, the refugees swarmed the buses.

In the end, migrants expressed their anger that they weren't given accurate transportation information. Bad travel agents, no doubt.
https://youtu.be/wYhRjBisBd0

From the Croatian side of the border, thousands of violent and enraged refugees tried to force their way into Slovenia. Migrants stormed fences, battled each other and police, and caused havoc. With depraved indifference, some migrants even carried small children to the front lines. Slovenian police protected their border with pepper spray and riot shields.
https://youtu.be/_5f0CyNrFPo

Refugees in Croatia scrambled to board buses bound for Hungary. In scenes repeating themselves all over Europe, the migrants pushed, shoved, and climbed over each other and

police officers in order to get onto vehicles. A heavy armed police presence seemed to keep things somewhat less chaotic.
https://youtu.be/FjXaZp9i6kI

As we have already learned, in September 2015 Johanna Mikl-Leitner, Austria's Minister of Internal Affairs pointed out that migrants that got to Croatia had, in fact, reached a "safe country." As such, the migrants were obligated to seek asylum there, and not move on.

Based on the evidence that these so-called asylum seekers rarely apply for asylum in Croatia, which is a safe country, Ms. Mikl-Leitner suspected that this behavior "suggests they are *not* looking for safety but are choosing the most economically attractive countries." And as we already know, Ms. Mikl-Leitner promised that "if refugees arriving from Slovenia and Croatia to Austria seek asylum, we will return them to Croatia and Slovenia."

We will include this revelation in the Slovenia section as well in case someone reads the Slovenia chapter first.

That people are figuring out that there is a lot of economic tourism going on is great. It's certainly a first step. But unless rules are vigorously enforced, nothing changes.

Then, of course, there's always Germany and free *everything*...
http://www.b92.net/eng/news/region.php?yyyy=2015&mm=09&dd=24&nav_id=95551

(11) CYPRUS

In March 2014, Amnesty International accused the Republic of Cyprus of abusing asylum seekers and other migrants.

This small island country, with a population of just over a million residents, was once known as a tourist hot spot destination for many years. In contrast, Amnesty International detailed how migrants were being held "in harsh prison-like conditions for prolonged periods, in some cases for up to 18 months or longer."
https://www.amnesty.org/en/latest/news/2014/03/cyprus-abusive-detention-migrants-and-asylum-seekers-flouts-eu-law/

Cyprus and its atrocities
It has been going on for a long time. Amnesty International's Greece and Cyprus campaigner had warned the world back in 2011 that Cyprus was keeping asylum seekers and migrants in prisons and other detention centers with no processing plans and poor humanitarian aid services.
https://www.amnesty.org/en/latest/campaigns/2011/12/inside-cyprus-migrant-detention-centres/

According to the UN, there were 8,102 refugees and asylum seekers residing in Cyprus as of June 2015. In September 2015, when Cyprus agreed to take up to 300 refugees from the Middle East, Socratis Hasikos, the Interior Minister of Cyprus, added "We would seek for them to be Orthodox Christians" as it would make their transition to life in Cyprus easier.

Certainly a reasonable sounding concern for a mostly Orthodox island. But lots of luck selling anyone on it.
www.unhcr.org/pages/49e48dba6.html

Cyprus – Alcatraz of the Mediterranean
According to the UK's Express, migrants avoid Cyprus since "it is isolated compared to the rest of the EU and difficult to exit." The Express also highlighted a video on their site that included an interview with some Syrian refugees at a detention center in Cyprus that they were literally trying to escape from.

A female Syrian refugee stated, "first we paid millions of (Syrian) pounds to leave Turkey for a European country, and now people take advantage of our weakness to get more money by promising to take us elsewhere. They've destroyed us materially. They destroyed us completely."

Later on, a male Syrian refugee related the story of another Syrian refugee who was able to get a forged passport for 5 thousand euros and escape to mainland Europe. When the man being interviewed tried the same thing, he was arrested and was apparently still in the Cyprus detention camp plotting his next escape attempt. With so much time on their hands and nothing to do, many migrants find their days consumed with escape planning.

The more we learned, the more we started to think of Cyprus as a modern-day Alcatraz – America's famous maximum-security prison built on a 22 acre island surrounded by the dangerous currents of San Francisco Bay. It had a reputation for being impossible to escape. For migrants stuck on the island of Cyprus, it must seem a lot like Alcatraz.
http://www.express.co.uk/news/world/603693/Christian-refugees-refugees-Socratis-Hasikos-religion-Muslim-European-Union

In the meanwhile, many refugees seem to find conditions in Cyprus so deplorable that they are gladly shelling out thousands of pounds to get into Turkey, so they can travel to mainland Europe.

As one frustrated female Syrian refugee said, "Honestly, we didn't think that a European country would treat us like this. Why would they have saved us if they wanted us to die here?"
http://www.dailymail.co.uk/wires/afp/article-2921282/Syrian-refugees-plot-Cyprus-escape-camp-closes.html

In October 2015, two boats carrying a majority of male Syrian refugees were abandoned by human smugglers near Cyprus. According to Cyprus Coast Guard Commander Marvi, "They probably told the refugees this is Greece or Italy and then they left. That's my guess, that's what they usually say. The refugees don't want to come to Cyprus, they want to go to Greece or Italy, because once they get to Cyprus they can't move freely as it's an island. So probably they just took the money and sped away. They usually charge them €3,000 to €4,000 each."
http://www.theguardian.com/world/live/2015/oct/21/refugee-crisis-syrians-rescued-at-british-base-on-cyprus-live-updates#block-56278acae4b020bd3060d61b

As seems to be a trend with most countries and states that aren't very welcoming to migrants, we could find no reported instances of refugee violence against native Cypriots, just lots of miserable refugees trying to flee elsewhere.

(12) CZECH REPUBLIC

In mid-2015, Czech President Miloš Zeman announced that the Czechs would take in 1,500 refugees. Up until then, there were only a few hundred refugees in the Czech Republic. Of course, Czech migrant shelters have been called "worse than prisons" by critics. Then, again, refugee crime in the Czech Republic is virtually unheard of... Why is that?

A practical man, Zeman mentioned that the migrants must be checked for infectious diseases, and to be questioned to determine if they are actually terrorists. Of course, the old-fashioned-controlled-media used his comments to paint him as some sort of uncaring monster. Seemingly unbothered, Zeman went on to tell the Blesk tabloid that all migrants need to be told three things upon arriving in the Czech Republic:
    #1. Nobody invited you here.
    #2. Once you're here, you have to respect our rules, just as we respect the rules when we go to your country.
    #3. If you do not like it, go away.
http://www.blesk.cz/clanek/zpravy-politika/334299/nikdo-vas-sem-nezval-vzkazal-zeman-uprchlikum.html

Predictably, President Zeman's comments sent Zeid Ra'ad Al Hussein, United Nations Human Rights Chief, into a tizzy.

Still unfazed, and referring to migrants from Northern Africa and the Middle East, Zeman said that they "had better fight for their home countries' future rather than flee overseas, (end up with) no work there and get by with welfare."

So Zeman thinks migrants should stay in their own countries and fight and struggle to make things better rather than take charity out of the pockets of taxpaying citizens from wealthier countries? What a firebrand!

Still speaking his mind, Zeman had this to say during a Blesk video interview – "They bring the children over in rubber dinghies, knowing they might drown... they (the children) serve as human shields for guys with iPhones to justify the wave of migrants.... most refugees do not deserve compassion because as a rule, they are young, healthy men with good material conditions."

Wow. No wonder the old-fashioned-controlled-media has tried so hard to ignore and marginalize Zeman.

Zeman also added that "a majority of the refugees were males with 'iPads' and 'iPhones' who had 'thousands of euros and thousands of dollars' in their pockets."

How much more honesty could the establishment put up with?

Not much. At some point, Vera Jourova, the European Commissioner for Justice, Consumers and Gender Equality, warned that people capable of influencing public opinion, like Zeman, should be careful not to spread prejudices or portray "refugees" as dangers to society.

Yes. Of course. But what if they are?
http://sptnkne.ws/X3D
http://www.praguemonitor.com/2015/10/26/zeman-most-refugees-do-not-deserve-compassion

Nooses for politicians, not migrants

What happens to migrants that "wander" into the Czech Republic? Czech police officers round them up and send them off to detention centers like the one in the village of Vyšní Lhotách where 220 men, mostly from Pakistan, Afghanistan, Syria, and Iraq await deportation.

Obviously, the word on the street is that the Czechs have no sense of humor when you try and take advantage of them. No wonder the migrants aren't lining up to sneak in.

Add in the fact that the Prague Police Department wasn't troubled the least bit in July 2015 by anti-immigrant protesters parading around Prague with mock gallows and nooses encouraging the execution of politicians who are "traitors" to the cause. Yes, that's right. The protestors walked around the town with gallows, complete with hangman nooses dangling, calling for the hanging of politicians they felt deserved to die.

In fact, the Prague police reportedly conducted an assessment and said that having nooses and gallows at a demonstration is absolutely *not* a criminal offense – freedom of expression lives.

The Czech Republic truly is a different world.
http://ostrava.idnes.cz/do-vysnich-lhot-privezli-prvni-bezence-d9a-/ostrava-zpravy.aspx?c=A150807_204036_ostrava-zpravy_jog
http://zpravy.idnes.cz/policie-resi-zda-mohou-byt-na-demonstracich-makety-sibenic-pny-/domaci.aspx?c=A150702_150511_domaci_kha

(13) DENMARK

Denmark's 2013 "Danmarks Statitik" report which analyzed criminal behavior in Denmark, stated that immigrants and their descendants made up 10.7% of the population, a majority of which were from non-Western countries. It was reported that employment rates among immigrants from Somalia, Iraq, and Lebanon were "very low." In fact, almost 40% of immigrants were on welfare.

Danmarks Statitik also reported that non-Western men were more likely to commit crimes than Danish men and men of Western backgrounds. In 2012, although only comprising 10.7% of the population, immigrants and their descendants committed a combined total of 16% of crimes. It was noted that among the young male 20- to 29-year-old criminal base – immigrants from Western countries represented a "remarkably low crime rate" while immigrants and their descendants from non-Western countries had a "very high frequency" of criminal activity. Interestingly, immigrants from the USA and China seemed to commit the least amount of crime

The report stated that most criminals originated from Africa (Somalia and Morocco) and Lebanon. Iraq, Iran, Afghanistan, and the old Yugoslavia were in the next tier. Reportedly, the most violent criminals were from Africa and Lebanon.

Of course, the report offered many explanations and excuses for these migrant overrepresentations in criminal behavior including unemployment and social inequalities.

My grandfather was a penniless refugee in Europe after World War II and never turned to crime. And when he got to the United States years later, again penniless and not knowing the language, he again didn't turn to crime. Could it be a mindset, not social inequalities or unemployment?
http://www.dst.dk/pukora/epub/upload/17961/indv2013.pdf

Sneak in and then complain endlessly
In September 2015, when a band of about 800 illegal aliens dodged police and broke through barriers to storm into Denmark, they actually hoped to register asylum claims in Sweden instead. Why would that be?

Seems Denmark protected itself by passing new laws to keep welfare assistance for its own citizens, thereby discouraging migrants who might otherwise show up and demand benefits.

For instance, an asylum seeker granted asylum in Denmark had his welfare benefits cut by 45%. Man, was he displeased. He lamented that Denmark "wants me to work!" and that he is "sad about this decision" to cut welfare, and felt discriminated against especially since "Sweden not make this. Germany not make this."

A spokesman for the Danish People's Party put it this way, "In the past we've taken a lot of refugees in Denmark and we've come to a point where we have to say enough is enough. We can't take anymore, we can't handle this type of immigration crisis... it's simply too heavy a burden on a small country like Denmark... let's just step on the brake..."

You think?

That any population could take in thousands of unexpected and unplanned-for migrants, and spend untold millions of dollars housing and caring for and feeding them, is rather remarkable. Especially when it is obviously at the direct expense of its own citizens. Make no mistake about it, the money is coming from somewhere, and that somewhere is out of the pockets of the citizens, and from the programs earmarked for and paid for by the citizens. Period.

While such altruism is commendable, it can also be rather dangerous and irresponsible, especially if one's own populace suffers because of it.

Troublesome, also is the gnawing fact that while Syrian migrants have endless complaints about their strife in Denmark, they never seem to question why their wealthy Arab neighbors in the Middle East are conspicuously quiet, and notoriously stingy in assisting.
https://youtu.be/8dcCLD6NoZc (video marker 1:21)
https://youtu.be/axOuN5Uj0AU

The media explains away the rape statistics
In an article titled, "Every Second Rapist Sentenced is a Foreigner," a major media outlet in Denmark reported that while migrants are only about 10% of the population in Denmark, they accounted for a majority of the rapists in 2010. And, over the last 7 years, more than one in three convicted rapists of Danish girls and women was an immigrant or had an immigrant background.

Callously, but not surprisingly, a major media outlet ignored the victims. Instead, they offered a manure pile of reasons to explain the rapes, including well thought out gems such as:
- The victims wore short summer dresses
- Migrants may not understand that a girl wearing a dress isn't inviting them to rape her
- Migrant values about sex and women just don't mesh with Danish sexual morality

- And, according to senior researcher Karin Helweg-Larsen at the National Institute of Public Health, judges may have an UNCONSCIOUS tendency to let nice Danish rapists off the hook more frequently than migrant rapists

Seriously? With the media providing ready-to-use excuses like these, who needs to worry? Certainly not the victims.

http://www.bt.dk/danmark/hveranden-voldtaegtsdoemt-er-udlaending

When reality sets in, Nigeria's the ticket

An illegal migrant in Denmark was interviewed on Denmark's publically owned TV2. The young African man said he was from Nigeria and had left his family to travel in 2010 to Europe and Denmark to "give my family a better life, that's *really* why I left Africa."

When the TV host followed up and asked him if there was any *war* or if he had been *threatened* in anyway, the young African said, "No, no, no, no, and there was no war."

The young man said he went from Morocco to Spain by smuggler's boat, and then made his way to Denmark. Asked about his new life in Denmark, he said he had "mixed feelings... Denmark is not my problem, the people here are very friendly... my problem is my inability to adapt to the system."

The man said he now wanted to return home to Nigeria.

In a dejected and disappointed voice, the young African man explained "I never knew it's difficult to get what you want in Europe... I was thinking when you come, within a short period of time... a couple of months... you get a house, you get a car, live a comfortable house. But I never knew that it's not true. It takes time."

Welcome to Europe. And yes, it *all* takes time...

https://youtu.be/wlW5gJ4bn34

Why not get migrants to pitch in and pay their way?
In mid-December 2015, Denmark decided that it would consider *seizing assets from migrants* to help defray the cost of providing healthcare, accommodations, and even education to the migrants. Wedding rings, watches, and other "sentimental" items were to be excluded.

The old-fashioned-controlled-media quickly fanned the flames around the subsequent outcry with terms like "extreme," "cruel," "hoax," "ugly," "petty," and some even likened the idea of having migrants pitch in for their care to Nazis taking possessions away from concentration camp prisoners – a stretch but that was the basic drift.

What many people missed was that in order to receive jobless benefits, unemployed Danes were forced to divest themselves of assets above certain stated levels.

One might wonder if it's good enough for native Danes, then why would a rather similar policy be "bad" for migrants.

Whose country is it anyway? Sorry – whose country *was* it?
http://www.theguardian.com/world/2015/dec/20/danish-mep-quits-ruling-party-plan-refugees-valuables

(14) ESTONIA

Estonia is a small northern country on the Baltic Sea next to Latvia and Russia, across the gulf from Finland. Its countryside features amazing castles, medieval towns, majestic architecture, and Orthodox and Lutheran churches.

When the Minister of Social Affairs for Estonia suggested a ban on burqas in 2015, Estonians across the country agreed and expressed a fear of losing their culture and identity. It wasn't that long ago that the nation was occupied by the Soviet Union, and tens of thousands of Estonians were shipped off to Siberian death camps under the watchful eye of Stalin and his murderous henchmen like Leo Reichman and Lazar Moses Kaganovich.

A member of the Estonian Association of Journalists put it this way, "We speak about the fears of a small nation, of the loss of its language, of the loss of a culture built on language, of the loss of a national identity... We know that it can happen. We have this Soviet experience, of somebody forcing us to behave differently." The burqa ban would be a small step towards keeping some of the foreign influences out.
http://www.dw.com/en/estonias-past-plays-into-refugee-debate/a-18740819

The Estonian Experience

According to the UN, in 2014 only 95 people applied as asylum seekers to Estonia. In that same year, 339 people *left* Estonia as "refugees" and 33 *left* as "asylum seekers." In 2015, Estonia received 136 applications in the first half of the year.

Estonia has long resisted being swept up into the rest of the European Union's refugee chaos. Estonian politicians have steadfastly refused to participate in UN migration schemes, instead looking for the causes of the migrant strife to be dealt with – unrest in Libya and Syria as well as human trafficking.

In 2013, it was reported that Estonia had defended its borders aggressively, to the point that asylum seekers had not gotten a chance to gain entry to have their applications filed.

At the same time, Estonia had lower living standards than neighboring nations, making it less attractive to economic opportunists. Some migrants had complained that Estonian expulsion centers for asylum seekers often dragged out application decisions; they didn't have a robust amount of services, especially for special needs migrants; and they didn't effectively forward materials sent to them by outsiders.

Add that to the fact that Estonia is also off the beaten trail that migrants favor, and you have a pretty well insulated country.
http://www.ipsnews.net/2013/06/estonia-not-on-the-refugee-way/
http://humanrights.ee/en/annual-human-rights-report/5030-2/situation-of-refugees-and-asylum-seekers/

In September 2015, at Estonia's only refugee shelter, was involved in good old-fashioned-controlled-media coverage because none of the staffers could tell the new asylum seekers what direction they needed to face to pray to Mecca.

When it was revealed that the refugee shelter would be expanded to house even more refugees, local residents expressed dismay. They were unhappy that so much money

was being spent on foreigners while they suffered economically.
http://www.politico.eu/article/estonia-migrants-refugees-asylum-eu/

The numbers are significant.

Migrant Privilege in Estonia
Migrants each receive about 1,000€ monthly in support payments, plus free housing, plus free meals three times every day, plus free education. All of this goes on for *at least* 6 years.

In contrast, while the average monthly wage in Estonia is just over 800€, in the town the shelter is in, it averages only 500€. Talk about a vast disparity. Estonian citizens who work hard every day earn about *half* the amount handed to migrants just for "arriving." How would *you* feel?

To drive the point home even more painfully, Estonian citizens who are poor and "in need" receive just over 60€ per month as aid, 1,600% less *than the migrants.*

Back to the townspeople.

They felt further abandoned as the refugee housing was maintained in beautiful condition, including new geothermal heating, while the locals struggled to make ends meet in their decaying buildings.

In a show of solidarity and support for the local townspeople, hundreds of motorcyclists from across Estonia rode to the town where the refugee center is located on Saturday, July 4, 2015. The residents, who had felt forgotten, poured into the streets cheering and waving in what would be a record-breaking crowd.

Oh, and by the time the motorcyclists had arrived in town, the shelter was long empty.

Was it an alien abduction?
Something like that, *minus the UFOs...*

It seems that clever government officials had arranged for the migrants to enjoy a full day of taxpayer-funded traveling around various cultural events in Estonia aboard luxury tour buses – including the zoo, "the Christian Song Festival, the Ukrainian Culture Centre, the Open Air Museum, and the lakeside." *Sweet.*

In the meanwhile, many local Estonian children took the opportunity to play in the town's playground, something they hadn't been able to do for a long time. It was reported that the migrant kids had kept them out of the playground by bullying them and throwing stones and rocks at the local children. Today, though, the children laughed and played, unafraid.

As the motorcyclists left, all was peaceful, save for the roar of the bikes.
http://www.balticbusinessnews.com/article/2015/6/19/estonian-bikers-get-involved-in-refugee-issue
http://news.postimees.ee/3250627/bikers-rally-turns-out-calm-and-quiet

In early September 2015, an external wall of the refugee shelter caught on fire damaging about 10 square meters of the outside wall. There were no reported injuries. A man with a fire extinguisher was able to put out the flame, and the police were investigating the fire as an arson. The media and endless critics hammered away, claiming the specter of "racism" had raised its ugly head, yet again.

We have been unable to find any follow-up stories to learn what actually happened after the police investigation.
http://news.err.ee/v/politics/bf9d55c4-aae8-49fe-9cf7-085d828767e0/roivas-demands-zero-tolerance-on-vao-arson

(15) FINLAND

It was reported that the number of rapes in Finland has risen 87% in the past six years. According to 2005 police crime statistics, although foreigners made up only about 2% of the population, foreigners committed over 20% of reported rapes. By 2012, the numbers would be much higher – 5.5% of the population was foreign and 34% of all rapes were committed by foreigners.
http://www.helsinki.fi/kriminologian-ja-oikeuspolitiikan-instituutti/
http://www2.hs.fi/english/archive/news.asp?id=20000822xx3

The United States Department of State's *Bureau of Diplomatic Security* reported that 2014 saw a serious spike in robberies in Finland, up 11% in that one year alone.
https://www.osac.gov/Pages/DocumentGenerator.aspx?generateDocument=true&documentLocation=Content%20Attachments/ContentReports/17950/Finland%202015%20CSR.pdf

Prime Minister graciously houses migrants in his home
After the Prime Minister of Finland offered up his personal residence to asylum seekers in 2015, he visited a crowded refugee shelter to hear people's concerns. Migrants complained to him that they weren't being processed fast enough for their liking. One migrant, who appeared to be easily in his late twenties, made a big deal about actually being able to prove he was only 17.

But none of this was the real *story...*

For those who were *watching*, and not distracted by all the many silly side stories, the video showed that the refugee shelter was occupied almost exclusively by young fighting-age men.

When the old-fashioned-controlled-media doesn't have time to edit or stage events, the truth slips through. Sometimes.
https://youtu.be/GdDf3rAnCCA

If you were at all puzzled moments ago when you read that the "Prime Minister of Finland offered up his personal residence to asylum seekers," here's some more info to put this "altruism" into prospective.

After Prime Minister Sipilä announced the opening of more refugee centers in Finland, the local townspeople who would be personally affected and imposed-upon expressed their utter disgust. That's when Sipilä, a wealthy millionaire, offered up "his personal residence to refugees." According to Finnish public broadcaster YLE, Sipilä quipped, "We should all take a look in the mirror and ask how we can help."

Well, except the house Sipilä offered up is one he rarely uses, since he already has a government-provided residence, plus yet another personal residence. Kind of like donating one of your dozens of pairs of expensive old shoes to a charity drive while expecting your neighbor, who only owns two pairs, to do the same. You just simply have to love those rich 1%ers!

Concurrently, less well-off Finns felt betrayed as they watched their country's resources, and their funds, funneled off to benefit economic opportunists. For their wealthy multi-home-owning Prime Minister to try and chide them into "sacrificing" their own futures to subsidize foreigners just seemed hollow.
http://in.reuters.com/article/2015/09/05/europe-migrants-finland-pm-idINKCN0R50RT20150905

Your Finnish food really stinks
A group of migrants at a Finnish shelter complained that they were not being assisted properly, that the food wasn't to their liking because it was "so bad and so strange," and they demanded money.

As one of them said, after "13 days the eat is not so good, and we want just money, *our money*... to buy something from supermarket."

The migrants went on "strike," adding, "no anyone care about us, no money, no medicine, they humiliated us... they don't give us anything, no clothes, no bed, no shoes, no anything... we are like animals here...."

What has this world come to?
https://youtu.be/WRPgIYBOzTw

Never ever blame the guilty
In March 2015, five African Somali males, 15-18 years old were arrested as suspects in another brutal gang rape of a young Finnish woman. In this case, the rapists began harassing the young woman on a train and then decided to pursue her off the train and gang rape her at the Tapanila train station of northern Helsinki.

In a disturbing old-fashioned-controlled-media trend, the emphasis was not on the victim. One pundit was quoted as saying "We are a society that decides to look the other away and not help people if they are in trouble. We left the woman to be raped, *the young boys to spoil their future* and the police to do a job they can't manage properly."

Oh, so in reality there were 3 sets of equal victims. And society was to blame for letting young boys spoil their future. Seriously?

The only one not being helped by this drivel was the victim.

The "young boys" are criminals. Rapists. Gang rapists. Hiding them behind the intentional moniker "young boys" is a perversion. The same writer later states that if only society could find diversions like "football teams for these kinds of boys," everything would magically get better.

> Naïve at best. Dangerous at worst. Oh, and here's a newsflash... *Rapists don't stop raping because they also belong to a football league.*

Following the "formula," the article ended by noting that, "Another problem is social media that appears intoxicated with hate as if their racism and rage have been vindicated by what happened." While it is unclear what that sentence really means, it would seem to imply that anyone on social media that gets angry about a bunch of gang rapists of immigrant backgrounds raping a Finnish girl are probably just raging racists.

Or maybe they're just angry about yet another rape!

So how did the old-fashioned-controlled-media come to the aid of the victim? Or jump at the opportunity to strike a blow against rape? Or expose the alarming trend of violent assault against Finnish women?

They didn't.

Instead, there was a detailed report about how the African Somalis in Finland were feeling racial discrimination and hatred after the arrest of the five African Somali gang rapists. Apparently, migrants were concerned that Finnish racism and retribution would injure them and harm them – that all Somalis would be blamed for the gang rape perpetrated by a handful of their own. Unlikely. But it makes for scary headlines.

But again, no mention of the victim.

No tears for the victim. No concern for the victim.

Endless articles can be found about whether or not to identify criminals, and how it may impact the criminals, and how it may impact others who share their ethnicity, et cetera, et cetera.

It's all about protecting the violent migrant criminals, and, *wait for it,* to hell with the victim!

Think about it.
http://m.iltalehti.fi/uutiset/2015031319350781_uu.shtml
http://yle.fi/uutiset/nuori_somalialaisnainen_huolissaan_raiskauskohusta/7871334

Yet again, crime stats tell their own story
The National Research Institute of Legal Policy (Optula) study published in 2014, "Immigrants as crime victims and offenders in Finland," found that the number of rapes committed by those born in Africa and the Middle East was 1,700% higher than those committed by native Finns.

Not surprisingly, many special interest groups attacked the report claiming that it was (a) flawed, since it relied only on police reports of rape, and (b) that its findings would be used to label and victimize migrants. *Really?* Those are all your concerns?

Again, what about the victims? The V I C T I M S????

Oh wait, sorry, we neglected to apply the formula... Protect the violent migrant criminals, and, to hell with the victim!

In an interesting twist, one investigator made generous allowances for various socio-demographic factors, removed these from the study data, and the number of rapes committed by those born in Africa and the Middle East were still 1,000% higher than those by native Finns. Further, it was reported that Finns involved in rapes were usually drunk, and raped women they knew. Migrant rapists were often sober and raped random Finnish females.

In the same media feed, we see a steady stream of apologists lined up to claim that rapes were caused by a variety of factors including:

- young men who feel that they don't belong
- men from foreign backgrounds who may not understand that they can't just rape Finnish women
- migrants from certain regions who see women as their inferiors, to do with as they please

Again, protect and excuse the violent migrant criminals, and, to hell with the victim!

Pretend-time
Imagine how much richer the pharmaceutical manufacturers will become once "apologist-itis," or "the unnatural need to apologize for and excuse horrific behavior without holding the perpetrator accountable," is finally added to known psychological disorders, and the newly concocted pills will be prescribed by the bucket-full.

The supply of fresh patients may be endless...
http://www.optula.om.fi/material/attachments/optula/julkaisut/tutkimuksia-sarja/XZ5bk8f2H/265_Lehti_ym_2014.pdf
http://yle.fi/uutiset/maahanmuuttajien_korkeaan_raiskaustilastoon_ei_loydy_yhta_patevaa_syyta/7877771

In the end, the Helsinki District Court freed two of the suspected African Somali gang rapists, and imprisoned the other three African Somali gang rapists – two of which gang raped the young woman as the other held her down.

Convicted of aggravated rape, and aggravated rape of a young person, the African Somali teenage gang rapists received very light sentences, due to their young ages at the time of the brutal gang rape assault. Prosecutors had hoped for 3+ year sentences, but felt that "exceptional publicity" led to extreme leniency.

Translation: The "power of the press" resulted in light sentences. Hope the press was proud to have helped...

What about the victim?

The court sealed the gang rape trial records for 60 years to protect the victim's privacy.

Intensely sad.
http://yle.fi/uutiset/tapanilan_raiskaajille_reilun_vuoden_tuomiot_kahden_syytteet_hylattiin/8097897

Another report, same story
In March 2015, Finnish news outlet ILTALEHTI posted a story that according to newspaper reports, "African males pose a particular rape threat to Finnish women." Although the researcher claimed "a large number of rape crimes committed by persons of foreign origin is difficult to explain," the numbers were staggering.

The number of rapes had risen 87% in six years. In one year alone, from 2013-2014, the number of rapes increased 18.7%.

According to the Ministry of Justice, in 2012, 34% of those convicted of rape were foreigners. The Ministry also revealed that foreigners committed 41% of all "serious rapes." Yet, Statistics Finland showed that by the end of 2013, foreigners only made up 5.5% of the population.

Less than 6% of the population was committing more than a third of the rapes in Finland. Think about it.

An experienced crime investigator and physician said that there were many different results when looking at native and foreign criminals and all the types of crimes they commit, *except when it came to rape* – foreigners and immigrants were at the top of the statistics in rape crimes.

Why is that?

The report looked at traditional excuses:
- The immigrants are largely young males
- Most of the young male immigrants live in major cities
- The young males have low incomes

After studying these factors, the conclusion was that "Population by age and gender (youth and male domination), low income and living in big cities did *not* explain this difference in rape crimes."

The newspaper reported that rapists from the Middle East and North Africa were overrepresented 1,300%, while Africans were overrepresented 1,200% compared to Finnish natives.

In the end, there was no easy way to excuse or explain away these terrifying statistics.

Apparently, the facts are the facts. Just don't talk about them.
http://m.iltalehti.fi/uutiset/2015031319350781_uu.shtml

Tourists, easy money, and a vacation
In October 2015, Finnish TV aired an interview with an Iraqi refugee who had been living in Finland since 2008. His family had fled Iraq for Syria after his father was shot dead, and they then sought official asylum in Finland which they received.

The Iraqi man, who learned Finnish and spoke it fluently, revealed that he had spoken to many "asylum seekers" and felt that 70% were not fleeing danger. He said that they lived in relative safety in southern Iraq. When the Finnish reporter asked him why they come, he said "because of the money. They believe they will get easy money from the social welfare office."

Asked if refugees should be deported, the man said "yes." He explained that many still had jobs in Iraq since they went to Finland on "temporary vacation." Their jobs, apartments, "everything" was still waiting for them in Iraq. "They are tourists here in Finland," he concluded.

How great is that? Take a vacation from your third world country. Travel around. Find a nice new gig. If it works out, you're set. If not, return to your old life as if nothing happened.

Think about it.
https://youtu.be/8gO1QTEnwQw

My sandbox, my toys, my way
By October 2015, almost 20,000 new asylum seekers arrived in Finland. Nearly 11,000 arrived during the month of September alone. 70% were Iraqis. According to Finland's Interior Ministry, the vast majority, about 75%, were young males mostly from Iraq, Somalia, and Afghanistan.

Finnish Prime Minister Juha Sipilä, who originally said 50,000 asylum seekers would be welcomed by Finland, cut the number down to 30-35,000 after realizing Finland's resources "are stretched thin." *Reality check...* Even 30-35,000 migrants would be "ten times as many asylum-seekers as last year" according to Sipilä.

While his country struggled to host these young male opportunists, the Prime Minister seemed not to be at all concerned. In his signature *my-way-or-the-highway* style, Sipilä said in November 2015 that he was "ready to dismantle his own government if he does not get his way over proposed reforms to health and social care."

Napoleon had nothing on this guy.
http://yle.fi/uutiset/asylum_seekers_from_afghanistan_topped_iraqis_as_majority_in_tornio/8422616
http://yle.fi/uutiset/pm_sipila_finland_at_asylum-seeker_capacity/8389972
http://yle.fi/uutiset/pm_sipila_govt_very_likely_to_fall/8435726

Finnish food isn't fit for dogs

In September 2015, about 60 Iraqi migrants from an emergency shelter held a noisy protest at a police station in Oulo, saying that "Finnish food isn't fit for dogs or women."

It seems that the Finns running the shelter had contracted with a popular local caterer that provides similar meals to schools and retirement homes. But the furious young Iraqi men would have none of it.

Barley? Potatoes? Porridge? Fish soup? What an outrage!

All these "horrible" traditional Finnish foods, apparently "not fit for a dog" are in the process of being replaced with something far more suitable for the angry Iraqi men.

> *Hey, Prime Minister Sipilä. Better start making some serious changes to your "horrible" culture to accommodate your new guests. While you're at it, maybe you should call your kitchen staff at the mansion you loaned to immigrants and tell them to stop watching animal food specials, and start watching Syrian cooking shows, so they can prepare meals with real food, not dog food.*

Ironically, on November 7, 2015, the Institute for Health and Welfare released research from a 7 year study that found that a traditional Finnish diet, a so-called "Baltic Sea Diet," is healthy and cuts down on obesity.

In fairness, the angry migrants probably wouldn't have been swayed by the report.
https://youtu.be/ZgYh61YvYDo
http://www.finlandtimes.fi/national/2015/10/01/20908/Refugees-stage-demonstration-in-Oulu
http://yle.fi/uutiset/study_baltic_sea_diet_reduces_obesity/8439199

Significant terrorist threats? Quick, protect the migrants!
In early November 2015, Security Intelligence Service Chief Pelttari warned the public of an increased terror threat in Finland. The high influx of refugees was at the center of his fear that Finland now faced "a significant threat to Finnish security."

In true Finnish fashion (say it three times), Chief Peltarri cautioned that the threat was really *dual!* It had two parts.

First, among the migrants, there could very well be violent people, and people fueling an interest in "extreme Islamist activity." He also felt this could lead to an increase in "terrorism-related support and recruitment activities."

Terrible. What in the world could be the other half of the threat?

Second, the Chief then went on to warn that neo-Nazi groups, and other anti-immigrant groups (notice that anyone who dares to question the open door policy is lumped in with the crazies), *might* commit "violent hate crimes, largely due to the growth in anti-immigrant sentiment." According to the Chief, the "neo-Nazis" had been "spreading one-sided and distorted information about asylum seekers."

The Chief didn't reveal what that "misinformation" was, but since the actual truth is so horrific – "34% of all rapes were committed by foreigners in 2012" – we understand why the Chief would be concerned.

Luckily, the Chief assured the public that all was well – that his agents were monitoring the activities of some 300 migrants who were *possible, but not proven, terrorists* and were freely moving around the country. The Chief's said that his agents were "particularly interested in their activities at asylum reception centers... We have information that some of the arrivals may include people who've been involved in fighting."

Then, Finland's Interior Minister Orpo calmed everyone down some more by stating that

> "roughly 70 fighters have left Finland to fight abroad, including among the ranks of IS; a couple dozen have returned to Finland... there are some asylum seeker cases where we have found indications or connections suggesting that they have participated in terrorist activities."

Oh, wonderful. Nothing to worry about except potential terrorists roaming the streets... well, the "evil" citizens of Finland are probably more of a threat than the refugees...

Well, yes, yes they are according to Minister Orpo.

In his statement to media giant "yle," Minister Orpo also stated that "the most concrete threat to national security remained attacks by Finns opposed to immigration and clashes with asylum seekers."

That's why Orpo asked that more police be assigned to shelters to help *protect the refugees from* his allegedly crazed and bloodthirsty countrymen.

Seriously.
http://yle.fi/uutiset/supo_violent_hate_crimes_refugee_links_to_violence_affecting_national_security/8428552

(16) FRANCE

Ah, France. The Eiffel Tower. The Seine River. The Bordeaux Wine. The Migrants.

Some years ago, PressTV reported "the widely accepted estimate" that 70% of the inmates in French prisons are Muslim despite only being 5-10% of the general population of France. The report claims that to find out why Muslims are so dramatically over represented would take a "political courage" that's nonexistent.

Interesting statement. What could it mean?

Think about it.
https://youtu.be/GmJ4-xleQsQ

Calais Re-imagined
Calais, France, is the closest town in France to England. On a clear day, from this beautiful and ancient town, you can see the famous White Cliffs of Dover on the English shoreline. Calais had at one time been under English control and known as the English Crown's brightest jewel due to its strategic location and wealthy port. Because of its sheer beauty and safety, Calais was very popular with travelers, and 10 million tourists visited annually.

That was then. This is now.

And now, Calais has an enormous squatters' camp, nicknamed *The Jungle*, with thousands of migrants. A reporter visiting the camp in the summer of 2015 said that from a distance, he could smell the stench of human sweat and excrement mixed in with garbage. Doctors volunteering at the camp said the diseases and injuries were plentiful.

To be clear, many of the injuries were sustained while trying to jump trains and sneak on trucks, breaking and entering into terminals, evading police, and jumping security fences. Certainly, lawless criminal activities can be dangerous!

Reportedly, there were political signs such as "NO BORDER – RESIST! REBEL! REVOLT!" which begs the question, why the migrants didn't "Rebel! Resist! Revolt!" in whatever country they came from, for it is curious to flee a country to a "safe" country only to then decide to "Rebel! Resist! Revolt!" in the country that is providing you refuge.

The reporter was apparently accused of racism by an Afghan migrant who said "with considerable venom" – "You in England, you don't like us... You English, I don't like you either." The migrant swiped his hand at the reporter to make him go away.

> *Interesting dynamic. The migrant is camped out in Calais desperately trying to sneak into England but is openly and loudly professing his disdain and dislike for the English to an English journalist. Wonder how that will play out when the migrant finally gets to England...*

Another migrant said he was trying to sneak back into England to live "the good life" after already having been deported once. As the reporter noted, "however hostile the public opinion, they will keep coming."

Indeed they will.
http://www.newstatesman.com/politics/2015/08/owen-jones-talks-calais-migrants-they-forget-we-are-human

Unrequited love
In a 2015 interview with African migrants in the Calais *Jungle* camp, one migrant complained that instead of the "good treatment" he expected when he showed up in France, he quickly found out that he would have to fend for himself and live in a tent. Yes, yes, France *did* provide free clothes and free food, but the water supply was inconvenient, and sanitation services were lacking.

Whether the migrants were actually illegal aliens, based on where they sought asylum first, was never revealed nor addressed in the video interview. Instead, the viewers were given the impression that they were simply bonafide refugees.

During the same segment, one African migrant complained that police chased him for *no reason whatsoever* and hit him in the nose and legs with their batons.

> *For the record, Calais sits across from England. As commercial trucks line up to go to England via the Eurotunnel, and as trains pass along the same route to England, migrants often attempt to jump onto them or break into them to gain illegal entry from France to England. Migrants are also reportedly habitually damaging property and cutting security fences to gain access to the tunnel. It is not uncommon for thousands of migrants* per night *to try to force their way into England illegally.*

Another African migrant told of the time when police chased him, *for no reason whatsoever,* and he fell, breaking his arm. The same callous police then called an ambulance to tend to his injury. Then "bad-treatment" France paid for the migrant's 20 day stay in the hospital. That he stayed in a hospital for close to a month for a broken arm, for which most Americans would have been sent home the same day, didn't seem to trouble the researcher reporting the story who glossed right over it.

Bad treatment indeed!
https://youtu.be/vI6H5uzgm-c

When in doubt, fight it out

In early summer 2015, hundreds of migrants from the *Jungle* battled over access to smuggling routes into England. Armed with knives, wooden clubs, and iron bars, two rival African gangs (Sudanese vs. Eritreans) rampaged through the streets of Calais for over six hours.

Besides rioting, and battling each other, the crazed migrants also committed acts of arson as well as property destruction. The vicious fighting and violence spilled from section to section and erupted in random areas as migrants beat and stabbed and cut each other. In the end, while many fighters were hurt, at least 24 migrants sustained serious bodily injuries. The mayhem lasted almost all night until police were finally able to disperse the bloodthirsty crowds.

This extreme violence and fighting between the African Sudanese and Eritreans became rather commonplace. On many occasions full scale battles would erupt and rage for hours. More and more migrants were seriously injuring each other.

By the end of September, French police began tear gassing unruly migrants and evacuating their makeshift camps, sometimes hundreds of migrants at a time.

It didn't make a dent.
http://www.thetimes.co.uk/tto/news/world/europe/article4457539.ece
http://www.telegraph.co.uk/news/worldnews/europe/france/11884297/Migrants-tear-gassed-by-French-riot-police-at-Calais-Jungle-camp.html

In September 2015 the BBC had a reporter spend time in Calais with a group of migrants who spoke about their organized schemes to gain illegal entry into England.

Inadvertently, the video also revealed visually the dirty secret the old-fashioned-controlled-media works tirelessly to guard – virtually all the migrants were young fighting-age males.

The migrants spoke of the many ways they routinely break the law: damaging property and cutting fences, jumping on trains, breeching security fences, and monitoring and relaying police activities using their cell phones to try and stay one step ahead of the law.

Surely, these skills that they are honing will serve them well once they settle into their new host countries.
http://www.bbc.com/news/uk-29074736

French Prime Minister Manuel Valls, whose given name was Manuel Valls Galfetti when he was born in Spain, became a French citizen at the age of 20. In the spring of 2015, he said, "I am against the introduction of quotas for migrants. This has never been in line with French proposals." He has since caved.

In September 2015, several French mayors spoke of their intention to only accept Christian refugees in order to be "certain they are not terrorists in disguise." Another mayor said "he would only consider taking in Christian families from Iraq and Syria because 'they are the most persecuted.'"

We suspect the spectacle of so many Christians being beheaded really made an impression. And the claim that "Christians were the most persecuted" was validated a few months later when the European Parliament Vice-President, Antonio Tajani, reported that "Every day, in every region of our planet, we register new cases of systematic violence and persecution against Christians. No other religious community is faced with such hatred, violence and aggression as is the Christian community."

Predictably, Prime Minister Valls condemned the French mayors for their views, firing back, "You don't sort (refugees) on the basis of religion. The right to asylum is a universal right." Also condemning the mayors' sentiments, the French Interior Minister said on television that he didn't understand "this distinction (between religions). I condemn it and I think it's dreadful."

Apparently, the Prime and Interior Ministers had not heard the late September 2015 warning from the German Police Chief who completely disagreed.

There has been an alarming growth in violence in German shelters housing Christian and Muslim asylum seekers. Hundreds are rioting and fighting, and scores are being injured.

"'I think housing separated according to religion makes perfect sense," deputy head of Germany's police union, told German newspaper Die Welt, "particularly for Muslims and Christians."

Better not mention your practical idea to any French Ministers. They will likely not understand the distinction, will condemn it, call it racist, and think it's dreadful.

But then again, they're just pontificating politicians and don't have your hands-on experience, do they Chief?

Ah, if only you could chat with them about theory vs. reality...
http://www.ibtimes.co.uk/france-pm-manuel-valls-slams-2-mayors-who-want-take-only-christian-refugees-1518996
http://www.telegraph.co.uk/news/worldnews/europe/germany/11896855/Christian-and-Muslim-refugees-should-be-housed-separately-says-German-police-chief.html
https://www.rt.com/news/259337-france-rejects-migrant-quotas/

Overwhelmed and struggling to make sense of a senseless situation, French police detained at least 18,000 illegal migrants in the Calais area in the first part of 2015. In the meanwhile, migrants were endlessly trying to sneak into England.

Breaking the law night after night is tiring work
Allegedly, the migrants typically rest during the day and create mayhem mostly under the cover of darkness. On a typical night in the summer of 2015, about 1,700 migrants had attempted to storm the tunnel. Violence erupted as about 1,000 were pushed back by French police. Afterwards, the migrants rushed to the roadways and used their bodies to block the tunnel and disrupt the orderly flow of traffic between France and England. Another 700 migrants that had broken into and entered a freight terminal, were removed by police.

This isn't a joke. The company that is responsible for managing the Eurotunnel keeps demanding help "to stop the 'organized' groups of migrants storming their terminal 'at will' every night."

While weary police were attempting to restore law and order, migrants attacked them, throwing stones and rocks. One African migrant hurled a rock at a police officer causing "serious head injuries." The migrant was arrested. But it didn't stop the hundreds and hundreds of others from hurling more projectiles.

The UK Daily Mail reported that "an organised gang of 200 (migrants) filmed chanting 'open the borders' and demanding to be allowed to walk to Britain" marched on the tunnel before being turned back.

Is this happening in the same country that gave us Voltaire, Rousseau, Hugo, Cézanne, Monet, Renoir, Degas, Debussy, Jules Verne, Brigitte Bardot, crêpes, and escargot?
http://www.dailymail.co.uk/news/article-3183668/Riot-police-pelted-stones-2-100-migrants-storm-Channel-Tunnel-Calais-weekend-chanting-Open-borders.html

Before we continue, please take a moment to imagine the professionalism and restraint French police must have shown in the face of all this violence and rioting.

You're a police officer. Not too long ago, while on routine patrol if you came upon someone breaking and entering into a building, you would have made a good arrest and maybe gotten a citation.

Now, thousands of unruly foreigners illegally entered your country, set up camps on your soil, and were now devoting themselves to figuring out ways to undermine the very laws you swore to uphold. Every day and every night they shamelessly break laws, destroy your nation's property, and create havoc, all the while taunting you, disrespecting your country, and you.

They rush you, mob you, throw stones, bricks, rocks, pipes, and other projectiles at you, your eyes, your head, and there is not much for you to do but try and stay calm as you push them back.

Restraint under these circumstances really does take people of exceptional character.

There is no end in sight

By November 2015, there were a reported 6,000 people milling about in the Calais camps, planning their next moves to gain illegal entry into England. One can only guess how this will all turn out.

http://www.telegraph.co.uk/news/uknews/immigration/11779615/Calais-crisis-Chaos-in-parts-of-Kent-and-the-Channel-Tunnel-under-siege-live.html
http://www.thetimes.co.uk/tto/news/uk/article4458919.ece
http://www.independent.co.uk/news/uk/politics/police-use-anti-terrorism-powers-to-detain-british-volunteers-taking-aid-to-calais-refugee-camp-a6724221.html

Lacking a 'migrant seal of approval'

Many "experts" have made outlandish claims that the fact that more refugees don't want to settle in France somehow looks bad for France. One migration specialist said, "France should be deeply concerned that more refugees do not want to come... (this) is a clear sign that the country is no longer attractive... (this) shows without doubt the economic situation in the country is no longer in good health and neither is the democratic situation."

After trying to analyze this "conclusion" that France must be in trouble since it doesn't have a seal of approval from refugees, we simply wrote it off as old-style Soviet doublespeak and moved on.

How can you tell a banker is lying? His lips are moving...

An "expert" at a French investment bank said France should scoop up as many refugees as it can in order to "expand its growth prospects." An "expert" at a German investment bank said refugees "could boost economic output in the Eurozone by 0.2%" by the end of 2015.

One organization put out an "expert" report that claimed refugee "costs to national budgets are minimal." A migration "expert" from the same organization said "no study has ever shown that immigration is bad for France." He also claimed that the goal of refugees isn't to receive welfare, it is to have a better life.

"Experts" also cautioned that refugees need to be given time to recover from the traumas they have suffered. Give them time. They can't be expected to become as productive as citizens for at least 15 years.

15 years. Think about it.

Of course, not one "expert" pointed to any actual real life case studies from countries that have multiple years of actual experience, not just theorems and hopeful optimism. Well, how about Sweden? No, that's a bad example. It's really not working. Or Lebanon? *Worse yet.* It's *really* not working.

For experts to boldly claim that masses of refugees will boost France's economy is wondrous. But where's the proof? Has this new model worked anywhere? You know, for years experts swore asbestos was safe, and doctors endorsed smoking cigarettes in ads seen by millions. How'd those claims without proof work out? Just asking.

You can see where this is headed. There is just way too much material here.

Connect your own dots.
http://www.thelocal.fr/20150916/refugees-offer-chance-for-france-to-boost-economy
http://www.telegraph.co.uk/news/worldnews/europe/france/11880391/Refugees-shun-France-land-of-red-tape-unemployment-and-poor-housing.html

Your donations in action

As far as all the donations, and clothes, and cash people are sending to support the poor refugees, more and more video evidence is surfacing showing that tens of thousands of dollars' worth of clothes and supplies are routinely being rejected, thrown out, abandoned, and even destroyed by unappreciative and increasingly demanding migrants.

In one September 2015 drive purportedly through France, you can see massive amounts of clothes lying in heaps all over the streets, like litter, discarded by migrants who had no use for the stuff.
https://youtu.be/TPv4a4b_FWQ

Church for sale

In Vierzon, a local community of 27,000 people with dwindling numbers of church-goers found that they had too many costly churches for their needs. So, in 2013, they decided to sell one of the unused buildings, the Church of St. Aloysius. Local Muslims, whose numbers are growing exponentially, immediately expressed interest in buying the church and converting the church into a mosque.

Instead, the Archdiocese decided to sell the church to a "nondenominational" charity coincidentally named "The Fraternity of St. Aloysius" which was collecting money to buy the church under the motto "Stop the Mosque."

Very French, n'est pas?
https://youtu.be/l82jXj5tHos

In fairness to past history, France experienced horrific migrant riots about a decade ago.

Do you remember when the US Government told US tourists to avoid travel to parts of France?
No? Here's a quick refresher.

In October 2005, French police were routinely investigating a break-in at a construction site. As police attempted to question a group of migrant youths in the vicinity, two male teens, one African and one Arab, fled. In their attempt to evade police, the migrant teens climbed the wall of an electric relay station.

Really bad idea. There's a reason there are DO NOT ENTER and DANGER signs all around electric stations.

Sadly, but not surprisingly, when the two trespassers came into contact with a high voltage transformer, they were electrocuted.

Shortly afterwards, hundreds of African and North African Muslim migrants, angered that the police chase was "responsible" for the electrocution of the teens, turned the housing projects on the outskirts of Paris into a burned-out war zone worthy of a Mad Max sequel.

The destruction went on for weeks. Violent and terrifying night-time riots and battles spread to other cities as well.

On one fateful Fall Saturday in France, some 250 rioters were arrested, including children carrying homemade fire-bombs.

Bomb carrying children in France. Think about that.

And almost 900 vehicles, including city buses, were burned, and countless properties were damaged. "Hit-and-run-arson attacks" spread through immigrant neighborhoods as hooded gangs of migrant youths, mostly Africans, demonstrated their hatred for France and the police.

Nothing was sacred. Many public and private buildings, including schools, post offices, churches, and businesses were targeted and burned to the ground. They rampaging youths also shot at police and random bystanders. Hoping to stop the rampant arsons, desperate authorities forbid the sale of gasoline to minors.

Migrant youths were apparently further infuriated that French authorities were taking a hard line against crime, calling the rioters "rabble," "dregs," and threatening to "clean widespread crime out of the suburbs with 'a power-hose.'"

As DW reported, "There were concerns over the fact the unrest was concentrated in neighborhoods with Muslim immigrants from France's former Arab and African colonial territories, a small proportion of whom have turned to radical Islam in the past few years."

When children go wild
By mid-November, it was reported that over 2,500 people, as young as 13, had been arrested and migrants had destroyed nearly 9,000 vehicles. Property damage estimates were astronomical, in the hundreds of millions of dollars.

Worse, more than 100 police officers and firefighters had suffered injuries as a result of the rioters. About a dozen police officers had been shot. A handful of innocent bystander were murdered by migrants as well.

Some youths interviewed by various news outlets claimed it was "fun" setting cars on fire. Others spoke of making acid bombs that spray acid, and nail bombs that shoot nail shrapnel when they explode. Yet others had seen people dropping metal cannon balls and bombs off high-rise apartment buildings at police patrolling the streets below.

Of course, none of the children admitted to participating themselves in any of this mayhem that they simply "witnessed from afar." Yet, in the south of France, police arrested a half dozen migrant children caught making about 150 bombs in a local building.

Bomb making children in France. Think about that.

One African teen, who blamed virtually everything on police harassment, explained that, "It's not going to end until there are two policemen dead" to settle the score for the 2 electrocuted migrant teens.

Goals and priorities. It's all about goals and priorities.
http://www.dw.com/en/french-leaders-meet-as-riots-spread/a-1766239
http://www.pages.drexel.edu/~pa34/PARISRIOTS.htm
http://www.nzz.ch/newzzEFW1EOO2-12-1.183284

Bus ride from hell
Back in July 2008, Muslim migrants attacked a French man on a city bus. As a security camera captured the horror, the man was targeted and then systematically robbed, picked apart, and when he tried to retrieve his property, he was beset upon by three or more young male Muslim migrants. The attack lasted for many long agonizing minutes and it is literally painful to watch this innocent random victim be beaten and kicked and tortured while other riders on the bus are also systematically and repeatedly punched and assaulted.
https://youtu.be/D24bK9mqKo4

Venting some frustration
In videos from July 2014, crazed young migrant men went nuts on the streets of Paris. The video showed them attacking and chasing police officers, using metal poles to break up sidewalks to loosen chunks of concrete to throw, and surrounding police cars as they kicked and dented and smashed the police vehicles while screaming. Instead of running their attackers over, the police cars made u-turns in their attempts to escape the attacks but were pummeled mercilessly.

The rioters tipped over a small van, collected and threw more and more projectiles, and created a load of property damage. When police used tear gas to try and restore law and order many rioters continued throwing dangerous items, and even began throwing some of the tear gas canisters back at police. The young migrant male rioters, often clad in flags of Muslim countries, destroyed local businesses, set fire to cars, and attacked random people. They rampaged recklessly, laying waste to what was a very high-end area with beautiful boutiques and shops, and caused endless suffering and pandemonium.

Along the way, they also destroyed maintenance trucks, city services, and lights as they vandalized, looted, and laughed and smiled and took selfies while waving Muslim heritage flags. They set fire to cars, buildings, dumpsters, and committed many acts of arson. And they attacked and taunted the police.
https://youtu.be/5eKutDQ8700
https://youtu.be/w45LwE-CkUs

The Times of Israel featured a video that allegedly showed a clash between pro-Israel and pro-Palestine militants in the streets of Paris. The Times of Israel noted that the video showed "what appears to be pro-Israel demonstrators tearing through the street in front of the shul, carrying sticks, and throwing tables and chairs in the direction of pro-Palestinian protesters."

The two groups went back and forth until the allegedly pro-Israel group ran behind a police line at which point the French police advanced on the pro-Palestinian group as the video ended. While it wasn't clear exactly what was occurring, it was clear that hatred and violence had spilled out onto the streets of Paris, yet again.

Imagine what next year will bring once all the new arriving migrants get established.
http://www.timesofisrael.com/watch-jews-clash-with-pro-palestinians-at-paris-gaza-rally/

As we were preparing this book for press, everything changed.

November 2015, Friday the 13th, in Paris, France
In Paris, one of the most gun-controlled cities in the modern world, horrific terror attacks left about 130 people dead and possibly triple that number injured. From restaurant and sidewalk shootings, to soccer stadium explosions and machine gunnings at a rock concert, the carnage was unspeakable. After we made some calls to contact loved ones to make sure they were safe, we dove into the news coverage.

Sometimes, in the early parts of a tragedy unfolding, there isn't much spinning. An apparently forged Syrian passport was found by the body of one attacker. The Guardian reported that "Greece's citizen protection minister, Nikos Toskas, said… the passport's owner had entered the European Union through the Greek island of Leros on October 3, 2015." The man was possibly "wanted" so he snuck into the EU via Greece on his forged passport. Or maybe the passport was planted. Other authorities agreed that at least one attack group had recently snuck in through Greece.

Police said that another attacker was on their "radicalized Islamist list" with a criminal record but no jail time. Consistently identified by the media as a "Frenchman," reportedly one of his parents was from Algeria and the other from Portugal. Other suspects were identified as "French nationals born in Belgium" - technically quite correct but the other half of the story is that they all had Middle Eastern parents.

Witnesses of the rock concert massacre said that shooters were yelling "Allahu Akbar" as they shot people and lobbed hand grenades.

Remember, back in September 2015, Lebanese Minister of Education Elias Bousaab warned British Prime Minister David Cameron that 2% of migrants were radicals looking to cause havoc. He said most had, and would, enter via Turkey into Greece. Apparently, the have and they will.

French authorities claimed most, if not all, of the killers were Muslims who had been trained in Syria by the Islamic State. French authorities also identified one of the three shooters that killed 90 people at the rock concert as a Muslim who lived in France, left for Syria in 2013 to fight alongside the Islamic State, received training and experience, and then returned to France to terrorize and murder the people of Paris. Reportedly, at least one of the terrorists had entered the EU with the other "refugees fleeing war."

Our deepest sympathies and thoughts to the people hurt and suffering from this tragedy. We are so profoundly saddened. It didn't have to happen.
http://www.dailymail.co.uk/news/article-3234458/Two-100-Syrian-migrants-ISIS-fighters-PM-warned-Lebanese-minister-tells-Cameron-extremist-group-sending-jihadists-cover-attack-West.html
http://www.latimes.com/world/middleeast/la-fg-foreign-fighters-20151208-story.html

Grand delusions
On November 17, 2015, António Guterres, the UN's High Commissioner for Refugees said that to blame migrants for terror attacks was "absolute nonsense." He added that the terrorist "strategy is not only to set Europeans against

refugees, but within Europe, to set citizen against citizen within communities, community against community within countries, and country against country in the Union."

Of course the migrants aren't to blame for the terror attacks.

Duh. Most migrants don't have time for such silliness and are really good law-abiding people looking for a better future. Could this explain why quite a few are simply way too busy over-representing themselves in the growing crime statistics we've seen spiking across Europe?
http://www.unhcr.org.mt/news-and-views/north-africa-situation/805-unhcr-chief-says-it-is-qabsolute-nonsenseq-to-blame-refugees-for-terror

The more the merrier
On November 18, 2015, the French President stated that France would be taking in another 30,000 refugees over the next two years, thus repeating France's commitment to migrants since that 30,000 figure had already been announced in September. At that time, France added the caveat that it "cannot welcome to Europe all those who flee dictatorship in Syria." Now, the caveat was, "France accepted playing its part in showing solidarity towards these refugees and towards Europe."

We wait to see how the refugees will return that solidarity in kind to France.
https://euobserver.com/migration/131175

Another bad train ride
On December 9, 2015, a group of young Afghan men tried to rape a 28-year-old woman on a Paris express train. The woman had gotten into an empty car but soon 10 Afghan men joined her. Maybe sensing danger, she got up and tried to move to another seat when three of the Afghan men followed her. They ended up grabbing her, groping her, one Afghan tried to strangle her with her own scarf, and a third Afghan pulled out a knife and put it in her face.

The attackers then began to take her clothes off. Luckily, the rapists were surprised by another passenger who helped the young woman escape.

The victim was so traumatized after the assault that she needed 2 weeks of work-leave.

Security cameras recorded images of the assailants and the woman identified them as well. Of the three attackers, so far two were arrested, and are asylum seekers from Afghanistan. They both denied the charges and had what they thought was a "perfect alibi." They said that they had actually been out looking to have sex with homosexual and transvestite prostitutes in the Bois de Boulogne park and had nothing to do with the assault. The police weren't buying their story after the woman's eyewitness identification and a review of the security cameras.

Damn those pesky security cameras.
http://www.leparisien.fr/versailles-78000/versailles-un-viol-evite-de-justesse-dans-un-train-07-01-2016-5428711.php

Marking the Hebdo Massacre anniversary
In Paris, on the 7th of January 2016, the anniversary of the *Charlie Hebdo* massacre, a foreign-looking man with wires hanging out of his clothes, a fake explosives belt, and wielding a meat cleaver tried to force his way into a police station and attack the police, screaming "Allahu akbar." Police shot and killed the would-be terrorist and locked down the surrounding neighborhood.

In the aftermath, many strange details emerged and were reported by Bild. The dead terrorist had been living in a nearby refugee center and used no less than 7 aliases. Since coming to Europe, at various times, the man claimed to be Syrian, Moroccan, Tunisian, and Georgian. He had been a very busy migrant, having registered in Austria, Germany, Italy, Romania,

Sweden and Switzerland between January 2011 and March 2015.

He had racked up a rap sheet that included the sexual assault of a 13-year-old girl, a dangerous assault, various drug offenses, threats, insults, theft, illegally having a gun, fraudulent acquisition of services, harassing and groping women at nightclubs, and he also beat up a homeless man and a passer-by. Three times he had been incarcerated in German prisons. Yet he had never been deported.

Unbelievable. Are there more than 3 strikes in German baseball?

The dead terrorist's former roommate told Bild, "He was very fast and aggressive, especially when it came to faith. All unbelievers would be worthless, would die."

A former *Charlie Hebdo* journalist remarked to CNN, "We know that it's going to be this way for the next years as long as the people who are giving orders from Syria are not disconnected."
http://news.yahoo.com/photos/paris-police-station-attack-thwarted-slideshow/french-police-secure-area-man-shot-dead-police-photo-121437940.html
http://www.cnn.com/2016/01/07/europe/paris-gunfire-charlie-hebdo-anniversary/
http://www.bild.de/news/inland/paris/das-ist-der-terrorist-aus-dem-deutschen-fluechtlingsheim-44093280.bild.html

(17) GEORGIA

Georgia is a small country between Russia, Turkey, Armenia, Azerbaijan, and the Black Sea. With a population of just over 4 million, Georgia has a total of over a quarter million internally displaced persons due to "internal occupations and strife," 587 asylum seekers, and 1,659 refugees according to the United Nations as of June 2015. At the same time, at least 14,000 people have fled Georgia as asylum seekers and refugees. With so much internal unrest, Georgia has its hands full.
http://www.unhcr.org/pages/49e48d2e6.html

In the meanwhile, Georgia has provided asylum to several thousand refugees, and has a *very low* rate of rejection. The Ministry of Accommodation and Refugees in Georgia is also committed to the "success" of asylum seekers, stating that "Our major goal is to help them have a livelihood in order to assure them that the *state aid is not the only way to survive*. After we provide housing and they can experience a feeling of property, we want to *change this psychological kind of addiction to state allowance* and show them *how to live independently.*"

Scary stuff if you're looking to live off the system.

So why else aren't there more refugees clamoring to get in to Georgia? It seems that many opportunists are now shunning the little country after realizing that since Georgia has been designated a "safe" country," they would be blocked from trying to move on to seek more lucrative asylum elsewhere.

And they would be stuck in Georgia where the government would expect them to become independent and responsible for themselves.

What's so unattractive about that?
http://www.economist.com/blogs/easternapproaches/2010/11/refugees_georgia
http://www.europeandme.eu/30brain/1660-georgia-refugee-haven

(18) GERMANY

"We have many examples where we showed we can respond. Remember the bank rescues? During the international financial crisis, the federal and state governments pushed through the necessary legislation in a matter of days."

Angela Merkel
Chancellor of Germany

Germany has been hot for immigrants for years. In 2012, the German Federal Ministry for Economic Affairs and Energy launched the "Make it in Germany" campaign to lure non-German "qualified professionals" to immigrate to Germany and have a wonderful future and make a lucrative living. Complete with an interactive website listing open jobs and other enticements, the idea was to attract immigrants to Germany to fill gaps created by retiring workers.

Spoiler alert: *the German vision of an "immigrant looking for work" is an experienced and qualified professional like a surgeon, nurse, lawyer, chemist, civil engineer, research scientist, database programmer, or IT wiz.*

In 2013, Chancellor Merkel was quoted as saying that "increasing diversity also means enrichment," and that Germany must transform into an "immigration country."

A "Success Through Diversity" award was set up and awarded 10,000 euros to German businesses that promoted diversity best. As the "Make it in Germany" website noted, "All the award winners agree that integrating international *qualified professionals* is well worthwhile. Not only does it enable them to fill posts faster and with exactly the right person; diversity is also a way of securing success for their business."

There's that "qualified" term, again.

In December 2015, current "in demand" professions listed on the "make it in Germany" website included doctors, trained nurses and medical support staff, engineers, scientists, and IT specialists. The website noted that prospects were "excellent" even for young people 15-25 where unemployment for their demographic was only about 8%.

The website concluded that "Given that qualified labor is crucial to the success of the German economy, skilled workers will remain in big demand for years to come."

Hmmm. Qualified. Skilled. Think about it.

Well, Merkel got her wish of massive immigration, but she blew the target by miles on the qualified or skilled part. And that could spell disaster.
http://www.make-it-in-germany.com/en

Tipping the scales
Germany has taken in more migrants than any other EU country. According to Germany's Federal Office for Migration and Refugees, of the refugees arriving in Germany in 2014, the majority were, *surprise surprise*, young males. The largest age group was, *surprise surprise*, males 18-25 years-of-age.

In August 2015, the Chairman of the Central Council of Muslims in Germany told reporters that "at least 80%" of the current and expected refugees to Germany this year are Muslims.

Both these trends seem to be continuing.
http://www.bamf.de/SharedDocs/Anlagen/DE/Publikationen/Broschueren/bundesamt-in-zahlen-2014.html?nn=1694460
http://www.tagesspiegel.de/politik/fluechtlinge-und-religion-die-zahl-der-muslime-wird-signifikant-wachsen/12242898.html

The bottomless pit
In 2014, about 200,000 migrants sought asylum in Germany. German authorities officially said the number would be around 800,000 in 2015, while Vice Chancellor Gabriel was quoted often as saying it might be "up to 1,000,000."

In late September 2015, the news from Berlin was bleak. The Boston Globe reported that Germany's Interior Ministry admitted that on top of everything else that was wrong, about a third of the refugees coming into the country were lying about being "Syrian" since Syrians were almost always guaranteed acceptance in the EU.

The UK's Telegraph reported that "In Bulgaria 10,000 fake Syrian passports have been seized, which is likely to be only a fraction of those in circulation elsewhere." In September 2015, police in Germany arrested a jihadist caught using forged papers to pretend to be an asylum-seeker.

The Telegraph further noted in late September 2015 that "The most recent EU figures show that only one in five migrants is Syrian, but at some border crossings it has been reported that up to 90 per cent of those entering Europe claim to be from Syria."

Think about that one for a moment. What a mess!

Also in September 2015, German Interior Minister Thomas de Maizière said, "'we cannot open Europe totally for millions and millions of poor people in the world or even for all of those coming from conflict zones. Impossible." Bet Chancellor Merkel wasn't pleased one bit. No one is pleased when their harebrained schemes start to unravel.

The confidential report that wasn't
In October 2015, a leading German newspaper cited what it called a confidential government forecast that expected the total of migrants entering Germany would top 1,500,00 by the end of 2015.

Question. *What* was Merkel thinking?

The report further revealed far graver scenarios. Breakdowns of resources and provisions. Health risks. Housing. Sanitation. And how about the families of the mostly young men of fighting-age? Each asylum seeker granted refuge could very well bring "an average of four to eight family members over to Germany in due course."

New question. *Was* Merkel thinking?

After all, Merkel must have been awake when she suspended the Dublin Regulation. Without the Dublin Regulation, which would have limited asylum seekers to those people that actually claimed asylum at a port of entry in Germany, Merkel basically created a free-for-all stampede. No questions asked.

In fairness, we now know that Merkel *was* busy. Busy taking selfies with refugees. One wonders if Nero would have done the same given the technological advances of today. Drop that violin and snap some shots of those dancing flames, man. It's cool. And warm, too. Click, click, click.

Let's do some basic math based on the "confidential" report's concerns of "migrants bringing over family members and/or other related parties." The potential numbers laid out in the report are truly staggering.

Lower end – each refugee brings over 4 relatives.
1,500,000 x 4 relatives = 6,000,000 additional people PLUS add back in the people already in Germany for a total of 7,500,000 potential guests.

Higher end – each refugee brings over 8 relatives.
1,500,000 x 8 relatives = 12,000,000 additional people PLUS add back in the people already in Germany for a total of 13,500,000 potential guests.

> *Perspective time:* out of the goodness of your heart, you host a party at your home and invite a dozen people who are down on their luck. You prepare a dozen place settings, and make sure you have some extra food and drink along with some really great desserts. Unfortunately, you find out that Merkel was in charge of the invitations, and suddenly each guest is bringing an average of 6 additional people along for the festivities. Your party is now 72 people strong... just like that. *Are you ok with that?*

No wonder Germans were concerned. It just gets better and better for the Rhineland. By the way, the German government denied any knowledge of the "confidential" report.

What report? No one knows anything about any report.
http://www.theguardian.com/world/2015/oct/05/germany-now-expects-up-to-15-mln-migrants-in-2015-report
http://www.dw.com/en/german-government-denies-reports-of-15-million-refugee-estimates/a-18762443
https://www.bostonglobe.com/news/world/2015/09/25/nearly-third-migrants-germany-falsely-claim-syrian-officials-say/lg7JDOrESUAILxhQ0HyiZO/story.html
http://www.telegraph.co.uk/news/worldnews/middleeast/syria/11880979/People-smugglers-using-Facebook-to-sell-fake-Syrian-passports-to-economic-migrants.html

Can it get any better?

Oh yes it can! At least the migrants are *well educated* and can jump in to help save Germany, right?

Not according to the German Federal Employment Agency.

The sad truth about qualifications
At the end of October 2015, the German Federal Employment Agency reported that most (81%) of the recently arrived refugees and migrants had *NO FORMAL QUALIFICATIONS*. In fact, as far as they could tell, only 8% had a college degree and a high number are uneducated and quite literally illiterate.

> *Luckily, scores of German universities have said they'll allow refugees to attend courses to help them out.*

The German Federal Employment Agency also reported that based on their research, and German's love their research, *at least 400,000 new welfare recipients* would be added to the system funded by Germany's already overburdened taxpayers.

Now that's a huge number.

And that was estimated *before* the influx number of new refugees topped over 1 million people.
https://assets.jungefreiheit.de/2015/10/BA-TOP_3_1_02.pdf
https://jungefreiheit.de/wirtschaft/2015/prognose-fuer-2016-400-000-neue-sozialfaelle-durch-asylkrise/

Statistics at odds
Ok, so the German Federal Employment Agency was convinced at the end of October 2015, that most (81%) of the recently arrived refugees and migrants had no formal qualifications and only 8% had a college degree, leaving a high number presumed uneducated and illiterate. Interesting that the UN claimed nearly the exact opposite during the period April to September 2015. *Gee. How could that be?*

UN profiles Syrians

On December 8, 2015 the UN reported the results of "surveys" they had done in Greece in 2015, saying that the process wasn't random but provided "a good overall picture of the 'profile' of Syrians arriving in Greece between April and September 2015."

Weirdly, the UN chose to grace the web page of the survey results with a photo of a Syrian "family" complete with a mother, two daughters, and a cigarette-smoking father. The choice was weird, not because it showed callous disregard for the health of young children from the known dangers of second-hand smoke, but because the vast majority of those surveyed were young men.

The UN reported that 85% of the people surveyed said they were Sunni Muslims and the "vast majority of those surveyed (78 per cent) were under 35." *No surprises so far.*

Curiously, in their press release, the UN left out whether those surveyed were male or female. So, we dug through the links to get at the actual report (complete with another deceptive cover photo – this time a defenseless little girl wrapped in a blanket). We discovered, *wait for it,* that 81% of those interviewed were males!

81% were males! *(Another non-surprise, but wow!)*

But it gets *sooo* much better. Read on, unless you get scared easily.

Fears confirmed, as a majority of the Syrians interviewed by the UN reportedly said

- they had lived in private accommodations in their country of transit or first asylum and only 3% had lived in refugee camps (*so they weren't fleeing anything anymore, were they?*)
- they had no legal documentation or identification

- they were planning to bring the rest of their family members with them once they got to their new asylum country
- they left their country of transit or first asylum because of *a lack of employment opportunities and a lack of financial assistance (welfare)*
- their goal was to get set up in Germany or Sweden

The UN seemed to feel all of this was good news. Try as we might, we didn't see why.

The UN also reported that 86% of Syrians interviewed by the UN *claimed* to have "secondary" or "university-level" educations. Many also *claimed* a variety of professional experience, all without documentation or substantiation. This led the UN to make the following bold statement, "Overall, the profile is of a highly-skilled population on the move."

Yet the German government said most of the recently arrived migrants in Germany as of October 2015 had *virtually no formal qualifications.*

Why such a grave disparity? Is the sacred fairytale unraveling?
http://www.unhcr.org/5666ddda6.html

Stop the hysteria and start embracing new ways!
Instead of all this fear mongering and silly hysteria, Germany should consider itself lucky to be able to immerse its adults and children, especially its young girls, in the new cultural experiences migrants will offer.

How about learning to dress properly not to get groped or raped?

Parents of students in a Bavarian school in the summer of 2015 received an emergency letter shortly after a Syrian refugee shelter, housing hundreds of migrants, opened next door to the school's gym. We'll get to the letter in a second, just know that the students are safe as the gym has been closed and all physical education classes are now taking place at another school.

Here are sections of the letter from the headteacher of the school:

> "Overall, about half of the Syrian population has been displaced as a result of the fighting in their country - more than half of those affected are children."

> "For the refugees, access to the school gardens and buildings is strictly forbidden. The same goes for the school grounds during the day. The number of teachers on duty during breaks has been increased."

> "The Syrian citizens are mainly Muslims and speak Arabic. The refugees are marked by their own culture. Because our school is directly next to where they are staying, modest clothing should be adhered to, in order to avoid discrepancies. Revealing tops or blouses, short shorts or miniskirts could lead to misunderstandings."

The letter caused a flurry of controversy, but was defended by a local politician who said it was "absolutely necessary." He added, "when Muslim teenage boys go to open air swimming pools, they are overwhelmed when they see girls in bikinis... These boys, who come from a culture where for women it is frowned upon to show naked skin, *follow girls and bother them without realizing."*

The school district administrator also defended the letter stating it contained nothing wrong and was a "necessary preventative approach."
http://www.welt.de/vermischtes/article143128131/Miniroecke-koennten-zu-Missverstaendnissen-fuehren.html

In a moment, you will see why the administrator may have felt justified in feeling nervous and concerned.

Way back in 2006, DW, Germany's "leading organization for international media development," reported that young immigrant males committed violent crimes 300% more frequently than their native German contemporaries.

One expert conclusion cited was that since criminals and violent offenders, "as a rule," start offending when they are 14-17 years old, that "teenagers turn to crime *not* because they lack prospects, but quite the reverse: that young immigrants lack prospects *because* they've embraced crime."

So, criminals cause their own trouble by choosing criminality? People are accountable for their actions? How revolutionary...
http://www.dw.com/en/identifying-the-roots-of-immigrant-crime/a-1953916

Sports cures everything
Anyone ever hear of a theory along the lines of keep young men busy with sports and everything will be fine?

In October 2015, a well-meaning Bavarian teacher put together a soccer game (*football* in Europe) between his students and a team of young migrants from Africa and Syria. No need to know the German language. Integration 101. Happy happy. Make some new friends over a fun game of soccer. Who doesn't love sports?

Ok. Honestly, This does *sound like a nice idea and all. What could possibly go wrong?*

Well, everything started out just fine. Until the migrant team decided to substitute an African player with a Syrian player. First the migrant teens had a heated and verbally abusive exchange. Next thing you know, the migrant teens were beating and kicking and punching each other. In the end, a 23-

year-old Syrian asylum seeker was hospitalized with head lacerations.

The Bavarian student team likely learned everything they needed to know as they stood on the sidelines and watched in disbelief as the migrants battled it out over nothing.
https://www.bsaktuell.de/31878/neu-ulm-fussballspiel-unter-asylbewerbern-artet-aus/

The red flags are everywhere
Social workers and other volunteers in the German state of Hesse area noticed that women and children at migrant shelters were being routinely abused by migrant males.

The situation became so pronounced that in mid-August 2015, four groups of social workers and women's rights advocates
- Der Paritätische
- Landesarbeitsgemeinschaf
- LandesFrauenRat, and
- Pro Familia

wrote a letter to the authorities in the parliament of Hesse warning that women and children, especially girls, were in jeopardy at shelters.

They reported on many disturbing issues including the fact that women traveling alone are often seen as "wild game" by those men that consider women as subordinates. The letter exposed the fact that there were "numerous rapes and sexual assaults" at shelters.

Additional chilling warnings included:

> "We are also receiving an increasing number of reports of forced prostitution. It must be stressed: these are not isolated cases."

> "Women report that they, as well as children, have been raped or subjected to sexual assault. As a result, many

women sleep in their street clothes. Women regularly report that they do not use the toilet at night because of the danger of rape and robbery on the way to the sanitary facilities. Even during daylight, passing through the camp is a frightful situation for many women."

"These facilities must be equipped so that men do not have access to the premises of the women, with the exception of emergency workers and security personnel."

That pretty much sums up the horror migrant women and children are facing at the hands of mostly migrant males.

But of course you already knew this having seen the endless reports in the old-fashioned-controlled-media, right? No?
http://www.soerenkern.com/pdfs/docs/gewalt.pdf

An article on Bavarian Broadcasting BR24 revealed in April 2015 that shelters around Bavaria were known for "rape and forced prostitution." With populations consisting of about 80% migrant males, and no locking doors, the women and children were at high risk.

According to a spokeswoman for the Coalition for Action, "the price for sex with asylum seekers in Munich's Bavaria Barracks is 10 euros."

Reports of rape are rare since "cases of sexual violence often do not come to light, because the women did not dare to talk about their experience... many women felt defenseless in the shelter," said an asylum lawyer.
http://www.br.de/nachrichten/oberbayern/inhalt/vergewaltigungen-bayernkaserne-100.html

Go ahead, I dare you
In Munich, in a video interview, a disgusted Syrian migrant boldly *threatened* to return to Syria if Germany didn't roll out the red carpet and accept Syrians.

What? What did he just say? *Someone, quick, "triple dog-dare" this guy to return.*

The migrant was staying at an old military camp turned into a shelter. Besides the Syrians, many of the migrants were Afghans, Senegalese, Albanians, Pakistanis, and Bangladeshis. The Syrian migrant arrived in Germany with his wife and two sons, one who was disabled and required special medical attention. Clearly revolted by the treatment he was receiving in Germany, the migrant said that if Germany tried to relocate him, he would immediately return to his own country of Syria. "I go back my country," he crowed, "I go to my country. Everybody. If you ask anyone, if Germany not accept people here, they will (go) back (to our) country... Germany or nothing... I back (to) my country, of course."

Of course, indeed!

Now, does that sound like a true, *running for my life*, persecuted refugee? Or are those the words and threats of an economic opportunist or a disappointed tourist?

Think about it.
https://youtu.be/Q_XHkgScOSY

Migrants rate Germany as a one-star dump
Migrants in Kassel, Germany, protested their conditions at shelters and held up signs demanding "to be transferred to apartments." In Heidenau, Germany, a female Syrian migrant called her shelter gross based on a lack of private bathrooms and no windows. For her, shared bathrooms were unacceptable and disgusting, even under these extraordinary emergency circumstances. She ended by saying Germany's facilities were "disappointing, it's not what I had imagined." She says that although she had mentally prepared herself for all sorts of hardships and bad situations, what she has faced in Germany's shelters was far worse than anything she could have imagined.

In the meanwhile, the German Red Cross defended the shelter, explaining that they had been given less than 48 hours to put together the emergency shelter since the migrants arrived without warning.
https://youtu.be/Q_XHkgScOSY

When in doubt, lash out
Violence by migrants in Germany is on the rise. Big time.

According to an October 2015 report on Spiegel.de, violent outbreaks in migrant hostels have been growing exponentially. And it's not just fists and punches. No, those lovable migrants are a clever bunch. Police in Bavaria discovered that migrants in a hostel had fashioned machetes from bed frames, constructed 3 foot long spears topped with knives, crafted clubs made from chair legs, and had an assortment of iron pipes. It is reported that migrants at shelters routinely break out into violent battles, and that the level of violence during one such fight between 200-300 migrants was so intense that even the hostel's security guards fled for their lives (Sinsheim hostel in Baden-Württemberg).

Police officers are routinely injured during fights, such as at the September 2015 Calden Airport shelter battle when more than 350 migrants went berserk. In August 2015, police were called 926 times to restore order at refugee accommodations in North Rhine-Westphalia.

Refugees at the Leipzig Trade Fair complex recently rioted and attacked each other as well as the German military and security guards. Police said at least 200 Afghans and Syrians began fighting and rioting after an 11-year-old Syrian girl had a knife pulled on her by a 17-year-old Afghan boy. In July 2015, the refugee center in Trier housed an enormous violent riot during a soccer game between Syrian and Albanian migrants. At least 70 police officers were required to regain control of the shelter.

After the Stuhl town refugee center was "severely vandalized" by rioting migrants who hurt a half dozen government workers, the Governor of Thuringia in Germany proposed separating migrants by religion. In contrast to the nasty accusatory reaction of the French Prime Minister when some French mayors came up with the exact same idea, it was reported that one of Germany's police unions called for migrants to be housed according to religion as well, in an effort to calm tensions at hostels in October 2015.

Not surprisingly, there is little support for this measure at the political level. The interior minister of Rhineland-Palatinate, Roger Lewentz, commented that separating asylum seekers by religion would be "nearly impossible." Spoken like a true politician. So easy to make pronouncements from on high. Maybe good old Roger would think differently if he actually had to be on the ground and restore order in these hell holes...

No rest for the weary
September 2015 has been a real opener for German authorities. Well, maybe not the bosses, but definitely the people working the front lines. Lack of respect and incredible arrogance seemed to be the norm, as migrants routinely stormed official buildings. Instead of lining up in an orderly fashion to register, get benefits, apply for aid, whatever, the same scene of chaos and violence played itself out, day after day after day, as migrants hit and shoved and pushed each other and government workers, to get to the front of lines. One government worker who was on 12 hour shifts while Germany tried to get a hold of this crisis said, "There is a lot of tension and aggression in the air."

It really is an alternate universe
Johannes-Wilhelm Rörig, German Government Commissioner on Abuse, expressed his concern about the steadily increasing sexual assaults on children and women in the shelters. But he may be trying to make pigs fly. After all, migrants have stated in past interviews, women just don't have many rights.

Since August 2015, various aid groups have been reporting an alarming number of rapes. Gays are also having trouble. For instance, in the Dresden shelter, Arabs, Afghans, and Pakistanis routinely harassed one gay migrant, calling him "girl," chasing him through the camp, demanding that he dance for them, and throwing rocks at him.

Considering the penalty for homosexuality in many Muslim countries is death, or close to it, this migrant probably got off easy. Hopefully he can settle in a part of Europe without an increasingly ever-present intolerant populace, or being pelted with stones may be the least of his worries.
http://www.spiegel.de/international/germany/asylum-shelters-in-germany-struggle-with-refugee-violence-a-1056393.html

Flipping and flopping
In October 2015, the German Police Union Chief warned of "widespread prepared and organized mass brawls and fights" in migrant shelters and camps. He stressed that he wasn't referring to mere brawls, but "proper power struggles between different groups who have different ethnic and religious backgrounds." He specifically said the police had taken note that *Christians were being attacked by Islamists*, but added that since most victims of Islamists in Islamist countries "are not Christians, but Muslims. A religious separation is therefore not effective."

Dead silence.

He also predicted if the migrant tsunami isn't stopped, full scale wars between migrant groups would spill into the streets of Germany. He said migrants often used weapons they bought or hand-fashioned themselves, such as "steel poles with tips."

When the interviewer wondered why the incidents of violence seemingly hadn't gone up with the arrival of hundreds of thousands of new migrants, the Chief said that "the public does not know everything" because the public is told "only a fraction" of the violence happening "in order not to unnecessarily terrify the public."

Once again, **the public is told "only a fraction" of the violence happening "in order not to unnecessarily terrify the public."**

So whatever you read or hear or see in the old-fashioned-controlled-media is watered-down and only a fraction of what's going on?

Positively terrifying. Think about it.

Probably in an attempt to lighten the mood, the Chief added that the German police are now facing "the biggest challenge in their police history since 1945."

Ok. That's big. *Uber big.*
http://deutsche-wirtschafts-nachrichten.de/2015/10/01/polizeigewerkschaft-zur-asyl-gewalt-die-oeffentlichkeit-erfaehrt-nur-einen-bruchteil/

Youngsters and crime in the age of selfies

How "open" are young criminals in Germany? In mid-October 2015, news giant Bild, showed examples of major social media sites featuring emboldened young criminals, street thieves around 16 years of age, posting photos of themselves on their social media pages posing with stolen merchandise (laptops, cash, expensive sunglasses, cell phones, etc.) and giving the police the middle finger salute. *Nice.*

One such pariah was arrested dozens of times, had over 20 cases of theft and robbery pending against him, but received special treatment by courts due to his asylum seeking status according to police who added, it was "incomprehensible that such serial offenders do not sit in pre-trial detention."

"Incomprehensible" is a fine choice of words. We prefer lunacy.
http://www.bild.de/news/inland/diebstahl/wird-von-klau-kids-verhoehnt-42988580.bild.html

And it's just not getting better.

In October 2015, in the late evening in Karlsruhe, two migrants aged 23 and 24, young fighting-age males, grabbed a 30-year-old German woman and dragged her into the bushes. They beat and punched her, and severely injured her according to police. The woman lived since she managed to call for help and the attackers ran. The asylum seekers were captured by police.

And migrants don't just attack native civilians. They can be just as violent with each other, and security personnel. Some shelter incidents in just one month (October 2015) included:
- clashes between refugees in a Hamburg shelter resulted in the hospitalization a young male migrant teen
- two teen migrants attacked security guards at a Hamburg shelter, beat one in the head and injured them both
- two African asylum seekers fought each other at a shelter in Bavaria until one ended up at the hospital with a bleeding wound to his head
- a 14-year-old migrant at a Hamburg shelter attacked a security guard with an antenna and a broken toilet seat and ended up hospitalized with a foot injury
- three young migrants of fighting-age fought in a shelter in Wohldorf-Ohlstedt, tried to strangle a security officer, prompting responding police to file criminal charges

Aren't these all perfect ways to impress your host country with your devotion to assimilating and becoming productive members of society?

Or maybe not.
http://www.swp.de/ulm/nachrichten/suedwestumschau/Frau-von-zwei-Asylbewerbern-angegriffen-und-geschlagen;art1157835,3503259
http://www.rosenheim24.de/rosenheim/mangfalltal/bad-aibling-ort28271/aibling-streit-zwischen-zwei-asylbewerbern-eskaliert-5691521.html
http://www.welt.de/regionales/hamburg/article148084717/Fluechtling-greift-Wachmann-mit-Toilettendeckel-an.html

Just like elsewhere in Europe, rapes are on the rise
In 1816, the picturesque town of Erding in Bavaria held its first Volksfest, an autumn festival which now sports carnival rides, games, music, and entertainment. It has grown to a large and much anticipated 10 day celebration of local pride.

In September 2015, after visiting the Erding Volksfest festival, a 37-year-old German woman and her 17-year-old daughter were walking back to their car just after midnight when a 23-year-old migrant man, a Pakistani citizen according to police, began following them. The women sensed danger and tried to run as the migrant jumped the mother, threw her to the ground, and attempted to assault the woman as he wormed and jammed his tongue into the woman's mouth. As her frantic daughter attempted to beat the attacker off of her mother, the desperate German mother bit the attacker's still-penetrating tongue, severing a piece of it. This stunned the attacker, and the mother and daughter fled to their car and found the police to tell of the sexual attack.

Police started a search for the assailant, but didn't have far to look. It seems that the would-be rapist migrant had returned to the Volkfest, either out of shock, or maybe he just wanted to scope out some other women to try and rape. But soon his severe tongue injury caught up to him. Bleeding quite profusely in front of one of the festival tents, he collapsed, and was taken to the hospital. The chunk of missing tongue made it rather easy for police to track him down and arrest him.

And the victims? The mother suffered lacerations and her daughter was suffering from shock. The police later found the victims' shoes and other evidence strewn across the crime scene. Horrible crime. But it could have turned out so much worse.
https://www.polizei.bayern.de/muenchen/news/presse/aktuell/index.html/226973
http://www.merkur.de/lokales/erding/erding/kronthaler-weiher-zwei-frauen-sextaeter-attackiert-5460548.html

Just a few more of the thousands of examples of migrant indiscretions, naughtiness, and misbehavior in Germany that got past the censors:
- October 2015: two male asylum seekers (ages 38 and 52) at a refugee center in Bavaria sexually assaulted a female member of the cleaning crew every day from October 1 to 10 until the woman got up enough courage to report them to police.
- October 2015: on the University campus at Magdeburg, a 19-year-old German girl was attacked and brutally gang raped by migrants. She was the fourth gang rape victim by refugees within a few weeks and had to be hospitalized for her serious injuries, and her psychological trauma.
- October 2015: a 24-year-old German woman was savagely gang raped in a cemetery in Magdeburg.
- October 2015: Two 19-year-old German girls were ambushed and brutally gang raped by refugees near Magdeburg.
- October 2015: Dessau Police unearthed the body of a 20-year-old Syrian woman that apparently had been gang-raped in Syria by three Syrian men, causing her to be deemed "unclean" by her Syrian family, and leading to her father and brothers stabbing her to death in an "honor killing" (where the victims are killed since they are considered not obedient, or too Western, or accused of some sort of alleged sexual impropriety).
- September 2015: a 31-year-old German woman was raped by a 31-year-old African asylum seeker in Dresden. The man attacked her using a shard of broken glass, dragged her into nearby bushes, and raped her.
- September 2015: a 7-year-old girl riding her bike in a playground in Chemnitz was grabbed by a 30-year-old North African who gagged her and brutally raped her before her nearby mother knew anything was wrong.
- September 2015: near a refugee shelter and train station in the Bavarian town of Mering, a man speaking

"broken German" and described as having "dark skin" raped a 16-year-old girl walking home from the train station.
- August 2015: two Iraqi refugees (19 and 23) who lived in Hamm were arrested for the rape of an 18-year-old German girl behind a school in Hamm.
- July 2015: a 14-year-old boy on a train between Heilbronn and Schwäbisch Hall, was lured to, and sexually abused, in the train's bathroom by a 30- to 40-year-old black haired Arabic-looking man.
- July 2015: An 20-year-old woman in Karlsruhe was raped by a 21 year-old asylum seeker from Africa.
- June 2015: a 13-year-old migrant girl was raped in the Detmolder refugee shelter by a migrant from the same country as the little girl was from according to police.
- June 2015: two Somali asylum seekers received 7 ½ year sentences for the brutal rape of a 21-year-old German girl in 2014 in Bad Kreuznach – during the attack, the pair of African migrants had beaten the girl severely, breaking her facial bones, and were caught with DNA evidence.
- June 2015: a 30-year-old African asylum seeker who had recently been released from prison for raping another woman, tried to rape a 20-year-old girl in a Munich disco bathroom, and got sentenced to prison again.
- May 2015: a 25-year-old African was arrested for attempting to rape a 21-year-old woman in the stairwell of a parking garage – security guards saved the woman who was then hospitalized.
- May 2015: a crazed 30-year-old Moroccan man received 4+ years for trying to brutally rape a 55-year-old school teacher early one morning in a schoolyard in Meissen – he punched her, ripped out her hair in bunches which were spread all over the crime scene, and even bit the woman's thigh.

- April 2015: an Iraqi asylum seeker received 3+ years in prison for raping a 17-year-old girl at a festival near Deggendorf after DNA evidence identified him.
- April 2015: a 29-year-old asylum seeker tried to rape a 14-year-old girl in Alzenauer in broad daylight and was arrested.
- March 2015: a pair of young male asylum seekers from Afghanistan were each sentenced to 5 years in prison for brutally gang raping a 21-year-old petite German woman near Stuttgart – minutes before committing the gang rape, one of the rapists had tried to rape, at knifepoint, another girl, 19 years old, but she broke free – the other rapist had previously been convicted of public masturbation.
- February 2015: a 28-year-old African migrant received a 4 year prison sentence for the rape of a 25-year-old German woman in the German town of Stralsund.
- February 2015: a 27-year-old African asylum seeker was arrested for multiple rape attempts – first he assaulted, choked, and tried to rape a 19-year-old girl on the street, but she broke away – next he broke into and entered the house of a 27-year-old woman and tried to rape her in her living room but her screams for help saved her.
- January 2015: a 24-year-old Moroccan asylum seeker was arrested after he followed a 29-year-old Polish girl, kept "hugging" her, and when she tried to get in her home to safety, the man kicked her down, and brutally raped her, biting her cheek – afterwards he stole her phone and backpack.

http://www.augsburger-allgemeine.de/friedberg/Nach-ungeklaerter-Vergewaltigung-werden-Fluechtlinge-wuest-beschimpft-id35508097.html
http://www.wa.de/hamm/uentrop-ort370525/vergewaltigung-hammer-osten-erster-verdaechtiger-u-haft-polizeiliche-ermittlungen-dauern-5339731.html
http://www.rnz.de/politik/suedwest/polizeibericht-suedwest_artikel,-Heilbronn-14-Jaehriger-auf-Regionalzug-Toilette-sexuell-missbraucht-_arid,116338.html
https://koptisch.files.wordpress.com/2015/08/vergewaltigung.jpg

http://www.liveleak.com/view?i=a50_1441757895
https://www.muenchen.tv/stachus-sicherheitsdient-verhindert-vergewaltigung-102690/
http://investmentwatchblog.com/4th-gang-rape-victim-in-magdeburg-this-month-19-year-old-german-girl-was-ambushed-by-refugees-around-4-am-and-brutally-raped/
https://mopo24.de/nachrichten/versuchte-vergewaltigung-meissen-7232
http://www.polizei.bayern.de/unterfranken/news/presse/aktuell/index.html/218884
http://www.westfalen-blatt.de/OWL/Lokales/Kreis-Lippe/Detmold/2069675-13-jaehriges-Maedchen-aus-Asien-von-Landsmann-missbraucht-Verdaechtiger-in-U-Haft-Polizei-aeussert-sich-nach-Berichterstattung-Im-Fluechtlingsheim-vergewaltigt-Oeffentlichkeit-soll-nichts-erfahren
http://www.stuttgarter-zeitung.de/inhalt.kirchheim-die-beweise-und-die-aussagen-der-opfer-sind-eindeutig.5ff66965-9e79-4f27-a62b-87ab1c77b43d.html
http://www.svz.de/mv-uebersicht/studentin-bedraengt-und-missbraucht-id8937191.html
https://youtu.be/lVDKkZBAlPQ
http://www.pnp.de/region_und_lokal/landkreis_dingolfing_landau/1576283_Zwei-versuchte-Vergewaltigungen-Taeter-27-festgenommen.html
http://www.radiodresden.de/nachrichten/lokalnachrichten/frau-an-nossener-bruecke-vergewaltigt-tatverdaechtiger-gefasst-1165298/
http://www.bild.de/news/inland/mord/sachsen-anhalt-dessau-leiche-in-gartenlaube-liess-mutter-ihre-tochter-erstechen-42916868.bild.html
http://www.br.de/nachrichten/unterfranken/inhalt/sexueller-missbrauch-fluechtlingsunterkunft-kitzingen-100.html

Still welcoming the refugees

"Ignorant," or "ignoring," in late October 2015, a thousand or more migrant supporters took to the streets of Heidelberg, some chanting and screaming "Say it now, say it clear, refugees are welcome here." The crowd of welcoming and smiling Germans were most likely also celebrating Chancellor Merkel's announcement that her "open-door" policy would include a few deportation plans.

In an earlier demonstration, in September 2015, African migrants from Eritrea served up a mouthful of anti-German hate rhetoric including:
- "your democracy for us is anti-democracy"

- "you are racists"
- "we are equal under the law"
- "the stick is in your hands, but I will assure you, we are not going to fear of you because we are more than stronger, *more* than yesterday, and we will be tomorrow *more stronger* and we'll defeat you"

Call me crazy, but that sounds like strange words from people seeking asylum, especially the part about "we'll defeat you."

In any case, thanks for the warning, dude. Now that the German authorities understand your true motives, and your open hatred for racist democratic Germany, and that you aim to "defeat them," we're certain something will be done.

Like letting in even more new refugees...
https://youtu.be/EiPR0zdPU0I

According to German government figures, among the million or more migrants that will swell Germany this year, it seems that nearly 200,000 are "economic migrants" (opportunists) living in Germany in search of the "easy life." Further, over 40% of the migrants that flooded Germany in September 2015 were not really fleeing war anymore. They had entered from "safe" countries.

Wow. Who would have thought? Merkel leaves the doors to her mansion open and a bunch of opportunists, almost 200,000, make themselves right at home.

The success Merkel will have with her plans to deport the economic migrants remains to be seen. Inviting someone in is often easier than evicting them.

Unless, of course you want to evict native Germans... read on.
https://www.youtube.com/watch?v=IZo_Y9WPnUM
http://www.independent.co.uk/news/world/europe/refugee-crisis-angela-merkel-signals-deportation-of-economic-migrants-from-germany-as-ec-president-a6703331.html

Migrants in, Germans out
In September 2015, a 51-year-old German nurse, who cared for asylum seekers over the years, and who lived in her apartment for 16 years, received an eviction notice. Seems the landlord and town needed the space for 30 refugees.

The nurse said in an interview with DieWelt, "I was completely shocked and I can't even begin to find the words to describe how the city has treated me. I have had to go through a lot of difficulties recently, and then I get this notice. It was like a kick in the teeth."

The town mayor said that the choice was between building a new shelter at a cost of 30,000 euros, or the nurse's eviction. "This solution will cost me nothing," the mayor told Die Welt.

Nothing indeed. Except a citizen's home.

The mayor then ridiculed the nurse for going public, said she had been given a generous amount of time to clear out, and blamed the trouble she was having in finding a new place on her pet dog. So there.
http://www.welt.de/politik/deutschland/article146825325/Fuer-Fluechtlinge-gekuendigt-Das-war-wie-ein-Tritt.html

Religious spat
August 2015 was an interesting time to be visiting Suhl, Germany. The most notable event took place in a large crowded migrant shelter.

For some unknown reason, an Afghan man decided to tear up a Quran and dump pieces of the holy book in a toilet. A large group of mostly Syrian men chased the Afghan, to exact revenge and punish him properly for desecrating the Quran.

By the way, according to Peter Bergen, a CNN terrorism analyst, "desecrating the Quran is a death-penalty offense" in many places including Afghanistan and Pakistan.

The Afghan desecrater was rescued by the shelter's security force. Well, the way the Syrians saw it, they wanted to avenge the desecration, and the pesky guards were keeping them from their righteous goal.

Not good.

The already enraged Syrians became further enraged, and they attacked the security guards. Things quickly spiraled out of control. Local police were called in to help, and when they took away the Afghan Quran-shredder, the Syrian crowd became even more furious. Instead of handing over the desecrator to them for punishment, now the pesky police were "protecting" him as well.

So much worse.

Boom. The vicious mob rioted and attacked the police. Violence ensued. Journalists present at the scene, trying to paint an old-fashioned-controlled-media "balanced" picture of events, instead found themselves targets as well. Instead of weaving typical drivel about the "poor conditions" that caused migrant violence, or providing excuses or apologies for migrant misbehavior, suddenly the journalists were literally running for their lives.

As reported by DKA, "The Syrian men, armed with iron rods, bricks and concrete blocks, went completely berserk. They smashed doors, windows, police cars, chased the journalists and tossed about furniture and other things... The rage was particularly aimed against the asylum center where they live, as they broke into the center's office and smashed everything..."

In the news video, you can clearly hear terrified journalists running for their lives. While they ran, what sounded like rocks, projectiles, and metal pipes can be heard hitting the ground around them, as people screamed. As they reached their car and started to drive away to escape, they are all out of breath and gasping for air.

In what can only be a vile and racist response, German authorities dared to "say that they will try to divide asylum seekers by ethnicity, in order to prevent a recurrence of the violent riots." Forget separation by religion, now authorities were looking at separating people by race.

WHAT? Separate the races? Are you saying races can't get along? You have to keep them separate in order to have peace? How outrageous! And don't tell the French Ministers. They'll think you're nuts!
http://denkorteavis.dk/2015/en-afghansk-asylansoger-skaendede-koranen-og-sa-gik-andre-50-i-blodrus-mod-alt-omkring-sig/
http://www.cnn.com/2005/WORLD/asiapcf/05/15/newsweek.quran/

Pass that collection plate
Eight young males, members of a Muslim criminal gang, were charged in mid-October 2015 with a multi-year crime spree in the Cologne area that allegedly helped finance jihadist ISIS activities in Syria.

According to prosecutors, the burglars targeted churches and "stole collection boxes, crosses and other objects 'dedicated to church services and religious veneration.'" They also targeted schools where they stole laptops and cash. Their signature move was to often cause serious property damage before leaving a robbery scene (like robbing a church or school wasn't enough of a statement). Three of the gang members were "also charged with supporting a foreign terrorist organization." Prosecutors further revealed that the gang's prominent member, a Muslim male from Africa, also posted an ISIS recruitment video on the internet encouraging other "Muslims to fight for ISIS."

Just another case of the migrant boys next door.
http://www.thelocal.de/20151020/cologne-gang-stole-from-churches-to-fund-isis

German health care gets super sick

November 2015 saw the beginning of the end of the "smooth" ride for the German health care system.

When you travel internationally, you ordinarily have to make sure your vaccinations are up to date and that you aren't carrying any dangerous diseases, et cetera et cetera. For goodness sake, you can't even bring half-eaten fruit into most countries.

But these are *not* ordinary times. Yet no one is doing much screening.

Let that sink in a moment.

With close to a million new foreign guests in their country, German doctors are beyond overwhelmed. As staff members are starting to suffer from fatigue and exhaustion, hospitals and medical facilities are slammed daily with record-breaking crowds of migrants, some suffering from a wide variety of serious and some high-fatality diseases. According to the Koch Institut, these include Crimean-Congo hemorrhagic fever, Ebola, hepatitis, diphtheria, HIV/AIDS, malaria, meningitis, measles, mumps, scabies, tuberculosis, typhus, polio, and whooping cough.

Ebola concerns are becoming routine with testing and suspected cases investigated in Hamburg, Saxony, Bochum, Cologne, and other locales I wouldn't travel to anymore.
http://www.kn-online.de/News/Aktuelle-Nachrichten-Schleswig-Holstein/Norddeutschland/Angst-vor-Ebola-Fluechtlinge-blockierten-in-Hamburg-Strassenkreuzung

Up close and personal with rare diseases

Medical staff that had only read about certain diseases will now be able to thank Chancellor Merkel for some practical hands-on experience to list on their resumes when they apply for new positions elsewhere.

Worse, German news giant DieWelt reported in November 2015 that German doctors are "on alert, because with the arrival of hundreds of thousands of refugees infectious diseases could enter the country. *This is not hysteria.* But simply a challenge for our health care system which hasn't faced anything like this in decades."

Honestly. If I lived in Germany, I'd be rather hysterical right about now. Sorry doc.

Could it get worse? Oh yes. Hang on.

German doctors reported that they are very concerned about another horror – "...there is a danger that a refugee is 'colonized' with dangerous germs... Every person carries bacterial germs in and on the skin. For healthy people they are harmless. They become a problem when they propagate in a clinic with critically ill and immunocompromised patients."

It was also reported that 5% of the migrants are infected with resistant germs.

What's 5% between friends? Tiny, right?

5% of the reported 1,000,000 new migrants is about 50,000 carriers of resistant germs. If 1,500,000 migrants show up, that would be 75,000.

In any case, that's scary. Real scary.
http://www.welt.de/gesundheit/article148378154/Fluechtlinge-erst-einmal-ins-Einzelzimmer.html

Tuberculosis (TB) is nasty. The World health Organization says about 10,000,000 people get it every year, mostly in third world countries. Of those infected, 1,500,000 die.

In November 2015, the director of a clinic in Parsberg went on Spiegel TV to say that although 8,000-10,000 migrants in

Germany have tuberculosis (TB), only a tiny number are quarantined. The better news is that to quarantine one migrant with TB takes up to 18 months and can cost more than 200,000 euros per person.

While the German government pretends all is just swell, quite a few medical professionals are panicking. One doctor said he's now facing "diseases that I have not seen in 20 years." Another was concerned about Germany's ability to cope with the influx of disease. Hundreds of medical professionals are volunteering around the clock but can't keep up.

Think about it. Diseases not seen in Germany in decades are now being welcomed and reintroduced in a huge way.

Bubonic plague, anyone?
http://www.tagesspiegel.de/berlin/fluechtlinge-in-berlin-medizinische-notversorgung-kann-nicht-nur-aufgabe-freiwilliger-sein/12499360.html
http://www.rki.de/DE/Content/Gesundheitsmonitoring/Gesundheitsberichterstattung/GesundAZ/Content/A/Asylsuchende/Asylsuchende.html
http://www.welt.de/politik/article147804092/Krankheiten-die-ich-seit-20-Jahren-nicht-gesehen-habe.html
http://www.spiegel.de/video/rueckkehr-der-tuberkulose-fluechtlinge-werden-zu-patienten-video-1622431.html

Calm down, vaccines will save everything
Please tell me there are plenty of vaccines to go around. That's right, isn't it. Oh don't tell me there's an issue with a vaccines.

There's an issue with vaccines.

In Germany, the Professional Association of Child and Adolescent Physicians is seriously concerned. Pediatricians across Germany are reporting finding more and more unvaccinated migrant children at shelters and in the course of running their medical practices. Many also have vaccination gaps. It seems that many migrants and many migrant children never were vaccinated for a host of diseases and illnesses.

Tell me it can't get worse. *Please?!*

Sorry.

The overwhelmed German health care system really didn't plan on having millions of extra vaccines on hand. The President of the Professional Association of Child and Adolescent Physicians, speaking in October 2015, said, "Much worse... is the lack of vaccines."

By year's end, Germany will reportedly not have certain vaccines, such as the vaccine against diphtheria, whooping cough, polio, and tetanus. There are major shortages across much of Europe due to the refugee health crisis. It is now likely that German doctors won't have vaccines for their native German children, or the migrant children alike.

Even though the CEO of a Chamber of Pharmacists went on the record saying, "the current refugee situation is one of the main reasons for the bottlenecks," one outspoken German politician, Schulz-Asche, warned that there are alternatives out there and "the current tense vaccine situation must not be *misused* to stir up public opinion *against* refugees... there is no reason for alarmism."

Oh. Ok. We'll believe the politicians over the doctors.

Let's see how that works out.

Hope you're right Schulz-Asche.
http://www.pei.de/DE/arzneimittel/impfstoff-impfstoffe-fuer-den-menschen/lieferengpaesse/informationen-lieferengpaesse-impfstoffe-inhalt.html
http://www.bvkj.de/presse/pressemitteilungen/ansicht/article/kinder-und-jugendaerzte-fordern-politik-muss-versorgung-mit-impfstoffen-sicherstellen/
http://www.apotheke-adhoc.de/nachrichten/politik/nachricht-detail-politik/impfstoff-engpaesse-schulz-asche-warnt-vor-stimmungsmache/

At least the refugees are grateful to get free medical care
With German resources spread thin, and medical professionals stretched to the breaking point, migrants are getting pretty damned pissed about all this German ineptitude and the lack of service they're getting for free.

In November 2015, German news outlet, RP, reported on the many instances of violent attacks on hospital personnel in 100 emergency rooms and hospitals across Germany, Austria and Switzerland. The majority, 73%, reported assaults against doctors, nurses, and staff by angry migrants. 43% reported a growth in the number of attacks in the past few years. Property damage was also a large issue as well.

Combat pay
Attacks by migrants against hospital staff in Germany have increased so dramatically that many facilities have increased security. ER doctors joke about "hazard pay." But it's no joke.

The attacks go way beyond insults and scuffles. They are often very violent and include punches and kicks and more.

For instance, one impatient migrant grabbed an emergency room staff member and put her in such a vicious headlock that she suffered bruises. In another facility, water is now only provided in paper cups after one migrant used a broken glass water bottle to go on a violent attack against staff.

Hey, I was here *way before* that guy with the bullet wound
Impatient migrants seem to be frequently lashing out if they have to wait for care. Migrants make the waiting situation far worse by using the ER as their personal doctor's visit. Instead of seeing a specialist they just go to the ER and demand services. With an ER full of coughs and colds and sniffles, the doctors try and help real *life-threatening* emergencies *first* – which only infuriates the migrants who "do not understand or refuse to understand."

Bodyguards

German FOCUS magazine reported on October 31, 2015, that more and more frequently, migrants have been punching and kicking the doctors and nurses trying to assist them. It is so bad that some hospitals have hired bodyguards to protect their staff from violent attacks.

Think about it. *Bodyguards.*

Hey, you, I'm *axing* you why you disrespected me

Doctors reported that migrants, "beat and kick around, trying to bite the caregiver, throw furniture around, damaging expensive medical equipment." Doctors also said that migrants arrive armed with knives and more.

On one occasion, a bodyguard was able to stop a migrant who had returned to the hospital with a brand new ax to "get revenge" because he felt the staff had slighted him somehow.

Far from being an isolated incident, it was reported that this was the new norm of violence, with "nurses and physicians increasingly encountering aggressive patients."

Vulgarities and threats are also the new norm. And it's not just expletives, dirty words, and filthy language. One staff member was told by an upset migrant patient that if he ever ran into her "outside," he would "cut her and let her bleed out."

Incidents of sexual assault have skyrocketed as well. Nurses and staff are trying to work in pairs to guard against "sexual harassment, sexist insults, being touched, and being physically pulled."

After particularly brutal attacks against nurses in Stuttgart, safety glass was installed at the receiving station.

That's good news, since in October 2015 it was reported that an average of 145 migrants sought medical attention daily in

Stuttgart with the most common issues being chickenpox, flu, scabies, measles, and dysentery.

Hopefully, the glass will help.
http://www.rp-online.de/nrw/staedte/moenchengladbach/gewaltausbrueche-in-der-notaufnahme-aid-1.5505841
http://www.focus.de/panorama/welt/schlaege-und-tritte-in-der-notaufnahme-manche-kommen-schon-mit-waffe-krankenhaus-mitarbeiter-klagen-ueber-pruegel-patienten_id_5052753.html
http://www.augsburger-allgemeine.de/politik/Wie-Fluechtlinge-das-Gesundheitssystem-herausfordern-id35879927.html
http://www.stuttgarter-nachrichten.de/inhalt.fluechtlinge-in-ueberfuellten-unterkuenften-breiten-sich-krankheiten-aus.dff26e94-2758-442f-a5cf-c2f9893b6a08.html

At least everyone is being registered and tracked, right?
Not even close.

At the end of September 2015, the new head of the German Federal Office for Migration and Refugees revealed that at least 290,000 refugees got into Germany without being registered.

Ooops.

Hopefully they will all go on to do great things.
http://www.zeit.de/news/2015-09/30/un-g7-kuenden-zusaetzliche-gelder-fuer-fluechtlinge-an-30111403

Call out the military, and quick
As Germany prepared for another 40,000 new refugees to arrive in *one* weekend in September 2015, authorities said that they would be placing 4,000 soldiers on alert. The *theory* was that soldiers could assist with setting up refugee camps, provide transportation for migrants, and other necessary services. The *reality* was that the military was there to help any federal states that needed actual *military* assistance with the migrants.

At the same time, hundreds of Muslim migrants spilled into the streets of Frankfurt and rioted. Apparently Turkish Muslims and Kurdish Muslims were at odds. Hundreds of migrants were seen fighting and battling each other *as well as* the police as authorities struggled to reestablish law and order. Even with decades of law enforcement experience, the situation was frightening. In other sections of Frankfurt, groups of hundreds of Muslims marched through the area carrying hundreds of Turkish flags and chanting in Arabic.

Clearly something was brewing. And it wasn't Turkish coffee.
https://youtu.be/j6arg2gTD3c

Young Germans should be forced to serve the migrants
In November 2015, a crackpot scheme that betrays just how desperate Merkel's new Germany is, was floated by one politician, Eckhard Rehberg who seriously suggested that German youth be given a choice of serving in the military for one year or spend one year serving the needs of all the migrants that Merkel let into the country.

A month earlier, several social media sites went berserk when a German school in Lubeck conscripted 13- and 14-year-old children from 8:30am till 1:30pm to clean refugee shelters, make beds, sort clothes, and help in the kitchen in an initiative, shrouded as "practical work experience," but called "Help for Refugees."

Thousands of post shares sent the message viral and comments from livid and furious parents included "refugees should clean their own mess with their own hands" rather than enlisting our children.

In the meanwhile, The Express reported that "a group of around 20 Syrians are even *suing* the German government because they had to wait longer than a week" to be processed.

You just can't please everyone... Wait. *Newly arrived refugees suing after a week?* Seriously? You're in a country 7 days, and already you know how to file a lawsuit? Cha-ching!

Think about it.
https://youtu.be/ChLlROqgHdg
http://www.express.co.uk/news/world/612208/refugee-crisis-asylum-seekers-Lubeck-Germany-Angela-Merkel

Silence the non-believers
In September 2015, Die Welt reported that Chancellor Merkel was caught inadvertently on an open mike at a UN summit pressuring Facebook CEO Mark Zuckerberg to monitor "hate speech posts." *Monitor hate speech posts?* We can only guess this means that Merkel means to silence anyone that "hates" her stupid ideas and crazy crackpot schemes. We also think that Comrade Merkel, *a former uniform-wearing Communist Youth Party member,* was apparently paying a lot more attention than we gave her credit for during those Communist propaganda lessons. (More on that coming up later.)

In the meantime, in Germany people that post or share what Merkel's posse consider "xenophobic" or "radical" views, risk losing *not only their jobs* but also their children since a family court will now also have to determine if the parent's views might be "endangering" the children.

Imagine if Merkel had been working for the British in 1776. There may not have been any American revolution based on her ability to squash "radical" discussions.

Tea, anyone?
http://www.welt.de/finanzen/verbraucher/article146904927/Nach-Hetze-ist-das-Umgangsrecht-in-Gefahr.html

Boo, scared you.
November 2015 saw German police evacuating the soccer arena in Hanover, 90 minutes before a Germany vs. Holland match was set to take place after investigating a suspicious

package, saying they had "concrete evidence" of a planned explosion, and added something about suspicious people. A late night press briefing revealed that no explosives were ultimately discovered.

Better safe than sorry in Merkel's new Germany.
http://www.dailymail.co.uk/sport/sportsnews/article-3322536/Germany-friendly-against-Holland-cancelled-security-threat.html

More "surprises"

In September 2015, Germany's Interior Minister revealed that "At least 25% of refugees claiming to be from Syria *are not from Syria*, but from other Arab or African countries." Since Syrian refugees get priority treatment, this is not surprising. A Bavarian border police officer noted that the impersonators know no shame stating that "all present themselves as Syrians even if they are obviously black Africans."

The heads of Germany's Police unions were nervous about the ramifications of absorbing so many migrants, and blamed the government's wishy-washy "back and forth" refugee policies as well as the overall "aimlessness" of the German federal government.

Might such honest concerns reveal xenophobic racism? Or is it just concern for one's country's safety?

Either way, will Merkel now start monitoring police officers' social media accounts searching for evidence of hatred?
http://www.n24.de/n24/Nachrichten/Politik/d/7230446/sturmwarnung---1400-fluechtlinge-muessen-evakuiert-werden.html
http://www.spiegel.de/politik/deutschland/fluechtlingskrise-was-die-deutschen-grenzkontrollen-bedeuten-a-1052819.html

Shocker: Merkel says multiculturalism has failed

So for all the criticism of Chancellor Angela Merkel, Time Magazine's 2015 *Person of the Year*, and her acceptance of a million+ migrants, what does Merkel herself think of multiculturalism?

Well, way back in 2010, *long before* she threw open the gates of Germany, Merkel said "the multiculturalism approach – saying that we must simply live side by side and be happy to be living with each other – this approach has failed, utterly failed." Instead, she stressed that true integration would be the real key to success.

So what exactly changed in the last few years that prompted Merkel to swing open the gates?

We have no clue since in mid-December, Merkel said "Those who seek refuge with us also have to respect our laws and traditions, and learn to speak German. Multiculturalism leads to parallel societies, and therefore multiculturalism remains a grand delusion."

A "grand delusion" indeed. Possibly as delusional as opening your front door wide open *after* you fully realize something is gravely wrong outside...
http://www.theguardian.com/world/2010/oct/17/angela-merkel-germany-multiculturalism-failures
http://www.theguardian.com/commentisfree/2015/dec/15/merkel-syrians-assimilate-germany-multiculturalism

Germans and migrants are *equally* criminally minded

Luckily for everyone, in mid-November 2015, a report from the German Federal Office of Criminal Investigation said crimes in Germany were increasing *only* because there were more people now in Germany, and not specifically due to the influx of migrants.

What a relief!

Ordered in October 2015 by Thomas de Maizière, Germany's Minister of the Interior, the report was *designed* to help the Minister "dispel rumors about an increase in criminal acts in Germany."

The saying "you get what you pay for" jumps to mind.

The report looked at crime levels in Germany between January–September 2015 and found that there was no increases that could be tied solely to migration factors. Of course, the report only looked at Germany, only looked at reported crime, and only looked at a time frame during which migrants were arriving. We wonder if a similar report done in a year or two will follow the trends you've seen in most other European countries. But for now, the "rumor" has been dispelled. Jauchzer!

Although the report did reveal that Iraqi and Syrian refugees were the most "likely to commit crimes," and that "sex crimes" accounted for less than 1% of the crimes the migrants studied committed, based on currently available statistics (January 2015 – September 2015), *the Minister predicted that refugees would not commit more crimes per capita than native Germans.*

Of course, this absurd prediction was made before New Year's Eve 2016. More on that mess at the end of the book.

Ouch...
http://www.dw.com/en/report-refugees-have-not-increased-crime-rate-in-germany/a-18848890

Merkel should admit her mistake
In mid-November 2015, Bavarian Minister of Finance, Markus Söder, said that Europe must
> "protect itself better from enemies who will stop at nothing... The era of uncontrolled immigration and illegal immigration cannot go on like this. Paris changes everything... Protecting the EU's external borders must finally be guaranteed. For too long it has been neglected. If that cannot be ensured, Germany must secure and protect its own borders."

Seems pretty straightforward and logical so far.

Markus Söder added that "it would be good if Angela Merkel would concede that the indefinite opening of borders was a mistake. We wanted to help and have helped, but now we are also overwhelmed. Therefore, there must be a limit."

Lots of luck waiting for *that* apology!
http://www.welt.de/politik/deutschland/article148851433/Angela-Merkel-soll-Fehler-einraeumen.html

So apart from this little bit of the "tip of the iceberg" we served up in this chapter, everything is *ausgezeichnet*.

Splendid indeed...

(19) GREECE

By 2010, Greece had become the "Mexico" of Europe – that is to say, it was a major point of entry for illegal aliens. According to a recent United Nations report, about 97 percent of the illegal immigrants who snuck into the US, did so across the almost 2,000 mile border between the US and Mexico. Similarly, it was reported in 2010 that nearly all illegal immigration to the European Union flowed through Greece. In fact, 132,524 illegal aliens were arrested in Greece in 2010. In 2006, the number had only been 95,239.

Those were the good old days.

Oh, to turn back the clock to those laid back times...
http://www.bbc.com/news/world-radio-and-tv-19269891
http://www.migrationpolicy.org/article/greece-illegal-immigration-midst-crisis/

Greece 2015

By the end of August 2015, the UN estimated that 160,000 people had arrived in Greece, 50,000 of which showed up in August alone. This number was about to change dramatically in the course of a few months.

In what could very well have been footage from the siege of Normandy, without the guns and armored vehicles, ferries "disgorged" thousands and thousands of migrants on the Greek port city of Piraeus in August and September 2015. As many as 12,500 people in one single week.

The sheer mass of people, a vast majority of them young males, was simply unbelievable, pouring out of the ferries, overwhelming Greek resources and authorities. Without much ado, they were handed documents that allowed them to stay in Greece for up to 3 months.

Not-so-ancient Greek ruins
Unfortunately, Greece never recovered from its economic collapse and there were little resources for migrants. And the migrants knew it. Most were on their way north to Macedonia, Serbia, Hungary, and then on to see open-armed Chancellor Merkel in Germany.

That doesn't mean they were going to pass through peacefully.

Macedonia, not a member of the EU, started to try and protect its borders in August 2015 as Macedonia's foreign minister said, "there has been a dramatic increase of inflow of migrants and we have reached numbers of 3,000 to 3,500 per day which obviously is not something a country of two million people, and our resources, can handle on a daily basis... We had to reinforce the control of illegal entry into Macedonia."

By September 2015, Macedonia had figured it out, like any game of hot potato, and was moving refugees, as quickly as possible, from the Greek border up to Hungary. Greece was thankful. Hungary wasn't.

Back to Greece. *So how bad is the economic crisis?*

Well, in November 2015, the results from a 3 year study of prostitution in Greece (it's legal, but workers must register) showed that prostitution had skyrocketed 150% during the economic crisis, and that 80% of the prostitutes were Greek female students aged 17-20. *Sad.* Many were only earning *a few euros per half hour* but kept working to cover basic expenses such as food costs. *Sadder.* It would seem that the times are rather desperate in Greece, even without a refugee crisis.

Think about it.
http://greece.greekreporter.com/2015/11/28/author-of-study-on-greek-female-sex-workers-denies-cheese-pie-comment/

Prisoner in your own home
In late summer 2015, tens of thousands of migrants swarmed the popular Greek tourist island of Lesvos, turning it into what looked very much like an occupied war zone.

As migrants rioted and fought on a regular basis, native Greek residents were routinely reduced to tears and terror as they became prisoners in their own homes. And there was no end in sight with a thousand new migrants arriving daily.

Honest reactions on the ground in Greece
A Greek man, a homeowner, tried to reason with trespassing migrants as he told them to stay off his property. "You guys are violating private property, respect Greece, this is Greece, not the Middle East," he shouted, as scores of migrants milled about. It is sad to watch the man act as if he really believed that his trying to explain Greek ideas and values to the trespassers would make a difference. It didn't.

A Middle Eastern migrant explained to the camera that every day Afghans, Iraqis and Syrians fight amongst each other in the streets and riot. As he spoke, right on cue, crazed rioters ran past him in the street, throwing garbage cans, stones, rocks, pipes, and other objects at each other.

In tears, a Greek woman spoke about the migrant invasion, telling us that it is the migrants who are at war, not the Greeks.

She also sobbed as she wished for things to go back to the way "they were before" the increasingly unruly and violent hoard descended on her town. The woman said all she wanted to do was go back to work, and her children just wanted to go back to school, but due to the migrant takeover of their town, they couldn't do either.

She tearfully explained that the Greek citizens were the real victims, *not* the invading migrants. She said "they have to take them from here."

If only it were that easy.
https://youtu.be/yfeCvrT0uaY
https://youtu.be/CleLxrz08Mw
https://youtu.be/8dcCLD6NoZc
http://www.bbc.com/news/world-europe-34026114

"Hellhole Kos"
In Kos, Greece, in 2015, migrants at a shelter detailed their heartbreaking plight dealing with broken windows, and drafty accommodations that lacked electricity. They lamented a lack of food and a washing machine for their dirty clothes. Worse, nine people had to sleep in just four beds.

To top it all, whenever the migrants went to the police station to complain, the police offered them the outrageous advice to "go back" to their own countries.

Sad. Why can't you drop everything to kowtow to migrants?

In late May 2015, the UK newspaper, Daily Mail, ran a story that called Kos a "disgusting hellhole." Boy did they catch major heat. Apparently, telling it like it is, is unacceptable. Social media sites were created to refute the "slanted" story and explained that nothing was amiss.

In fairness, we weren't there, so who knows, but the photos we saw seemingly told it all – hundreds of marching young male migrants, decrepit shelters, squatters, shops and restaurants blocked by enormous crowds of young male migrants, hundreds of people sleeping in courtyards and living in the streets, piles of garbage, migrants washing themselves and their clothes in the sea and hanging clothes to dry all over the place, et cetera.

In the meanwhile, holiday travelers to Kos in 2015 were reporting the most "disgusting" state of affairs on this once popular destination island. Allegedly, migrants were lying in the streets, on sidewalks, on park benches, and in alleys. Rubbish and waste was everywhere. Migrants sat outside restaurants and intently watched vacationers as they ate. Others called the newly dilapidated island "really dirty and messy."

Travelers said they were "sure they will never return."

As the formerly beautiful seashore was transformed into a massive clothes washing zone, with garments hanging to dry, litter accumulated. Thousands of migrants milled about. Shops and restaurants were losing more and more business each and every day. And that was many months before tens of thousands *more* migrants would arrive... sometimes daily!

For Greece, already in the throes of its worst financial disaster ever, a drop in tourism is more economic death.

No good deed ever goes unpunished. Again.
https://youtu.be/Q_XHkgScOSY
http://en.enikos.gr/society/29654,Kos-turned-into-a-disgusting-hellhole-says-the-Daily-Mail-PHOTOS.html
http://www.dailymail.co.uk/news/article-3099736/Holidaymakers-misery-boat-people-Syria-Afghanistan-seeking-asylum-set-migrant-camp-turn-popular-Greek-island-Kos-disgusting-hellhole.html

The flood gates remained wide open

By the end of October 2015, it was reported by the UN that 8,000 migrants were pouring into Greece daily, probably hoping to get there before winter set in. The UN also said that the new total number of migrants entering via Greece had now topped 500,000.

Whatever you do, don't strand the migrants

In the meanwhile, the media noted that while the host countries were overwhelmed and struggling to keep up with the ever increasing needs of these economic opportunists, that to close their borders would leave migrants "stranded." This is certainly another attempt to garner sympathy for people who have, in many cases, intentionally and recklessly put themselves in harm's way.

How often have you heard the old-fashioned-controlled-media say that a burglar was "stranded." The implication is that the burglar has some sort of right to your property and that by your closing your doors, or locking your windows, you somehow "stranded" the burglar on your porch. Really? On what planet?

Think about it.
http://www.bbc.com/news/world-europe-34585088

Epic tourist fail

The trusty old-fashioned-controlled-media finally reported, in November 2015, that Greece's tourist industry, one of the few saving graces of the failed and decimated Greek economy, "may get hurt" by the refugee crisis.

Well, yeah...

If you are trying to relax, why in the world would you spend enormous sums of money to be surrounded by the sights and sounds and smells of thousands of economic opportunists and migrants mixed in with your beautiful travel destination? Or risk your safety or your family's safety by risking confrontations when you know that the authorities are saying that desperate people, many who simply melted into the countryside and are wandering about, are looking for opportunities to do whatever it is they think they want to do?

Think about it. Or, of course, you can wander about and pretend nothing will happen to you. You're special. And maybe nothing will happen to you or yours. Maybe.

Since 20% of the total GDP of Greece comes from tourists, if travelers forsake Greek destinations, the impact could be staggering. As expected, Greek authorities are pretending everything is fine. And, as expected, so are travel agents. But then again, both these groups have a vested interest in your time and money.

Yet all the assurances and reassurances and declarations and platitudes didn't mean a thing to one Dutch tourist who will probably never forget the vacation to Greece.
http://www.cnbc.com/2015/11/02/migrant-crisis-may-hurt-vital-greek-tourism-industry.html

Travels to Greece – finds something missing for decades
According to the World Health Organization:
> Cholera is an **extremely virulent** disease. It affects both children and adults and **can kill within hours if left untreated**. It is an acute diarrheal infection caused by ingestion of contaminated food or water. Recently, **new variant strains** have been detected in several parts of Africa and Asia. Observations suggest that these strains cause more severe cholera with higher case fatality rates. Every year, there are up to 4.3 million cholera cases resulting in up to 142,000 deaths annually worldwide.

http://www.who.int/mediacentre/factsheets/fs107/en/

In October 2015, the Centre for Disease Control and Prevention confirmed that a tourist to Greece was struck down with symptoms of cholera, a disease most common in Africa and Asia. The World Health Organization said Greece hadn't seen cholera since 1993. Over two decades of being cholera-free, *and poof*, cholera *may* be back on Greek soil. And the lucky tourist from the Netherlands *may* have found it. Had the symptoms turned out to be nothing much, we would have expected to see big headlines to that effect. You know, "No Cholera Here!" Instead, we saw nothing. The whole situation is depressing but really not surprising at all. Remember the warnings from the doctors in Germany in the last chapter? Tens of thousands of people coming in from countries *known* to have certain diseases – living in filthy conditions in makeshift camps with poor sanitation and washing facilities – and what would you *reasonably* expect?

By October 2015, the Syrian American Medical Society reported that Syria had experienced a cholera outbreak, with at least one death so far, and that the cholera outbreak was a "real threat." Since up to 80% of infected people don't exhibit symptoms, and cholera is *highly infectious,* it is a challenge to manage. Worse, concurrently over 1,200 cholera cases were confirmed in Iraq, including a half dozen fatalities, over the course of a few weeks.
http://www.express.co.uk/news/world/609553/Migrant-crisis-cholera-Kos-island-refugees-Syria-Afghanistan-Europe
http://www.independent.co.uk/life-style/health-and-families/health-news/syria-cholera-outbreak-sparks-fears-of-international-threat-a6708436.html

It's really bad so how can we make it so much worse?
In a bout of really bad timing, Greece was "forced" by its international creditors to allow all the directors at its public hospitals to be "evaluated." The result was that in November 2015, about 90% of Greece's public hospital directors were removed from their jobs. The Greek government was scurrying to fill the positions, a process which they thought would take three or so months.

Let that all sink in. Slowly.

So, your nation's economy is a sick joke. You're also facing the potential onslaught of serious diseases from an endless tsunami of migrants. Concurrently, a bunch of bankers that loaned you money force you to "evaluate" the directors of your public hospitals, and afterwards you agree to fire 90% of the hospital directors all at the same time? 90%! *And now you need a quarter of a year to replace the leaders of your public hospitals? I mean, an idiot wouldn't have to break a sweat to generate several plausible conspiracy theories around this one...*

Maybe it's all good. Maybe it'll all be just dandy. With any luck, the new directors will hit the ground running and make everything fine again. But we're seriously betting the bankers will be doing their elective surgeries elsewhere...
http://www.ekathimerini.com/202162/article/ekathimerini/news/hospital-directors-about-to-undergo-job-evaluations
http://apokoronasnews.gr/most-state-hospital-directors-to-go-after-failing-evaluation/#ixzz3qKTSUE8c

In the meanwhile, dillusionists were busy flooding the internet with claims that the migrants carry no greater risk of disease than anyone else, that they will be a *boon* to the economies of Europe, and that *there are no militants sneaking in* as well.

Crazy, right?

One particularly well written article from October 16, 2015, entitled "3 Damning Ways European Leaders Have Tried To Curb Sympathy For Migrants" included a section called "**Myth: Militants enter Europe by posing as migrants**." In debunking this "myth," the author wrote that "Government officials have not just warned about Islamist militants crossing into European countries. Some have conflated security fears with xenophobic notions of national identity."

Wow. Who could possibly have thought to cram so many loaded topics into one sentence: Government, Islam, Militants, Warnings, Conflation, Security, Fear, Xenophobia, National Identity.

The author also skillfully went on to link "far-right" with those that worried about militants. The author then penned the phrase that begged to be examined... "Those who have followed the issue most closely, however, have said that the fears are overblown." The clear implication was that anyone that expressed fears was a nut job, and that the "real experts," those following the issue *most closely*, unlike us "nut jobs," were saying the concerns were "overblown." Or Islamophobic. Or Xenophobic. Or claustrophobic. Or whatever-phobic.

But the media spin was crystal clear. If you had concerns that among the tens of thousands of migrants pouring into Europe there may very likely be militants, you were a right wing, far-right, Islamophobic, xenophobic, racist, nationalist, nut job.

As a further debunk of *militants enter Europe by posing as migrants,* the author quoted a person she identified as helping to "lead an Italian parliamentary committee on immigration and security" as saying that "Italy has not seen any militants posing as migrants." Strange journalism considering that in May 2015, Italian police arrested in Italy an illegal migrant from Africa that arrived on an illegal migrant boat who was wanted for a deadly museum attack in Tunisia. That's pretty militant.

But who has time to check facts anymore?

Of course, let's not forget when Italian police in April 2015 arrested a bunch of Pakistani and Afghan immigrants who had been planning a "big jihad" of the Vatican. Back then, Reuters reported that "Italian officials are also concerned that members of terrorist groups might be hiding among the thousands of migrants who arrive on Europe's shores every week." So, barring some sort of ulterior motive, for this writer to try and craft an article designed to make unaware readers think that "experts weren't worried" is beyond strange.

The author also added a message from the vice chair of the European Union's Parliamentary Subcommittee on Security and Defense who was quoted as saying "The only thing I have seen evidence of has been *European citizens* going into Syria and committing terrorist acts. I have not come across any evidence the other way around."

Well, after this "preponderance" of evidence and testimony that the author heaped on us, one could *only* reasonably suspect one's self of being a closet far-righter if you were still fearful that a militant might sneak through the *blockade-less* blockade...

And we certainly had hoped that the fears were overblown and that this overconfident "author" was right in their pontifications and righteousness. The November 2015, Friday the 13th, Paris terror attacks which left about 130 people dead and more than double that number injured, showed all the lecturing and doublespeak about *no militants entering Europe clothed as migrants* for what it was – pure fantasy.

Chilling. But oh so predictable. Except, of course, if you were an expert who "most closely" followed the issue. Then you must have been completely caught off guard.

Even a conservative estimate is a nightmare

Remember back in September 2015, when the Lebanese Minister of Education Elias Bousaab warned British Prime Minister David Cameron that radicalized migrants most *had* and *would* enter via Turkey into Greece. He wasn't kidding. And then he specifically said that 2% of migrants were radicals looking to cause havoc.

2% sounded tiny, right? Like itty bitty. Insignificant. As in, a 2% raise is a joke... Until you do the math...

Then the potential number of militants is staggering. If Germany hits 1.5 million migrants, and the Minister is right, that will be a minimum of 30,000 militants setting up shop.

Just how will Merkel deal with that? Or anyone else.

Again, our deepest sympathies and thoughts to the people hurt and suffering from this tragedy. The people on the ground, with nowhere to go and nowhere to hide. We are so profoundly saddened.

And again, it didn't have to happen this way.
http://www.who.int/mediacentre/factsheets/fs107/en/
http://www.dailymail.co.uk/news/article-3169178/Greek-islands-Lesbos-Kos-host-thousands-migrants-shocking-conditions.html
http://www.euronews.com/2015/11/14/paris-attacks-what-we-know/
http://thinkprogress.org/world/2015/10/16/3713380/migrant-fears/
http://www.telegraph.co.uk/news/worldnews/europe/italy/11617369/Italy-arrests-Tunisia-museum-terror-attack-suspect.html
http://www.reuters.com/article/2015/04/24/us-italy-security-pakistan-idUSKBN0NF0DO20150424#G5KARoLwf0jcpA4m.97
http://www.theguardian.com/world/2015/nov/14/syrian-greece-refugee-paris-attacks-killers
http://www.dailymail.co.uk/news/article-3234458/Two-100-Syrian-migrants-ISIS-fighters-PM-warned-Lebanese-minister-tells-Cameron-extremist-group-sending-jihadists-cover-attack-West.html

Send in the TSA
Remember when the legendary motorcycle enthusiast, Sonny Barger, offered to go to Viet Nam with fellow members of the Hells Angels and help out?

Well, if Greece continues to be unable to secure its external border and do a better job of screening migrants, maybe America can send over an army of our TSA agents. They are extremely adept at screening travelers at US airports. They have cool blue uniforms and are used to dealing with irate tourists and passengers.

The migrants would be no match for US TSA agents!

And *everyone* would be screened. Maybe even twice! And patted down, if they refused to be x-rayed. Compliance would be guaranteed, and we'd finally get to see exactly what it is the migrants are carrying with them in their bags and backpacks.

Imagine how many nail files, scissors, nail clippers, pocket knives, cork screws, baseball bats, lighters, butter knives, sharp sticks, foreign foods, plants, seeds, sharpened items, drugs, axes, hammers, electronic chargers, batteries, saws, and possibly even guns and hand grenades could be weeded out.

The results could be very interesting.

Don't forget to take off your belt and shoes! Do you have any liquids? Step off the line. Are you carrying cash in excess of $10,000? I need to pat you down. Do you have anything to declare? And put your watch and coins in this small tray...

(20) HUNGARY & MEDIA SPIN

Overwhelmed by tens of thousands of migrants storming her borders, Hungary declared a state of emergency. In September 2015, after almost 10,000 migrants entered Hungary, officials installed more barbed wire fencing in an attempt to stop migrants from sneaking in from Serbia, and closed the border.

One migrant was portrayed by CBS News as having a hard time trying "to understand why they've been locked out."

Wait. What was that?

Locked out? Of what? A country they were trying to trespass through? Seriously? Do would-be trespassers have a hard time understanding why stores lock their doors?

Good old fashioned media spin subtly at play. It's time to delve into the subtle art of media spin. Let's use the way some stories about Hungary were spun. Stay alert!

But that's what the viewers were *prompted* to think. "Hungary locked the poor struggling man out." The irritated migrant continued, "We are asking what time you will open, what happened, *what will you do for us*? Nobody answering any questions."

So call me old school, but if I'm fleeing strife and get to a friendly country, I'm probably going to have a different approach. Just saying.

At a minimum, I'll be *asking* for help, not demanding to know *what will you do for us*?
https://youtu.be/AMQUe1qvz1s

To paraphrase – I knew Jack Kennedy. Jack Kennedy was a friend of mine. And Jack would caution you to ask not what your country *can do for you* – ask what *you can do for your* country. *Actually, now that I think about it, I guess this is a moot point since most of these migrants have* abandoned *their countries...*

The CBS report continued with this gem, "Migrants who arrived just moments too late were simply cut off."

More media spin. Try this on for size, "The home-invader got to your front door moments too late, as you had already locked up, and so he was simply left standing outside..."

Media spin is as easy as it is dangerous. It has tremendous power. Most people don't realize that their opinions are being craftily nudged, if not flat-out created. Learn to recognize media spin. Stay alert!

As Hungary began to enforce its laws, and arrest illegal entrants, CBS News said, "Unlucky for the first men arrested in Hungary's crackdown. Now, anyone caught trying to enter the country illegally faces the prospect of 5 years in prison."

Not sure how anyone can think that Hungary *actually enforcing its laws and protecting its citizens* is a negative. But this is the new Europe, right?

Then CBS News reported that the crisis at the Serbian border had "reached a breaking point" and that "hundreds if not thousands of migrants are pressing up against the border trying to break free, and they are not being given any information."

Did you catch the *multiple* media spins? Let's go through them, one by one.

> *"Breaking point?" What is it that's supposedly breaking? The only thing I saw breaking was the migrants breaking Hungarian laws, and quite a few fences, too.*
>
> Trying to "break free?" *Break free of chains? Handcuffs? Getting out of a prison? A cage? The implication is that somehow Hungary had imprisoned migrants.*

The truth was – thousands of migrants were trying to "break in" and NOT to "break free."

> *"Not being given any information." Ok. So I try to break into your house, you lock the doors, and then I get indignant when you won't tell me anything. Seriously?*

As journalist A.J. Liebling famously wrote in The New Yorker magazine in 1956, "People everywhere confuse what they read in newspapers with news."

Once you get the gist of media spin, catching it is *sooo* much fun... Unfortunately, once you are aware, you won't be able to read or watch or listen to the old-fashioned-controlled-media the same way ever again. You will see what is being done to consumers of news like you. And it is no longer fun. You've been warned.

Instructive American media spin example – "fabricating"
For a classic example of media spin, think "the George Zimmerman 911 call."

No matter what side you're on, the facts are the facts.

A Hispanic American male named Zimmerman shot and killed an African American male teen named Martin.

The old-fashioned-controlled-media apparently wanted their audiences to believe that Zimmerman was a racist and that's why he killed Martin.

The 911 call segment you were *allowed* to hear on NBC's Today Show supported their spin with Zimmerman speaking the sentence, "This guy looks like he's up to no good, he looks black."

Wow! Most would agree that this statement could be strong prima facie evidence of racism.

Except that's not exactly what transpired.

The 911 tape played to America had been *edited* by NBC to produce a deceptive and inaccurate media spin.

According to court documents, Zimmerman, while performing a neighborhood patrol, called in a suspicious teen to 911 saying,
> "This guy looks like he's up to no good. Or he's on drugs or something. It's raining and he's just walking around, looking about."

The 911 dispatcher asked Zimmerman,
> "OK, and this guy — is he black, white or Hispanic?"

> *By the way, why didn't anyone question the 911 dispatcher about racial predilections since the dispatcher obviously mentioned the choice "black" before white or Hispanic?*

In any case, that was the first time Zimmerman mentioned race, when he answered the 911 dispatcher's direct race question with,
> "He looks black."

Frankly, with the right software, you could edit a White House Press Conference to make it sound like President Obama was admitting to the Kennedy assassination...

Worse, instead of showing journalistic integrity and accuracy, the old-fashioned-controlled-media endlessly repeated the edited sound bite designed to make Zimmerman appear racist.

How could you seriously ever trust a "news" source that took part of one sentence *and* the answer to another question *and so craftily pieced the bits together and fabricated it to sound like one racist and presumptive sentence?* Think about it. *The obvious question is "What else have they lied about? Misled about? Edited? Misrepresented? Embellished?"*

Liar, liar, pants on fire... once a liar, always a liar... cry wolf...

Even after NBC apologized for airing the edited clip (after they were sharply criticized by a media watchdog group), the "damage" had been done. But, then again, didn't the old-fashioned-controlled-media know that all too well? Ooops!

Unfortunately, 99% of the masses won't see beyond the curtain. Too bad for the countless victims of media spin. Far worse, for years after the "truth" has been finally revealed, *usually with no fanfare on some obscure part of a nearly unread back page*, people still will be repeating the initial lies they were fed. It's human nature. They gleefully remember and repeat the "big lie" long after it has been disproven.

That's the *real* power of the media!
http://www.foxnews.com/us/2012/04/03/nbc-issues-apology-edited-zimmerman-11-call/

Instructive American media spin example – "ignoring"
Another example of media spin, this time accomplished by misdirection and ignoring an elephant-in-the-room, was the law enforcement siege and subsequent assault on the church

and compound of a religious group known as "Branch Davidians" near Waco, Texas in 1993.

No matter what side you're on, the facts are the facts.

In the aftermath of the event, 4 US Government law enforcement agents and 82 Branch Davidian church members were dead. The media seemed to neatly make this into a "crazy religious cult" versus law enforcement event. And a "gun nut" event since guns were seized. And a "child abuse" event since there was concern about underage sex and physical abuse going on at the compound. And "everyone" seemed to get the impression that the "cult" members were weak-willed, dumb, gun-toting, poor, white people who were flat-out weirdos.

For some mysterious reason known only to themselves and their handlers, the old-fashioned-controlled-media either completely missed, or intentionally chose to ignore the one glaring elephant-in-the-room – half of the dead weren't white.

Half (actually a bit more than half... 52%) of the church members who died during the siege and assault were minorities (29 were black, 6 were Hispanic, 6 were Asian, and 2 were Polynesian). *A minority event!* Also, 40% were not even Americans, and included people from England, Australia, Canada, New Zealand, and even one Israeli. *An international event!* And that almost 70% of the dead were women and children. *A women and children event!*

Think about it. More than *a third of the dead* Branch Davidian church members were black, and not a peep out of the old-fashioned-controlled-media. No rallies. No marches. No mention. *Had the internet been in full bloom in those days, would the racial component gotten airtime?*

So, for the old-fashioned-controlled-media, sometimes *ignoring* facts is as effective as *fabricating* stuff. Think about it.
http://carolmoore.net/waco/waco-victims.html

Real people, real violence
In September 2015, hundreds of violent young male migrants attacked Hungarian police at a border crossing. Trying to gain illegal entry into Hungary, they attempted to swarm a locked gate which they managed to break open. They furiously kicked at fences, rammed wire, threw rocks, bottles, bricks, stones, metal, and just about anything else they could find. They kicked at Hungarian police officers, who showed great restraint, and apparently only pepper sprayed the rioters. At some point a woman is heard screaming in perfect American English, "We are real people here. These are real people."

As opposed to "fake people?" Like the ones in Hollywood? I suppose the take away is "real people who commit real violent criminal acts should not be held accountable when they are migrants." Very interesting spin.

While we're on it, who are these "talking heads," these people that mysteriously appear at so many events lately and blurt out sound bites that often are aptly contrived and so perfectly push a slanted agenda?

Seriously. Think about it.

Oh and it got so much worse

Let's put the children to use!
At some point, the migrants got the incredibly callous idea to place some little children on the front lines, right by the fences and police. Then, the migrants tried to push through the border fence, using the terrified crying children as shields or hostages or whatever. Seriously?

Who does something like this?

Listen up, Ms. Merkel. What the migrants did and were willing to do to children at this border crossing should give you a crystal clear insight into some of their mindsets. When's the last time you put one of your children in harm's way, intentionally? Scratch that. You put your whole country in harm's way. We withdraw the question because the answer is so obvious.

Luckily, the Hungarian police officers didn't play into the rouse and repelled the hoard of violent migrants once again.
https://youtu.be/-LD2BGT26qI

Who are all these "journalists?"
As an aside, there also seems to be a load of "journalists" covering each of these "events." And many are filming from the migrant side of the fence. Of course, the moment the migrants go berserk, the "journalists" are stumbling over themselves to get to the safety of the police officers – ironically, the same officers the "journalists" would probably, no doubt, vilify in a heartbeat in their extremely one-sided but highly *marketable* "struggles of the noble migrants" stories.

Cash is still king.
https://youtu.be/KIIonTos1vI

No good deed goes unpunished
Flash forward to a local Hungarian man with a large bag of items and food he was handing out to newly arrived migrants at Budapest's Kelet train station. What a wonderful and kind act of love and caring for your fellow human beings. What could possibly go wrong?

How about good old-fashioned robbery?

Within moments of walking into one area filled with refugees, the well-intentioned man was surrounded by a group of migrant children who came at him from all sides and literally stole all his items *including his bag* which they ripped from his shoulder. Some may say that this was just an innocent act of "overzealous self-dealing" by children grabbing for themselves what they wanted, without regard for anyone else, and hardly a "real" robbery. And we say, what would *you* call it if someone ripped your bag off *your* shoulder and ran off with it?

Shocked, the do-gooder walked away shaking his head. He probably didn't know how to react to such blatant disregard for law and order. Hey buddy, did you check to make sure you still had your wallet and watch? Welcome to the new Europe.
https://youtu.be/Ls_iQusP9BY

In September 2015, some people drove their car up to Budapest. Along the way they filmed the incredible debris, garbage, and filth that was strewn and dumped by the passing refugees along the highway and countryside. People in emergency suits were surveying the mess that their "guests" left at this particular "party" scene, which was in ruins. It went on for miles and frankly, was disgusting. And it was probably just the tip of the iceberg.

The old-fashioned-controlled-media spun this particular story by *not covering* it. Now you know another particularly effective way the media can spin – by not spinning at all – by not paying any attention to stories. Total media silence. Media blackout.

Or, as the Soviets might have called it, censorship.
https://youtu.be/SIfF6huzZzA

The "noble" struggle continues
In September 20015, a lot of footage was circulating showing desperate refugees trying to reach the Hungarian border as overwhelmed police struggled to protect their country. Alongside the refugees were journalists filming and photographing the events.

Did you catch the media spin?

Here are the planted terms/phrases: *desperate, immigrants,* and *trying to reach.*

Desperate: Desperate for what? Most are young men seeking their fortunes. Many migrants say they left perfectly safe homes and secure jobs in search of wealth. So *desperate* really seems to be a poor descriptor – unless you're spinning.

Refugees: Possibly immigrants, or maybe migrants, or economic opportunists, or any number of other things, but to paint all of the people in the crowd as "refugees" is as deceptive as calling all of the people, including staff and visitors, in a hospital "sickly." Some are, some aren't.

Trying to reach: No, not just *reach*. It's *breach*. Trying to *breach*. The only reason they were running is because they wanted to *breach* the border – break through.

Now you know.
https://youtu.be/Pdm0rVp5gac

Damned if you do and damned if you don't

After over 150,000 migrants stampeded through Hungary causing mayhem and destruction, Hungary set about protecting itself. It made it clear that it would be a crime to illegally cross Hungary's borders, and made it clear that causing damage (property destruction) to its new razor-wire fence would likewise be a crime.

The EU went nuts and threatened Hungary. Hungary simply replied that they were taking their EU obligations seriously.

In September 2015, Hungarian police used tear gas, water hoses, and officers to protect their country as migrants attempted to break though locked border gates.

Apart from the highly sanitized videos carefully edited to make a one-sided report even more biased, the migrants were *violent*.

Determined to trespass, the migrants broke through several border crossing areas and clashed fiercely with police, injuring at least 20 police officers.

While the Associated Press complained that one of its cameramen was "compelled" by Hungarian police to delete footage of what they claimed was a police dog knocking over a refugee (Hungary disputed the story), no footage was aggressively aired by any major media outlets of the mostly young male migrants lashing out at the police, destroying property, or anything else in a "negative" migrant vein.

Why is that?

Speaking of being "compelled" to delete things, we hear journalists claiming that they were "compelled" to erase "cops behaving badly" footage. Do you ever wonder *who* "compelled" the journalists to delete all that "migrants behaving badly" footage? Or do "journalists" delete that stuff themselves since they know there is no market for "that" side of the story?

Think about it.
http://www.theguardian.com/world/2015/sep/16/refugee-crisis-escalates-as-people-break-through-hungarian-border

Conspiracy theorists take note
In the meantime, outwardly fearless Hungarian Prime Minister Orban told the Swiss newspaper Die Weltwoche (November 12, 2015 issue) that,

> "No one raised the question of whether the essence of the matter is more about our existence, our cultural identity and our way of life... the suspicion arises that none of this is happening by chance. I am not brave enough to publicly talk about this as a certainty; *the suspicion inevitably emerges, however, that there is some kind of master plan behind this."*

Prime Minister Orban added that "Let us then look at the situation from a moral point of view, as well: how do we define our own moral responsibility towards war refugees? I believe that our Christian responsibility does not lie in offering them a new European life. Our responsibility lies in enabling them to return to their old lives, once their own countries have stabilized – even if this takes years."

"Liberalism today no longer stands up for freedom, but for political correctness – which is the opposite of freedom."

Anyone else find these to be very interesting insights from an insider who senses something is up? Who else senses that there is some "master plan"?

You may not be alone this time.
http://hungarytoday.hu/news/viktor-orban-defender-europe-swiss-weeklys-interview-hungarian-leader-full-50008

Migrant-chic
Norbert Baksa is a talented Hungarian fashion photographer, whose clients include Nike, Maxima, Elle, Red Bull, Glamour, and Adidas. At some point, he decided to do a photo editorial featuring popular fashion model Monika Jablonczky.

Ok so far?

Mr. Baksa added a twist. He had the model don all sorts of "refugee" clothes and pose by barbed wire fencing, and even included an obligatory "hostile police officer" in some shots. The model was featured in various poses and designer head scarves, heels, and boots, was posed taking selfies of herself with a cell phone complete with a Chanel logo, and showed a rather plentiful amount of uncovered breast in some shots. To make sure his audience didn't miss the point, Mr. Baksa called the spread "Der Migrant."

The reaction was swift.

Wickedly wrong. Sick. Art gone berserk. Very problematic. WTF?! Utterly sick. Can photography get any lower than this? Tasteless. And these are among the nicer comments that we can actually put in print. Social media was in an uproar.

Mr. Baksa defended his work on his website posting, "The shooting is not intended to glamourize this clearly bad situation, but... to draw the attention to the problem and make people think about it." He added, they "never meant to offend anybody" and "did our best to respect people's faith and conviction and not to cross certain boundaries." His website no longer features this particular work nor the rebuttal.
http://www.ibtimes.co.uk/hungarian-photographer-norbert-baksa-blasted-refugee-chic-fashion-shoot-featuring-monika-1522723

Where there is scorn, someone may be telling the truth
Sometimes to get to the truth, it pays to look at people that the old-fashioned-controlled-media relentlessly disparage.

So, back to Prime Minister Orban. Here are some more of his insights:
- "This is a migratory movement composed of economic migrants, refugees and also foreign fighters. This is an uncontrolled and unregulated process."
- "Does it comply with the freedom of information and speech that media usually show women and children while 70% of the migrants are young men and they look like an army?"
- "... the factual point is that all the terrorists are basically migrants. The question is *when* they migrated to the European Union."
- "Liberalism in Europe now concentrates not on freedom but on political correctness. It became a sclerotic ideology. Dogmatic, may I say. The liberals are enemies of freedom..."

In mid-November 2015, Prime Minister Orban added, "In light of this terror attack (the Paris killings), Brussels cannot challenge the right of member states to defend themselves. Mandatory resettlement quotas are dangerous because they would spread terrorism across Europe."

Actually, they already did.
https://euobserver.com/migration/131175
http://www.theguardian.com/world/2015/oct/23/refugees-look-like-an-army-says-hungarian-pm-viktor-orban
http://www.politico.eu/article/viktor-orban-interview-terrorists-migrants-eu-russia-putin-borders-schengen/

In late December 2015, Prime Minister Orban told Lidové Noviny, the Czechoslovakian daily newspaper, that
- "the European political elite is sitting in a closed, ideological shell, which means it has hardly any connection to reality."
- "Europe must abandon its suicidal tendencies, and must stand on both feet..."
- "We have the suspicion that there is also a secret – or not openly acknowledged – importation of voters into Europe."
- Speaking of Christianity and other national traditions, "Europe has forgotten who or what it actually is, and what the truly important things are... in order for it to become strong again, we need a Europe which has self-esteem and a sense of identity."

http://www.lidovky.cz/orban-nedovolme-aby-nam-do-zivota-bez-kontroly-napochodovaly-davy-uprchliku-1sq-/zpravy-domov.aspx?c=A151218_183756_ln_domov_gib

Will migrants assimilate?
These discernments were in-line with Orban's previous comments in Die Weltwoche, the Swiss weekly where the Prime Minister noted that,
"We enlightened and liberal-called Europeans think that all people behave just like we do. If Europeans were to emigrate to Syria, they would try to be part of Syrian life. We would not want to change Syria to our ways, but would accept the country as it is. Therefore, we believe that

people who come from Syria would behave the same. *But that is not the case.* They have different attitudes and they want to keep them."

This is clearly demonstrated across the globe where Muslims set up their own community centers, maintain their own traditions, and except for maybe getting a driver's license or registering an automobile, they really don't blend in, nor do they aspire to assimilate. Instead, they build what Orban and others have called "parallel lives."

Orban's comments on Europe's Christian roots and traditions, and his desire to maintain the same (just as Muslims and other groups are encouraged to maintain their traditions and customs) were equally balanced and seemingly even keeled, although he was again maligned by the old-fashioned-controlled-media. Orban was quoted saying that

"Christian Europe - I look at this as a cultural concept - has a common recordable identity. This does not mean that this Christian Europe is better or worse than the Islamic world, it is just different, with different rules and beliefs... we have to say, 'These are our values, our history, our way of life, and we will defend it.' (But) we do not... Whenever I speak to the European Council about Christian Europe, they look at me as if I come from the Middle Ages."

Were his comments so outrageous? So horrible? Or were they right on point? After you read Orban's words for yourself, and made up your own mind without old-fashioned-controlled-media spin, what did you conclude?
http://www.weltwoche.ch/index.php?id=555458

The Jewish Press warnings fall on deaf ears
Most amazingly, by the end of 2015, quite a few of the influencers and leaders in Europe and beyond had started to echo many of Orban's early warnings, concerns, and positions.

In October 2015, the Jewish Press said that "Hungarian Prime Minister Viktor Orban *wisely warned* that the wave of mostly Muslim refugees coming to Europe threatens to undermine the continent's Christian roots... All too obvious is the dearth of Christian and Jewish refugees who truly need asylum from the jihadists."

Exposing yet another example of the old-fashioned-controlled-media's imagery duplicity, the Jewish Press added that "The BBC's website of 200 images is also dishonest in its refugee presentation – providing a 53% focus on children, 36 percent men, and 10 percent women, whereas the United Nations Refugee Agency revealed that 75 percent of 'refugees' were young men."

There goes that "70-80+% young men of fighting age" statistic again. But Is anyone listening?

Citing another prime example of spin, the Jewish Press noted that "The (Jewish) Federation's announcement (in favor of population redistribution) contained a particularly deceptive photo of a wide-eyed, blonde toddler complete with Teddy bear..."

Again, where are the shots of masses of young Muslim men of fighting age?

Laying out their perception of the complete insanity of the situation, the Jewish Press continued, "...but the refugees are primarily able-bodied young men, weaned on anti-Semitism and hatred of the West and democracy, who are seen stomping on or burning our flags, brandishing rifles, hurling fire bombs, and wielding swords for decapitation. These are Islamists who have waged wars against Jews and Christians, and brought their savagery to Europe, complete with their methods of intimidation – riots and rapes of children and women."

The Jewish Press concluded that "The Jewish Federations (including AIPAC, AJC, B'nai B'rith Int'l, HIAS, ORT America, and National Council of Jewish Women), Catholic Charities, World Council of Churches, and other 'altruist' counterparts are conspiring against democracy, unintentionally or deliberately, to destroy Western civilization. To support them is to hasten some very Syrious and irreparable consequences."

Is anyone listening?
http://www.jewishpress.com/indepth/analysis/a-very-syrious-matter/2015/10/18/

Then, Hell froze over
In late December 2015, featuring an unflattering photo of Prime Minister Orban which made his face look as though he was contorted with grief or a serial killer, the New York Times reported that "European leaders have started to echo many of his (Prime Minister Orban's) points."

Good story, lousy photo. Seems you never get both when you're on the "wrong" side of things.

While stating that European leaders were beginning to see the wisdom in Orban's beliefs and views and stances, the New York Times did use the opportunity to dredge up and publish a whole litany of disparaging labels used in reference to Orban including: "self-declared scourge," "shrill," "bigoted," "hate-mongering," "repelled," "nasty snarls," "bizarre conspiracy theories," "tinged with racism and anti-Semitism," "belligerent tirade," "the Devil," and "mocking."

Guess the lousy photo wasn't enough.

And, guess it just wasn't enough to say Orban might have been right all along...

Nine paragraphs into the article we learned that the President of the EU's European Council, Donald Tusk, said that

Chancellor Merkel's open-door policy for migrants was "dangerous" and that Tusk, "endorsed the view long promoted by Mr. Orban – that most of the asylum seekers entering Europe were not Syrians fleeing war but economic migrants seeking jobs."

Man, that's huge!

"Most of the asylum seekers were... economic migrants seeking jobs."

The New York Times noted people were wondering if "...Mr. Orban had a clearer view of the scale of the migration crisis and its potential hazards than technocrats in Brussels and leaders in Berlin and other European capitals."

What would have happened had Orban succumbed to the initial smear campaigns and caved-in or shut up?

Think about it.
http://www.nytimes.com/2015/12/21/world/europe/hungary-viktor-orban-migrant-crisis.html

(21) ICELAND

Known as the most peaceful place on Earth, Iceland is an 85% Christian country famous for its hot springs, geysers, and waterfalls. While most Icelandic police officers don't carry guns, reportedly more than one third of Iceland is armed.

Initially, Iceland had capped its refugee count at 50. A country of around 300,000 inhabitants, they were called on to do more for Syrian migrants by a local author/activist on her social media page. In September 2015 over 10,000 Icelanders had responded to the "Syria is Calling" page which featured an impassioned plea for help including:

> "Refugees are our future spouses, best friends, or soulmates, the drummer for the band of our children, our next colleague, Miss Iceland in 2022, the carpenter who finally finished the bathroom, the cook in the cafeteria, the fireman, the computer genius, or the television host."

Moved by the appeal, generous Icelanders offered to house the migrants in their own homes and teach them Icelandic. Some spoke of being eager to assist and help the Syrian migrants to integrate into the Icelandic culture and adapt to society.

At some point the correlation between the most peaceful place on earth and only 50 refugees currently residing in Iceland may be researched. For now, we can only look at what has happened to similarly situated countries that have opened their doors and expected to integrate their new friends.

If history repeats itself, or flows along the same tried and true paths, it won't work. First, as far as the whole "integration" concept, exactly where in the other European countries has it been a smashing success?

Spoiler alert – it hasn't, has it? Not even a little. Hmm. So why would it work in Iceland?

The silence is deafening.

Next, if the Syrian migrants in Sweden were offended by the cross on that country's flag, well the Icelandic flag featuring its cross would have to go. The national anthem probably isn't suitable for all people, and better rethink the whole Icelandic language thing. And best get your farmers up to speed on halal meat slaughter techniques including the necessary blessing prayers.

We have no idea if this will apply to Hrútspungar. Considering the charming migrant in Denmark that led a large protest and proclaimed the traditional Finnish morning porridge "unfit for dogs," we're guessing you'll have your hands full between the Skata, shark, horse, fish soup, and Svið.

If you're Icelandic, you know what I mean. If not, just let it go. Trust me, let it go.

As for wine, start instituting prohibition now.

And that whole "Miss Iceland 2022" goal – sorry to burst your bubble but two serious flaws in your fantasy spring to mind.

First – with 70-80+% of the migrants being young fighting-age males, chances are you won't get many females to groom into beauty contestants. Second, your new houseguests will likely require you to cover up your scantily clad Icelandic women, in their heavy pants and knit sweaters and all. The swimsuit competition, unless it features a head-to-toe burka, will be a no-show. Third, the strict prohibitions and parameters on music would need to be fully investigated before any participation could be even contemplated. And just like that, there go the deliriously naïve visions of "Miss Iceland 2022."

A sociologist at Northern Michigan University said that "Iceland's low crime rates are rooted in the country's small, homogenous, egalitarian and tightly knit society." So, once that is dismantled, what then? And what will you tell your children when they ask you "with all the evidence from all over Europe, what were you thinking?"

Maybe, like Merkel, you weren't.
http://www.theguardian.com/world/2015/sep/01/icelanders-call-on-government-to-take-in-more-syrian-refugees
https://www.washingtonpost.com/news/worldviews/wp/2015/02/18/5-countries-where-police-officers-do-not-carry-firearms-and-it-works-well/

(22) IRELAND

Ah, the land of St. Patrick, ancient Christian churches, four leaf clovers, Celtic lore, and magical legends. And soon to be the end of the proverbial rainbow, and pots and pots of leprechaun gold, for some lucky new migrants.

According to the UN, by June 2015, there were about 5,853 refugees and 4,300 asylum seekers living in Ireland. Recall that Ireland was in a good place with the EU and its refugee scheme – according to EU law, the EU couldn't legally force Ireland or England to join in the migrant scheme, and Denmark had a "blanket 'opt-out." But, being good caring global citizens, the Irish decided to "opt-in" and help out anyway.

The new math where 4,000 = 20,000
In September 2015, Irish authorities and politicians announced Ireland would welcome 1,800 Syrian refugees. Then they said that they would take in around 5,000 refugees. Then it was 4,000 refugees where it sat for a while. Then, Irish authorities admitted that by the time the 4,000 new refugees exercised their rights to "family reunification," where all their family members from wherever would get to join them in Ireland after some time, the number would likely rise to over 20,000.

Picking and choosing who gets to come into your country and who doesn't (children, Christians, women, Muslims) ordinarily gets severe and feverish criticism. Case in point, remember that the French Prime Minister condemned several French mayors for wanting to take in only Christian refugees and said, "The right to asylum is a universal right." And the French Interior Minister said on television that he didn't understand "this distinction. I condemn it and I think it's dreadful."

So along the same lines, if countries were to discriminate along the lines of sex, rather than religion, wouldn't that also be dreadful? Just saying it was interesting that when the deputy Prime Minister of Ireland said that "women and children, including displaced children, would be prioritized" there was zero outcry – particularly peculiar since that means Ireland will be overlooking assisting the 70-80% of the refugees who are fighting-age young males.

Irish President Higgins chimed in and claimed that "racism and xenophobia" were again rearing their ugly heads in a few countries in the EU. Higgins thought that "people should not be afraid of an influx of refugees" since they are simply "people fleeing persecution, slavery and smuggling."

Some, for sure, were fleeing persecution, slavery, and smuggling. But based on the voluminous migrant interviews we've reviewed, we're finding plenty of empirical evidence that suggests many are just looking to better themselves economically. That overwhelming majority of the refugees who are fighting-age young males appear to fit into that opportunist category very neatly. And remember that Donald Tusk, President of the EU's European Council, now agrees.

Irish Justice Minister Frances Fitzgerald said that helping 4,000 refugees would cost Ireland about 48 million euros per year. The first 600 refugees would arrive by the end of 2015. She said, "We will put in place all the necessary supports to ensure that those coming to Ireland can integrate…"

Wait. What? Integrate?

After all the evidence about, *and directly from*, migrants who have no intention of taking on your alien and infidel European ways, with your beer and uncovered women and disregard for Sharia law, and you actually believe that you can be successful with "integration"? Seriously?

Does anyone else think that a rude awakening is on the way? Just check out the "integration" shenanigans in Sweden, or Denmark, or England or Germany, or... well you get the picture.

Call it welfare. Call it kindness. Call it blind humanity. Call it gullibility. But dare not call it integration or assimilation. Based on everything we've seen, that just ain't happening. And to stick your populace with the burden of implementation while you hide away in your gated communities with armed guards and private planes is simply unconscionable.

A nation once again. Indeed.
http://www.bbc.com/news/world-europe-34208805
http://www.thejournal.ie/refugees-germany-makes-billions-available-2315567-Sep2015/
http://www.irishtimes.com/news/politics/ireland-to-take-4-000-refugees-in-new-programme-1.2346948
http://www.rte.ie/news/2015/0904/725569-ireland-refugees/

(23) ITALY

By 2007, Italy was already in trouble. While the rate of criminality when comparing native Italians and *legal* immigrants was not noticeably different, according to the Italian Interior Ministry, foreigners, *mostly illegal aliens*, committed 35% of all crimes.

That's terrible.

Let's see if there was any noticeable trend. Forget pickpocketing, beatings, burglaries and other silly nuisances. How about a really bad crime? How about murder. Yes, that's pretty heinous and final. Let's check out historical murder rates in Italy.

In 1988, foreigners made up less than 1% of the population yet committed 6% of the murders. In 1998, foreigners made up 1.7% of the population yet committed 18% of the murders. In 2006, foreigners made up less than 5% of the population yet committed 32% of the murders.

Why is that? And could that be a trend?

Fast forward to February 2015. Data from the Italian Department of Prisons showed that approximately a third of all detainees were foreign-born. As for crime, foreigners dominated prostitution committing 78% of the offences, 36% of drug offences, 30% of attacks against people, and 25% of property crimes (in the meanwhile burglaries had gone up 127% in 10 years). Yet, foreigners only made up 8.3% of the Italian population in January 2015.

8.3% of the population was involved in a third of the crime.
http://www.rainews.it/dl/rainews/articoli/Istat-crescita-zero-popolazione-Italia-8-2-per-cento-immigrati-02a8ba3a-5a2b-4fee-b333-0a7df9cd2abc.html
http://immigrazione.aduc.it/notizia/viminale+reato+tre+commesso+immigrati_99097.php
http://www.iltempo.it/cronache/2015/03/14/droga-ordine-pubblico-furti-e-rapine-un-reato-su-tre-commesso-da-stranieri-1.1390627

Bye-bye police car
In August 2015, a group of about a half dozen African migrants expressed their anger with Italia by demolishing a police car.

As someone filmed the attack on video, and other migrants watched from close by, the rioting men proceeded to use bats and sticks and poles to demolish the Italian police vehicle. At one point, one of the African migrants jumped on the roof of the car to get better leverage, as he smashed in the windshield.
https://youtu.be/kXurSjsE9tw

I'm firing my travel agent
In October 2015, in Padova Italy, with the camera on, a migrant from Ghana expressed his disgust that the shelter provided by the Italian Government and paid for by the Italian people was "no good." He explained that the accommodations were no good, since it was "too hot, and the food we eat is no good, no television, no air condition, you need a comfortable place, because the place we sleep is no good..."
https://youtu.be/Q_XHkgScOSY

In August 2015, in Milan Italy, at a Red Cross migrant camp, an African wearing what appeared to be a new running suit was seen on video aggressively asking for help, stating that they were "sleeping in bad conditions, try to help us, we are dying, we are dying, we beg you, we beg you, we suffer too much here, try to help us... so many are here from Africa..."

As he took us on a tour of his allegedly "deplorable" conditions, we saw emergency shelter tents set up in rows occupied by migrants. In one tent we were shown where some water leaked onto the floor after a rain storm.

As to the "bad" conditions, for emergency shelters set up for uninvited migrants, there didn't seem to be anything so terrible. Except, as the previous man pointed out, there was a lack of air conditioning and television sets. At some point, rowdy African protesters began running through the compound and ended up at the gates where scores of Africans were pummeling police officers. As the officers pushed back with their riot shields, the migrants moved back into the camp, stopping to further taunt and jab at the police as they screamed and yelled and threw things.
https://youtu.be/rYGmazGwa-g

Planning a trip to Rome?
Before you pack your bags, better figure out which areas are "no-go" areas due to migrants and their invasion of that ancient city. Concerns center around migrant criminal activity and migrant waste and disease, literally.

In mid-June 2015, the Daily Mail reported that the huge surges of migrants had led to more than 500 cases of scabies in 2015 alone. Common in prisons, scabies is a skin infection caused by mites laying eggs under the skin resulting in a pimply rash that itches intensely and is spread by contact. Hundreds of migrants, mostly from Eritrea in Africa had been swarming around Milan's train station causing security concerns.

Piles of human waste, the stench of urine, scattered garbage, and other contaminants were making the Italian health authorities nervous as well.

In one video clip, you can see an aid worker handing out water bottles when she is suddenly overwhelmed by African migrants who shove her and try to snatch all the bottles from her hands. Luckily, the person videotaping quickly shut off the camera so we couldn't see how the melee ended. We can only guess it's all part of keeping the image of migrants clean and orderly and pristine. Except when you walk around Rome a bit.

Come see it, and *smell* it, for yourself. Just hire a few armed bodyguards. Far from a tourist haven, the migrants were quickly transforming parts of Rome into a living toilet.

In the meanwhile, business owners were panicking as tourists were avoiding areas overrun by hordes of lawless and increasingly violent migrants. The media won't cover it, so ask around. Maybe chat with the leaders of the three most affluent areas in Italy, that have already accommodated about 15% of the latest migrant swarm. The leaders said they were further concerned that the "sight of African migrants would have a 'devastating effect' on the country's tourism industry."

Italy is bursting at the seams as the latest influx of migrants is overwhelming their already strained resources. The Italian government was expecting that 200,000 migrants would show up in Italy by the end of 2015. That was way up from 2014, when the number was 170,000.

Rome has been economically teetering for years. In a 2011 Guardian report, we met an angry African migrant who got refugee status from Italy, but expressed his anger that Italy, "they haven't given us houses." Instead of getting the houses the refugees imagined they would receive, migrants were sleeping all over the streets, lying on sidewalks, following tourists and asking for aid. Italian charities help as much as they can but are overwhelmed.

One migrant in Italy told his story of sneaking into England, where he was instantly given a one bedroom apartment and enrolled into Bedford College within a week. Plus, England gave him 55 pounds spending cash each and every week for doing absolutely nothing. That is until they found his fingerprints, and realized he had initially claimed asylum in Italy so they deported him back to Italy. Boy, was he upset. One migrant summed up the situation by saying that Europe is a bunch of liars who aren't helping them.

In 2010, angry and violent African migrants protested poor conditions in Rossano, in Southern Italy. Hundreds of migrants were sleeping in the streets and abandoned buildings, and the protesters were demanding better treatment. As the protest progressed, the migrants suddenly chose to rampage and riot, destroying businesses, shops, motor vehicles, and property. Quite a few were arrested as police tried to restore order in the once beautiful town.

This was in 2010 and 2011.

It has only gotten worse. A lot worse.
http://www.dailymail.co.uk/news/article-3124612/Parts-Rome-turning-no-areas-sanitation-security-issues-caused-migrants-claim-local-businesses.html#ixzz3oaSRhb7k
https://youtu.be/f1bK-KaNZ-0
https://youtu.be/UGqwE72NPl0
https://youtu.be/rKEcJ0-15gs

Can't wait to feed the Christians to the lions in the Coliseum? Why not just drown them?

Considering all we've seen so far, this April 2015 Italian police report will certainly not raise any eyebrows.

For those of you who missed it, apparently 105 African migrants were on a slow boat to Italy from Libya. At some point, the boat developed a leak, and one of the migrants, a Christian boy, innocently began praying to Jesus for help.

Big mistake.

Witnesses, quoted in the Daily Mail, said Muslims warned the Christian boy to stop praying, saying "Here, we only pray to Allah." When the boy continued his Christian prayers, the Muslims pitched him overboard amongst screams of "Allah is Great." The boy drowned. Other Christians who tried to help the boy were pitched overboard. And they drowned as well. This scenario repeated itself about a dozen times.

Yup. They'll be integrating into Europe real well...

After a rescue boat arrived, Italian Police arrested 15 Muslim migrants from Western Africa (Ivory Coast, Mali, and Senegal) for the murder of 12 Christian migrants, also Africans (from Nigeria and Ghana).

Police in Palermo reported that the death toll would have been higher, but, after the first dozen Christians were murdered, other would-be victims "strongly opposed the drowning attempt and formed a human chain."

As to motive, Italian Police stated that the 12 victims were murdered because they were Christians, and officially charged the alleged killers with "multiple aggravated murder motivated by religious hate."

All is well! Really!
But all is well in the land of the Vatican, and the Pope. Well, at least that's what Italian Prime Minister Matteo Renzi made it sound like when he was questioned by a reporter about the Muslim-on-Christian drowning hate crime. Renzi said,
> "I think there are not problem of clash of religions in Italy. Maybe yesterday, maybe there were one case about it, but *the problem is not a problem of clash of religions. It's a*

problem of human dignity. We are absolutely committed to solve this problem, and I am confident if this become a priority, we achieve a great result."(sic)

Oh, now we get it, Renzi. Italian Police put 15 African Muslims under arrest for "aggravated murder motivated by religious hate" after tossing a dozen African Christians overboard and drowning them for being Christian, and you think it's really a *human dignity problem...*

Well, thanks for clearing that up! We never suspected that eating too much gnocchi could cause one to hallucinate, but there you go. We'll sleep near the piazza with the front doors unlocked tonight...
http://www.cnn.com/2015/04/16/europe/italy-migrants-christians-thrown-overboard/
http://www.dailymail.co.uk/news/article-3044584/Pray-Allah-ll-throw-overboard-Muslims-ordered-Christians-punctured-dinghy-African-migrants-sank-Mediterranean.html
https://www.whitehouse.gov/the-press-office/2015/04/17/remarks-president-obama-and-prime-minister-renzi-italy-joint-press-confe

Same tired old songs
In the summer of 2015, a boisterous group of around 100 African migrants, almost exclusively young men of fighting-age, with no identification, tried to push into France from Ventimiglia, Italy, carrying "We want freedom" banners and screaming in English "We are not going back. We need to pass."

The unruly group was stopped by quick acting French police who received orders to enforce EU rules – "People without papers must be readmitted to the country they came from, in this case Italy."

In the previous week, playing by EU rules, French police had caught a "record 1,439 undocumented immigrants" trying to sneak into France and had turned over 1,000 back to Italy.

One migrant said that they risked their lives to cross the Mediterranean Ocean to get aid, only to find "Nothing. No humanity."

And no chest of imagined riches at the end of the rainbow.

The angry migrant had no problems accepting and consuming the free food provided by the Red Cross. He also threatened that they were "ready to cross the sea again" but failed to indicate in what direction he meant. He added "we're ready to die " but didn't indicate for what or why.

In an attempt to manipulate the French authorities and force them into breaking EU rules, the migrants at Ventimiglia staged a peculiar so-called "hunger strike" in which some of the men refused to accept the free food from the Red Cross, although others, including the few women and children with the group, ate as usual.

French authorities weren't swayed, and the Italian authorities began talking about establishing a shelter in Italy for the migrants. Italy's Interior Minister, Angelino Alfano, went so far as to claim that France's insistence on following EU laws and not permitting the migrants to trespass through France was "a punch in the face to all the European countries that want to close their eyes" to this crisis.

What that quite actually meant was unclear but the old-fashioned-controlled-media loved the "punch in the face" sound bite.
http://www.euronews.com/2015/06/13/french-police-block-african-immigrants-trying-to-cross-the-border-from-italy

Clean up or ship out
The sound bite no one picked up was blurted out by an Italian governor who ordered all migrant tents and shelters to be cleared out since "their presence would have a 'devastating' impact on tourism in the region around Venice."

Ultimately, Italian police began rounding up these and hundreds of additional African migrants that had snuck into the area. While the vast majority of the migrants were young men, the old-fashioned-controlled-media "just happened" to capture and run photos of the handful of African women who were being moved as part of the enormous group. Headlines screamed that the police "forcibly removed" migrants. The fact that a police officer was hurt by migrants was underreported. Some remarked that yes, when you break the law and trespass, especially when you aren't a citizen, have no identification, *and* are not doing the right thing, you shouldn't be surprised when the police actually enforce the law and remove you.

Police placed those migrants they could find onto buses that took them to temporary shelters run by the Red Cross at various train stations across Italy. The area filled up yet again with migrants and a second and final removal of squatters took place at the end of September 2015. The Bishop of Ventimiglia intervened to help the migrants stop another sit-in, and convinced them to board buses.

Is this the same country where Roman legions once ruled the "world" and detractors were crucified by the thousands?
http://www.english.rfi.fr/africa/20150613-migrants-sitin-france-italy-border-french-police-block
http://www.telegraph.co.uk/news/worldnews/europe/italy/11678459/Migrants-clash-with-police-forcibly-removing-them-from-French-Italian-border.html

Unsettling events continue
It was also at the end of September 2015 that a young woman came forward with details of her gut-wrenching abuse at the hands of some of the African migrants from that "shelter."

The young woman, around 30 years of age, a volunteer with the *No Borders* activist group that advocates for and supports immigrants, was working with and helping African migrants in Ventimiglia. She had devoted a month of her life helping the migrants.

Then one Saturday night, as migrants enjoyed a loud party complete with blaring music, a gang of African migrants allegedly trapped the girl in a "shower block set up near the camp in a pine forest." Her cries for help and screams of terror were muffled by the blaring music.

Then the gang of Africans allegedly proceeded to rape and gang rape the woman as she struggled and screamed in vain.

According to major Italian national news source *Corriere Della Serra.*, the woman said she was convinced not to report the incident by *No Borders* colleagues since it might cause a scandal, it might harm the migrants, and it might "delegitimize the struggles of *No Borders*, a group born during the refugee emergency in Ventimiglia to support the protest of asylum seekers."

Corriere Della Serra reported that, in their defense *No Border* activists claimed the woman reported the rape *only to spite them* because of some other controversy.

The woman said she finally decided to report the incident to the police on the advice of a friend.

In the meanwhile, the alleged perpetrators were long gone.
http://www.express.co.uk/news/world/610376/woman-gang-raped-refugee-camp-activists-Italy-border-France-Ventimiglia
http://www.theguardian.com/world/2015/jun/16/italy-forcible-removal-eu-mediterranean-migrant-crisis-french-border-refugees
http://www.corriere.it/cronache/15_settembre_25/attivista-stuprata-un-migrante-mi-chiesero-tacere-non-creare-scandali-496d3388-6370-11e5-9954-7c169e7f3b05.shtml

Money. It's all about the money.
In a video published in October 2015, a young male migrant (aren't they all young males?) being interviewed at a refugee camp set out the horrible conditions the migrants were facing rather eloquently, "Well, uh, the problem. We come here but we finish our money. Everyone, you see them? (He looks at

some migrants.) The families. The women, the men, finish their money. They want money."

Succinct. Direct. Nicely said. "They want money."

Don't we all?
https://youtu.be/aVy-OKOxzGM

On November 27, 2015, Italian police seized almost 800 weapons (shotguns/rifles) on a truck from Turkey headed to Belgium, Germany, and the Netherlands.

One can only guess...
http://www.independent.co.uk/news/world/europe/paris-attacks-almost-800-pump-action-shotguns-seized-by-italian-police-on-way-to-belgium-germany-and-a6752106.html

Ciao, Italia.

(24) KAZAKHSTAN

Kazakhstan has a rather strong economy, bolstered by natural resources such as oil, gas, and minerals. Sporting a 99% literacy rate and a stable banking sector, the country has a robust tourist industry with almost 5 million people visiting from 2011-2015.

Part of the spike in tourism may have inadvertently resulted after the controversies surrounding the highly irreverent 2006 comedic film "Borat." The bawdy "mockumentary" was about a man from Kazakhstan filming a documentary in the US detailing why he thought America was a great country.

At first, Kazakhstan attempted to block the raunchy film's release. Then Kazakhstan tried lawsuit threats. Then the movie won a bunch of awards and grossed over a quarter billion dollars. And then a strange thing happened.

Instead of Kazakhstan being a laughing stock, tourism went through the roof. By 2012, the foreign minister said that tourist visas had gone up tenfold since the movie's release.

But we digress. Back to the migrants.

By June 2015, 662 refugees and 149 asylum seekers were living *in* Kazakhstan, and 2,242 refugees and 1,187 asylum seekers had originated *from* Kazakhstan.

Since the early 2000s, Kazakhstan has reportedly not been a great place for refugees. Few employment opportunities for outsiders, huge difficulties getting medical services, high housing costs, geographically far from just about everything, and poor integration prospects all added up to "not much opportunity to enrich one's self." Maybe that's why Kazakhstan has been pretty much shunned by migrants.

Curiously, in September 2015, Poland said it was in the process of taking in refugees *from* Kazakhstan –primarily ethnic Poles.

Not much more to report here.
http://www.irinnews.org/report/28306/kazakhstan-afghan-refugees-seek-third-country-resettlement
http://data.worldbank.org/indicator/ST.INT.ARVL
http://www.kazakhstannews.net/index.php/sid/238128567
http://www.bbc.co.uk/newsbeat/article/17826000/kazakhstan-thanks-borat-for-boosting-tourism

(25) KOSOVO

Kosovo, formerly part of Yugoslavia, was formed when it declared independence from Serbia in 2008. By February 2015, about a third of the country was living in poverty and more than a third was unemployed. Tens of thousands of people from Kosovo had been sneaking through Serbia into Hungary, after which many tried to reach Germany. Thousands reached and applied for asylum in Germany in January 2015 alone.

The president of Germany's Federal Office for Migration and Refugees said that although Kosovar applications for asylum were prioritized (hey, they are fellow Europeans, right?), few were approved, explaining that "their hope of finding a better life in Germany is in vain, as the recognition rate of asylum applications from Kosovar citizens is close to nil. We know that the economic situation is difficult in Kosovo. But poverty alone, according to the Geneva Convention, is not sufficient grounds for asylum – neither in Germany nor in other EU countries."

Aha! Now we know why all of those other economic migrants all seem to have the necessary elements in their prepared and rehearsed asylum stories. *Poverty alone* is not enough! Loose lips sink ships, buddy!

In the meanwhile, an exacerbated and slightly embarrassed Arifete Jahjaga, Kosovo's President, asked her fellow Kosovars to "carry the weight of building" Kosovo, adding that "the solution is not to run away."

"The solution is not to run away." *What a great concept.* Maybe that is the key to this whole mess.

Ask people to try and fix their countries rather than run away. Kind of like what the American colonists did. Instead of acquiescing to things they felt unfair, or running to Canada or Mexico or into the woods, they banded together and stood their ground. Some perished, some lived. It wasn't easy. But they held firm and in the end, with a lot of effort, heartache, and a load of military maneuvering and fighting, they created the country they envisioned.

Or, if violence isn't your thing, check out Leo Tolstoy's disciple Mahatma Gandhi. Tolstoy's book, *The Kingdom of God is Within You*, as well as his belief that passive resistance and love rather than violence were the keys to effectuating change influenced Gandhi to use the same as he pursued his nationalist political goals and transformed India.

"The solution is not to run away."

Think about that sound bite.
http://www.dw.com/en/kosovo-population-drain-challenges-germanys-refugee-policies/a-18245189

(26) LATVIA

In 2014, the United Nations highlighted the story of a Syrian refugee living in Latvia whose family was still in Syria. The refugee said "I have never felt in any way discriminated here. On the contrary – I am really glad and in general very satisfied with regards to the level of culture and societal attitudes towards foreigners." The man reportedly spoke fluent Russian, certainly useful in Latvia, and also organized a church charity concert to benefit Syrian children.
http://www.unhcr-northerneurope.org/news-detail/a-syrian-refugee-in-latvia-bashar-builds-a-new-life-in-riga

Migrants not welcome
In mid-October 2015, Public Broadcasting of Latvia announced that 55% of Latvians, "like many other people in Europe," don't want any refugees accepted into their country.

Latvian Public Broadcasting also asked and answered, "What is Latvia's past record on accepting asylum seekers? It's pretty bad... Latvia has the lowest rate of approving asylum seekers, having accepted only 8.3% of asylum seekers from January to June 2015."

By now, you saw that media spin, right? "Evil" Latvia accepts too few migrants! Or could it be that Latvia is far more selective and that's why it has far less migrant trouble?

In any case, Latvia agreed to accept about 530 refugees from Greece and Italy over two years, and possibly another 245 from Hungary.

Latvian State Secretary of State Ilze Pētersone-Godmane said the following are Latvia's preferred groups:
- Families with school age children who can learn Latvian
- At a minimum, one of the two parents speaks a European language
- Migrants with ID
- Migrants with an education

The Prime Minister added that migrants with a "similar mentality" would be preferred, likely meaning "Christian refugees."

Considering that we've seen that 70-80% of the migrants are young fighting-age males, a majority are Muslim, and most are uneducated, it would appear Latvia will be hard-pressed to meet the goal of 531 refugees over two years if Latvia tries to stick to its preferences.

Of course, the EU will likely be shocked and repulsed by Latvia's honest and straightforward assessment of potential integration hurdles and getting the right mix for assimilation into Latvia.

Edgars Rinkevics, Latvia's Foreign Minister, warned that Latvia's "failure to adopt an official position on refugees" caused Latvia to end up "in international isolation and risked losing Europe's support in various areas, such as security and EU funding."

While the esteemed minister may have some valid concerns, they only hold water if you see the EU as the giver of life. If the EU is truly capable and willing to punish member countries by withholding security and money, then why not get out of the EU now? No one needs that kind of sword dangling over their heads. What kind of union is based on a fear of *what might be withheld*? Barbaric. Truly barbaric.

Minister Rinkevics also said in October 2015 that the EU should "strengthen its borders, and 'be made more effective by means of EU institutions actively engaging in a dialogue with third countries to achieve that they meet their obligations on return and readmission of their citizens.'"

This means that the esteemed minister is warning third world countries that their refugees will be returned to them, sooner or later.

Think about it. That is the essence of providing asylum. It is a temporary shelter until you can return to your home, sweet home.

Well said minister!

Except we're betting that most of the 70-80% fighting-age males that are barreling north aren't the least bit interested in repatriation or going back home. They have set out to seek their fortune as economic opportunists. And they are planning on eventually bringing over their relatives as well.

How exciting.
http://www.lsm.lv/en/article/features/latvia-and-the-refugee-crisis-a-primer.a150836/
http://news.xinhuanet.com/english/2015-09/18/c_134634890.htm
http://www.lsm.lv/en/article/politics/foreign-minister-has-his-two-cents-worth-on-refugees.a150090/

(27) LIECHTENSTEIN

Liechtenstein is a principality next to Switzerland with a constitutional monarchy, no military, less than 100 armed police officers, under 40,000 residents, and one of the lowest crime rates in the world. Liechtenstein has one of the world's highest GDPs per resident and virtually no unemployment.

The UN reported that as of June 2015, it had a combined total of 182 refugees and asylum seekers. Not one person left Liechtenstein as a refugee or asylum seeker during the same time frame.

Liechtenstein is reportedly the world's largest producer of false teeth. Talk about a specialized niche. Maybe Liechtenstein will be cajoled into taking in a refugee or two. Maybe not.

It probably won't matter, one way or another.
http://www.liechtensteinusa.org/

(28) LITHUANIA

In September 2015, the EU decided that going forward, the EU would scrap the current voluntary migrant resettlement structure and instead impose a coercive mandatory program allowing EU leaders to make decisions on how many and where migrants get resettled. The mandatory program is troubling since it is akin to handing over control of watering your garden to a distant neighbor. Just enough water makes for a healthy crop yield. But if he decides to open the nozzle full blast for months on end, your once promising garden could quickly turn into a useless swamp of ruined crops.

Instantly seeing through the potential totalitarianism, the President of Lithuania, Dalia Grybauskaitė, stated that "Without a doubt, none of us would want solidarity to be based on some coercive mechanisms. We are equal countries that are friendly towards each other, therefore, we would want to solve matters by consensus and in a friendly way."

As of June 2015, 1,055 refugees and 54 asylum seekers already lived in Lithuania. Lithuania agreed to take in, over the next two years, another 1,105 refugees. And that's that.
http://bnn-news.com/week-lithuania-lithuanian-companies-refugees-replenish-countrys-weakened-workforce-132919

(29) LUXEMBOURG

According to the UN, by June 2015, there were 1,192 refugees and 831 asylum seekers in Luxembourg, a wealthy nation (actually a "Grand Duchy"- don't ask...) of about half a million inhabitants.

Luxembourg has been largely unaffected by the migrant crisis.

In November 2015, Jean Asselborn, the Foreign Minister of Luxembourg warned that the *EU could break up in months* if countries *insisted* on controlling their borders in light of the migrant crisis.

Here are some of his quotes:
- "The European Union can break apart. That can happen incredibly fast, when isolation instead of solidarity, both inwards and outwards, becomes the rule."
- "We may have only a couple of months."
- "The glue that holds us together is still the culture of human values. And this false nationalism can lead to a real war."
- If Schengen falls, the "greatest achievement of the European Union also falls."

Oooo. Scary stuff. But what is the esteemed minister talking about?

"The European Union can break apart."

Well, yes, anything can break apart. And like a bad marriage, sometimes a break up is for the better.

"That can happen incredibly fast, when isolation instead of solidarity, both inwards and outwards, becomes the rule."

Isolation implies bad. *Solidarity implies* good. *I get his clever spin. But with many of his fellow EU countries being overrun and overwhelmed, for the esteemed minister to try and stigmatize any country that moves to protect its people under these extraordinary times is shameful.*

"We may have only a couple of months."

So what? So, in a couple of months the EU becomes Europe again. Who cares? A married woman in an abusive dysfunctional relationship throws in the towel and gets her life back. She'll change her credit cards back to her old name. Hey, chances are she might be much happier and safer...

"The glue that holds us together is still the culture of human values. And this false nationalism can lead to a real war."

Ok. Honestly, this is one of those quotes that reaches for the stars and is intended to be lauded and quoted. Except it's no "road less travelled." Scalpel please... Glue that holds us together.... Pretty innocuous so far. "Still" implies that an ideal or greater good is desperately clinging on for its life. We "still" have a chance. He "still" respects life. They "still" have a chance to do good. Seizing the moonshine, the feds broke up Cousin Earl's "still."

"Still the culture of human values." This is the next big turn. Culture is the whole. It is the way of life for a particular group.

Human values could be a part of that culture. But traditions, values, customs, beliefs, behaviors, symbols, and attitudes make up "culture" as well. Is he implying a love for all humanity? Or human values, maybe as displayed by the new migrants as well as the old? Who knows. So saying "the culture of human values" sounds grandiose but means nothing.

"And this false nationalism can lead to a real war" is yet more drivel. First, "nationalism" has been hijacked as of late as a code word for racist. So that's bad. This concept of "false nationalism" is confusing since it seems to condemn fake nationalism yet in today's politically corrupt (correct) climate, any nationalism, false or real is bad, right? And how will it lead to a real war?

Oh, and don't get me started on what a fake *war might be, as opposed to the quoted* real *war. Considering Luxembourg's volunteer army recently totaled about 900 soldiers, their perspective on "war" could be understandably different. Compare that to New York City's 34,000 cops. Just saying...*

And finally, if Schengen falls, the "greatest achievement of the European Union also falls."

Schengen is the agreement which allows free travel between many EU countries. Kind of a Europe without borders. The theory is, once you officially get in to the EU, you've been identified, checked out, cleared, and can now roam around freely between many countries with no more border checks.

First. If "Europe without borders" is truly the "greatest achievement of the European Union," get a refund. It wasn't worth it. Look at what has happened!

Second. To cling to an experimental idea that isn't capable of providing proper protection for citizens during the current out-of-control extreme state of emergency, is quite delusional. Like a pathetic and pitiful spouse that refuses to end an abusive relationship because they cling to "how it was supposed to be" and ends up dead. Was it worth clinging to something that is failing dangerously?

Europe likely needs to reassess its unbridled altruism and figure out a better way to deal with and help true refugees. At a minimum, the EU needs to wake up and face reality, show some leadership and get control over its immigration.

Instead, the esteemed minister criticizes people for being full of fear as hundreds of thousands of foreign migrants storm through their streets and fields; labels those leaders that try and protect their countries and their people; and pontificates about what the EU countries facing the stampede should do and think. Clearly incapable of empathy, even in the face of this crisis of biblical proportions, the esteemed minister still doesn't think that the outer borders should be closed.

Think about it.

It actually reminds me of Woodstock. THE Woodstock in 1969. Well, White Lake, actually. A real estate agent showed us a really neat house near White Lake in early August. We must have liked it since we left a deposit. We were on our way back to see it again the weekend of August 15 completely oblivious that about 400,000 people were on their way to the same vicinity to see Jimi Hendrix, the Who, Santana, and so many others at a rock concert on a farm. Traffic jams galore. We had to return the next weekend which is when we saw exactly what hundreds and thousands of people "walking around" can do to a property. The front lawn was mud. The backyard was mud. Everywhere you looked you saw garbage, broken fences, quite a bit of excrement, and it smelled. Really bad.

Since then, when I hear people telling other people what they should and shouldn't allow on their property, I remember Woodstock. Until you live through the damage, and have a firm understanding of how bad it can be, don't pontificate.

If you've spent any amount of time cruising the internet, you've seen the current damage. The crisis is beyond words, indescribable, and seemingly endless. And still the esteemed minister won't even consider securing the borders.

Well, in fairness, Luxembourg really is very far from the beaten path. Maybe if the migrants were walking across the Foreign Minister's lawn, dumping garbage here, breaking a fence there, defecating here and there, things would get fixed real quick.

Alrighty then. Rock on.
https://euobserver.com/migration/131019
www.armedforces.co.uk/Europeandefence/edcountries/countryluxembourg.htm

(30) MACEDONIA

Formerly part of Yugoslavia, beautiful Macedonia and its two million inhabitants are in the cross hairs of the latest migrant crisis. Unfortunately, with a shared border with Greece, migrants were passing through Macedonia regularly. Since many illegal migrants walked along railroad tracks, and many were killed when they walked too close to speeding trains, Macedonia generously changed its laws to allow migrants to move freely through Macedonia for 72 hours. No need to sneak around and walk deadly railroad tracks. Keep moving though. Macedonia had been, and intended to remain, a "transit" country, so no true shelters were built either.

Since few migrants want anything to do with Macedonia and its unattractive welfare packages for asylum seekers, authorities have created a pass-through system. Refugees show up at the border. Following a brief rest, they are loaded on buses and trains headed north towards the promised lands in Germany and Sweden.

When the numbers of migrants jumped to 1,500-4,000+ per day, in August 2105, Macedonia declared a state of emergency, protected its borders with its military, and used tear gas and stun grenades to protect themselves from migrants. The borders were closed, opened, overrun, closed, overrun, opened, partly opened. Although the state of emergency was still in effect in November 2015, ultimately the border was reopened, and the pass-through transit process continued.

Ill treatment by whom?
In September 2015, Macedonia was accused of having "ill-treated" migrants. One caption on a press photo identified as "Macedonian authorities beat refugees trying to cross border" only showed Macedonian police at a border crossing trying to hold back an attempt by a large group to breach their border illegally. Any police officer will tell you that they are allowed to use physical force when faced with physical force. Maybe the caption could have just as easily read, "Migrants try to illegally cross a border and physically attack police, as police push back trying to protect their country and their citizens."
Guess it depends on your editor's perspective. Predictably, a majority of the shared photos featured children and families while the several wide angle shots showed a majority of fighting-age males. No surprise.

In October 2015, Macedonia stopped issuing certain paperwork and concentrated on streamlining the transport process as uninvited migrant arrivals increased to an overwhelming 10,000+ people daily. As refugees passed through Macedonia, many were afforded medical care, clothes, food, and even legal advice.

Rain and cold reveals true motives
As cold temperatures moved in, and torrential rains served up thick mud as far as the eye could see, the Telegraph reported that, "for some, the chaos, the cold and the rain were unbearable. One Iraqi man was asking anyone he could find how he could return home. He wanted to fly back to Iraq, he said, he couldn't bear the conditions any more to reach Europe."

Start those engines.

Fence-time

In November 2015, following the terrorist attacks in Paris, Macedonia began clearing southern border areas in anticipation of installing fencing to better control migrants. Macedonia's State Security Council stressed that a fence would be a last resort, and the idea wasn't to close the border "but to restrict the flow of migrants, in line with the number of migrants/refugees that would be accepted by those European countries where they might be headed."

http://www.telegraf.rs/english/1533432-terrorist-attack-in-macedonia-40-armed-albanians-beat-and-bound-police

http://www.b92.net/eng/news/region.php?yyyy=2015&mm=04&dd=13&nav_id=93784

http://www.telegraph.co.uk/news/worldnews/europe/11856124/Refugee-crisis-Thousands-hit-by-torrential-rains-and-thick-mud-in-Macedonia.html?frame=3435232

In the future, however distant it might be, if Macedonia *did* ever decide to fence themselves in, this "prep" work would allow a 3-level fence to go up in less than 8 hours.

Nothing like being prepared.

http://www.avaz.ba/clanak/205531/macedonia-prepares-to-raise-border-fence-as-last-resort?url=clanak/205531/macedonia-prepares-to-raise-border-fence-as-last-resort

(31) MALTA

By 2013, weekly boats filled with hundreds of migrants from Africa were arriving on Malta's shores. In the previous decade, at least 17,000 illegal aliens had shown up on the tiny island of 400,000 people. But known for its overcrowded migrant shelters and mandatory *up-to 18-month* detention for illegals, it certainly wasn't on many must go lists for economic opportunists. By June 2015, about 6,520 refugees and asylum seekers were living in Malta according to the UN.

Malta was also the site of meetings between EU leaders and African leaders discussing the migrant crisis.

In April 2015, DW News posted a video report on the plight of migrants in Malta called "Migrants Don't Feel Welcome in Malta." The report showed some migrants from Africa milling about on a street corner. One claimed to have snuck into the country by boat and was "euphoric with hope" only "to discover the locals' hostility."

Ok, you caught that? Me too...

The illegal alien complained that the locals were "racist" and called him "black" and harassed him and he's "not feeling so happy." Malta is a tiny and densely overpopulated island with little room for its own citizens. In their own defense, locals asked *where do the migrants think they're going to work? Where will they live when the houses are already very full?*

Good questions.

A priest that ran a mission for migrants said that the government was overwhelmed and couldn't handle the current migrants, let alone take on new ones, and asked for other EU states to share the burden.

DW News opined that since other EU states simply won't help out, Malta "tries to deter the migrants by making life here miserable for them."

Here are some sadistic ways Malta "tortures" migrants:
  a) Newly arrived migrants start off in a "closed camp" (with walls and fences).
  b) Migrants may be kept in the facility for months while their legal status is determined.
  c) Migrants are provided food and drink.

Another unidentified migrant called the camp "a kind of prison" hall with "200 people from Somalia, Ethiopia, and Eritrea... it's the worst thing I ever seen.. I am in Europe (where) everyone gets his rights...No! I didn't get *my rights*, for sure..."

What rights Europe *owed* African migrants was not addressed. But soon, a special conference held in Malta would decide that very question.
http://www.theguardian.com/commentisfree/2013/aug/04/malta-needs-eu-help-immigration-crisis
http://www.unhcr.org/pages/49e48eba6.html
https://youtu.be/QfdjYG0VCsI
http://www.dw.com/en/migrants-dont-feel-welcome-in-malta/av-18419874

It's pretend time again
Imagine the following scenario.

Pretend you're rich and live in a big house. I live next door in a small house with my kids. Over the years, you've been a fine neighbor and have even helped me out a bit. Now, my kids are regularly sneaking through my yard into your yard and are making themselves at home in your house. Instead of calling the police, you try to be nice and look the other way. (Maybe you feel a little guilty since I'm constantly accusing you of being a privileged wealthy pig.) You can't figure out if I keep *sending* my kids, or am *allowing* my kids, or *encouraging* my kids, or *abusing* my kids, or whatever, but they are endlessly sneaking in. As you watch your weekly food and electric bills explode you're getting nervous – so you call a meeting with me to figure out a neighborly solution. After all, we have "a common problem on both sides of the yard." And my problem is obviously "an even larger problem than the one" you have. (These outrageous claims will become clear momentarily.)

As we chat, I see my opportunity. *Hey, you're rich.* I'll offer to solve *your* problems (*my* kids sneaking constantly into *your* house) for a big fat fee. *Cha-ching!*

Seeing potential relief from my trespassing kids, you agree to give me money even though you've been helping me for years.

That was easy. Why not try for more and more and more?

So I get you to agree to set up a trust fund for my little trespassing darlings. *Why not?* Then I get you to agree to fork over extra money *every time* one of my kids gets caught in your house in the future so that I come over and get them out *quickly*. Of course, you'll also throw me some additional cash to help transition my kids back into living in my less luxurious house. Maybe even buy them stuff, too. How cool is that?

An endless gravy train.

No more pretend-time
In November 2015, EU leaders and African leaders met in Malta to discuss the refugee crisis coming out of Africa. The Central African Republic Delegate, Eloge-Armand Issa-Gadenga told reporters that although he felt that the "atmosphere was charged and it was difficult, but African and European leaders must find a way to compromise."

The bottom line seems to be that Africa will be getting a lot of money to quickly take back deported migrants. According to a German delegate, Europe gave Africa "a great many concessions."

The EU also set up a 1.8 billion euro trust fund to strengthen African countries, fight poverty, and end conflict. Jean-Cladue Juncker President of the European Commission said that "We have a common problem on both sides of the Mediterranean, and we have to support the Africans because they have an even larger problem than the one we have."

What common problem? Just how many migrants are fleeing Europe to settle in Africa?

This mysterious quote borders on meaningless codswallop. That people are actually elected or appointed, and then paid to come up with such poorly thought-out plans is scary. Seriously scary. Unless of course you follow the money.

Money, money, money.

Oh yeah, that'll solve everything...
http://www.dw.com/en/money-for-refugees-offered-at-malta-summit/av-18844518
http://www.dw.com/en/18-billion-euro-trust-fund-for-africa/av-18845255

(32) MOLDOVA

Situated between the Ukraine and Romania, with a population of about 3 million people, Moldova is known for its fine wines and is home to the world's largest underground wine cellar. It is also rife with corruption, bribes appear to be commonplace, and the murder rate is one of the highest in Europe. Moldova did promise to take in 50 refugees in 2014 making the total of refugees and asylum seekers in the country 484. During the same time period, 3,697 people left Moldova to seek a better life elsewhere.

In November 2015, Moldova was also facing a few little internal problems – the head of the central bank resigned, the former prime minister was under arrest for a billion dollar fraud, the current prime minister was suspected of corruption, the latest new government was voted out, and the economy was close to collapse.

As far as being a player in the current Syrian refugee crisis, Moldova has its own problems to deal with first.
http://globalriskinsights.com/2015/11/crisis-in-moldova-presents-opportunity-for-russia/

(33) MONACO

Located on the French Riviera, Monaco is a tiny principality and one of the most densely populated places on earth. About a third of the residents are millionaires, it has *no* income tax, is known for its beautiful beaches and casinos, and enjoys a mild climate year-round.

As you might expect, while Monaco is part of the Schengen area (free borders), hosts many meetings for many special interest groups, and is also a very popular vacation destination for the ultra-rich, as far as being on the front lines of the current refugee crisis, well, not so much. According to the UN, as of June 2015, Monaco had no asylum seekers and 33 refugees living alongside its 37,000 residents.

Obscene wealth has its privileges.
http://www.unhcr.org/pages/49e48ec16.html

(34) MONTENEGRO

Formerly part of Yugoslavia, Montenegro has just over 600,000 residents and is a tourist magnet with its spectacular old forests, ancient structures, the deepest canyon in Europe, and beautiful beaches on the Adriatic sea.

As of June 2015, according to the UN, just over 6,200 refugees and asylum seekers lived in Montenegro. In September 2015, Montenegro's Zdravko Soc, Vice President of the Liberal Party, said that considering that 20% of Montenegrins are migrants themselves, "the duty of the state of Montenegro and Montenegrin society is to actively participate via Government assistance, citizens' donations, campaigns of mobile operators, and the Red Cross of Montenegro" to help with the refugees.

Think-tank-toe
In October 2015, a Montenegrin think-tank discussing migrants sensed that there was probably no tidal wave of migrants headed for Montenegro. There had been about 1,541 requests for asylum, but since July 2015, when migrants were actively rolling through Macedonia and Serbia, all asylum requests to Montenegro virtually stopped. Because Montenegro is considered a "transit state," most people feel migrants, *if any*, will simply be moving through.

Witch hunt! Light the torches!
The think-tank members might have overlooked all the Nazis under the beds of Montenegrins had it not been for a stroke of good fortune. Luckily, a representative from the human rights group CEDEM set everyone straight. She said she wasn't so sure that migrants would just "move through" Montenegro. She worried that they might stick around for a while, especially in the winter. She also worried about potential trouble *not from the migrants* (it's *never* the peaceful tolerant migrants), but the local Montenegrin *racists* and *xenophobes,* adding that

> "misinformed citizens can start creating attitudes and opinions colored by xenophobia and racism... so it is necessary to prepare the local public and notify them on Montenegrin responsibilities."

While she's at it, maybe she should have those misinformed racist Montenegrins chat with the over-informed racist French people in Calais for a real taste of the migrant experience.

October 2015 saw Montenegro put together some plans, locations, and facilities *should* any migrants actually arrive.

But the migrants were the least of their troubles. In November 2015, thousands of Montenegrins took to the streets to protest their Prime Minister whom they accused of decades of corruption, nepotism, and self-dealing. Political unrest was in the air as torches burned and angry speeches echoed through the streets and squares. Thievery and corruption! Apparently a not so uncommon complaint in the Balkans.

Montenegro may not have its political house in order, and may not be a darling of the migrants, but at least Montenegro will be ready for some refugees, *if* they ever come.

http://www.cdm.me/english/soc-montenegro-to-assist-in-dealing-with-consequences-of-refugee-crisis
http://www.cdtmn.org/EN/index.php/civil-society/490-how-prepared-is-montenegro-for-refugee-crisis

(35) NETHERLANDS

In 2009, the Justice Minister of the Netherlands reported to his Parliament that of the perpetrators of serious crimes (murder, manslaughter, violent robberies, extortion, arson, public acts of violence, and sexual crimes) among criminal youngsters aged 12-17, 63% were of migrant origin. Further, the Minister reported that of *all* the serious crimes committed, 14% of the perpetrators were Africans from Morocco.

Of all young criminal offenders, most were likely to be 16-17 years of age, except in the case of sexual offences, for which the 14- to 15-year-olds were the biggest group, followed by 12- to 13-year-olds who made up a disproportionately large share.
https://web.archive.org/web/20130208101230/http://www.nisnews.nl/public/180309_1.htm

In Rotterdam, in 2009, more than half of Moroccan men aged 18-24 years old had run-ins with the police. The same statistics showed that "90% of boys with a Moroccan background were repeat offenders." As far as towns go, Amsterdam had the most Moroccan criminals.

In a fascinating 2010 Netherlands study of crime, "Criminality, Migration and Ethnicity," the results were shocking:
- 50% of Moroccan males committed a crime before turning 22

- 33% were repeat offenders with 5 *or more* police records
- Moroccan girls committed 300% more crimes than native Dutch girls

In the meanwhile, as the trends go from bad to worse, many native Dutch people don't seem to be content to sit around and see how this multi-cultural experiment turns out. The 2011 official emigration figures revealed that "in the first 6 months of 2011, more than 58,000 people *left* the Netherlands (nearly 5,000 more than in the same period for the previous year.) The increase in emigrants is largely due to native Dutch leaving the country to settle elsewhere."

By 2013, "work" was cited as the main reason for emigrating. Well, yes, "work" in a less dangerous environment... Guess someone was paying attention to statistics and trends.

And there they go.
http://www.elsevier.nl/Nederland/nieuws/2009/6/Schokkende-cijfers-criminaliteit-Marokkanen-Rotterdam-ELSEVIER236094W
http://www.gouda.nl/ris/dsresource?objectid=19921
https://openaccess.leidenuniv.nl/ldap-login
http://www.cbs.nl/en-GB/menu/themas/bevolking/publicaties/artikelen/archief/2011/2011-050-pb.htm
http://www.bloomberg.com/bw/articles/2014-09-18/norway-exports-inmates-to-netherlands-to-solve-prison-crowding

Shelter of horrors
In the Netherlands, well dressed and healthy looking but indignant migrants complained about and detailed the "horrible" treatment they were receiving at the hands of their would-be saviors in an emergency camp set up to save their lives. In a very telling and representative video interview, multiple migrants listed grievances that included: a lack of proper entertainment resulting in boredom with nothing to do but eat and sleep; breakfast and lunch portions that were simply too small; cold nighttime temperatures; not enough

variety of clothes to choose from; and "the slow internet, it's sooo bad."

No seriously, that is a direct quote, the internet is too slow!

Another migrant demanded money so that he could "smoke" and "send cash to his mother" in Syria. The irony of the Netherlands taking money from its tax-paying citizens to hand over to cigarette smoking opportunists who will then also send some of that money to people in Syria is sweet.

The interview clip ends with all the migrants agreeing that they are simply just not getting any service from the operators of the Emergency Shelter. "We get no service!" is their meme.

Seriously, you can't make this stuff up.
https://www.youtube.com/watch?v=Q_XHkgScOSY

About that assimilation plan...
As reported in 2012, Bellmore was a planned city area in Amsterdam, designed by architects to be a model city of the future, to offer Dutch residents a wonderful lifestyle, with plenty of space and conveniences. Except that immigrants from Africa and former Dutch colonies have settled in and made it their own parallel universe, so to speak.

Reportedly, migrants who've lived there for a decade still haven't bothered to learn the Dutch language nor are many interested in learning about or following the "Dutch way of life." One African migrant blamed the Dutch and explained that the Dutch are "greedy." A Turkish migrant explained that he and fellow Turks stick together, listen to Turkish music, speak Turkish, and follow Turkish customs.

Another migrant, a Muslim leader, criticized the legendary Dutch love of soccer, saying soccer was a waste of time and calling it "poison for the people." He also denounced all other Dutch society values, and spent his time planning and executing protests against Dutch values and ways.

Why aren't migrants trying to assimilate, instead of fighting the cultures of their protectors?

What happened to all the plans for utopian assimilation and integration and culture sharing?

Maybe the culture sharing just isn't catching on because the cultures are so diametrically opposed to one another.
https://youtu.be/2sJ7eMUBBzc

Children pregnant with children
A pregnant 14-year-old Syrian girl was reported missing from a Dutch Asylum center in September 2015. The police issued notices with her picture and were concerned since she was already 9 months pregnant and might need medical assistance.

Hold on there. 14 years old? 9 months pregnant? The legal age for sexual consent in the Netherlands is 16. So where is the outcry?

Wait! All is fine. The girl is actually a "child bride."

Apparently, the Dutch are facing a new challenge. Seems that there are a growing number of "child-brides" among the migrants.

What to do?

Your own laws forbid pedophilia. The legal age of consent is set at 16. Now you have these new guests, 13 or younger, who are "married."

Do you just have to get used to the idea?

According to Dutch news station RTV-Noord, the Dutch have already granted about 20 youngsters, ages 13-15, the legal right to rejoin their older "husbands" in various shelters.

There has to be another name for this ...

Member of the Dutch Parliament, Attje Kuiken told BBC that "a 12-year-old girl with a 40-year-old-man – that is not a marriage, that is abuse... we're talking about really young children, girls 12, 13 years old. I want to protect these children."

To that end, the Dutch government is seeking to change its own laws so that in 2016, only marriages between people at least age 18 are lawful for purposes of immigration reunification applications.

In the meanwhile, Member of Parliament Kuiken boldly calls the practice of child brides "abuse" and she sounds genuinely concerned.

Of course, chances are that the old-fashioned-controlled-media will accuse her someday of just not being an accepting person, and simply not open to immersing herself fully, *yet*, in the wonders of other cultures and practices.

What do you make of all this?
https://www.politie.nl/en/wanted-and-missing/missing-children/2015/september/fatema-alkasem.html
http://www.bbc.com/news/world-europe-34573825

(36) NORWAY

Bloomberg News reported in 2014 that prisons in Norway are "the most luxurious in the world." Features include "private bathrooms, and flat screen TVs... a sauna and tennis courts; inmates wear street clothes and are free to roam as they please among the cottages where they live and the buildings where they work and eat."

So maybe it wasn't that surprising when towards the end of 2014, Norway's Minister of Justice announced that Norway had so many more criminals than space, that Norway would be sending several hundred convicts to jails in the Netherlands.
http://www.bloomberg.com/bw/articles/2014-09-18/norway-exports-inmates-to-netherlands-to-solve-prison-crowding

Hide the truth, feel better
In Oslo, Norway's capital and most populous city, police reported "a record number of assault rapes in 2009 committed exclusively (100%) by non-Western immigrants." Worse, police reported that the assault rape numbers had doubled from the year prior. The vast majority of the victims were native Norwegian females. It wasn't uncommon. During the years 2007-2010, 100% of the perpetrators convicted of assault rape had non-Western background and were often asylum seekers, and their victims were mostly native Norwegians. When reporters asked the police if they were

worried that releasing such statistics might *stigmatize* them, the police said, "The aim is to tell the truth and create a better society."

You caught that, right? Telling the truth could lead to you being stigmatized. Really? On what planet?

Statistics Norway's 2011 study revealed similarly disturbing facts – as crime skyrocketed in Norway, statistics showed that migrants were overrepresented in a big way. Africans from Somalia were 440% more likely to be convicted felons than ethnic Norwegians. First generation African immigrants and Iraqi immigrants were 300% more likely to be convicted felons, and Pakistani immigrants were 260% more likely, than native Norwegians. Second generation immigrants (Asians and Africans) were convicted of almost 200% more felonies than first generation immigrants.
http://www.nrk.no/norge/rekordmange-overfallsvoldtekter-1.6944861
https://www.ssb.no/a/publikasjoner/pdf/rapp_201121/rapp_201121.pdf

Connect the dots, then hide the diagram
Here are a few more *really* inconvenient truths.

Norway's *The Local*, in September 2014, reported that a study from the Norwegian Directorate of Immigration showed that in 2010 there were about 18,000 asylum seekers and illegal aliens in Norway making up a tiny part of the population, only .4% (.004). Yet, they were over-represented more than 200%, having committed 2.5% of the crime in Norway in 2010, with men and young asylum seekers also over-represented. Certainly not a "crime wave" according to the researchers, but still very telling.

Then, in November 2014, the newspaper Dagsavisen ran an article that showed a correlation between deportations of immigrants and a drop in crime.

Deport immigrants. Watch crime rates drop. Who would dare even think *such a thing?*

Kristin Kvigne, manager of Norway's National Police Immigration Service, said that in 2014 "of the 5,876 people who have been expelled so far this year, many were criminals, or people who had previously been expelled from Norway - and who had illegally returned."

Norway planned to deport 7,100 people in 2014, and another 7,800 in 2015. Kvigne said the deportations, "save Norwegian society much money. It costs money to process people in the courts and to jail them." She also added it is "important to view the high number of deportations made by Police Immigration Service in the context of falling crime rates across the country."

Well, yes.

In November 2015, The Local reported that Abdul Hakim Sanchez Hammer "a Norwegian fighter for the terror group ISIS predicted that the group would send an army to conquer Norway and establish Sharia law once it is victorious in the traditional lands of Islam."

Luckily, a researcher for the *Norwegian Defense Research Establishment* said such talk "should not be taken too seriously."

Oh, okay. We'll sleep like babies.
http://www.dagsavisen.no/samfunn/sendte-ut-rekordmange-i-oktober/
http://www.thelocal.no/20140909/norway-reveals-immigrant-crime-crisis
http://www.thelocal.no/20151111/is-will-conquer-norway-and-impose-shariah-fighter
http://www.nrk.no/norge/norsk-is-kriger-til-nrk_-_-lederen-var-vil-sende-en-arme-og-ta-over-deres-land-1.12640781

Occasionally, journalists have no more tales to spin

Even some journalists have realized things are amiss. According to CBN News, Hege Storhaug, who called herself a "naïve left-wing journalist," had a life-changing experience in 1992 when she encountered a "young Norwegian born Pakistani woman" who was forced to marry her second cousin in Pakistan by her parents who, the girl said, "were willing to kill me if I didn't enter into this marriage, to protect their own honor."

So much for assimilating into the Norwegian cultural experience.

Moved by this and many other experiences, Storhaug became a full-time protector of female immigrants, trying to save them from arranged/forced marriages, barbaric female genital mutilation practices, beatings and other violence stemming from issues of "honor."

Storhaug mentioned that she was upset that Norway had "abandoned" these women and didn't protect them. She gave the example of the African immigrant parents of four Norwegian-born girls who sent the children (ages 3-9) back to their old country in Africa, Gambia, to have the girls' genitals ritually mutilated.

As the BBC reported in 2013, "The hold such traditions (female genital mutilation) have in The Gambia was made apparent... (by)... Muhammed Alhajie Lamin Touray, the country's most senior imam and president of the Islamic Council in Gambia who said,
> 'Apart from the religious reasons in favor of female genital mutilation, I have heard on reliable authority that the clitoris makes a woman itch, making her want to scratch all the time and that the clitoris makes water leak from her private parts.'"

http://www.cbn.com/cbnnews/world/2011/August/Culture-Crisis-Norway-Tackles-Muslim-Immigration-/
http://www.bbc.com/news/uk-23933437

And what about this Norwegian journalist turned protector of immigrant girls and women? For her hard work and dedication to *keeping women safe*, Hege Storhaug has been labeled an "Islamophobe" and a "racist."

Seriously?

It's always the victim's fault, isn't it?
In 2008, upon the release of an Oslo Police report showing a disturbing increase in Somali rapists and Somali gang rapes of Norwegian girls, P4 (the Norwegian media broadcaster) went to Oslo and interviewed three men (ages 26, 30, and 35) from Somalia and Senegal. Not surprisingly, the Africans didn't want to be identified, but spoke rather freely, if not disturbingly, about the rape epidemic from the African immigrant point of view.

When the conversation turned to Norwegian girls, the Africans casually blamed the way Norwegian girls dress for them being raped.

When the reporter from P4 asked,
"You're saying that Norwegian girls are asking to be raped?"

The 26-year-old Somali answered,
"Not exactly asking, but when they go out almost completely naked and get completely drunk in Frogner park or go to a party together with some friend, and then they complain about being raped? It's their fault."

The 35-year-old Somali defended a recent gang attack where Norwegian girls were thrown to the ground and stripped of their clothes in a park. His defense? "Weren't these boys young? Such as 13-14 years old? I think this was curiosity as to how girls look. They were so young that they didn't know what they were doing."

The 30-year-old Senegalese man was asked why young African men attack Norwegian woman and he answered,
"Such things happen now and then. When we drink too much and get drunk it happens that we attack them, but if we don't drink, we don't attack Norwegian women – but respect them."

The 26-year-old Somali noted that he believed his and his comrades' points of view were representative of the attitudes of many members of the Norwegian Somali community.

When asked if he thought people would be scared of his views, he answered, "Just broadcast it, because this is true. That's the way things are - it's the facts. I'm not lying. I've never been with a Norwegian lady, but I've been with many Norwegian girls - they are fairly nice and very skilled in bed."

Well. I mean... there are no words.
http://www.p4.no/story.aspx?id=272134

By November 2015, Norway's News-in-English reported that there was a noticeable trend in "asylum seekers" in Norwegian shelters getting cold feet and withdrawing their applications for asylum on a daily basis.

The "refugees" were voluntarily leaving Norway to seek their fortunes elsewhere. Reportedly, long approval waiting times, "disgusting" local foods, *poor or no internet access*, and "shabby" accommodations had turned them off to the whole Norway experience. Norwegians may be tiring of the whole migrant experience as well. Near Sarpsborg, when a group of refugees charged that their shelter wasn't clean enough "Justice Minister Anders Anundsen issued a curt reply: 'Do the cleaning yourselves.'"

According to Norway's branch of the International Organization for Migration most of the migrants deciding to leave Norway cite "family reasons," and "most want to travel back to Lebanon, Turkey, Jordan and Russia."

Well, if Lebanon and Turkey and Jordan are a better bet than Norway... you have to wonder if these "asylum seekers" were really seeking asylum in the first place. Really.
http://www.newsinenglish.no/2015/11/16/asylum-seekers-changing-their-minds/

(37) POLAND

Poland has had a rough time. It suffered numerous atrocities under German occupation during World War II and many Poles died. Poland has since publically and privately touted a distrust of Germany. Some even called the refugee crisis a "German crisis," and not an EU crisis. So when the president of the European Parliament, Martin Schulz, a German, accused Poland of happily taking money and security aid from the EU while not pulling its weight with the migrant crisis, the Polish Interior Minister called Schulz's statements "another example of German arrogance."

The UN reported that 18,426 refugees and asylum seekers were living in Poland at the end of 2014. In late 2015, Poland had agreed to take in an additional 5,000 Syrian refugees over the 2,000 they originally agreed to house. Shock of all shocks, Polish Prime Minister Kopacz expressed a preference for Christians, possibly in light of the increased beheadings of Middle Eastern Christians. Concurrently, Poland was already dealing with a large number of Ukrainian refugees.

But following the November 2015 Paris attacks, Poland seemed to get cold feet and made official statements that it would have to reevaluate its position altogether.

Nobel Laureate pulls no punches

Even before the terrorist attacks in Paris, former Polish President, Lech Walesa (yeah, *that* Lech Walesa, the guy who brought down Communism in Poland in the 1980s, was the hero of the decade, and even won the Nobel Peace Prize) warned against opening Europe's doors to the current migrants.

Lech Walesa was quoted in 2015 in the Jerusalem Post as saying that these immigrants were "different."

Punch to the nose

Walesa said that unlike Polish immigrants and refugees who "respected the local culture and laws. These immigrants are different. Even second or third generations – look at France, for example – who got good education and made money still turned against their host countries."

Right hook

Walesa also noted that during Communist rule, when there was serious trouble in Poland, he had the opportunity to run away, yet he chose to stay and fight for his country – in stark contrast to the many migrants he sees today abandoning their countries.

Upper cut

According to Lech Walesa, he understands why Poles fear the migrant waves since they come from "places where people are beheaded. We are worried that the same will happen to us."

Left hook

Walesa also wondered if all of the migrants were really true refugees or if many might be seeking to simply improve their living standards.

Knock-out punch

In a most curious observation, Walesa noted that "We in Poland have small flats, low salaries and meager pensions.

Watching the refugees on television, I noticed that they look better than us. They are well fed, well dressed and maybe even are richer than we are."

Clearly the major networks at the old-fashioned-controlled-media need to do a better job of editing out all those well-heeled migrants and focus in on the ones that better fit the official narrative. If it becomes too difficult, maybe Hollywood can green-screen some appropriate content.

Also, isn't it interesting that a Nobel Peace Prize laureate seems to be on the same page as Hungary's Prime Minister? Could it be that they are both evil xenophobic racists? Or are they just thinking people with a load more common sense than the politically ~~corrupt~~ correct?

Think about it.
http://www.krakowpost.com/10477/2015/09/poland-to-accept-5000-refugees
http://www.reuters.com/article/2015/11/17/us-europe-migrants-poland-schulz-idUSKCN0T61RK20151117#XIgm4cJedmRlHy5c.97
http://www.jpost.com/Israel-News/World-Affairs-Simple-solutions-for-a-complex-world-416499
http://www.independent.co.uk/news/world/europe/poland-plans-to-backtrack-on-migrant-commitment-following-attacks-in-paris-a6734521.html

Saving women, one at a time
Radio Poland reported in January 2014 that the Polish Defense League was organizing patrols to defend the honor of Polish Women, and to keep Polish women safe from rapes and gang-rapes by Muslims by keeping an eye on Polish women at bars and nightclubs, and walking them home to safety, especially if they were drunk.

Online, the Polish Defense League posted a warning:
"In Poland, there will be NO Sharia law. NO headbanging or shouting Allahu Akbar in the streets. NO insulting our religion and our culture. NO burning cars like in France. NO burning down police stations. NO imposing your ways

on us. NO calling us the sons of apes and pigs. If you do, we will be the ones waging jihad...on YOU!"

Succinct statement. Leaves little to the imagination. So it must be some version of xenophobic racist hate speech, or something similar, that means you're standing up for your national culture against foreigners who disrespect you.

That stuff used to be called patriotic speech. My how times have changed in *former-Communist-party-member* Merkel's new European experiment.
http://www.thenews.pl/1/9/Artykul/158678,AntiIslamic-group-patrols-clubs-to-defend-Polish-women

No system to catch and prevent crimes *before* they happen
In the meantime, Poland hasn't been the country of choice for migrants either. After all, Poland is almost exclusively Polish, and demographically 99% European. And rather set in its traditional ways.

In September 2015, the International Business Times (IBT) picked up on a scathing Amnesty International report and blasted the Polish for excluding many groups from their current hate crime legislation including disabled people, homeless people, gay people, lesbian people, transgender people, bisexual people, intersex people, and others. IBT added that "While steps have been taken to tackle hate crimes fueled by racism and xenophobia, other minority groups still face daily fears and harassment." There was also a reported lack of procedures in place in Poland to catch and prevent crimes of hate *before* they occur. (*What!? No mind-reading equipment?*)

With an atmosphere like this in Poland, no wonder refugees are seeking other destinations. Or, maybe that's the plan.
http://www.ibtimes.co.uk/poland-abandoning-hundreds-victims-lgbt-other-hate-crimes-1520082

People on the street speak out
One politician running for Parliament, created a broadcast segment where he asked young Poles at a massive street

demonstration what they thought about opening Poland to migrants in October 2015. One young father said that "What they are saying on TV, that these people will assimilate and it will be normal, is propaganda. It's a lie. After they set up their ghettos, we will have to support them forever. And we need to talk about the rapes in Sweden and about Rochdale in England... And that the people who talk about this are branded fascists..."

Another Polish man said that migrants come to the EU "and expect to get on (welfare) benefits."

And another Polish man said "We don't want those barbarians in Poland... just look what is happening in France and England and Germany... Italy... we don't need the same troubles... better to prevent it before it happens, not after... they want handouts..."

One young Polish lady said she had no interest in letting Muslims into Poland since Muslims "do not respect our laws and culture."
https://youtu.be/qco51zahONg

In mid-November, Poland's EU Affairs Minister made Poland's position very clear when he said, "in the face of the tragic events in Paris, Poland sees no political possibilities for implementing the decision on the relocation of refugees."
https://euobserver.com/migration/131175

The migrant crisis has definitely not gone unnoticed in Poland. November 2015 saw Poland's right wing party win control of the Parliament in a landslide election. We wouldn't have given them a second look until Polish Newsweek and other agents of the old-fashioned-controlled-media immediately labeled them the "worst government," "an embarrassment," "great disaster," and the "biggest political fraud in 25 years."

Who are they?

A strong woman prime minister, some hyper conservatives, a few nationalists, a retread or two, and a conspiracy theorist.

Compared to the usual purchased and handpicked politicians supported and lauded by the old-fashioned-controlled-media, this is a very daring lineup.

We are most eager to see what happens.
http://polska.newsweek.pl/sklad-rzadu-pis-nowy-rzad-ministrowie-w-rzadzie-beaty-szydlo,artykuly,373704,1.html
http://wiadomosci.onet.pl/kraj/tomczyk-nowy-rzad-najwieksze-polityczne-oszustwo-ostatnich-25-lat/v7p42r

(38) PORTUGAL

In May 2015, the Algarve Daily, in its article "Portugal to benefit from refugee quota," gleefully reported that Portugal would now get 700 refugees, a huge increase over the 40 people it took in the year prior. As the Algarve noted, "This number is a leap forward for Portugal's current intake process which has been characterized by sloth, indecision and a notable lack of effort despite the *long term economic benefit* an influx of new blood could bring." (The key term is "could." *Could* bring, not *would* bring and not *will* bring. And based on the real life reports and experiences of other European countries we've studied, *won't* bring.)

With Portugal's serious economic woes, and the worrisome exodus of its own residents in search of a better life, how the migrants will be taken care of or what opportunities to build new lives they will be afforded is quite unclear. As one reader noted, where will the migrants find work? This is not an insignificant concern. As we've seen, with young males making up 70-80% of migrants, and Portugal's youth unemployment rate at *over 30% for residents*, exactly where will migrants find legal work? Think about that one.

September 2015 unemployment figures were dismal. About 19% average long term unemployment, 12.2% regular unemployment, and 31.2% youth unemployment.

If you actually count everyone, it's a lot worse
Portugal's actual unemployment figures are likely far higher. Some researchers from Centro de Estudos Sociais pointed out in 2015 that Portugal reports figures without including an army of unemployed who are classified as inactive – but who are unable to find work, "discouraged," have given up, are part-timers who can't find full-time work, or are part of the "300,000 mostly young, well-educated people who left Portugal (seeking work) in other countries during the crisis years."

In the meanwhile, Portugal has created "temporary job schemes" where the unemployed must work non-paid positions in order to continue to receive their welfare checks. The government loves this scheme since they get labor in return for their welfare disbursements. The problem is that the government can now *fire* the full-time workers that had been doing the full-time jobs which are now being done by the unemployed welfare recipients. And reap huge savings in future pension payouts and benefits. *Quite obscene!*

It was reported that in order to further bolster "official" unemployment figures, that "Companies were in some cases given grants in order to 'employ' unemployed people on an unpaid basis. The unemployed were required to take on these often pointless jobs because they would otherwise lose their welfare payments." *Same scheme, just in the private sector.*

The bottom line is depressing. As one researcher said, "One of five Portuguese citizens who is able and willing to work can't find a job. Maybe one out of four. Those are the real numbers."

And into this well-honed and superbly oiled apparatus, more worried about statistics than people, more worried about *looking* good than *doing* good, we will now gleefully drop in a load of newly arrived refugees who "need to work."

Think about it.

With just over 1,000 refugees and asylum seekers in Portugal at the end of 2014 according to the UN, in September 2105 Portugal offered to take in another 1,500 refugees over the next 2 years. After some EU politicians complained, Portugal upped its total to 1,400-1,500.

Then, Portugal's Deputy Minister of Development added

> "What I can say is that Portugal surely is able to accommodate a larger number of refugees, hoping that this same solidarity and capacity also exists in the other European states."

> "...the Portuguese position is that we should not contribute to a climate which further hinders the reception of refugees and the reception of immigrants. We must have a European policy for this matter which does not promote the worsening of the humanitarian crisis."

In November 2015, the President of Portugal reiterated Portugal's commitment to assisting with the refugee crisis even though no refugees had yet arrived.

To date, Portugal has skirted much of the refugee crisis. Too bad its own economic situation remains so incredibly bleak.
http://algarvedailynews.com/news/6570-portugal-is-willing-to-accept-more-refugees
http://theportugalnews.com/news/portugal-prepares-for-migrants/35809
http://www.algarvedailynews.com/news/7096-portugal-and-bulgaria-s-presidents-call-for-solution-for-refugee-crisis
https://ycharts.com/indicators/portugal_youth_unemployment_rate_lfs
http://www.dw.com/en/dodgy-stats-understate-portugals-unemployment-rate/a-18414326
https://www.cia.gov/library/publications/the-world-factbook/fields/2075.html

(39) ROMANIA

By mid-2015, according to UN figures, 2,858 asylum seekers and refugees were living in Romania. At the same time, about 3,200 people *left* Romania to seek their futures elsewhere.

In September 2015, the EU smacked together some new refugee distribution figures. Ireland, England, and Denmark were all excused because they weren't legally obligated to participate. Hungary, Italy, and Greece were left alone since they were already teetering with an overage of refugees. Which left about 20 potential destinations.

The EU told Romania that it would be expected to take in 6,351 refugees. Romanian President Klaus Iohannis shot back that, *nah*, the "quotas" are voluntary and Romania can only take 1,785 tops. He added that as far as migrants simply storming through Romania, "this can't happen… we're not part of Schengen (open borders), and migrants must fulfill some rules if they want to enter Romania."

Then-Prime Minister Ponta said that "Romania's position is a solidarity and support one, to respect our obligations. Our capacity is 1,786 seats… we cannot engage to receive more than we can take."

Ponta would later resign in November 2015 after a deadly fire in a night club set off street protests "over government corruption and poor safety supervision." Protesters called for Ponta to step down amidst allegations of financial impropriety.

Go figure.
http://www.romaniajournal.ro/ec-asks-romania-to-shelter-a-total-of-6351-refugees-romania-sticks-to-voluntary-quotas-position/

Just say no to **Romania**
Rumor has it that refugees are intentionally avoiding Romania. In September 2015, the Romanian Aadevarul Roadevarul reported that hundreds of refugees in Hungarian shelters who thought that they might be forced to seek asylum in Romania revolted and protested saying that they "will not go to a country that has nothing to offer them."

One young male (aren't they all?) from Iraq had done his homework and told a reporter, "I have no reason to choose to go to Romania. *It is a poor country and has no money.* We want to have a country that can help us. I heard about Romania and I know how hard the situation is. "

Another migrant added "Maybe someone does not want to go to Romania. It's not fair that some refugees arrive in Germany and others in Romania. We want to get in a country like Germany, not in a poor country... We need to find jobs where we come. "

Yet another Syrian asylum seeker said he didn't consider Romania suitable since "I come from a warm country... I want to settle in a hot country."

Oh, and winters in Germany or Sweden will be a sauna?
http://adevarul.ro/international/europa/fotogalerie-refugiatiinu-vor-romania-e-tarasaraca-nu-bani-1_55e96e2bf5eaafab2c3f3856/index.html

Near the end of September 2015, Romanian authorities were still gearing up for the arrival of refugees who just don't come. The police held a refugee shelter drill, set up 50 tents, food stations, and toilets. Local farmers watched as they worried that marching refugees might destroy their crops like has happened elsewhere in Europe.

In the end, no refugees came.
http://adevarul.ro/locale/timisoara/reportaj-vecin-tabara-refugiati-romania-sorin-isi-aduna-linistit-cocenii-porumb-trebuie-cazati-undeva-1_55fec84cf5eaafab2ccef599/index.html

Journalists slinging mud are ignored
In mid-September 2015, INSCOP did a survey and claimed that while 95.8% of Romanians had heard of the refugee crisis, 56.2% of Romanians didn't think refugees should be received in Romania. 65.3% definitely didn't want them settling in Romania. For the record, it wasn't revealed if the survey also asked Romanian's if they knew that many of the refugees were actually migrants seeking economic betterment, or that the vast majority of the refugees were primarily fighting-age young males. In any case, apparently expressing your honest opinions in Romania will get you set upon by a bunch of self-hating Romanian journalists who used the survey results to mock their own countrymen for their honest opinions, and tried to label them "xenophobes" and "racists." Except the old over-used and tired scare tactics and labels were beginning to ring hollow. *No one even flinched.*

Some have argued that instead of publishing hate speech against their fellow citizens, maybe the journalists should move to Malmö in Sweden and live amongst the migrants for a few years. If they survive the regular grenade attacks, avoid the savage gang rapes, and dodge the many other crimes, then they should return to Romania and spread their message of cultural enrichment based on first-hand experience. *Interesting challenge. We wonder what the journalists will do.*
http://www.digi24.ro/Stiri/Digi24/Extern/EXODUL/SONDAJ+Cati+romani+vor+ca+Romania+sa+primeasca+refugiati

(40) RUSSIA

Russia has pretty much marched to the sound of its own drummer for centuries. The geographically largest country in the world, it remains an enigma. Women in Russia got the right to vote before the women in the United States. And while technically they never had slaves in Russia, they did have white "serfs" – whom they liberated long before the United States freed their black slaves. And before Communism, Russians freely mixed religion with the tsar and the government.

From its Viking roots to its hijack and near destruction by murderous Bolsheviks, to its relatively recent rebirth as an apparent representative democracy, Russia continues to do things "Russia's way."

According to the United Nations, by mid-2015, 317,736 refugees and asylum seekers resided in Russia, and 95,412 refugees and asylum seekers had *left* Russia. To date, Russia had approved 2 (two) Syrian refugees for asylum in 2015.

In September 2015, it was reported that Russia wouldn't be involving itself in any of the EU refugee settlement schemes. Russian President Vladimir Putin explained that the refugee crisis was a "completely predictable crisis. We said that there would be problems on a massive scale if our so-called Western partners pursued what I always said was a mistaken foreign policy... the imposition of your own standards without taking into account the historical, religious, national or cultural peculiarities of these regions. Above all, these are the policies of our American partners. Europe blindly follows within the framework of its so-called duties as an ally, and then is forced to bear the burden."

The old-fashioned-controlled-media couldn't contain itself as it bashed and trashed and lashed out at Putin and Russia. Where was Russia's humanity and concern and sympathy? Subservience to the "migrant cause" ahead of defending your nation! Leap, and don't look, you racist xenophobes!

> *For the record, every time I hear or write "xenophobe" or any of its derivations, the only thing it conjures up is an image of someone scared of the legendary female action hero "Xena: Warrior Princess."*

Then, as the refugee crisis worsened, the criticism cooled.

Don't underestimate Russian bears
By mid-October 2015, the Washington Times opined that President Putin "may in the long run be seen as the man who ended the mass migration of shell-shocked Syrians."

While US President Barrack Hussein Obama joined other European leaders to wring his hands and sound alarms, others thought that President Putin's "reinforcement of Syrian President Bashar Assad could be the difference-maker, ending the strife and enabling desperate Syrians to stay put."

Towards the end of November 2015, Bavaria's Prime Minister Horst Seehofer lambasted Chancellor Merkel's refugee "policy," calling for "a culture of reason, not a culture of welcome." He noted that since September 2015, over half a million refugees and migrants had shown up in in Bavaria and "no one can be forced to shoulder more than they can carry." Seehofer went on to announce that he would seek to gain Russia's help and cooperation stating that "we have to face the fact that without Russia we cannot solve many things. We won't be able to solve them."

First leaders started to echo the sentiments of Hungarian Prime Minister Orban. Now more leaders have started to express agreement with Russian President Putin. The times they are a changing...

Who would have thought?
http://m.washingtontimes.com/news/2015/oct/15/editorial-valdimir-putin-may-end-syrian-refugee-cr/
http://www.themoscowtimes.com/news/article/putin/529404.html

(41) SAN MARINO

San Marino, founded in 301 AD and a constitutional republic, is home to about 30,000 people. A wealthy and sheltered country, San Marino has active tourist and banking industries. Italy imports 90% of San Marino's manufactured items such as clothes, furniture, fabric, ceramics, tile, and wine. According to the United Nations, by June 2015 no refugees lived in San Marino although two (2) people had left San Marino to seek refuge and asylum elsewhere.

As to the refugee crisis, in mid-November 2015 San Marino announced it would be contributing 20,000 euros to a bank "Migrant and Refugee Fund."

I feel all better now. Pour the *Brugneto di San Marino* vino.
http://www.coebank.org/en/news-and-publications/news/san-marino-supports-migrant-and-refugee-fund/

(42) SERBIA

A rather mountainous country, Serbia was settled in the 7th and 8th centuries by ancient Slavs, established itself as a kingdom in 1217, and lived through many foreign invasions and conflicts. More recently, it was a part of the old Yugoslavia in 1943, and became a stand-alone independent nation in 2006 when the State Union of Serbia and Montenegro was dissolved. It is home to about 7 ½ million people.

The picturesque capital city, Belgrade, has a history spanning 7,000 years and sits where the Danube and Sava rivers meet. For whatever reasons, Serbia also desperately wants to be an official part of the EU and has officially applied for membership. (*Maybe they're desperate to lose their nation's sovereignty? Or perhaps they just wish to become indebted to the banksters? Note to self – it all ends up the same way once you inject EU into your system...*)

In an encouraging dialogue captured on Belgrade's TV Pink in December 2015, Michael Kirby, the US Ambassador to Serbia, went on the record saying Serbia's major problems are poverty and unemployment but stressed that the US has "helped Serbia in many ways."

According to the United Nations, several hundred thousand refugees, displaced persons and others are residing in Serbia, and several hundred thousand have left Serbia.
http://www.unhcr.org/pages/49e48d9f6.html
http://inserbia.info/today/2015/12/us-ambassador-i-believe-that-we-have-helped-serbia-in-many-ways/

In late October 2015, it was reported that over 200,000 migrants had crossed *through* Serbia on their way to other European destinations. No stranger to human crises, years ago Serbia had dealt with the effects of various wars and entanglements yielding half a million Kosovar and Bosnian refugees and about a quarter million Serbs ejected from Croatia. But today is different. These new refugees didn't share any similarities in language, culture, or religion. So the Serbs helped them along, but kept them moving.

With mounting pressure to actually settle thousands of migrants *in* Serbia, the EU appeared to be using Serbia's EU candidacy as leverage. But the Serb's figured it out and one Serbian politician even stated as much, adding "Serbia must oppose the dictate from Brussels that plans to turn Serbia and other Balkan states into the largest refugee reception point, an immigrant colony, as it might thus become another condition of Serbia joining the European Union."

And you're joining the EU *why*?
http://www.ibtimes.com/eu-refugee-crisis-serbia-quota-condition-pending-european-union-membership-will-turn-2137179
http://www.slate.com/articles/news_and_politics/foreigners/2015/11/serbia_is_leading_the_way_in_europe_s_refugee_crisis_it_knows_what_is_needed.html

Mid-October 2015 saw continuing bottlenecks as more than 10,000 migrants were stalled in Serbia after Croatia (where refugee camps were full to capacity) and other countries slowed or closed border crossings. At some points, a steady onslaught of 5,000+ migrants, mostly young men, were crossing into Serbia from Croatia daily.

"Kill, slaughter, so that there is no Serb."
In the meanwhile, after Albania qualified for the European Football Championship, Albanians living in Serbia celebrated by spilling into the streets chanting a variety of joyous slogans such as the crowd-pleasing "Kill, slaughter, so that there is no Serb." Pretty strong hate speech, if there ever was any.

So, did the Serbian Police strike fear into those calling for the literal killing and slaughter of their very own ethnic Serbs?

Nope.

The Serbian Police didn't react much at all. Maybe they feared upsetting the ethnic minority Albanians, while native Serbs hid, scared to death in their own country.

A day or two later, the Serbian Police stated that they *had* actually "reacted within its authority" (we're guessing that means they *watched* intently) but that *now* the Police and the Prosecutor's Office were conducting a criminal investigation to round up the people who had incited intolerance against race, religion, and the nation.

Timing is everything.
http://www.theguardian.com/world/2015/oct/19/refugees-stranded-on-serbian-croatian-border
http://inserbia.info/today/2015/10/presevo-albanians-chanted-kill-slaughter-so-that-there-is-no-serb/

The BBC reiterated in September 2015 what everyone already knew and knew well – refugees have no interest in settling in Serbia. When Hungary tried to send people back to Serbia, even the UN faulted Hungary since Serbia doesn't have the capacity to deal with large groups.
http://www.bbc.com/news/world-europe-34261357

An import for an import
Following squabbles over border crossings, border closures, and which side to break eggs on, Serbia banned imports from

Croatia, and Croatia no longer allowed vehicles registered in Serbia into Croatia. Croatia was angry especially since their economy has been a disaster for more than half a decade and any dip in exports to Serbia will cut deeply. On top of all this, Hungary's border closures had redirected tens of thousands of migrants *into* Croatia. The war of words continued as Serbia and Croatia accused each other of all sorts of bad sportsmanship and collusion. Hungary's foreign minister jumped in with claims that authorities in Croatia, Greece, and Romania were liars

While the old-fashioned-controlled-media lamented that seemingly "many" migrant families had been detached from their children, horrors of horrors, during all these disagreements, luckily the number of the separated is doubtless miniscule in the grand scheme of things since 70-80+% of the migrants are young fighting-age males. Ultimately, the European *Council of Foreign Relations* explained everything by saying that "These societies and states feel that they are threatened and have been abandoned by the EU. The EU was the glue that held them together, so now their neighbors are the easiest targets."

With glue like that, who needs to sniff it?
http://www.aljazeera.com/news/2015/09/tensions-croatia-serbia-rise-refugees-150924193440477.html
http://www.newsweek.com/2015/10/09/europe-refugee-crisis-fans-old-balkan-tensions-377714.html

Silence isn't necessarily golden
From the absence of contrarian voices, one might think, *wow, the people of Serbia sure are behind the migrant thing.* After all, as opposed to the loud protests in Greece and Germany and England and Spain and Austria, and etc. etc., Serbians aren't complaining a bit.

Well... there is a real story behind the supposed silence...

As summer 2015 came to close, and large groups announced rallies and protests, Serbia's Interior Minister, Nebojsa Stefanovic, broke out the cases of duct tape and gags, and made it illegal to protest against migrants. No, *seriously*.

In rhetoric reminiscent of the Soviet-era dictates, the government stated that

> "We will not allow the expression of intolerance and hatred to be something that is characteristic of Serbia. The Ministry of Interior will *not allow any meetings* against migrants and people passing through Serbia, who were *forced to do so because of difficult conditions* or war in their country."

Notice the devilishly clever wording which puts "difficult conditions" before "war in their country" since most savvy politicians are aware of the fact that most of the migrants are economic opportunists – and theoretically can be made to fit in the "forced to do so because of difficult conditions" box quite easily under any variety of linguistic legerdemain.

Shockingly, Serbia must have been desperate to make the curtailing of freedom of speech stick since they had Interior Minister Stefanovic unabashedly throw in "gay rights" to further stigmatize anyone who questions "migrants." A lawyer who combats LGBT hate crimes in Serbia stated that "The fear of refugees are (sic) irrational and I feel sorry that some organizations are trying to emerge from anonymity by mobilizing and abusing people with anti-gay propaganda and xenophobia."

Quite the opposite, many gay people we have heard from are positively petrified about what the influx of migrants who deny the rights of LGBT people will mean to Europe's gay communities. No one we heard from feels it will end happily.

When all else fails, start labeling
The Serbian government tried to marginalize and shut down concerned Serbian citizens who wanted to express sincere worries about migrant assimilation by quickly labelling them xenophobes, racists, and fascists.

Well, that pretty much covers the whole smear-bucket, minus Nazi, satirical artist, and baby killer.

While the accusations had the desired effect, and shut down all discussion and debate, legitimate and unanswered questions from the LGBT community remain.

> What will it mean to LGBT people in Europe as hundreds of thousands of migrants who openly don't support (just ask them) the rights of LGBT take up residence in their towns and cities and introduce Sharia law?

> Will the approved and many-state sanctioned practice of physically stoning homosexuals to death be another topic that Interior Minister Stefanovic will forbid people to question and discuss?

The "created" pro-migrant environment has made Serbia the darling of the old-fashioned-controlled-media which has singled out Serbia as the "model" for how to deal with migrants. Of course, currently the migrants are just passing through... Wait till they set up shop.

Duct tape or no duct tape, EU or no EU, once migrants start settling in and demanding their welfare payments, free accommodations, free health care services, and begin suing for cash settlements if they feel snubbed, we wonder if Serbians will be allowed to express their opinions then, free from the fear of imprisonment and/or the stigmatization as racists, xenophobes, and fascists.

For now, we'll have to make do with the highly sanitized, painfully politically correct propaganda manufactured and disseminated by the authorities.

There was an old joke from the Communist-era Soviet Union that went like this...

Two men were assigned to the same cell in a Siberian gulag. One asked the other, "What are you imprisoned for?" The man answered, "For making *anti-Stalin* statements." The first man smirked and stared at the grey wall. "Interesting. I'm in for making *pro-Stalin* statements."

All is going great. Just great, I tell you...
http://www.balkaninsight.com/en/article/civil-sector-wows-ban-of-anti-migrants-protest-08-26-2015
https://youtu.be/1IqBmDjoxIE
http://www.balkaninsight.com/en/article/serbian-police-open-to-undue-government-control--12-07-2015

(43) SLOVAKIA

In 2014, the United Nations reported that about 1,000 refugees and asylum seekers were already living in Slovakia, and another dozen or so had been granted asylum. Pressured by the EU, in August 2015 Slovakia agreed to take in some Syrian refugees – 200. And, according to the Slovakian government, they had to be Christian since Slovakia has zero mosques. The EU had told Slovakia to take 800 refugees, and then upped it to 2,287 as part of the "quota."

The self-important old-fashioned-controlled-media instantly labeled Slovakia's attempts at "planning ahead to stack the odds for integration success and asking for Christian refugees" as bigoted, xenophobic (fear of foreigners, not fear of *Xena: Warrior Princess*), racist, paranoid, and a host of other tags.

Actually, Slovakia's planning reminded me of the way a nearby school, that hosts many foreign exchange students, decides how to place children. When they can, Jewish children live with Jewish families, Christian children with Christian families, Muslim children with Muslim families, et cetera.

I always thought that it was a kind and thoughtful way to make a student feel a little more welcome during their time in the home of strangers in a foreign country. Little did I suspect that such care and thought was secretly dripping with racism and hate. Wow. Now that I've seen the error in their ways, I am writing an accusatory letter to the PTA and school board to demand that they never repeat such horrible outrages when planning children's accommodations.

The town of Gabcikovo gained a bit of notoriety when residents voted overwhelmingly (97%) to *not* reopen an existing but dormant refugee center. That center had been active several decades ago when some 5,000 migrants and refugees from Chechenia, Iran, Sri Lankan, Romania, Afghanistan, India, Iraq, Moldova, Pakistan, Russia, Syria and Viet Nam came and went.

In 2006, the Gabcikovo refugee shelter took in many refugees from a neighboring town's shelter when the migrant children at that other facility were playing with a cigarette lighter and burned that shelter to the ground. Most recently, the Gabcikovo shelter had been dormant.

Smoking is dangerous.
http://www.pluska.sk/spravy/z-domova/premier-fico-nemozeme-tolerovat-prichod-moslimov-stavanie-mesit.html
http://www.unhcr.org/4506d7634.html

We aren't helping economic migrants
According to the Financial Times, in August 2105, Slovak Prime Minister Robert Fico accused EU leaders of lying about who most of the migrants streaming into the EU really were. Fico was blunt. He said, "Ninety-five per cent of these people are economic migrants...We will not assist this foolish idea of accepting anybody regardless of whether or not they are economic migrants."
http://www.ft.com/intl/cms/s/2/ef5179bc-4ff7-11e5-8642-453585f2cfcd.html#axzz3kSi3wjWA

No means no. And we're suing your butts.
Near the end of September 2015, Prime Minister, Robert Fico, said that not only will Slovakia not participate in the EU quota pronouncements, but that Slovakia intended to sue the EU.

Furious that other countries had created the migrant crisis and now wanted to force "innocent" countries to pick up the pieces, Fico added that "We have been refusing this nonsense from the beginning, and as a sovereign country we have the right to sue."

Remember that Prime Minister Fico's outrage was in September 2015. Imagine if it had been two months later when the total number of economic opportunists attracted by Chancellor Angela Merkel's scheming had been revealed to be not 120,000 but 1.5 million!

Every time one looks around, the highly demonized and marginalized, yet outspoken, Balkan nations seem to be making decisions more in line with protecting their countries and their people than the major players.

Excitedly, the old-fashioned-controlled-media predicted this hard stance from Prime Minister Fico would be his xenophobic demise – pure political suicide.

Instead, a curious thing happened. His popularity at home grew and grew.
http://www.express.co.uk/news/politics/607480/Europe-migrant-crisis-Syrian-refugee-quotas-Brussels-Slovakia-court
http://www.euractiv.com/sections/justice-home-affairs/slovakia-pushes-ahead-legal-action-over-eu-migrant-quotas-318139

Anger and more complaints
Remember Gabcikovo? Well, by mid October 2015, with the Austrian shelters overflowing, Prime Minister Fico agreed to help out his fellow EU country and to house up to 500 Syrian refugees temporarily.

At the shelter it was reported that migrant "children played games, but the adults sat about for hours, fiddling with their phones on benches or drinking beer and smoking cigarettes."

Although the Slovakians were just trying to help the overwhelmed Austrians out, the refugees were displeased and some were downright furious.

Refugee complaints included:
- not having a say in whether or not they wanted to stay at a shelter in Slovakia
- being in an isolated village
- being in Slovakia
- wasting time and not having the ability to prepare for their new future "life" in Austria
- no assistance with Austrian integration while in Slovakia
- only two German language teachers
- not enough books and pencils in the classroom
- Slovakian country life was very, very boring
- not having a proper family life
- "They give us some money but it's nothing - it's not enough"

One young male (aren't they all?) Syrian refugee lamented, "Sometimes I think *if I never left Syria* that might have been a *better choice.*"

Ah, the wisdom of youth, and the power of hindsight.
http://www.topky.sk/gl/315591/1626867/Gabcikovo-par-hodin-pred-prichodom-migrantov--VIDEO-Zabery-zvnutra-uteceneckeho-tabora-#infopanel

(44) SLOVENIA

Slovenia was formerly part of Yugoslavia. It is home to just about 2 million Slovenians. The Slovenian ambassador to Germany announced that Slovenia would welcome up to 10,000 refugees. With Hungary protecting its borders, migrants were finding new ways to sneak through Europe and Slovenia found itself in the cross-hairs.

In September 2015, it was reported that many migrants were pressing their way through Croatia and Slovenia. Slovenia initially was passing people through, but started to seal its borders in late September 2015 due to an overwhelming surge of angry and indignant migrants demanding entry. In a scene too often repeated, violent migrants fought with each other, clashed with police, and swarmed trains, climbing through windows, to make their way out. Reportedly, even Red Cross workers were appalled and disgusted.
https://youtu.be/znCVdMaBdtI
https://youtu.be/5CuMolvV5no

On September 19, 2015, Slovenia had to resort to using riot police to protect its borders as thousands of migrants tried yet again to gain illegal entry. The police needed tear gas to stop one of the migrants trying to lead the hoards attempting to knock over and break through the Slovenian border cordons.

As we have seen many times before, but rarely in the old-fashioned-controlled-media, the migrants became increasingly violent, threw dangerous objects including sticks and bottles, and attacked police.

Later, hundreds of migrants pitched tents and camped overnight in the Slovenian town of Obrazje, adding to the pressure Slovenia was feeling from these lawless mobs that do as they please.
http://www.express.co.uk/news/world/606386/Migration-crisis-Syria-refugees-Europe-Croatia-Hungary

Safe-country? We don't need no stinkin' safe-country!
September 2015 saw Johanna Mikl-Leitner, Austria's Minister of Internal Affairs point out that migrants that got to Slovenia had, in fact, reached a "safe country." As such, the migrants had to seek asylum there.

Based on the evidence that these so-called asylum seekers rarely applied for asylum in Slovenia, *which is a safe country,* Ms. Mikl-Leitner suspected that their behavior "suggests they are *not* looking for safety but are choosing the most economically attractive countries."

Well, yes. Of course. Anyone with a brain has figured that out already.

Ms. Mikl-Leitner promised that "if refugees arriving from Slovenia and Croatia to Austria seek asylum, we will return them to Croatia and Slovenia."

We hope so. Maybe that will send a message to these economic opportunists.

Maybe.
http://www.b92.net/eng/news/region.php?yyyy=2015&mm=09&dd=24&nav_id=95551

Arson, migrant-style

In late October 2015, young migrant men wearing hoodies committed arson by setting fire to their own tents at a migrant camp in Brezice, Slovenia. Then, in true asylum-seeking fashion, they took selfies. One Middle Eastern migrant can be seem smiling ear-to-ear taking a selfie as he flashes a two fingered salute in front of temporary housing and other personal property engulfed in orange and red flames.

Following the classic proverbial migrant style of *cutting off your nose to spite your face*, these young male criminals were already upset with the "crummy" shelter-food situation and accommodations. Then they apparently got really angry and rampaged wildly upon learning that it would take a minimum of *24 hours* to process them and get them to the Austrian border. *How dare we be delayed!*

Furious and with only a few dozen alternatives (*waiting in a shelter peacefully just isn't an option, right*?), the migrant youths chose to express their frustration by torching the place. Under the same circumstances, wouldn't you choose to do exactly the same thing?

One angry Iraqi migrant said, "We did not think Europe is like this – no respect for refugees, not treating us with dignity. Why is Europe like this?"

In fairness, the camp was designed for 250 people but the day before the arson, almost 4,000 refugees showed up unexpectedly and tried to push their way through.

Slovenia's police and military struggled to maintain law and order. Lots of luck.
http://www.express.co.uk/news/world/613809/European-migrant-crisis-refugees-set-fire-tents-Slovenia-selfies-travel-UK-Germany?_ga=1.86623259.2001237940.1442673819

(45) SPAIN

According to the Spanish National Statistics Institute (INE), in a 2008 study, Spaniards committed 70% of all crimes committed in Spain, and foreigners committed 30% of all the crimes in Spain. No rejoicing yet, since at that time, foreigners only made up about 15% of Spain's population. So, sadly, foreigners were 200% over-represented in crime statistics.

Where have we seen that before?
http://www.tercerainformacion.es/spip.php?article10906

In July 2015, King Felipe VI of Spain spoke to the European Parliament noting that "hundreds of thousands of refugees... pursue a project of hope, and see the Union as a land area of peace, prosperity and justice. We cannot let them down."
http://www.europarl.europa.eu/news/en/news-room/content/20151007STO96397/html/King-Felipe-of-Spain-Europe-cannot-let-refugees-down

Over the years, the gracious King has championed the causes of various minority groups, and was the first monarch of Spain to entertain, invite, and recognize "representatives of associations of gays, lesbians, bisexual, and transgender Spaniards" at the Royal Palace in 2014. Only a mere 30 years ago, homosexuality was a crime punishable by imprisonment in Spain.

When the new migrants that King Felipe so desperately wants to assist introduce Sharia law to Spain, hopefully they will follow in King Felipe's footsteps and be as open and welcoming, and will embrace Spain's LGBT community. And hopefully, they will not want to reinstitute the old anti-gay laws. Or add laws from some of their home countries which make imprisonment look like a walk in the park.
http://www.lasexta.com/noticias/nacional/reyes-reciben-primera-vez-colectivos-gays-palacio-pardo_2014062400197.html
http://www.europarl.europa.eu/news/en

Spain and its happy little weapons industry
Luckily, a 2014 report from the Delàs Center of Studies for Peace stated that since 2009, Spain hadn't sold any weapons or arms to Syria. Wouldn't it be a travesty if any country were to help arm the conflicts at the heart of, or the cause of some of the refugee migrations?

Not to say Spain isn't cranking out the guns.

A 2014 report from Amnesty International reported that Spain was selling weapons like crazy – the Saudis alone bought almost half a billion dollars' worth of weapons in 2013 alone. And of course the Saudis wouldn't ever slip a few of those guns to buddies elsewhere. So all was good.

More impressive, from 2004-2013, Spain's weapons industry sales had gone up 1,000% from just under a ½ billion dollars to more than 4 ½ billion dollars. Surrounded by an economy that resembles malaria, those sales increases are a welcome boost.

Ironic, right?
http://www.centredelas.org/images/stories/informes/informe24_cas_web.pdf
https://www.es.amnesty.org/uploads/tx_useraitypdb/Jugando_con_fuego.pdf

Complaint desk, take a number
The UN reported 13,323 asylum seekers and refugees living in Spain at the end of 2014. In the summer of 2014, Syrian refugees were complaining to the media that conditions in Spain were very bad for refugees and that "98% of Syrians" had moved on to destinations with nicer accommodations and more lucrative economic assistance. Think Germany, Sweden, or France. Not that it's just about the money, but it could be. Plus, Spain's 22-25% (or possibly far higher) unemployment rate didn't help.

One official said that even though Syrian refugees are set up with clothing, housing, food, job training, language classes, and a monthly allowance –
> "They don't stay. They leave because they think their chances are better in other countries. *They ask to leave the same day they arrive.* They say they have relatives in Europe."

One young male Syrian "refugee" who took an airline flight to Spain asked, "Why does Spain offer less help to refugees and take longer to process asylum applications than Germany or Sweden? If I had known it, I would have travelled to another country."

Such honesty is refreshing. We wonder if it will be contagious.
http://www.ipsnews.net/2014/07/spain-a-precarious-gateway-to-europe-for-syrian-refugees/

Bad Spaniards?
The old-fashioned-controlled-media made a big deal about Spain's apparent sluggishness and "insensitivity" to refugees. Many Spaniards were goaded into action and suddenly thousands of people volunteered to help refugees, from donations, to providing services to literally opening their homes to strangers.

Let's put that in perspective.

In September 2015 it was reported that 1/3 of all the foreclosed empty houses in Europe, *3,400,000 vacant homes,* were in Spain. The Spanish government reported an additional 500,000 abandoned "partially-built" homes as well.

Read that again slowly and think about the numbers.

Many Spanish politicians, worried purely about aesthetics, pushed for banks to face stiff fines for letting the properties languish. At the same time, the European Union reported that there were at least 4,100,000 homeless people in Europe (*not* including the newly arriving refugees).
http://www.theguardian.com/world/2015/sep/10/barcelona-fines-banks-60000-for-empty-homes

Europe is flooded with vacant homes? Seriously?
The number of vacant homes across Europe is epic! Ireland 400,000; UK 700,000; Germany 1,800,000; France 2,400,00; Portugal 735,000; Italy 2,700,000; Greece 300,000; and 3,400,000 in Spain.
http://www.theguardian.com/society/2014/feb/23/europe-11m-empty-properties-enough-house-homeless-continent-twice

Embarrassingly, no one connected the dots and thought to offer to house the millions of native European homeless in European-foreclosed-homes. Until now!

Well, there is a *slight* twist.

Certain groups in Spain have called upon Spanish banks to release portions of the enormous volume of foreclosed properties they were holding *to help house the refugees.*

So after seizing 95 homes *per day* from Spaniards who could no longer afford payments, special interest groups are demanding that the banks make those very same homes available for refugees. *Seriously?*

Wait. So, millions of your own citizens are economically downtrodden and destroyed by your poor conditions and poor economy, and your answer is to sit by and watch the seizure of their homes by banksters, and then consider handing their seized housing out to refugees? Really? What are your priorities?

Spain initially said it was "saturated" and could only agree to take in 2,749 refugees. Shamed by the EU, Spain later agreed to let in another 14,931. In retrospect, now that so many more refugees will be arriving in Spain, it is quite fortuitous that the banks seized so many homes out of the hands of Spanish families so that they now may actually be able to house the new migrants in style.

It is *so* good to be *so* filthy rich and *so* very out of touch...
In 2014, one of Spain's richest aristocrats, the Duke of Arjona, took in two Syrian refugee families to live in his ostentatious palace near Seville. The Duke claimed that after reading an article about a "highly educated" urologist migrant sleeping on the streets of Spain, he just had to help. He learned that the doctor's medical office had been bombed out during some combat. Well, no "highly educated" man was going to be living on the streets of Spain on the Duke's watch. No sir! And that's how the Syrian doctor and his family, and another Syrian family, ended up living with the Duke in his palace.

Of course, the Duke has a few palaces – Liria Palace in Madrid *(a huge more modern palace with dozens of rooms, featuring a priceless art collection including El Greco, Titian, Rembrandt, Renoir, Goya, letters by Christopher Columbus, old armor, elephant tusks, a 28 person dining room, a small 35 x 50 foot antechamber with 20 foot ceilings* – most of the other chambers are far larger - *and so much more)* and the palace near Seville called Palacio de las Dueñas *(it originally had 9 fountains, 100+ marble columns, 11 patios – one patio remains– enormous courtyards, long passageways, huge sitting rooms, vaulted ceilings, tons of priceless art, massive rooms that would dwarf a giant, palm trees, mounted bull heads, tiled walks, mosaics, floor to ceiling tapestries, a private church chapel, fruit orchard, walls dripping with historical artifacts and culture, and apparently now a resident urologist).*

Isn't it grand to see to what extent the super-super-wealthy will go to help foreigners?

It must be a source of great comfort to the 95 Spanish families a day, that were systematically evicted out of their homes, to know that there were such kind people in their own country ready to help foreigners.

Hopefully, some rich Syrians will read about the houseless Spaniards and be similarly moved, and offer them new lives in their homes.
http://www.theguardian.com/world/2015/sep/15/spain-refugees-indignados-safe-cities
http://elpais.com/elpais/2015/09/01/inenglish/1441099525_412620.html
http://www.thelocal.es/20150907/spanish-duke-takes-in-two-syrian-families-at-his-country-home

Spain in Africa

Melilla is the Spanish city bordering Morocco in Africa. Spain established the autonomous port city in the 1400s and considers it a legal part of the Spanish state. Morocco considers the area "occupied territory" and wants Spain out.

For many years, opportunistic migrants had been sneaking into Melilla from Africa to gain access to the EU. At some point, around 1999, the illegal entries became so brazen that Spain replaced their old border (a bunch of rolls of barbed wire), with an imposing super-fence complete with razor wire, infrared detectors, cameras, microphones, and armed patrols. Migrants that were caught in Melilla were reportedly roughed up before being returned to Morocco where police often roughed them up again. None of this stopped the illegal aliens, yet many now started using boats to go across the sea to try and sneak into Southern Spain directly.

Mixed messages
Long before Chancellor Merkel's open invitation, the EU financed a coastal patrol operation in 2004 to turn the migrants back to Africa. The unsuccessful migrants gathered together by the hundreds outside of Melilla, and would organize mass assaults on the border, illegally scaling the fences. Overwhelmed border patrols on the Melilla side would try to return the illegals to the Morocco side, where Moroccan patrols would often drop the migrants off in the desert.

Remember that the technical differences between actual *asylum seekers* and *migrants* makes it difficult to sort things out, especially since we've seen that most crafty migrants know what to say in order to benefit from asylum seeker status. Then add in a tiny city all on its own, literally a sea away from its mother country, trying to maintain its sanity as hundreds of people try and rush its borders on a regular basis. Not an easy scene.

Deadly complaints
Many of the illegal aliens complained that as they tried to scale fences and swarm the borders, Spanish and Moroccan border guards would assault them. Quite a few migrants were shot and killed as they tried to trespass into Melilla. In one representative incident, Moroccan guards shot a half dozen aliens near the fence, claiming self-defense because the migrants were heaving stones and rocks at them. Whatever the case, the guards were never charged with any wrongdoing.

Overwhelmed Moroccan forces busied themselves with removing hundreds and hundreds of migrants, possibly including asylum seekers, and detaining or removing them elsewhere.

Resistant migrants would camp around the fences and bide their time, sometimes *years*, waiting for a chance to swarm the fence into Melilla, often 500-800 men at a time. It got so desperate that around the year 2005 the EU helped finance an even bigger fence to protect Melilla. We're talking really tall, with multiple, parallel fences, state-of-the-art detectors, and watchtowers.

None of it helped. The migrant onslaught continued.

Migrants game an unbelievably naïve "honor system"
The migrants knew the scam only too well. Get into Melilla at any cost. Once there, claim to be an "asylum seeker." Authorities will either say "yes" (unlikely), or say "no" and put you on *a free ferry ride to Spain* complete with paperwork saying "you're expelled so go home" *all* based on an "honor system." Seriously. Spain expected proven law-breakers, who had just gained illegal entry into Spain, to do the right thing and leave of their own accord after being transported for free to mainland Spain in Europe. Alrighty then.

Clearly, no one actually went way back "home" once they got to mainland Spain.

And so it went.
http://www.theguardian.com/world/2010/apr/17/melilla-migrants-eu-spain-morocco

Old habits are hard to break
Finally, Spain closed its own loophole and no one got on the free ferry to the mainland anymore. This "uncaring" act of actually enforcing its own laws "stranded" hundreds of migrants.

Feeling guilty for looking out for its own national interests, Spain set up dormitories and provided regular nutritious meals for illegal aliens. But not much else.
http://www.spiegel.de/international/europe/europe-tightens-borders-and-fails-to-protect-people-a-989502-2.html

News of the new highly unwelcoming nature of Melilla spread. Yet attempts to illegally cross its borders didn't slow.

In the first couple of months of 2014, more migrants jumped the border fence than in all of 2013. 2014 turned out to be a particularly bad year as 19,000 swarmed the fence and about 2,100 migrants actually made it over.

One if by land, two if by sea
In 2014, swarms of migrants tried to gain illegal entry into Melilla by sea and about a dozen drowned. Migrants bitterly accused border guards of firing rubber bullets and tear gas to turn them back. Still, no guards were investigated.

What a difference a year makes. By September 2015, out of a reported 3,700 trespass attempts, only about 100 migrants got in. And since May 2015, reportedly no one successfully jumped the fence. *What happened to stem the flow?*

Among the new successful defenses being used against the onslaught, a new Spanish "citizens security" law allowed border guards to instantly return fence jumpers to Morocco before they could claim asylum. (They literally whisked them back out through a special little gate.) Spain also provided some heavy reinforcement to the border patrol. *In*creased manpower and *de*creased criminal activity. Then using good old inventive smarts, the Spanish coated their fences with a material that made climbing extraordinarily difficult. Not willing to be left out, Morocco also built up some of its own barriers, bolstered patrols, and cleared out migrant camps.

Still, by the Fall of 2015, almost 6,000 migrants reportedly had snuck in, mostly by sea, or by hiding in cars or trucks, or by using falsified documents and forged passports.

Where there is a criminal intent, there is a means.
http://www.theguardian.com/world/2015/sep/08/melilla-fences-spain-morocco-migration-europe
http://algarvedailynews.com/news/6614-melilla-is-calmer-but-refugees-still-gain-entry

(46) SWEDEN

"...I can't think of what Swedish culture is. I think that is what makes us Swedes so envious of immigrants. You have a culture, an identity, something that ties you together. What do we have? We have Midsummer's Eve and such corny things.. Swedes must integrate into the new Sweden. The old Sweden is not coming back."

Mona Sahlin
Former leader Sweden's Social Democrats
Euroturk Magazine, March 2002

Since corny Mona Sahlin so famously professed amnesia and turned her back on more than a thousand years of rich and honored Swedish identity and culture, instead, only to blindly drip with lust for the "cultures" she fancied immigrants brought with them (hey, not everyone is lucky enough to practice female genital mutilation, or polygamy, or revile music and alcohol, or force children to be brides, or stone homosexuals to death, or commit honor killings, or murder non-believers, or whatever else corny Mona may have been so deeply impressed with), she would likely be rejoicing at the latest statistics. *Corny or not.*

Sweden proudly revealed in October 2015 that it had already taken in almost 100,000 asylum seeking applicants in 2015.

With all that wonderful new culture to replace the huge gaping deficit corny Mona identified in 2002 in the Swedish culture bank, it is interesting that Prime Minister Stefan Löfven stated publically that "Sweden is approaching the limit of its capacity." *So there is a limit to importing better cultures?*

The Swedish government also admitted underestimating the number of *young adults* and unaccompanied children that would be arriving in Sweden. From their original estimate of 12,000, the Swedish Migration Board nearly tripled their numbers to about 30,000 expected migrants. By January 1, 2016, the Swedish Migration Board's estimate had gone up to 35,369 unaccompanied "children." ("Children" is in quotes since you will learn later on that many "children" are really adults lying about their age for a variety of twisted reasons.)

The numbers have long been large, and growing. 7,049 children arrived in Sweden by themselves and sought asylum in 2014. That's a staggering increase of more than 80 percent over 2013's numbers. An now 35,369 in 2015? Daunting.

Honey, have you seen the kids?
In an even more disturbing story, a southern Swedish town reported that of the roughly 2,000 unaccompanied *young adults* and children that "showed up" in their area in October 2015, about half had run off even though they had been provided free food and shelter.

Strange. Super strange.

Commenting on the 1,000 or so young migrants now loose in the countryside, a town official stated that "we don't know where they are... We don't have the possibility to stop them leaving. We can't wait by their beds day and night."

In the meanwhile, a group of 1,000 unsupervised unaccompanied young adults and children was roaming around, doing who knows what.

Scary. Super scary.
http://www.thelocal.se/20151021/lone-refugee-kids-in-sweden-to-top-30000
www.hd.se/nyheter/sverige/2016/01/01/rekordstor-okning-av-ensamkommande/

Magical disappearances are commonplace
At the end of November 2015, Sweden's Immigration Agency officially handed 21,748 people in Sweden deportation orders ordering them to leave Sweden. But based on the story you just read above about the young adults and children who vanished, can you guess what happened next?

Exactly correct. Many thousands simply disappeared.

Instead of taking their orders of deportation seriously, more than 14,400 foreign nationals simply went underground. Well, no one could have seen that one coming... The Head of the National Border Police told reporters, "We simply don't know where they are."

Oh, and it's been happening a long time.

In May 2015, it was reported that only about 41% of illegals earmarked for deportation actually permitted themselves to be deported. With no real penalties, no risks, and a system stacked in their favor, about 60% of foreigners earmarked for deportation simply decided to hide out in Sweden, knowing that *if they claim to be Syrian* and if they can successfully evade detection for 18 months, they will likely score a place on the lucrative welfare rolls provided by Sweden's generous taxpayers.

Good payoff if you can pull it off.

In 2014, the Swedish Immigration Agency reported that at least 11,000 migrants had gone "underground." The Immigration Agency also revealed that they were "powerless to enforce deportation orders." Now, an additional 14,400 more migrants were "missing" and the year hadn't even ended.

Obviously, this begs the question, had the Immigration Agency announced that they had the *power to enforce deportation orders* against failed asylum seekers, would they have all been labeled by the Swedish press as "racist" for using hate speech?

Think about it.
http://www.thelocal.se/20151127/14000-illegal-immigrants-disappear-without-trace
http://www.thelocal.se/20150503/more-illegal-immigrants-going-underground-in-sweden

It's good to be warm and unaccountable
Back to Sweden's Prime Minister Stefan Löfven who claimed that "[It warms my heart] when I see the work being carried out. It makes me warm and proud to be prime minister in Sweden."

Hopefully, those words provide warmth and comfort to the millions of native Swedes paying for this grand scheme and those who might also find themselves on the receiving end of all this unrequited love.
http://www.thelocal.se/20151021/sweden-is-approaching-the-limit-of-its-capacity

So, why isn't there a really loud outcry and protest?
We will now add the following note on censorship and prosecution in Sweden today.

If you scratch your head and wonder why more people, especially native Swedes, aren't raising an uproar over the twisted course of immigration and migrant escapades, look no further.

At the end of 2014, under the guise of protecting children who are bullied online, the Swedish Parliament *actually changed its Constitution* to make the prosecution of Swedes MUCH easier for the "crimes" of "insulting government officials, immigrants, LGBTs, Muslims, and other minorities on the internet."

Ironically, since native Swedes aren't considered an ethnic group, they are not protected under this new change.

In Sweden, everyone is equal *except* for the native Swedes themselves. So if much of the population now uses the web to communicate, and you now know you might end up in court or jail for "insulting" someone that belongs to very specific groups, including government officials and immigrants, on the internet, then you shouldn't really be surprised why there is little substantive challenge to Sweden's iron fist crushing the windpipe of freedom of expression and free speech.

Let the insults fly!
http://swedishsurveyor.com/2014/12/05/swedish-christmas-present-censorship-law

Utopia vs. those damning statistics, again
Four decades after the parliament in Sweden voted unanimously to make Sweden into a multicultural utopian society, the results were in: violent crime was up 300% and rape was up 1,471%.

Worse yet, "according to figures published by The Swedish National Council for Crime Prevention (Brottsförebyggande rådet; known as BRÅ) – an agency under the Ministry of Justice – 29,000 Swedish women, during 2011, reported that they had been raped (which seems to indicate that less than 25% of the rapes are reported to the police)." We can't even fathom how bad the actual rape numbers really are based on this shocking revelation of massive under-reporting. But for now, we will work with the officially reported accounts.

Police statistics showed 6,620 rapes reported in 2014. Sweden was now #2 in rapes worldwide, second only to the Lesotho kingdom in Africa which had a higher per capita rape rate.

Sweden was setting records everywhere you looked as it was fast becoming not only the rape capital of Europe but also the bomb detonation capital of Europe as well. We'll look at the bombs a bit later.

Apologists for rapists have tried to dissuade concerns about the statistical increases with a variety of peculiar explanations including:

- Changes in laws made more offences into rapes
- More Swedes have started to report crimes
- Swedish men, incapable of dealing with women's equality, are becoming more violent towards women

In most of the rape cases, the BRÅ's report showed that:

> "In 58% of cases, the perpetrator was entirely unknown by the victim. In 29% of cases the perpetrator was an acquaintance, and in 13% of cases the perpetrator was a person close to the victim."

So, most of the time, Swedish women were being raped by complete strangers.

What a dangerous time for women in Sweden!
http://www.expressen.se/kvallsposten/antal-sprangningar-i-Malmö-rekordmanga/
https://www.bra.se/download/18.22a7170813a0d141d2180005382/1371914740842/2012_NTU_2011_Kap_3_Utsatthet_2012.pdf

90+ red flags don't impress authorities
Would you let a convicted child molester adopt a child?

What if his victim had been a 5-year-old girl? And the child he wanted to adopt was a 10-year-old boy? Sick right? It's about to get so much sicker.

And what if he had also been convicted of, *sit down*, more than 90 other crimes (NINETY) including child molestation. And he was known to carry on internet chats with underage girls. Oh, yes, and he was also a suspect in the rape of a teenage girl. Oh, and a social services ruling said he had to be supervised when he was with his own children.

Well, apparently, if you are in Sweden, it's all ok. In fact, Swedish authorities gave this man permission to adopt the young boy. It will all be ok, they claimed...

On what planet? Planet Sweden, apparently...

Think about it.
http://www.thelocal.se/20131129/convicted-swedish-paedophile-allowed-to-adopt

Oh no, no-go, literally
NO-GO ZONE: a military term meaning a hot area under enemy control, too dangerous to enter without appropriate military capability.

In 2015, Sweden's leading scientific journal Forskning & Framsteg reported a fast increase in gun violence in Sweden, the proliferation of Middle Eastern criminal gangs, and the growth of ghettos, from 3 in 1990 to 156 by 2006. Forskning & Framsteg also interviewed a police officer who worked in Sweden's "dangerous" zones who they quoted as saying,

> "The situation is slipping from our grasp. If we're in pursuit of a vehicle, it can evade us by driving to certain neighborhoods where a lone patrol car simply cannot follow, because we'll get attacked with stones and face riots. These are No-Go Zones. We simply can't go there."

In Swedish suburbs, shootings are now commonplace, according to the article. And street gangs have become more powerful and dangerous than motorcycle gangs. Some blame the dramatic increases in criminal activity amongst younger migrants on their parents. Something along the lines of – *the migrant parents had to work so hard that they ended up neglecting to raise their children properly*. Others claim the young thugs simply grew up in loveless migrant families. Still others lay the blame on a lack of standards among young migrant males.

Curiously, no one seems to have thought to hold the perpetrators accountable for *their* choices and actions. Plenty of excuses and explanations, but little accountability. And the violence increases.

Sadly, all indications point to the fact that without drastic changes the trend towards violence will continue to grow. And the crimes are getting more and more serious.
http://fof.se/tidning/2015/5/artikel/darfor-okar-de-kriminella-gangens-makt

Scared gang rape victim not "helpless" enough
In 2013, a young girl was gang raped in Tensta, Sweden. During a party in the mostly African and Arab suburb, six migrant boys in their late teens abducted the Swedish girl, locked her up in a closet, and proceeded to sexually assault her.

Initially charged with and *convicted of aggravated rape*, the boys were allowed to walk free after an Appeals Court ruled that the girl wasn't truly "helpless" during the assault, just scared.

The Appeals Court saw the girl's testimony as credible but expressed concern about just how much a girl locked in a dark space and surrounded by strangers could accurately observe details. The Appeals Court also found that the girl might have been in a precarious situation, *but wasn't legally so*, thus they didn't feel they should charge the 5 boys with rape and the sixth with attempted rape. Finally, they didn't charge the boys with a host of milder offenses since the prosecution would have had to prove the boys "had the intent to harass the victim in a way likely to violate her sexual integrity."

Really? Really????

There they go again. Protecting the criminals at all cost.

Seriously.
http://www.dn.se/sthlm/tonarspojkar-frias-fran-gruppvaldtakt/

Sweden and Criminal Activity

In the 1996 Swedish Government BRÅ report "Criminality amongst immigrants and children of immigrants," which looked at crime statistics from 1985-1989, it was found that migrants committed about 14% of all crimes, and were more than 200% as likely to commit crimes as native Swedes.

Apologists tried to explain away this overrepresentation by saying that the higher rates were simply due to the fact that young males made up a greater number of the immigrants, and young men statistically commit a greater number of crimes. Mystery solved.

But apologies aside, if such reasoning is correct, and knowing what we know about 70-80+% of the migrants flooding Europe, that they are young men of fighting age, then Europe could be in for a really rough time.

The report showed that criminals in Sweden were generally beginning their criminal behavior younger and younger – usually between the ages of 10-14. Disturbingly, immigrants were overrepresented, again, in certain violent crimes, and rape convictions revealed that 61% of rape convictions were of immigrant-background rapists.

The report was painfully specific. North African-born immigrants were 2,300% more likely to commit rape than native born Swedes. Iraqi-born immigrants were 2,000% more likely to commit rape than native born Swedes. And African-born immigrants were 1,700% more likely to commit rape than native born Swedes.

As the years progressed, it got worse.

In the 2005 Swedish Government BRÅ report "Crime among persons born in Sweden and other countries," which looked at crime statistics from 1997-2001, it was found that criminals of foreign backgrounds committed more than 40% of all crimes, and were more than 250% as likely to commit crimes as native Swedes. More specifically, about 25% of crimes were committed by purely foreign-born migrants, and about 20% of crimes were perpetrated by people born in Sweden but of foreign backgrounds.

Sweden's Council for Crime Prevention noted that while the study looked at stats for people "suspected" of offences, there existed "little difference" in the stats of "suspects of crimes" versus "people actually convicted."

Do age and welfare dependency play a role?
The study found that people of foreign background living in Sweden were 400% more likely to be involved in lethal violence and robbery. And "persons from families registered as having received social welfare benefits" were 600% more likely to commit crimes than non-welfare recipients.

Statistics showed that immigrants who arrived at a very young *pre-school age* did not often have run ins with the law. Alternatively, immigrants of "school age, up to and including the late teenage years, when they arrived in Sweden, comprised the group whose members were most often registered in connection with crime."

Wow. Hopefully this proven statistical finding is hogwash since the current migrant wave is comprised of 70-80+% young fighting age males, not the statistically less-criminally prone preschoolers the report references. However, if the finding is even remotely accurate, then Europe could be in for an even rougher time than anyone suspected.

The study noted that for certain very serious crimes such as rape, manslaughter, homicide, and robbery, immigrants were *exponentially* more involved than native Swedes. In fact, people in Sweden of African descent were found to be 450% more likely to commit crime than native Swedes, while immigrants of South Asian and Western Asian descent were 350% more likely to commit crime than native Swedes. In the cases of violent assaults, immigrants were 300% more likely to be investigated. As far as sex crimes were concerned, immigrants were 500% more likely to be investigated with people of North African descent and Western Asian descent very overrepresented in related criminal activity.

Good news
The National Council for Crime Prevention (BRÅ) made sure to end the report with good news.

It's not the fault of the migrants!

While the risks of criminal behavior amongst migrants may be higher, everything was easily explained away since

a) moving to a new country is hard,
b) migrants themselves are victims of *"poorer social opportunities and a worse social situation than the average Swede," and*
c) Sweden is to blame as Sweden has "flaws in the reception received by immigrants" based on prejudices and negative discrimination which causes segregation and is an enemy of assimilation

How about the victims? Oh please! When is it ever about the victims?

If you are shaking your head after reading these explanations that seem to excuse migrant criminality, you're not alone.
http://www.bra.se/download/18.cba82f7130f475a2f1800012697/2005_1 7_brottslighet_bland_personer_fodda_sverige_och_utlandet.pdf
http://www.pdf-archive.com/2011/05/08/br-1996-2-invandrares-och-invandrares-barns-brottslighet-1/br-1996-2-invandrares-och-invandrares-barns-brottslighet-1.pdf

Brave migrant reveals how really bad Swedes are

In Sweden, migrants seeking asylum complained on video that they had to walk long distances just to eat. Worse yet, they said you had to bring your own glass with you for drinks. If it rained, they noted, they got rained on. And the food facility was small, lamented a migrant who said it was fine for now, but what will happen when the snow comes?

Most concerning, the upset migrant claimed that the clearly callous and uncaring people at the Swedish restaurant providing free food and drink were only giving each and every migrant *one* sandwich per person per meal time. No super-sizing! *The horror!*

"A lot of people came outside (of the restaurant), they still hungry" after eating just one free sandwich he complained. Another migrant complained that his family walked a half hour to get to a store. He was also upset because there was no school for his children. When the alert interviewer corrected him and said that, in fact, *there was a school nearby*, the migrant changed the subject, complaining that he needed his family to be closer to the center of things.

The migrant ended the video with, "We need a place to have a good life. We came to Sweden... the land of freedom. We think they are lying to us."
https://youtu.be/Q_XHkgScOSY

Staggering numbers of "children" likely frauds

In August 2015, in a span of seven days, over 8,300 asylum seekers, most from Syria, Afghanistan, and Iraq, stormed

Sweden. 1,836 were unaccompanied children (young males), mostly from Afghanistan.

Before you feel too sad for the children, ID-less migrants lying about their age has been going on a long time, across Europe. In 2010, it got so bad in Norway that authorities resorted to using x-rays of teeth. They allegedly found that 90% of "unaccompanied refugee children" were actually adults over the age of 18!

90%!!!

In November 2015, a famous Swedish whistleblower and blogger stated that Immigration Service workers had "received orders that if the person does not appear to be 40 years or older we should accept the claim that they are children."

If that's true, well, now you're just asking for trouble.

You really can't make this stuff up...
http://tundratabloids.com/2015/10/sweden-8-000-muslim-settler-in-seven-days/
http://sverigesradio.se/sida/artikel.aspx?programid=159&artikel=3491113
https://twitter.com/MeritWager/status/662213236092239872

Tear down the crosses
In September 2015, Swedish newspaper and news site svt.se/Nyheter reported that the world's first openly lesbian Bishop, the Bishop of Stockholm, called for the Seamen's Mission Church in Stockholm, Sweden, to remove its crosses and other Christian symbols *so as not to offend Muslims*, and to mark the direction to Mecca to accommodate potential Muslim worshippers.

The Bishop referred to the expected Muslim worshippers as "angels" and explained in her blog that not removing symbols of Christianity would be "stingy towards people of other faiths."

How thoughtful and welcoming. When's the last time a mosque removed Muslim symbols to let Christians pray and worship?

Hopefully, when the Bishop visits a mosque in Iran, no one will find out she is a devout lesbian, since Muslim laws are very specific about what her punishment will be. According to the Guardian, in Iran in 2012, the punishment for "*mosahegheh* (lesbianism) is 100 lashes for all individuals involved, but it can lead to the death penalty if the act is repeated four times."

Considering the Bishop is married, we guess she will be eligible for the maximum penalty at the hands of her "angels."
http://www.svenskakyrkan.se/default.aspx?id=1318087
http://www.svt.se/nyheter/regionalt/stockholm/biskopen-vill-ta-bort-kristna-symboler-i-sjomanskyrkan

Malmö Mal-mess
Malmö is Sweden's third largest city. Malmö got its charter in the 13th century, and is home to castles, wondrous historic buildings, and amazing modern architecture. It ranks as one of the most bicycle friendly cities on the globe, with world-class museums, a 14th century church, endless cultural centers, and home to many innovative biotech and IT companies. Almost half of its residents have foreign backgrounds. And Malmö has a secret. *Rosengard.*

In October 2015, the Central Finland newspaper ran a detailed report on the Rosengard district in Malmö. They reported that Rosengard, now 90% inhabited by mostly Iraqi and Bosnian immigrants almost half of whom are 18 years of age and younger, is completely gang controlled.

In 2014, Rosengard gained some notoriety when it saw four bombings within a five hour window *all* in one day. It hasn't gotten better. Gang members patrol the borders of Rosengard aggressively. Police will only show up in minimum groups of 4 patrol cars, and officers rarely exit their vehicles. Ambulance drivers are scared to respond to calls after many violent

attacks on ambulances by gangs. Fire trucks will only show up if they have police escorts. How's that for a reality check?
http://www.ksml.fi/uutiset/ulkomaat/eiko-teita-pelota-tata-ruotsalaista-korttelia-pelkaavat-ambulanssikuskitkin/2144887?pwbi=2d5b9e1a012113e2952c01a87da14521

How is this being allowed to happen?
In September 2015, some migrants went on the record and told video viewers why they chose Sweden as their final destination.

- First, they can get full citizenship in only 4 years.
- Next, some of them are safe to be openly gay, which in Syria, would have meant torture and the death penalty.
- Third, the migrants get incredibly generous welfare benefits.

Apparently overflowing with cash and generosity towards foreigners, the Swedish government was planning to accept another 100,000 Syrian migrants in 2015 which would increase Sweden's population by 1%.

Since politicians are so often not in step with their constituents, such plans seemed ridiculous to many native Swedes.

It should come as no big surprise, then, that the most popular single party in Sweden in late 2015 was the Sweden Democrat Party, staunch supporters of Sweden and Western values. These mostly native and proudly patriotic Swedes expressed feeling powerless and excluded, as sweeping immigration decisions were being made without any serious debate or input from the populace. Sweden Democrat party members were also increasingly alarmed that their legitimate concerns were being marginalized by the seemingly magical and increasingly more often used rebuke, "racist."

Instead of serious consideration or discussion, the still effective hand grenade, "racist," was lobbed at any attempt at reasonable discussion. As the debates, or lack thereof, raged, someone had to pay for all this altruism. Sweden was planning to raise taxes by $7 billion – in a country with about 9.5 million people, that's just over $700 out of the pocket of every man, woman, and child in Sweden. Of course, since many of the migrants, who make up 15% of the population of Sweden, don't work or are collecting welfare, the burden on native working Swedes will be much higher.
https://youtu.be/axOuN5Uj0AU

More horror stories you likely missed

At the same time as Sweden rushes to make room for more migrants, there have been dozens of grenade attacks all over the city of Malmö, the place that most migrants go to first. Add in a steady stream of stabbings, shootings, rapes, gang rapes, and arson, mostly perpetrated by migrants, and you have the makings of a real disaster.

The devil is in the details

On Monday August 10th, 2015, several native Swedish citizens, shopping in an IKEA furniture store outside Stockholm, were randomly selected, and viciously attacked by a recently arrived Eritrean African migrant.

In Sweden for less than a month, this miscreant and his friend rampaged, as bystanders, apparently quite used to such attacks by migrants, yelled, "Stabbing spree! Stabbing spree!"

Store cameras captured one of the African migrants picking out some large kitchen knives, one for each hand, then viciously attacking and killing a Swedish mother and her son, and initial reports alleged he attempted to behead the woman.

IKEA responded by reportedly temporarily halting the sale of kitchen knives.

The Swedish Free Times stated that the pair of African migrants were roommates, at a Swedish shelter for migrant aliens. After the attack, one African confessed to the killing, saying that the other African was only tagging along and was actually innocent, so police let the accompanist go.

It has been further reported that the African migrant murderer, had just left the Swedish Migration Agency, where he had been told that he would be deported to Italy soon. Apparently enraged, the African migrant went to IKEA with his buddy, sought out some native Swedes, and butchered them.

In a post murder psychiatric assessment, in which he was found quite sane, the killer said he **chose the "most Swedish-looking" victims he could find** *– adding, he was seeking revenge for Sweden's plans to deport him and that "if an enemy is bothering you, you have no choice but to defend yourself."*

Can you guess what the Swedish authorities did immediately following the butcher murders carried out in the presence of these newly arrived African migrants?

Did they, (1) quickly alert local communities, so that they could protect themselves, lest any other angry migrants decide to take out some more Swedes?

Did they, (2) go to alien asylums and warn migrants that they must follow Swedish laws, and that murdering, or butchering Swedes, to vent frustration, will not be tolerated?

Or, did they, (3) rush to see how they could help their own citizens, and the families of the innocent victims, cope with this atrocity?

Sorry. It was none of the above.

"Dark" forces in society

Following the random butchering murders of two of their own citizens, Swedish police quickly rushed to protect *migrant* communities. And what exactly did the Swedish police think, that the migrants needed protection from?

According to the Swedish Police, the migrants needed police protection from what the police called, "dark forces in society."

So migrants are involved in the killing of two of your own, and your response is to be all worried about, and rush to protect other migrants? Really? Think about it.

When the bloodthirsty African migrant murderer confessed to the double homicide, unbelievably, Swedish authorities stated, that even if convicted of the double homicide, the migrant would likely not be deported, since he had rights. You read that correctly.

Worse, some have speculated that, faced with deportation, the recently arrived African migrant murdered the Swedes to ensure that he would be incarcerated in Sweden. After all, Sweden has some of the world's most luxurious prisons, and the inmate would be assured gourmet food, leisure time, exercise rooms, entertainment centers, and so much more.

A revolting and extreme plan, to say the least, unless, of course, you're an angry violent migrant facing deportation with no real plans for the future...

The killer was convicted at the end of October 2015, given a life sentence, and told that after he served his sentence he would be deported.

Ok. You're thinking to yourself, what a mess, but at least there was some justice meted out, since after he finishes serving his "life sentence" he'll be dead. Right?

Well, it *is* Sweden, so he'll likely get a reduced sentence after spending some time in prison.
https://youtu.be/YhIrgcaaXS8
http://vlt.se/ikeamorden/1.3213362-mordarens-val-av-offer-de-sag-svenska-ut-

No worries

Eritrean migrants from Africa are the second largest group of asylum seekers in Sweden these days. Another famous Eritrean migrant from Africa that caused mischief in Sweden is Henok Weire Fre. Fre committed a most gruesome, brutal, and violent rape in 2007.

Although convicted, Fre's sentence was a mere 3 years. And before he could be expelled back to Africa, concerned activists rallied, and argued that Fre would certainly face *inhuman treatment* in his home country of Eritrea (treatment, no doubt, along the lines of the way he brutally raped his victim). So, in 2009, he was allowed to stay in Sweden even though no one knew how many more rapes he might have been responsible for in the past.

Crazy, right? *Yet, it gets so predictably worse...*

In 2011, Fre did what Fre does best. He committed yet another brutal assault rape. This convicted serial rapist, turned loose unnecessarily by a twisted system, brutally beat a woman walking home from work, dragged her into an elevator and viciously raped her. Beyond eyewitness identifications, Fre's DNA was found at the scene. Case closed.

Well, it might have been closed except Fre disappeared into the shadows. To this day, Fre remains at large, undoubtedly causing similar mischief wherever it is that he is these days.
http://www.d-intl.com/2015/08/13/ledare-varfor-vagrar-polisen-dementera-ryktet-om-halshuggning-pa-ikea/

Underwear protests
Did you hear the one about the 30 Syrian asylum seekers in Sweden who stripped to their underwear to protest not being able to compose music and not liking the climate?

I bet you didn't. Pull up a seat...

It was early 2015, and 30 Syrian migrants were being transported by coach bus to Grytan, near Östersund from Malmö. Once they arrived in Grytan, the Syrians wouldn't leave the bus. They demanded to return to Malmö. (Malmö is the third largest city in Sweden, and occupied by a majority of foreigners – that's right, native Swedes are now a minority in their country's third largest city.)

Making threats and issuing demands is serious business. So what exactly had so upset the migrants to "force" them to take such drastic measures?

Among the reasons the Syrian migrants gave for being disgusted by the idea of leaving Malmö to live near Östersund included:
- DANGEROUS ROADS
"I am 75 years old and come from the Middle East. Then I get sent to a place that looks like this," a man from Syria told Östersunds-Posten, pointing to the icy road. "It is dangerous for me to be here."

- INABILITY TO COMPOSE
"Normally I play music and write songs. That's not possible here, I become completely dead inside from living here."

- POOR LIVING CONDITIONS
"Yes, we don't demand much. But now we must live 8 in each room, people with different backgrounds and ages. It is cold outside and cold

in the rooms. I doubt that, for example, Germany treats its refugees like this."

ISSUANCE OF SYRIAN MIGRANT THREAT #1

The Syrian migrants also issued their first threat.

> "Either they take us out of here to a better establishment, or we start a hunger strike."

Interestingly, one of the migrants complained that living near Östersund would isolate him from the "service he had been expecting to get." Surprised by his claim, the reporter interviewing him revealed that she was from Östersund to which the migrant replied, "Yes, but we are Arabs. We cannot live here in this kind of weather."

Proper planning, son. Proper planning.
During their "protest" the migrants stripped to down to their designer underwear for reasons known only to them. Interneters seized the opportunity to republish the semi-nude photos with witty captions. On Twitter, one of the migrants was featured in a tweet that showed him clothed in a new expensive winter jacket. Many former migrants went on Twitter to express their disgust at the shenanigans, culminating with a Lebanese woman who travelled to Grytan simply to confront the migrants and yell at them.

Police refused to move the migrants for fear of upsetting the Swedish press and being called inhuman, racist, or worse. For two long days, the migrants held out until finally the Swedish officials apologized and agreed to return the migrants to Malmö within 3 months.

The migrants next staged a protest in the dining hall of their new home, demanding official certification from the Swedish Government, *in writing,* that they will receive apartments within 1-3 months in Malmö or Stockholm. That's when the migrants issued their next threat.

ISSUANCE OF SYRIAN MIGRANT THREAT #2

> "If we don't get written guarantees of apartments in Malmö or Stockholm we will leave and seek asylum in Norway or Finland."

Ok. Honestly, if I were the hostage negotiator on this one, I would immediately have prepared transport to Norway or Finland in an air-conditioned coach bus. I would have probably driven the bus myself. But no one dared think that in today's Sweden.

Speaking of driving the bus, the bus driver from the original transport reported that the migrants had stolen his laptop and had ruined his New Year's plans as he waited out the protest alone in a hotel. But to hell with the native Swedes. To hell with the citizens. Protecting the rights of migrants is where it's at.

By the way, there are many more instances of refugees refusing to get off buses at other shelter destinations because they found them not to their liking. From Trängslet to Limedsforsen, refugees were routinely refusing to accept shelters they deemed too remote or otherwise unattractive. Luckily, the Swedish Migration Board worked overtime kowtowing to refugees and negotiating with them, to coax them into trying out the new facilities.

Think about the raw spirit of privilege and entitlement that these migrants must have to issue the demands and threats that they came up with. And they're not even citizens yet.

Just you wait, Sweden, just you wait.
 http://swedishsurveyor.com/2015/01/02/yes-but-we-are-arabs-we-cannot-live-here-in-this-kind-of-weather/
 http://www.ltz.se/jamtland/ostersund/lt-tv-tumultartat-nar-flyktingprotester-mottes-av-kritik-i-grytan
 www.dt.se/dalarna/alvdalen/asylsokande-vagrar-lamna-bussen-i-trangslet

Private jets

Another story you likely "missed" is from mid-December 2014. Life is so incredibly good for migrants in Sweden, that some are actually sneaking in via private jets. No, seriously. Like a Cessna 680 luxury private jet. On December 15, 2014, a Cessna 680 touched down at around 9 pm at Malmö Airport. The passengers consisted of 10 "asylum seekers" from Beirut, Lebanon.

Does the mention of Beirut conjure up notions of a third world city languishing in decay, surrounded by war and poverty?

Wrong.

In 2009, the New York Times named Beirut as one of the *Top Places to Visit in the World*, and Lonely Planet called it one of the world's liveliest cities. Beirut is reportedly a comfortable if not pricey place to live. From its pristine beaches to its amazing cuisine and wonderful climate, Beirut was chosen as Conde Nast Traveler's best city in the Middle East and as one of the New 7 Wonders of Cities in 2014.

Which makes the whole "asylum seekers showing up in a private jet" thing that much more peculiar...

After some sort of Swedish police investigation into possible "people smuggling," the 10 "asylum seekers" were allowed to stay in Sweden while the two Egyptian pilots and a young Lebanese woman, who apparently staffed the flight, were released from custody and sent on their way. Back to the luxuries and comforts of Beirut, no doubt.

Only in Sweden...
http://www.svt.se/nyheter/regionalt/skane/piloterna-fick-resa-hem

When the stats are bad, stop publishing them

The last report, that indicated crime by ethnicity, was issued by the Swedish National Council for Crime Prevention in 2005. It showed that immigrants were 500% overrepresented. 500%! And that's a ten-year-old report relying on numbers that are 15-20 years old. In any case, under a humane and caring regime, such statistics would be made available to all citizens so they could act accordingly.

Instead, since 2005, no more such reports have been issued. Clearly it must have gotten SO MUCH WORSE! Or why not issue updates? Unless, maybe, the Swedish politicians, officials, and even the media have colluded to keep the truth about the destructive and violent consequences of Sweden's experiment with multiculturalism hidden.

Of course, citizen journalists on the internet might reveal the truth. Oh wait. Remember the story at the start of this chapter? Maybe that's why the spineless Swedish Parliament changed its Constitution. Gag the truth!

Think about it.
http://www.bra.se/download/18.cba82f7130f475a2f1800012697/2005_1 7_brottslighet_bland_personer_fodda_sverige_och_utlandet.pdf

The case of the 8 "Swedish" rapists
Or, how the old-fashioned-controlled-media spreads lies...

There is a popular Viking Line ferry that cruises between the Finnish port of Turku and Stockholm in Sweden. It is popular with Swedes and other tourists who can relax and party on the overnight voyage. The dark secret is that in the years 2006-2010, the number of rapes reported by ferry passengers has doubled.

In February 2015, there was yet another rape. The old-fashioned-controlled-media reported that "8 Swedes" were being questioned in relation to a violent gang rape of a Swedish woman on a Viking Line Ferry in Finnish waters. Media outlets trumpeted the "8 Swedish alleged rapists" sound bite and headline incessantly. In the meanwhile, they reported that 6 of the Swedes had been captured in Finland, while 2 of the Swedes had snuck back to Stockholm before being rounded up. One newspaper added that several of the 8 Swedes arrested had criminal records or other run-ins with the police.

Horrible that these evil Swedes were committing such heinous acts of abuse and violence. Shame on you Swedes! Shame!

Here is the one fact that the old-fashioned-controlled-media left out – they weren't Swedes.

Not one was a Swedish citizen! Not one!

Seven suspects were African Somalis, and one suspect was Iraqi. Of the four eventually charged with the brutal gang rape, all four were African Somali citizens and Muslims.

A culture where the media regularly deceives the public is a sign of worse things to come. Unbelievably, not one reporter saw a red flag when the "Swedish" rape suspects needed a Somali interpreter during their police questioning in Finland. Sadly, most of the public simply accepted what the media was saying, that 8 of their fellow Swedes had committed an unthinkably brutal and violent crime.

By intentionally mislabeling African citizens as Swedish citizens, it would almost seem that the media was trying desperately to hide the criminality of the violent migrants. The game plan couldn't be more clear. Protect the criminal migrants, and to hell with the victim!

And worse yet, not one journalist who intentionally deceived the public with the "8 Swedes" lie was ever fired for gross negligence. Not one was sued for damages. Not one was shamed for lying. No consequences! Isn't there a penalty for making up stuff and printing it as truth, when you KNOW the truth is something different?

Or have members of the media convinced themselves that by lying about the truth, covering up facts, and misleading the public, that they are somehow "noble champions" protecting the violent and criminal migrants from racism? *Really?*
http://www.thelocal.se/20150202/eight-swedes-questioned-over-ferry-gang-rape
http://snaphanen.dk/2015/02/08/sondagskronika-nar-journalister-valdtar/
http://www.msn.com/sv-se/nyheter/other/%C3%A5tta-svenskar-misst%C3%A4nks-f%C3%B6r-f%C3%A4rjev%C3%A5ldt%C3%A4kt/ar-AA8Rrmd

And the media cover-up has been going on a really long time.

Media intentionally uses deceptive artwork to hide facts
In 2004, after a brutal assault with a baton and brutal gang rape, two Swedish women clung to their lives and one underwent many surgeries. The four attackers were identified as "Swedish" and one media outlet even went through the trouble of *fabricating generic silhouette cutouts* to make the gang rapists appear to be "European."

Except, as you probably guessed by now, nothing could be further from the truth.

The four "European" gang rapists turned out to be African Somali migrants. In an all too familiar scenario, three of the rapists received mild punishment by the court.

What about the victims?

It's *never* about the victims so let's catch up with one of those lightly-sentenced gang rapists. Energetically, he went on to commit quite a few more brutal crimes. Then he was caught in 2010 repeatedly raping an 84-year-old woman in her home. Although the news made sure to report that the lawyer representing this serial rapist wanted everyone to know that his client "feels really bad," no one reported how the 84-year-old victim felt...

In the meanwhile, the media continues to try to hide all mention of ethnicity, save when they can eagerly announce a Swede has done something bad.

Sick. Really sick when the truth "needs" to be censored.
http://www.expressen.se/nyheter/23-aring-misstanks-for-valdtakt-pa-84-arig-kvinna/

Stop the deportation, I'm a Christian now! I profess I am now a devout follower of Joseph Christ. Or is it James Christ? Or, wait, wait, is it Jacob Christ? Wait, I can get this. Christ Christ?? Help me out here... You know, the one who leaps tall buildings, faster than a speeding train... Right? Hello? Why don't you believe me? Are you a *racist*?

In 2005, the rape of children under the age of 15 was reportedly 6 times as common as it was a generation ago in Sweden. It's only gotten worse. To that end, here is the particularly sickening story about a clever Muslim child rapist, Mohamed *(not his real name, but a pseudonym assigned by a news reporter)*, who figured out a loophole at the zero hour.

Even though this 21-year-old Afghan asylum seeker, who snuck into Sweden in 2010, had been denied asylum and was supposed to be deported, like so many others, he slipped through the cracks and wandered around Sweden.

In 2013, 21-year-old Mohamed, the Afghan illegal migrant, got a 14-year-old Swedish girl crazy-drunk in a parking lot and proceeded to brutally rape and assault her while she was "practically unconscious." The court sentenced him rather lightly (2½ years) due to his tender young age of 21, but also added deportation for ten years.

At some point while serving his sentence, the clever Afghan child rapist again applied for permanent residence, but with a twist. After the rape arrest, Mohamed claimed that he had converted from Islam to Christianity. Since he would be persecuted in Afghanistan for being Christian, he demanded asylum in Sweden and insisted on no deportation. The perfect plan!

Save for one small little insignificant detail.

Unfortunately, Mohamed couldn't answer even the most basic questions about his new religion, Christianity, during his asylum hearings.

It was almost like he was making the whole thing up...

Possibly a bit panicked, Mohamed then also threw in the fact that he *deserved* asylum since he had impregnated his cousin when he was 11 years old, and if he was deported to Afghanistan, that impregnation could cause problems for him. And now that he was also a "Christian convert," *oh boy* would that be tough...

Swedish authorities were skeptical and denied his newest request for asylum. So *bye-bye*? Case closed? *By now you know the answer to that question...*

Mohamed appealed! Seriously. This convicted child rapist who still couldn't answer basic questions about his "new" religion, appealed! And the Swedish Migration Court granted Mohamed *permanent residency* as well as *welfare support for life.*

Swedish taxpayers, who will foot the bill for this debacle, have just got to be SO proud! So VERY proud!

Wait! Not done yet!

The District Court then reversed the decision based on some *timed residency requirements*, so Mohamed will have to wait a bit longer to see if he fulfills his dream of permanent tax-funded residency on Swedish welfare. We bet he will be successful. Remember, protect the violent criminal migrants.

As to the victim? Apparently, to hell with the victim, yet again.
http://www.friatider.se/ahmed-21-v-ldtog-svensk-flicka-fick-permanent-uppeh-llstillst-nd-trots-att-han-var-d-md-till

A slice here, a stab there
In 2005, police caught a 21-year-old "young man" who had arrived in Sweden a few years prior. Seems he was going to dance clubs looking for sex, hitting on women, and slashing or knifing them if they rejected his aggressive advances.

He cut and slashed no less than 8 different women.

There have been many attacks like these, with women suffering long wounds, some requiring as many as 36 stitches. Police also said that this "young man" was furthermore accused of raping a girl at a private party, and molesting another woman in an apartment.

Not surprisingly, the charming migrant referred to Swedish women as "whores" and "sluts."
http://www.expressen.se/nyheter/knivskar-dem-som-nobbat-honom/

Pools and migrant predators
In 2005, at the Husby public swimming pool in Stockholm, a 17-year-old Swedish girl was raped as 30 people milled about. According to published reports, the girl was approached first by a 16-year-old boy who molested her in a hot tub. The girl got away from her attacker, but he followed her, cornered her, tore off her bikini, and raped her, aided by his accomplice. The victim said people just stared, and no one came to her aid.

After a trial and conviction, the 16-year-old migrant rapist was ordered to pay about $9,800 to the girl for her pain and suffering and was sentenced to three months of "youth custody," but was released because of his young age. Why risk tarnishing the reputation and future prospects of a youngster? And his accomplice? He wasn't sentenced. The young people were positively coddled. How generous.

And the victim?

Things didn't work out so great for her. The girl was in a psychiatric center. After the rape, she couldn't sleep anymore. She had recurring nightmares. She suffered from panic attacks and debilitating anxiety. Oh, and she tried to commit suicide multiple times.

But, it's never about the victim.
http://www.aftonbladet.se/nyheter/article10720801.ab

And we're no way near done.

When pre-teens attack
Do you remember good old Trollhättan? Where the Muslim intern refused to shake his supervisor's hand because she was a woman? And then got paid a load of money to settle his discrimination allegation?

In July 2014, in Trollhättan, there had been maybe a dozen or more sexual assaults. Police worked hard to solve the cases. What they found was sickening. It wasn't the work of separate rapists or sexual predators. It wasn't a psycho lone nut. And it wasn't a gang of savage teens.

Nope. This time it was little children. Seriously.

A gang of pre-teen migrant boys, ages 8-12, were discovered by police to be responsible for *no less than* 8 of the cases of sexual assault.

8- to 12-year-old little boys. Think about that.

And the little migrants had no shame or fear. Police said that the dangerous deviants would gather in groups of around 5 boys, and would target young girls whom they would surround and sexually assault, usually in public places.

The victims were young girls 10-16 years-old. While they were at it, the gang also targeted some adults for verbal abuse and to spit at.

Ultimate *Get-Out-of-Jail-Free* card
Luckily for the "misguided" boys, police said that there couldn't be any "criminal proceedings" since the youngsters were so young. With Sweden's criminal age of responsibility pegged at 15 years of age, little 8-, 9-, 10-, 11-, and 12-year-olds are apparently pretty much free to do as they please, including raping and sexually assaulting girls.

Shame about all the emotionally and physically scarred victims! That's the one group that is *consistently* left flapping in the wind.

But by now you know that it's never about the victims.
http://www.thelocal.se/20140714/pre-teen-boys-behind-sex-assault-spree

The more you look, the more you find.

You can go swimming, but refrain from raping
Back to the Husby public swimming pool in Stockholm. Now it was 2011. A Swedish family was having a party for their 11-year-old girl and her similarly aged friends.

At some point, about 20 African and Arab 17-year-old asylum seekers from the Attendo Care refugee camp arrived. Attendo staff reported that they had held a meeting with the asylum seekers prior to the trip to the pool and explained to them that *they had to control themselves and not rape or molest girls in the pool in any way.* Nonetheless, when the migrants saw the 11- and 12-year-old girls, they made sexual advances. Then they grabbed at the terrified little girls, sexually molesting them.

Police would later claim that only 5-7 of the migrants actually molested the children and the migrants *only* "touched the back, legs, and butts of the little girls."

On the other hand, internet reports, including a report in the European Union Times, told of migrants tearing the swimsuits off the terrified youngsters, that several little boys who tried to protect the little girls were beaten by the migrants, and that as the young girls tried to escape they were cornered as the assault escalated. Internet reports also alleged that at least one of the 11-year-old girls was raped by the migrants. An alert lifeguard allegedly was able to stop the assaults.

Arriving police looked into the event, found that the migrants didn't have any identification with them, and no arrests were made, adding some credence to the version that no child was "technically raped." But since even the police admitted that migrants groped and touched and grabbed at the private parts of 11- and 12-year-old girls, shouldn't there be some sort of punishment? Apparently not.

The EU Times also added that with each migrant costing Swedish taxpayers about $150,000 annually to accommodate, angry Swedes are asking if it was worth the millions of dollars they spent on these child molesters to keep them in Sweden.

Great question.
http://www.eutimes.net/2011/03/20-refugees-suspected-of-gang-rape-at-stockholm-public-swimming-pool/
http://www.thelocal.se/20110301/32336

"Unprecedented in Swedish criminal history"
In 2012, seven young Afghan men with an average age of 22 were sentenced to prison for the brutal December 2011 marathon 7-hour-long gang rape of a 29-year-old mother of two young children.

A group of possibly a dozen migrants at a refugee housing center in Mariannelund decided to get themselves a Swedish girl to rape. One of the migrants went off and lured the woman to the apartment complex.

A lifetime of second-chances
The young and naïve Swedish mother of two didn't know it, but the friendly migrant tasked with luring her had previously been convicted of raping a young woman in 2008, had done two years in prison, but was allowed to stay in Sweden by the generous and forgiving Swedish authorities especially since this trustworthy soul claimed to be less than 15 years-of-age when he came to Sweden. And he had been investigated for the 2011 rape of another woman. Also in 2011 he was likewise convicted of assault, unlawful threat, unlawful disposal, use of counterfeit documents, drug crimes, drunken driving, and driving without a license. And in 2010, he was convicted of drug offenses. And in 2008, he was convicted of assaulting a former girlfriend after he threatened to kill her, calling her a "whore," "slut," and "racist." Busy in 2008, he was convicted of assault, illegal threats, and violent resistance. Not quite done in 2008, he committed another rape. And in 2006, he had been sentenced for fraud and abuse. And in 2004, he had been sentenced for assault. *And that's just what he was caught doing.*

Amazing how busy this migrant had been since arriving in Sweden to seek asylum from the troubles in Afghanistan.

This convicted rapist dropped the woman off at what she thought was just a party at an asylum center apartment hosted by some asylum-seeking refugees. Quickly, things got violent.

Without warning, a group of Afghan asylum seekers dragged the woman into a bedroom and held her down. At least seven, and maybe up to nine, men brutally gang raped her repeatedly as she struggled and thrashed. The woman recalled that the migrants were "clapping their hands and laughing" and no one tried to help her. The rapists apparently called her a "whore" as they ganged up, took turns assaulting her, did drugs, partied, and drank alcohol during the attack.

When the young convicted rapist migrant that had brought the woman to the "party" returned to the apartment some time later and saw what was happening, *he immediately joined in and raped her as well.* According to court documents, he also raped her again after the gang rape was over and while she was quite incapacitated.

The assault itself was too graphic, gruesome, and brutal to describe in detail. And it lasted 7 long torturous hours. This prompted the prosecutor to call it the "most gruesome rape marathon in the history of Sweden."

The victim eventually escaped after some men left and others fell asleep. She alerted police who investigated and gathered evidence.

While all the men said they were "innocent," massive amounts of DNA evidence from the woman's body and at the crime scene helped to convict them. The youngest who claimed to be under 21 got 4 ½ years. The other gang rapists got prison time from 6 to 6 ½ years.

And what about the victim?

Some papers didn't report on her condition but did say she would be entitled to a bit over $40,000 in restitution. Other news sources reported that she had gone into shock during the attack and had been "heavily traumatized" ever since. Allegedly she is wheelchair-bound "due to damages to her abdomen, and suffers from fecal incontinence." She also was suffering severe mental stress and was under psychiatric care.

This case was apparently so horrific that even the old-fashioned-controlled-media steered clear of making any stupid explanations or excuses. Instead, they simply turned their attention elsewhere, which is almost as effective.

Ignore it. Out of sight, out of their minds.
http://www.thelocal.se/20120411/40208
https://parnassen.wordpress.com/2012/03/14/atta-pa-en-kvinna-valdtakten-i-mariannelund-vi-ska-hamta-en-tjej-och-knulla/

Bored and just killing time
In March 2015, a pair of Afghan men, at least one who had lived in Sweden for more than a year in Malmö, and one with a prior drug conviction, were bored.

To occupy their time, the two men decided to abduct a Swedish woman – which is what they did. Then they decided to imprison her in an apartment in Malmö. Then they thought they should rape her. And for a torturous *week*, they brutally gang-raped the imprisoned woman.

While the police were very close-lipped about the details of the case, the prosecutor said the two Afghans committed the gang-rape "jointly and in concert with others." Clearly, other rapists were thought to be involved.

Oh. My. Living. God.
http://www.friatider.se/kvinna-h-lls-inl-st-och-gruppv-ldtogs-i-en-vecka

A shoulder to lean on
During the summer of 2015, a 23-year-old woman was sitting on a park bench in Södermalm island crying.

Two young male migrants from Africa approached her and attempted to cheer her up by taking her to a nearby lookout point from which you can see the natural beauty of the Stockholm area.

Clearly, by now, you sadly know where this is going.

After consoling her for a bit, the young African men suddenly became violent, threw the woman to the ground, beat her savagely, tore off her clothes, and began gang raping her.

The attackers also phoned some African migrant friends to join in and in the end the woman told police she had been gang raped by at least four different rapists "six times by the group, some of which laughed at her during the savage attack."

As the woman received medical treatment, police K-9 dogs found three of the African gang rapists in a nearby refugee shelter. The men, who appeared to be 15-18 years old, had no identification and claimed to be 13-16, likely hoping to get lighter sentences. Two denied the rape altogether. Sadly for them, DNA evidence proved they were lying. The remaining attacker testified he had met the woman while walking home from his mosque and insisted it was all consensual. Ultimately, the court gave the 2 deniers six months detention and the other rapist got nine months.

6 months? 9 months? That's all? Seriously?

Oh. Wait. How about the victim?

The woman said that her attackers' ridiculously short sentences were "sick," that she felt "bloody awful" after the attack, and now has to live the rest of her life with some permanent injuries.

Is anyone else feeling sick? Prepare to get sicker.

It was later revealed that medical assessments proved that at least two of the youngsters were in fact adults over the age of 18. But they were still treated as children since the court could not definitively decide that they were adults. Far worse, one of the rapists was eventually *completely exonerated*, not because he was innocent, but because the Court of Appeals decided that "one of the men should be completely cleared of rape because it has not been proven that he was over 15 when the crime was committed because he completely lacked identity documents."

The court even chose to not take into consideration the fact that the now-former-rapist migrant had, himself, declared he was over 15 during an asylum investigation. Screw the facts, exonerate him!

It really is all about protecting the migrants. *Seriously, you can't make this stuff up.*
http://www.aftonbladet.se/nyheter/krim/article21984148.ab
www.exponerat.net/hovratten-friar-ensamkommande-valdtaktsman-pga-att-hans-alder-inte-kan-faststallas

Yet another party invitation
In December 2015, Fria Tider ran the story of a 45-year-old Swedish woman that had survived a brutal and ruthless gang rape by about a half dozen Eritreans migrants in an apartment in Ludvika in August. It seems the Swedish woman was simply waiting in an apartment building common area for a friend to arrive when eight African migrants invited her to wait in their apartment where they were having a party.

Sadly, by now, you know the way this will likely end.

The woman accepted the invitation but soon decided she should leave and said she'd continue to wait for her friend elsewhere. Instantly, the Eritreans threw her to the floor and held her down. As they raped her, the victim said that they "laughed... and had great fun." She also testified that "it felt like fingers and hands were everywhere. Fingers penetrated both my vag**a and an**. It was very painful. I felt their nails."

And the brutal gang rape continued until two migrants started fighting over whose turn it was to rape the woman next. During this distraction, the victim tried to escape but one of the African migrants smashed her in the head with a cooking pot and knocked her unconscious. After she came to, the terrified and distraught woman threw herself out a window to escape, and reached a neighbor who called police.

Since the court couldn't determine exactly who had done what to the woman, and one African even testified that he had been forced to rape the woman while blindfolded so he couldn't offer any details, in the end only one of the six alleged rapists was convicted of rape. He got 5 years. His other buddies got away with 10 month sentences for failure to disclose the rape.
http://www.friatider.se/sex-eritreaner-d-ms-f-r-v-ldt-kt

Blackmail
At the same time Swedish police were warning that a trend towards filming or recording gang rapes was developing. Rapists would use the footage to blackmail or silence their victims, many who were girls only 14- to 15-years-old, some as young as 12.

What a living nightmare for the often very young victims!
http://www.friatider.se/flyktingbarn-f-r-l-ga-straff-f-r-bestialisk-gruppv-ldt-kt
http://www.thelocal.se/20151106/teens-sentenced-for-gang-rape-on-hipster-island

When it gets this commonplace...
And don't think that living with the looming threat of rape hasn't impacted some minds. Teenage entrepreneur Nadja Björk, a girl from northern Sweden, began thinking of ways to protect women upon learning of an active rapist in a neighboring town who raped women over the period of 5 years. Her fear of being the next rape victim spawned creativity. Nadja invented a chastity buckle. Worn on a regular belt on your pants, the special buckle locking mechanism is designed to keep an attacker from opening your belt quickly and easily – *it takes quite a bit of effort and two-handed skill to get it open* – and as Nadja says, "it gives the victim a chance to fight back, scream, and use other products for protection."
https://fashionagainstrape.wordpress.com/

Migrants complain some more
In the meanwhile, migrants have long been unhappy with the terrible treatment they claim they are getting at the hands of "useless Swedes." In 2011, in a small town in Sweden, African migrants from Somalia staged a loud protest in the streets demanding free housing, more money, justice, and better services.

Holding up signs saying "STOP EVICTIONS," the mob was also upset that some Somalis had been evicted from housing for not paying their rent. The whole "you have to pay for what you use" concept seems to continue to elude some migrants.
https://youtu.be/2IDBxPLp3i0

40 long endless minutes of pure sadistic torture
In 2012, while Swedish media aggressively covered stories of alleged discrimination and harassment of Somali immigrants in parts of Sweden, a gang of immigrants, led by a Somali immigrant male, robbed a Swedish teenager, tortured him, and left him to die after setting him on fire.

According to a hospital bedside interview, the burned and scarred teen victim told of his harrowing ordeal at the hands of attackers. He had been waiting for a bus near Stockholm after a night out with friends. Having dozed off, he awoke to three immigrants robbing and beating him.

According to Sweden's news outlet *The Local*, "then he was subjected to 40 minutes of torture by his three attackers, who were aged 16, 18 and 23," eventually leaving with the victim's bank card and pin number. But they soon returned to continue their brutal attack after unsuccessfully trying to use the card.

They allegedly stole the teen's jacket and shoes and continued their nightmarish beating of the boy. They dragged him off into the nearby woods. "They kept kicking me in the head and the upper body until I almost passed out," recalled the bandaged teen.

But it was about to get so much worse.

The teen remembered feeling wetness on his back and smelling lighter fuel, only to realize to his horror that he was on fire, and that "my back and my hair were burning." As the teen struggled, the Somali attacker ordered him to "let it burn," and stepped on the back of the victim's neck to let the flames take hold. Miraculously, the teen was able to break free and rolled to extinguish the fire. Shirtless, beaten, and suffering from severe burns, the boy was somehow able to find his way to a house for help.

The boy's whole body was covered in abrasions and bruises. He was hospitalized in intensive care to treat the severe damage to his scalp, neck, spine, and other areas where he was burned. He also ended up needing skin transplants and grafts.

Three immigrants, including the Somali, were eventually arrested for the attack. After trial, the Somali was sentenced to only 5 years 9 months prison time, which included a separate charge for "threats against an officer" stemming from death threats the Somali apparently made against police while in custody. In addition, he is supposed to pay the victim around $14,400 in damages, and will be expelled from Sweden for a period of 20 years after serving his prison time.

During the trial, the Somali claimed innocence, stating that while he actually did "aid and abet" in the robbery, he wasn't the one who used violence. He couldn't explain why his jeans were covered in the victim's blood. Then, he blamed one of his two friends for actually burning the victim. He described how the other two assailants participated in the crime.

In the end, the Somali was found guilty of two counts of aggravated assault, robbery, and making "threats against an officer."

And what about his two buddies, the other two accomplices?

Apparently, throwing the book at one immigrant had been hard enough for the Swedish court. To convict *all* of the perpetrators would have been just impossible.

So even though the convict had implicated his accomplices, and all the evidence and ATM videos and the rest pointed to collusion, and the *teen victim identified the attackers,* the other two suspects were completely exonerated!

That's right. Completely free to go and do more of whatever it is they do.

What in the world happened?

Well, the two accomplices turned the tables in their favor when they revealed that they, too, would have suffered injury had they not "tried to save the victim's life." And it seems the court was all too happy to believe that these robbers had actually spent all their time trying to keep the violence to a minimum.

When asked about the testimony of his two newly crowned "protectors," the teen victim said that they "just sat there and lied, I was angry and wanted to tell them." But he never got the opportunity. They walked out free men.

As to the most violent of the three? The victim said, "Now he cannot hurt anyone for five years." Well, maybe 5 years is better than nothing, considering the victim has lifelong scars and limited use of his right arm – doctors feel the damage will be permanent.
http://svenssonsfortvivlan.blogspot.com/2012/09/somalis-torture-set-teen-on-fire-and.html
http://www.thelocal.se/discuss/index.php?showtopic=53267
http://www.aftonbladet.se/nyheter/article15640926.ab

Military NOT welcome at public holiday celebration
June 6 is Swedish National Day, a public holiday annually celebrated to commemorate King Vasa who is credited with founding modern Sweden in 1523 when Sweden became

independent from Danish influence. Celebrations, flags, parades, singing, the works. But more recently, the day has been used to "welcome new Swedes" (immigrants) into the fold. Some groups even mark the day by burning Swedish flags.

In 2015, it was reported that the Swedish Armed Forces, Försvarsmakten, that often participate in Swedish National Day celebrations, were *no longer welcome* at the festivities in the municipality of Umeå. According to the official letter uninviting them, the presence of the Försvarsmakten could "undermine the celebration of the new Swedes."

And why is that?
https://www.swedishweekly.com/swedish-armed-forces-not-welcome-at-national-day-celebration/

Flying an Israeli flag gets a man beaten
In 2014, a man who displayed a small Israeli flag in Malmö, almost paid for it with his life. Apparently the man had a dispute with a group of "people" after he hung the small Israeli flag in the window of his apartment. The group smashed his windows.

When the man went outdoors, the group of about a dozen people beat him with iron pipes, according to police. He was hospitalized with serious injuries. The police suspected this was a hate crime and officially noted that the man "was attacked because of the flag." As the Jewish Telegraphic Agency noted, Malmö has about 300,000 residents, one third of them are "born in Muslim countries or whose parents were born in those countries." And the kicker? It now appears the victim wasn't even Jewish.

He was reportedly a Kurd who just supports Israel.
http://www.sydsvenskan.se/Malmö/grov-misshandel-pa-seved/
http://www.jta.org/2014/07/07/news-opinion/world/man-beaten-in-Malmö-for-hanging-israeli-flag
http://www.frontpagemag.com/point/235768/sweden-muslims-beat-man-wiron-pipes-hanging-daniel-greenfield

Boom, boom, boom
Sweden is becoming Europe's Detonation Capital as grenade and bomb attacks rock its streets on a fairly regular basis.

Remember Malmö, Sweden's third largest city? Where about 41% of the people are of foreign background? By July 2015, at least 18 explosions had already rocked Malmö. That was on track to be a huge increase over 2014's 25 explosions. By mid-September 2015, a reported 40 detonations from hand grenades and bombs had rocked Malmö. While violent incidents between the city's Kurds and Turks were commonplace, the police, true-to-form, didn't often comment on any possible connections. Maybe all the hand grenades and bombs are simply attributable to spontaneous combustion.

And that's just in *one* city.

Wait. Wait. Wait...

Explosions in Sweden? Loads of them? Now that's something my travel agent didn't mention...

Not just any old explosions. Hand grenades, pipe bombs, big bombs, car bombs. A Syrian refugee living in Malmö said it was "like being back in Syria." Most shockingly, the violence has become so commonplace that the papers rarely devote much space to the many regular attacks.

Can you even imagine living in a city where arson, stabbings, bombings, shootings, and grenade attacks are so regular that they are largely ignored or downplayed by the old-fashioned-controlled media? Seriously?

Worse yet, the police and the old-fashioned-controlled-media don't report on who is behind the attacks or what they are trying to accomplish with their bombings.

When people are caught, details are sanitized to the point of absurdity. In one case a young male bomber was arrested but due to his young age, details were blocked. Of course, the old-fashioned-controlled-media and the police did remind the public not to be racist, xenophobic, haters and blame immigrants.

Don't. Blame. The. Migrants. For. Anything. Ever!
https://youtu.be/t1pUXh5xCjM
http://www.aftonbladet.se/nyheter/article21171816.ab
http://www.thelocal.se/20150723/malm-attacks-part-of-spiral-of-retaliation
http://www.expressen.se/kvallsposten/15-aring-gripen-for-bomb-pa-rosengard/
http://www.aftonbladet.se/nyheter/article21403714.ab

Have a year-end blast

At the end of December 2015, a huge explosion rocked a commercial district in Helsingborg. The explosive device caused extensive damage to many buildings in an area where a hand grenade had been detonated in the fall.

The Swedish bomb squad ruled out a hand grenade this time, and determined that the blast had been likely caused by a much stronger explosive. Police added that the bombing was, "a heinous act against our people and our society."

Amazingly, there were no reported injuries.

And there were yet no suspects.
www.hd.se/lokalt/helsingborg/2015/12/28/kraftig-explosion-i-klubblokal/

Fireworks, migrant-style
Who would have thought to repurpose fireworks as weapons?

New Year's Eve 2016 featured some fireworks and rocket attacks in Helsinborg aimed at the Dalhem School and the Wieselgren School. Reportedly, the Dalhem school had damage including broken windows and a smoke condition, but escaped fire. A car was apparently also set on fire Blåkullagatan. Sadly, none of these were isolated events.

On December 26, 2015, Smålandsposten newspaper reported that a substantial amount of fireworks were stolen from a shipping container in Växjö in the afternoon.

Later on that night, large gangs of violent youths started fires and when police and emergency services responded, the young migrant males fired rockets at police and firefighters in Växjö. They tried to blind police officers by shining laser lights into their eyes. They also heaved stones and rocks at the officers.

Understaffed and overwhelmed, police called it a "violent riot" as they called for emergency reinforcements. Even when additional units from three towns arrived, police were hesitant to confront the ferocious and unruly youths, and waited for things to calm down.

After a security guard in the area was attacked and stoned, police issued warnings to security companies, taxi companies, and home health care workers not to enter the area. One witness on the scene told reporters, "There is total chaos with rockets everywhere." After many hours of violent rioting, police announced that the rioters had calmed down and that one 20-year-old male had been "arrested on suspicion of rioting and assault."

In late 2014, reportedly gangs of violent youngsters, 13-15 years of age, attacked people with fireworks and firecrackers in Norrköping. When the police responded, they were fired upon and attacked as well. In late 2015, the youngsters were at it again in Norrköping., throwing stones and shooting fireworks at people and buildings, injuring at least one person. They also decided to try their hand at arson and started fires.

When police responded, the young people stoned them and shot at them with fireworks.

But, clearly, none of this is a trend or pattern.
http://www.hd.se/lokalt/helsingborg/2016/01/01/fler-raketer-i-dalhemskolan/
www.smp.se/vaxjo/fyrverkerier-stals-ur-container/
www.smp.se/vaxjo/polisen-beskjuten-med-raketer-och-gron-laser/
http://swedishonlinearticle.blogspot.com/2014/12/young-people-shot-at-people-with.html

Top cop tells it like it is
In August 2015, the Swedish press reported that according to retired Chief Superintendent Elofsson (42 years on the Malmö police force), crime in Sweden was up and that criminals in Malmö had taken crime to a new level – routine and regular use of hand grenades, shootings, and increased drug sales. The spike in crime was alleged to be enabled by a liberal criminal policy, flourishing migrant criminal activity, and a "political hesitation when it comes to giving police and prosecutors the resources they need."

With the criminals having the upper hand, police morale was sinking pretty low and apathy was taking over. Malmö was (and is) seriously dangerous, and only getting worse. All of this adds to the lessening of the quality of life, the deterioration of an area, a concept any rookie cop will attest to... While everyone was distracted by and busy chasing the "big" problems, lesser offences were allowed to slip, so "vandalism, graffiti, littering, traffic offenses, and minor disturbances" usually went uninvestigated. Chip, chip, chip. *Crack...*

The ex-Chief also thought that one of the things the Malmö police needed to do was to *concentrate on stopping the hand grenade menace.*

Yeah. Pretty much.
http://www.sydsvenskan.se/opinion/aktuella-fragor/Malmö-bor-bli-forst-i-landet-med-en-kommunal-polis/

3 strikes
The owners a long-established local Malmö grocery store finally gave up. After being robbed 3 times within a short period of time they closed down.

2015 saw about a 15% increase in robberies in Sweden, and store robberies involving guns increased 36%. Of all robberies in Sweden, 45% targeted grocery stores. With odds like these, it is no wonder that the owners had enough. The last robbery which was particularly violent sealed their fate as the migrant robbers used knives during their robbery, threw one owner in a stairwell, and beat the other store owner bloody.

Sometimes, the writing on the wall is HUGE.
www.exponerat.net/tvingas-stanga-kvartersbutiken-efter-tre-ran/

Schools under attack
In March 2015, Varner Rydén, a junior high school in Malmö was closed due to a high incidence of crime and violence following the addition of students from a troubled school, Örtagård, that had been closed down the year prior. While the teacher's union fought against adding the students from the problem school to Varner Rydén, it was done anyway for "cost-saving reasons."

Threats, violence, and even visiting adult criminals were just some of the things that led to chaos. The teacher's union said Varner Rydén had become too dangerous for students and teachers, and that "Fighting among the students means that security can't be guaranteed." Union officials also stated that, "It has been unstable for some time now... There hasn't been as much progress as we would have liked to see for it to feel like a safe place to work." An administrator added, "Some groups of students spread so much trouble that teachers can't handle it."

Bureaucrats in Malmö were looking into hiring private security firms to police troubled schools. In the meanwhile, the school

reopened under "new management" and claimed fewer reports of violence.
http://www.stockholmnews.net/index.php/sid/230691629
http://www.thelocal.se/20150301/malm-school-too-dangerous-for-students

Racist Swedes just don't understand migrant privilege

In November 2015, KvällsPosten reported that the Grönkulla School in Alvesta was closed down. Apparently, the school principal had received threats via social media and police were onsite. One parent was quoted as saying that "there is apparently a lynch atmosphere in Alvesta today." The school website claimed vandalism was responsible for the closing after 24 windows were broken. There were also reported illegal threats, harassment, and defamation against municipal employees.

Threats. Police. Lockdowns. What in the world happened?

Plenty. According to the Fria Tider news site, the parents of several young girls attending the middle school were complaining to school officials about allegedly highly inappropriate and aggressive sexual behavior by several Somali migrant male students.

In particular, the parents of one 12-year-old Swedish girl attending the school complained to school management that their daughter was being aggressively sexually harassed by another student, a Somali migrant boy. It got so bad that the father of this Swedish victim went to school authorities with his allegations of sexual groping and his concerns. The father said he "had a meeting with the teacher and the deputy headmaster." Surely, that would solve everything.

Here come the explanations and excuses. Ready?

The father was reportedly told that "boys will be boys" and that "they are driven by their curiosity, and a lot is happening in their bodies." The father stated he would be going to the police to make a report, but the deputy headmaster allegedly said *that he did not need to involve the police*, and that the school "would take care of it."

You may have already guessed, this will not end well for the naïve and trusting native Swedes.

Unbelievable, instead of providing for the safety of the girls, the deputy headmaster reportedly also noted that she felt that "human equality" was the issue and suggested that the concerns of the father and the other parents were due to their prejudice and racial stereotyping. She further reportedly lectured the worried parents that there is no dividing them into "us and them" and that "we must keep this on an individual level." Empowered and full of righteous indignation, Ms. Deputy Headmaster then made the fateful, and some would say reckless, decision to allow two of the African boys in question to continue attending the school.

And now you have likely guessed this will not end up well for the little Swedish girls.

Fria Tider reported that soon after, while the two girls were playing in the schoolyard, the two African boys attacked again. This time one boy was successful and reportedly raped the 12-year-old girl behind some bushes. The other African boy grabbed the other girl and attempted to rape her behind some cars but she was able to escape when other people walked by.

The father of the girl who had been raped phoned the school and was allegedly met with a "total indifference to what happened." When he told Ms. Deputy Headmaster he would be keeping his daughter safe at home until the predators had been removed from the school, can you guess what response he got?

Oh, it so much more twisted than you can imagine. Maybe not.

Reportedly, Ms. Deputy Headmaster suddenly turned the tables on him and "threatened the parents with legal consequences" warning that "there is actually compulsory schooling." The father was quoted lamenting that, "she showed no respect whatsoever for our children at all, but it was compulsory school attendance that mattered."

Although police were conducting a criminal investigation into charges of child rape and sexual molestations, regardless of what the evidence eventually might show, the African boys had zero chance of being tried in a court because they both claimed to be under the age of 15.

Referring to the authorities at the school, the girl's father said that they feel free to "spit on us because we are Swedes."

He added that *had* his daughter dared to utter any anti-migrant sentiments there would have been an instant "outcry" and that the school would have "contacted social services at once, and (my daughter) would had gotten a special training course to learn how to think and believe." Start contrast to the school's non-response to charges of sexual molestation and assault.

Predictably, Ms. Deputy Headmaster hid from reporters' questions and instead issued a written response stating –
> "The investigation into the incident lies with other authorities. The school takes action when something happens so everyone involved should feel safe. We have not been able to answer questions at the individual level because of confidentiality."

In the meanwhile, after such blatant insanity, and a sneaking suspicion that the school administration had firmly sided with the perpetrators, quite a few families reportedly expressed their decision to pull their children out of the school. Parents also supposedly felt betrayed saying the school had never informed them of the brewing problems and what was being done (if anything) to safeguard their children.

Remember the rule – protect the migrants over everyone else, at all times, and in all circumstances.
http://www.expressen.se/kvallsposten/skola-i-alvesta-stangd--ledningen-fortegna/
http://www.friatider.se/rektorn-bortf-rklarade-tafsningarna-pojkar-r-pojkar-sen-v-ldtog-ali-sin-klasskamrat-p-skolg-rden

Nonsense & poison gas

None of what is going on in Sweden is much of a secret to the locals. It is just never discussed openly and honestly.

In 2010, a journalist for Swedish Television, who had worked as a social worker for a decade, came forward and revealed that he found that over the course of 25 years, over 80% of the "refugees" granted permanent residence in Sweden were classified neither as refugees nor as in need of protection. He called Sweden's claim to be accepting refugees due to a duty to "protect the most vulnerable" – *a complete load of nonsense.* He also claimed that the politicians and media outlets perpetuated the fairytale. He was disappointed and ashamed of the press for not revealing the truth to Swedes and the world, but understood that to expose any of the shenanigans would be financial and career suicide.

As a social worker, he initially wanted to expose what he saw but said he quickly learned to keep his nose down. He turned a blind eye as he granted "asylum seekers" *vacation visas* to the very countries from which they claimed to have *escaped* or *fled.*

> To *vacation* in a country that you claim that you *fled from* is clearly a new concept. How does that work?

The social-worker-turned-reporter also admitted to approving and paying welfare to foreigners whom he suspected had jobs off the books. (*So the migrants were collecting welfare checks funded by taxpayers while getting paid cash for jobs and not paying taxes. How can that be?*) He admitted that he played along in order to "avoid unpleasant confrontations." He also said, as a social worker, he lacked both the experience and the courage to stand up and expose the system.

Then, as a journalist, he claimed he was specifically told how stories involving immigrants were to be handled by his editor. Also, he said it was understood that it was good to make audiences sympathize with refugees and never to dig too deeply into any other sides of the story.

He said that political correctness in Sweden had destroyed any debate like a "poison gas." And he added that the "dreaded label *xenophobe/racist* still works as a choke and deters many" from discussing the truth.

The staggering costs to Sweden for their work with migrants has been questioned time and time again. The reporter said that untold billions are spent annually yet municipalities reported in the early 2000s that after a half decade, only 50% of migrant men and only about 35% of migrant women had gotten legal jobs, leaving the rest on the welfare rolls.

Well, there you go.
http://www.dn.se/debatt/journalisterna-morklagger-sanningen-om-invandrarna/

Migrants free to chant violence
In October 2015, hundreds of "Boycott Israel" protesters took to the streets of Malmö and were videotaped "chanting in Arabic about slaughtering Jews and stabbing soldiers."

The Israeli Ambassador to Sweden, Isaac Bachman, posted a video of the protesters. Writing about the video, Bachman's wife said, "Swedish people: Is this what you believe in? Is this what you bargained for? Are these your morals? Since I know the answers I feel ashamed in your name." In the meanwhile, Israel sent loads of monetary aid to help refugees but also built walls – and hasn't accepted any of the current refugees into their nation.

Maybe Sweden should study Israel's approach and learn a thing or two.
http://www.jpost.com/Arab-Israeli-Conflict/Protesters-in-Malmö-chant-slaughter-the-Jews-427534?utm_source=dlvr.it&utm_medium=twitter

Ingrid lays bare Sweden's lack of native culture
In 1997, after 8% of Swedish youth surveyed were allegedly unclear about the existence of the Holocaust, the Swedish government started a Holocaust information campaign called "Living History," and commissioned Holocaust historians to write a book named "Tell Ye Your Children ... a book about the Holocaust in Europe 1935-1945" which asked questions such as "Could Sweden have done more during the war? What role did Swedish xenophobia, racism and antisemitism play in shaping the nation's wartime policy?" The book and dissemination campaign became a permanent fixture with the establishment of the Swedish Ministry of Culture's "Living History Forum."

Ingrid Lomfors, the famous Jewish historian, was the 2015 government-appointed head of the Swedish Ministry of Culture's "Living History Forum."

In October 2015, the continuously self-flagellating Swedish government held a meeting in Stockholm themed – "Sweden Together" which reportedly demonstrated that Swedes were racists that needed to do more for immigrants.

The government announced a "100 Club" where Swedish businesses would each promise to employ 100 new migrants over a period of 3 years. Where the money would come from or what the migrants would do was not discussed. Attendees were admonished to respect the religious beliefs of Muslims especially because their numbers will grow and Swedes need to "treat them right."

As the King, Queen, and Prime Minister of Sweden, and many others sat and listened, Ingrid Lomfors, who had been asked to

speak about immigration, made her presentation where she maintained in her projected slide that,
1. migration is nothing new
2. we are all a consequence of immigration
3. there is no indigenous Swedish culture

Wait... What?

Sweden which was settled 12,000 years ago, enriched by its Vikings for centuries, and resulted in an established kingdom and empire has no culture??

Seriously?

Lomfors's attempt to claim Sweden had *no native culture* was met with instant mocking and criticism. "Absurd," "troubling," "denier," "traitor," "racist," "lunatic," "hater," "anti-Swede," and "embarrassment," were some of the more mild and publishable comments that flooded the internet, from disgusted Members of Sweden's Parliament and outraged citizens.

Ridicule of Lomfors reached such intensity that Lomfors herself quickly backpedaled and claimed that it was the audience that had gotten it wrong and had taken her comments out of context, now saying that –
> "I was asked to give a historical perspective on immigration to Sweden. To help me, I used a slide. It was taken out of context and created an uproar, especially on social media. I understand that, and I regret it."

Regret *what*? That you were *misunderstood*? It was all *taken out of context*? Even though your spoken words, and written slide, were *crystal clear*?

Lomfors, *possibly protecting her lucrative government job,* backpedaled even further in her blog by writing,
> "Obviously there is a Swedish culture. I'm writing right now in the Swedish language and am a part of this culture.

A culture that I value and appreciate, it's a part of me and I of it."

Yeah, whatever. Sweden heard you the first time.
https://youtu.be/YNXECcltt9U
http://avpixlat.info/2015/10/12/regeringen-holl-vackelsemote/
http://nyheteridag.se/ingrid-lomfors-pudlar-det-finns-en-svensk-kultur/

More anti-Semitism
Jews in Sweden have reportedly been feeling rather nervous for a while now.

Armed police guard Jewish schools with machine guns, guards are stationed outside synagogues, and security concerns forced the cancellation of a popular Jewish winter camp for children. Shopkeepers are pressured not to buy goods from Israel. Cemeteries and synagogues are desecrated. Jews report having to hide their Jewish identities or suffer abuse or violence.

One Jewish woman even officially filed for asylum in 2013, citing religious persecution by the Swedish government after the Swedish parliament banned kosher slaughter and moved to ban non-medical circumcision rituals.

"Saying that Jews are the only nation who don't have the right to self-determination, smearing Israel as a modern incarnation of Nazi Germany or apartheid South Africa, asserting that the 'Israel Lobby' manipulates American foreign policy from the shadows is unmistakably anti-Semitism," says Ben Cohen who claims social media has joined together leftists and Islamists.

In the meanwhile, according to the Tower Magazine, "in Malmö, Sweden, the local Chabad rabbi had experienced 90 anti-Semitic incidents, including one in which the word 'Palestine' was scratched into his car.

Pro-Israel rallies in Malmö have seen participants pelted with eggs, bottles, and firecrackers. On one particular occasion, the

city's mayor stated that "Malmö does not 'accept Zionism,' and that Swedish Jews can avoid anti-Semitism by publicly opposing the occupation of the West Bank."
http://www.thejewishweek.com/features/jw-qa/spotlighting-anti-semitism-sweden-and-beyond
http://www.haaretz.com/jewish/news/1.667887
http://www.thetower.org/article/the-scandal-of-scandinavia/

Daily school fires?

Let's not even start looking for excuses for the *daily* fires at Swedish schools. Daily. Once a day. Let that sink in.

One. School. Fire. Once. Every. Day!

Sweden Radio interviewed the author of a book, "F*ck School," who tackled the issue and seems to have explained away the behavior which apparently results from kids who are tired of having to attend school. In preparation for the interview, Sweden Radio stated on its website that

"There is at least one fire per day in [Swedish] schools according to the latest fire investigation. It often starts in a waste paper basket, a locker, or something similar, that can sometimes turn the school building to ruins."

According to the Swedish Fire Protection Association, *school arsons* have gone from 95 in 1996 to a whopping 300% increase, 297, in 2008. And it was trending...

School fires over the 2004-2013 period have averaged 498 per year. Definite arsons averaged 232 annually, plus an additional annual average of 60 "unknown origin" fires.

As the Fire Protection Association notes, for the money lost each year (500 million) to these school fires, you could hire and add an extra 1,200 teachers and staff to the Swedish school system!

The Association also notes the tragic aftereffects – young men can face long prison sentences. More often, they are sentenced to pay for the damages. This punishment leaves them "living with a debt for the damages (and can) destroy job opportunities, housing and driver's licenses."

How very Swedish to worry about criminals being held accountable for their crimes.

What has this world come to?
http://sverigesradio.se/sida/artikel.aspx?programid=1637&artikel=5897345
http://www.stockholmnews.com/more.aspx?NID=5029
http://www.brandskyddsforeningen.se/pa-arbetet/valj-omrade-har/anlagd-brand

No papers? No problem!
Rest secure in the knowledge that while all this commotion was going on, at least 90% of the asylum seekers and migrants to Sweden showed up with no documentation or identification.

None. Zip. Nada.

Migrants are pretty much who they say they are. And what age they say they are. Nothing more. Nothing less.
What a great time to reinvent yourself!
http://www.svd.se/nio-av-tio-saknar-id-handling_7936334

Oh, and if you feel the need to vacation to, or return to, the Middle East, and fight alongside ISIS for a while, "when a person wishes to leave a violent extremist group or is coming home from combat overseas," Stockholm has reportedly pledged to provide:
- ✓ customized inclusion efforts
- ✓ coordinated local cooperation
- ✓ volunteer organization support and advice
- ✓ psychosocial support
- ✓ social services
- ✓ social psychiatry
- ✓ drug units
- ✓ health centers
- ✓ psychiatric services

- ✓ income support
- ✓ employment and assistance with job placement
- ✓ cooperative housing

Blow off some steam and some heads, and when you're ready to return, you'll be set with health care, housing, and financial support until you get settled in a good job? *Seriously?*
http://insynsverige.se/documentHandler.ashx?did=1798005

And how to pay for all of this Swedish hospitality?
Raise taxes and cut deductions, of course!

Effective January 1, 2016, the Swedish government announced it would be raising taxes on many different services and products while cutting or eliminating certain deductions.

Donations to non-profits will no longer be deductible.

Let that one sink in... Statistically, people tend to donate more, and more often, when they are able to deduct their donations. In this day and age, who thinks that eliminating charitable deductions is a good idea?

Thrift stores run by charities were to see a 25% sales tax (since repealed, but what a pathetic way to extort funds!).

Fuel taxes would skyrocket, and a special progressive tax equal to consumer price index plus 2% would guarantee gasoline costs would rise year after year.

The inheritance and gift tax would be reintroduced. Property taxes would get a bump up. Per-person deductions would be cut in half, and various household services deductions would be cut down or completely eliminated.

Under the guise of "going green," new additional taxes were earmarked to "discourage use of dangerous chemicals in everyday life," and would be levied based on product and weight. "Dangerous chemical" products such as computers, cell phones, stereos, televisions, vacuums, freezers, refrigerators, microwave ovens, and similar items would be all fair game for the tax man's new tax. Those items are now classified as *dangerous chemicals?* So they can be taxed more? Crazy!

A new special payroll tax would specifically target elderly workers. *The elderly!*

The new tax laws would also eliminate tax deductions for saving money in a private pension, and would raise taxes on savings accounts. So the incentive to save for your future just got chucked out the window.

At least the economy is robust, NOT!
Luckily, Sweden's key economic indicators are impressive. Impressive in a negative kind of way, that is.

While politicians, bureaucrats, and the old-fashioned-controlled-media broadcasts a very successful and rosy picture of Sweden's economic situation, a look at the latest statistics reveals a country in distress. And it will only get worse as more immigrants overwhelm the nation's resources.

Sweden's actual adjusted GDP growth rate per capita and productivity are at their worst levels since World War II. Oddly, between 2006-2014, Sweden seemingly *abandoned* the GDP "per capita" standard in their official government budgets. *Another instance of hide bad results?* In any case, the last few years have seen a stagnant growth rate.

For the period 2010-2012, the unemployment rate for males and females was just about 8%. Long term unemployment (people out of work for a year and more) was between 17-18%. At the same time, the "dependent population" (people under 15 and people over 65) was about 35% of the total population. This was all way before the latest migrant influx.

If this doesn't cause most hard working tax paying Swedes to leave the country and apply for asylum in Denmark, what will?
http://www.di.se/artiklar/2015/3/27/regeringen-hojer-skatterna/
http://www.scb.se/
http://stats.oecd.org/
http://www.scb.se/sv_/Hitta-statistik/Statistik-efter-amne/Nationalrakenskaper/Nationalrakenskaper/Nationalrakenskaper-kvartals--och-arsberakningar/Aktuell-Pong/22918/Tabeller/376985/

Hunt down the Swedish teens

Let's take a break from all the serious crime and general mayhem and enjoy a little soccer ("football" in Europe).

Held in Sweden's second largest city, Goithenburg, the annual Gothia Cup soccer tournament is a BIG deal. It is billed as "the world's largest and most international youth football tournament. Each year, around 1,600 teams from 80 nations take part and they play 4,500 games on 110 fields." Enormous crowds of fans show up to watch the youths play.

Ever heard of the unsportsmanlike behavior displayed by some foreigners during the unsanctioned 2010 post-game "Swedish soccer team manhunt?"

It was 2010, and an under-16 (all players were under the age of 16) game between the Swedish and Iraqi soccer teams was being played. After a particularly close and competitive game, the Swedish team beat the Iraqi team 1-0.

Time to celebrate? Shake hands, smile, and let all the glory sink in? *Hell no, run for your lives!*

Without warning, hundreds of enraged Iraqi fans rushed the field and charged the terrified young Swedish teens. Some Swedes tried to hide, others ran for their lives.

Video footage captured the scenes of violence as Iraqis threw Swedish teens to the ground, hit them, stomped them, and according to some newscasters, reportedly threw rocks and stones at the fleeing youngsters. One referee was also reportedly kicked in the back as the Iraqis hunted down the Swedish players for retribution.

Police responded and, after a while, restored law and order.

Think about it. And connect your own dots.
https://youtu.be/Sbw2auygtGE
http://www.101greatgoals.com/blog/iraqi-fans-attack-ifk-gothenburgs-u16s-after-their-side-are-beaten-at-the-gothia-cup-video/

Free bus rides for migrants only
In the summer of 2015, the local government in Kalmar realized that the new migrants would be better off if they had free bus rides. So they concocted a scheme that would cost taxpayers about $700,000 to provide migrants free unlimited access to the city bus system.

The migrants were thrilled to be able to expand their travels beyond their free housing, meals, and stipends. Migrant privilege at its best!
http://m.thelocal.se/20150727/asylum-seekers-in-swedish-county-get-free-bus-passes

Space is running out
In 2015, it was reported that a German company trying to open up a satellite office in Stockholm, Europe's fastest growing city, spent a year unsuccessfully looking for housing for its 30 workers. With literally no space available, they scrapped their plans. It seems Sweden has spent much of its resources investing in the needs of current and future migrants and dropped the ball on its own infrastructure. There is a reported 8-20 *year* waiting list for "rent-controlled public housing."

Not surprisingly, market rents are out of control. Clearly, no housing for skilled workers means less ways to grow your economy and that's bad news for everyone.

And if workers can't find accommodations, where do you find room for migrants when you're hell-bent on saving the world?

More on that in a moment.
http://www.thelocal.se/20151204/housing-forces-startup-to-scrap-stockholm-move

No room at the Swede Inn
By November 2015, Sweden was scurrying to stop the flood of human travelers that they so carefully created and cultivated. 2015 projections were now 160,000 asylum seekers, double the number that arrived in 2014. Panicked Swedish Immigration Minister Johansson made emergency statements to migrants to *stay in Germany* as Sweden had run out of the ability to accommodate them.

Honestly, who could have ever predicted such an outcome...

But it was about to get even worse.
http://yle.fi/uutiset/ruotsalaisministeri_turvapaikanhakijoille_pysykaa_saksassa_taalla_ei_ole_asuntoja/8435539

No single women
In late November 2015, Swedish news center, Allehanda, reported that there was a late night disturbance at a refugee shelter in Nora. It seems that a group of 30 angry Muslim migrants tried to break into one of the rooms in order to rape a migrant woman and to kill her teenage son.

Her crime? According to one version, Muslims felt that because she was travelling alone, without a husband, she could be raped. When the mob couldn't break down the woman's door, they screamed their threats, including death to her teenage son. Shelter staff called police resulting in assault complaints. The Migration Board moved the woman and son elsewhere.
http://www.allehanda.se/angermanland/kramfors/mobb-skulle-valdta-kvinna-och-doda-sonen-anmalda-for-olaga-hot
http://www.allehanda.se/angermanland/kramfors/efter-dods-och-valdtaktshoten-nu-flyttas-den-drabbade-familjen-fran-asylboendet-i-nora

Taking some time off to kill

In November 2015, the Prime Minister of Sweden, Stefan Löfven, lamented that "It's completely unacceptable that people can take part in terrorism and return [to Sweden] without being held responsible." The Prime Minister's reference was to the common practice in Sweden of some Muslims taking time off to travel to Syria and/or Iraq to take up arms and fight alongside ISIS, and then to return back to Sweden as if nothing happened. The numbers are significant with a reported 300 foreign-background Swedes having joined up with ISIS over the past few years.

According to Swedish authorities, "There is a violent Islamist environment in Sweden that influences people to go. The core of about 200 people who support the logistics, money and recruitment has been fairly successful here."

Of the 115 "Swedes" that have so far returned from their ISIS adventures, Swedish authorities worry that "those who come home are sometimes treated like rock stars and become role models for other young people."

In December 2015, two men from Sweden were on trial. They were like any other happy and worldly foreign-born Swedes, except that during their recent vacation travels to Syria, they armed themselves, hooked up with a terrorist organization, went on a rampage, and ended up in a group that beheaded two men. One of the suspects allegedly held down one of the victims, and the other suspect participated as well.

Of course, both men claimed to be "innocent," which might have worked save for one little bit of evidence. *Instant replay.* That's exactly right. According to the prosecutor, video taken during the commission of the murders was all she needed to throw the book at the duo.

In one screen shot displayed during the trial, you can see at least ten armed men, surrounding the crime scene, with at least 3 men videotaping the executions on their cell phones. Apparently even murderous killers in Syria are into the whole cell phone videotaping and selfie lifestyle.

Based on the exhaustively graphic video evidence of two beheadings in Syria which featured the duo in jubilant and joyous attendance, the duo got life in prison on December 14, 2015. Of course, they are appealing. The sentence, that is.
http://www.thelocal.se/20151130/swedish-prosecutor-movies-show-men-killing
http://www.thelocal.se/20151214/swedish-pair-get-life-in-jail-for-syria-terror-crimes

Back to Sweden.

As *Säpo,* Sweden's government security service, searched the country for suspected terrorists, Prime Minister Löfven added that "Sweden has been naïve."

What caused the Prime Minister's momentary awakening? Maybe it was Sweden's recent world record.

Sweden makes history
In November 2015, for the first time in recorded history, Sweden went on "HIGH ALERT" meaning, according to the elite Swedish government security service *Säpo* that "the probability that players have the intent and ability to carry out attacks is high."

Warning the country at a press conference of a credible terrorist plot against Sweden and putting the nation on HIGH alert, the head of Säpo added that "violent Islamism is still the biggest threat against Sweden."

A historical first. A "HIGH ALERT." Swedes must be so very proud of their government's accomplishments.
http://www.thelocal.se/20151118/sweden-reported-to-be-raising-terror-threat
http://www.thelocal.se/20151004/300-swedes-have-left-to-join-extremist

Cruising the ocean blue

Forget the HIGH alerts and terrorists next door, with about 190,000 new migrants arriving in Sweden by the end of 2015, space was tight. How would they accommodate all those new arrivals in style?

Wait! How about... luxury.... cruise lines? Yes!

Undeterred by HIGH alerts and ISIS bound militant warriors, the ever-inventive Swedish Migration Agency announced that several Swedish cruise lines had offered to house thousands and thousands of migrants on their luxury ocean liners.

Since it takes about a year for Swedish authorities to "investigate" new arrivals to see if they should be granted "asylum," the accommodation chief of the Swedish Migration Agency said,

> "These ships should serve as proper asylum accommodation where asylum seekers can be throughout the period of investigation which is usually about one year." The plan is to have the ships docked at large Swedish ports and to board the first cruise "guests" around Christmas 2015.

Imagine a cruise ship filled to capacity with thousands of young males who are aboard a luxury liner for the first time. What a wonderful learning and assimilation experience!

We can only hope that the boat's social coordinator has some fun activities planned for all those young men. Hopefully, the tuxedo requirement at the Captain's dinner table will be suspended. Since most of the cabins on even the nicest cruise ships are really tiny, hopefully the migrants will be understanding, and make due. Beyond pools and casinos, at least there is always room service.

http://www.thelocal.se/20151113/five-myths-about-swedens-refugee-crisis
http://www.thelocal.se/20151124/cruise-ships-to-house-swedens-refugees

Protecting the family jewels
During the summer of 2012, poetic justice took a wild turn to the very far right and drove off the road.

Can you guess what happened when members of the dolefully out-of-touch Swedish Royal family met a male Somali migrant? Did they listen to his tale of woe? Did they throw him a few extra gold coins to help him out? Were they at all concerned that they knew virtually nothing about him, and that he was undocumented and had no proper ID?

No!

Instead, they reportedly partied with him at clubs and hung out as friends. At some point, the Princess and her husband arranged for the migrant to win the "lottery." Well, figuratively. You see, they apparently invited the young male Somali migrant to live with them at their home near the Royal Palace whenever he wanted. Reportedly, he received full access to the pad and became a "part of the family." How Swedish! (It'll get a *lot* more Swedish in a moment.)

The migrant got so chummy with Princess Christina that she reportedly called him "the child of the house." And Princess Christina's businessman husband, commoner Tord Magnuson, apparently served as the young man's mentor teaching him and advising him regularly about the-gods-know-what. When he wasn't being mentored or admired, the enterprising young migrant passed the time by busily and methodically searching through the couple's home. One day he discovered a fake bookshelf that held a key. Next he uncovered the location of the couple's safe. *Jackpot!* The houseguest then proceeded to steal over 850,000 kronor worth of jewelry including a diamond encrusted tiara, a unique golden-thread bracelet, gold rings, elaborate cuff links, and the like.

Reportedly, the migrant planned to frame the cleaning lady for his crime. He sold most of the jewelry to some marijuana dealers he knew for a tiny fraction of their value. When his thievery was discovered, he confessed and apologized, telling police that while he had stolen things before, this time he felt bad since he felt he had destroyed his "real" friendship with Princess Christina and her husband Tord.

Now just you wait. Don't be so hard on yourself!

Tord reportedly accepted the man's apology, had a hard time not crying as he testified at the thief's trial and said, "It's a sad day." Although the migrant was convicted of two cases of aggravated theft, luckily (hey, it's Sweden), since the man was so young (19 he claimed) he only got probation. *And* was allowed to stay in Sweden. *Whew!*

Tord was quoted as saying, "Justice has been served. It was a fair sentence. The important thing is that he has the care he needs now... I still think about him." *Double whew!*

By the way, isn't Stockholm where they invented the Syndrome?

Oh, and no jewelry has been recovered to date.
http://www.thelocal.se/20120614/41442
http://www.expressen.se/nyheter/tord-magnuson-efter-domen-sorgligt/
http://www.aftonbladet.se/nyheter/article14976888.ab

Night train, but hard to blame
In October 2015, a 28-year-old Iraqi man traveling on the night train between Umeå and Sundsvall was arrested for allegedly raping a Swedish female passenger.

The Iraqi migrant apparently had left Finland after becoming disappointed with bad conditions for migrants in that country. He was travelling around Sweden seeking a better life. On the train, he befriended a Swedish woman who reportedly had a soft spot for the plight of suffering migrants. The Swedish woman even bought him food and drink.

When she fell asleep, the Iraqi man allegedly wasted no time in repaying her kindness and began raping her. The woman was able to break free and found a railroad attendant.

A shocking testament to Stockholm Syndrome in action, and the success of the mass-programming of Swedish minds, *for a while the rape victim actually struggled with whether or not she should report the rapist!* According to court documents, she allegedly *pitied him, and feared for his safety should he get deported.* Seriously??

Finally, she broke out of her trance, and notified police who arrested the man. After trial, the Iraqi rapist was sentenced to one year in prison and subsequent deportation, but will be able to return after 5 years. We're guessing he'll take a train…
http://www.exponerat.net/asylsokande-irakier-besviken-pa-finland-akte-till-sverige-och-valdtog-pa-nattag/
http://www.friatider.se/missn-jde-asyls-karen-talas-f-r-t-gv-ldt-kt

Talking to the walls
At the end of August 2015, a former Swedish Migration Board asylum officer went public with his belief that ISIS terrorists could easily gain entry into Sweden. He said that in spite of warnings from high ranking officials in NATO, British intelligence, US sources, and the Libyan government, Sweden blissfully continued its lackadaisical "screening" process.

He noted that Swedish Migration personnel faced intense pressure to clear Syrian refugees quickly with minimal time allocated to screening. In fact, he said with reviews and individual salaries tied to how effectively officers cleared refugees, the opportunity to correct the system would be minimal. He added that the Migration Board's attempts to screen out terrorists were "insufficient," "lax," and "superficial."

Was anyone listening?
http://www.aftonbladet.se/debatt/article21319209.ab

Women prohibited

A female reporter for Norrköpings Tidningar set out to cover a large Muslim meeting in Norrköping in 2014. While helpful, none of the Muslim men would shake her hand as she tried to report on the gathering. They all *did* shake her colleague's hand, her fellow journalist, a male photographer. When asked why, the answer was pretty straightforward, "A man should not come in contact with another woman."

When the reporter asked why women weren't welcome at this gathering, the answer was again straightforward, "Islam differentiates between men and women. We do not mix." The bewildered journalist was also told that Swedes artificially exaggerate equality between men and women since "it is a culture that has been built up over many years. It has become like a religion to you." *Hello. Hello? Anyone?*
http://nt.se/nyheter/norrkoping/inga-kvinnor-valkomna-pa-stor-muslimsk-samling-9894356.aspx

Back to the 30-year-old "children"

Visions of unaccompanied refugee children, running for their lives, fleeing horrors, all on their own! The problem is, most of it really is just a vision, a mirage. In October 2013, an estimated 86% of refugee "children" were in fact adults lying about their age. Some sliced a cool decade or more off their "age."

For refugees one advantage is that children are often processed far faster than adults. Another huge advantage is that if they are caught getting involved in any criminal activity, they receive reduced children's punishments instead of adult punishments. And they get to attend school with youngsters. Since old-fashioned-controlled-media reporters just don't spend the time checking out sources or facts, many examples of obviously older men pretending to be children abound.

Here are just a few of the many cases.

In one wacky instance, the Gothenburg-Post featured a heart-wrenching story about the struggles of a 16-year-old refugee child from Afghanistan. He came over with his smartphone but no ID. It's a real human interest story till you look at the photos that litter the article and realize they show what is clearly a man, 25-30+years-old, cavorting amongst 16- and 17-year-old girls and boys.

Weird, right?

Unfortunately for the old-fashioned-controlled-media trying so hard to manufacture emotional concern for poor downtrodden refugee "children," another media outlet did some fact checking. It was quickly found out that this "poor child refugee" had a rather extensive social media presence complete with snapshots of himself travelling the world and many *years* of activity on an adult hook-up site. So, based on his claim to be "only 16 years-old," and some basic math, he would have had to sign up on the adult site at the age of 8, and then upload "aged" photos of himself. *Busted!*

The daily Kristianstadsbladet newspaper ran a story in 2012 of a 14-year-old boy whom the paper crowned "the fastest 14-year-old in Sweden."

The photos in the newspaper told a *whole* different story. The migrant was seen running alongside actual children, and clearly looked to be old enough to be their father. No joke. Their father. Not older brother, but *father*. Further, he towered over them, sported a five-o'clock shadow, and was obviously not a regular youngster. *Fact checking,* anyone?

In an equally laughable story, SVT ran a story about an alleged unaccompanied child from Afghanistan with no ID.

This "boy" had reportedly just turned 14-years-old two weeks before the story ran on December 21, 2015. In the news photos, the boy clearly *towers* over his fellow 14-year-old

Swedes and sports a robust hairy beard while his "peers" haven't even started shaving. Are the reporters blind or just really inept or so focused on feeding the fairytale that they suspend reality? The pictures show an adult man.

The blind acceptance *without any skepticism* must stop.
https://meritwager.wordpress.com/2013/10/09/en-migga-116-av-134-pastatt-minderariga-bedomdes-inte-vara-minderariga/
https://web.archive.org/web/20151021031437/http://www.gp.se/nyheter/reportage/1.2866002-ensam-i-nytt-land
http://avpixlat.info/2015/10/20/ensambluff-i-nytt-land/
www.svt.se/nyheter/regionalt/sormland/efter-veckor-i-sverige-ar-mohammad-en-i-laget

Attacking the elderly confined to wheelchairs
Founded way back in 1837 when life was far more simple, the Nya Wermlands-Tidningen (NWT) Newspaper reported on the Christmas Eve 2015 savage attack on a 70-year-old wheelchair bound invalid Swede in a bathroom at the Bergvik shopping center in Karlstad in the afternoon.

The elderly handicapped victim was beaten unconscious and left on the floor, bleeding from a head wound. Stolen were his watch and prescription medicines. The victim described his attackers as "two dark-skinned men" wearing hoods. Police were reportedly looking over surveillance cameras for clues.
http://nwt.se/karlstad/2015/12/27/man-i-rullstol-ranad

Violent young male migrants at asylum centers monopolizing police resources
In mid-December 2015 according to NWT, Värmland Police said they were averaging at least a call per day to rowdy refugee shelters. Reported examples of calls included brawls, threats, assaults, and even a 50-person knife fight at which responding units were unable to find the knives.

As migrant shelter violence and disturbances have been increasing, so have the excuses and explanations which ranged from "overcrowding," "stress," and "boredom" to "misunderstandings based on the many different cultures mixed into one space."

Wait! So now it's permissible to blame multi-culturalism in a tight space for misunderstandings and violence? Really?

Luckily, the head of the local Värmland Migration Board explained everything. You see, according to her, all the increased criminality and misbehavior was due to the fact that the number of refugees had doubled in a short period of time. So naturally there were more police calls. *Case solved!* Plus, she added, "We have 8,200 residents in Värmland. A very small percentage of those are involved in the scuffle. I think that police statistics show that Swedes are arguing more!"

Oh. So that's it. Swedes are arguing more!? Honestly, we can't begin to guess what the Migration Board head meant by her off the wall comment.

Curiously, at the same time, it was reported that only about 50% of police responses to the refugee shelters resulted in police reports. Hmmm.

If you don't record it, it didn't statistically happen – a tried and true way to cook the books and make crime stats appear lower.

Is this an isolated issue? Not at all. Off to Jamtland.

On December 25, 2015, newspaper Östersunds-Posten reported that police in the Jamtland area were called to refugee shelters at least 91 times in November 2015, averaging about 3 calls per day. This trend continued in December.

The police reported that so much of their time was now being spent on criminal behavior and unrest at migrant shelters and at group homes for unaccompanied migrant "children," that it left them virtually no time for regular policing duties or to devote any efforts to dealing with any other unrelated crimes.

One high-ranking officer stated that they were so backed up that, "we are not likely to catch up with some of the (non-migrant) crimes committed at the same pace as we could before."

How incredibly uncomforting.
http://nwt.se/varmland/2015/12/09/fler-brak-vid-boendena
http://www.op.se/blaljus/anstrangt-ar-for-polisen-med-omorganisation-och-flyktingkris-polischefen-varnar-vi-kommer-inte-att-racka-till-fullt-ut

Arson by any other name

Many asylum shelters and refugee facilities across Sweden, and Europe, have been mysteriously going up in flames. It was always assumed by the old-fashioned-controlled-media and politicians that xenophobic racist natives were responsible.

On December 24, 2015, an asylum shelter in Gamleby was set on fire. However, there was little material damage and no injuries according to newspaper VT.se. And low and behold, an asylum seeker from the shelter was arrested for torching his own facility. The fire received a load of coverage. The identity and ethnicity of the arsonist, not so much.

Why is that?

Interesting that while many Swedish asylum shelters have fallen prey to some degree of arson, the old-fashioned-controlled-media routinely made it seem like the work of local racists. Yet now it's starting to seem that more and more arsons are really the work of the migrants themselves.

So where is the corresponding flood of news coverage?

For instance, in October 2015 there was a fire at an asylum center in Munkedal in Bohuslän. Almost immediately, Swedish Migration Board Deputy Director General Mikael Ribbenvik claimed that the arson at the shelter was a "ruthless" attack "directed against people" while the old-fashioned-controlled-media jumped on the bandwagon and labeled it a "racially motivated attack." The fire had been set in the dead of night while people were sleeping which was conspicuously vile, and *obvious* proof of racist xenophobes. And since the fire alarm system didn't go off, "evil racists" theories mushroomed.

Politicians and authorities made an embarrassingly huge show about how hiding the locations of shelters would be hard and that protecting the migrants was a priority and that Sweden was a racist xenophobic powder keg. The arson at Bohuslän was even called a terrorist attack against the Muslim refugees.

Even Swedish Prime Minister Löfven got in on the accusations, calling the fires "terrible" adding that "I am absolutely convinced that most people in our country do not want to see this. It is not the Sweden we are proud of."

He even had the nerve to say that, "Now is not the time for campaigns and to stir up the people to different things."

That's right, Löfven, most Swedes "don't want to see this." That's why most Swedes probably aren't committing the arsons! And no one is stirring people up, except for maybe the migrants doing it to their own. Wake up Löfven! And for the sake of all the gods, man, check your facts before so quickly blaming your long-suffering constituents.

And then a funny thing happened.

The facts just don't matter that much anymore
Police determined that the arson at Bohuslän was likely set by the asylum seekers themselves, intentionally, inside the building. And that while it wasn't clear why the fire alarm system hadn't gone off, many of the migrants routinely smoked indoors and were in the habit of disabling smoke sensors to cut out the automatic fire alarm system, which may easily explain its "malfunction."

It was further reported that almost 60% of local asylum fires allegedly blamed on "racist" Swedes were definitely not arsons.

Were these new facts and revelations trumpeted with the same fanfare and fervor as the originally disseminated lies?

No. They floated away without a whimper.
http://vt.se/nyheter/man-anhallen-for-mordbrand-8650434.aspx
http://www.friatider.se/brand-p-asylboende-startade-inomhus
http://www.gp.se/nyheter/sverige/1.2869330-14-flydde-asylbrand-samvetslost

Anti-biotic resistant infections DOUBLE in 2015

According to one of Sweden's largest newspapers, HD (Helsingborgs Dagblad), in a January 2, 2016 report, 102 cases of MRSA was discovered in Sweden in November 2015 alone – more than *twice* the number of MRSA cases discovered since 2015 began.

Drug-resistant MRSA has the potential to cause a deadly flesh eating disease. The Mayo Clinic says it is an "infection caused by a type of staph bacteria that's become resistant to many of the antibiotics used to treat ordinary staph infections."

Not fun.

Not safe.

According to the Swedish Public Health Agency, the MRSA increase "has its explanation in the extensive refugee quarters... Many refugees who come here with both sores and blemishes are infected."

"Many refugees... are infected..."

The antibiotic-resistant intestinal bacteria "ESBL-carba" is also on the rise in Sweden. Since it is resistant to almost all antibiotics, treating ESBL-carba infections is difficult and

patients usually require quarantine and drastic measures. 2015 saw 100 reported cases of ESBL-carba, more than twice the cases reported in 2014. Prior to 2012, only 40 cases of ESBL-carba had been reported in Sweden. "Most cases have been linked to hospital treatment abroad, mainly in India, Greece and Iraq."
www.hd.se/nyheter/sverige/2016/01/02/flyktingstrom-bakom-stor-okning-av-mrsa/
http://www.mayoclinic.org/diseases-conditions/mrsa/basics/definition/con-20024479
http://www.folkhalsomyndigheten.se/amnesomraden/smittskydd-och-sjukdomar/smittsamma-sjukdomar/esblcarba/

Still protecting the criminals at all costs
In late October 2015 it was reported by Speisa, Swedish Radio, and other news sources that a 40-year-old migrant man at a Tingsryd refugee shelter had brutally raped a 3-year-old girl.

Quick! Put on your Sweden Hat and predict how this absolutely sickening tragedy will play out.

Upon learning of the child rape, did
  a) the Asylum Center management call the police?
  b) the Swedish Migration Board start deportation proceedings?
  c) all of the above
  d) none of the above

ANSWER (D) None of the above.

Actually, the heroes at the shelter and the Migration Board quickly moved the man to a safe location, fearing for his well-being. *Read that again.*

Seriously now, is this the former homeland of the mighty Vikings?

Reportedly, eight hours after the rape, upon discovering the horrible crime, friends of the little girl's mother contacted the police. After arriving at the shelter, police were met with resistance, as shelter staff appeared to be protecting the rapist and his whereabouts. They reportedly wouldn't cooperate. The rapist had already been moved to a new location to keep him safe so police were at a loss.

Only "top-level pressure" on the Migration Board finally revealed the identity and location of the suspect. Police were finally able to arrest the middle-aged migrant, and according to news source Kvällspostenile, police stated that they had also "heard from witnesses, and the forensic medical expert performed a DNA test."

It would seem that Sweden's got some serious problems.

By the way, what exactly are the priorities in Sweden?
http://www.delfi.ee/news/paevauudised/valismaa/rootsis-vagistati-avalikult-kolmeaastane-tudruk?id=72776415
http://www.ohtuleht.ee/700324/rootsis-vagistas-40aastane-mees-pagulaskeskuses-kolmeaastase-tudruku

Tears and great sadness, *but not for Swedes*
By the end of November 2015, a seemingly panicked Prime Minister Löfven announced that now Sweden would be taking in only the "EU minimum level" of asylum seekers.

He added a list of other highly restrictive measures as well including time limits on "family reunifications," only temporary residence would be offered in many cases, permanent residence permits for asylum seekers would no longer be issued, strict ID checks would be enforced on public transportation, and "children" traveling by themselves would have their "claimed" ages verified medically since many older men refugees were claiming ages as young as 14 or younger.

No surprises to readers of this book, but the Prime Minister sure seemed somewhat surprised and shocked. But the surprises kept on coming...

Deputy Prime Minister, Åsa Romson, visibly and reportedly "choked back tears" and could be seen crying during her televised announcement of the new stricter migrant measures, tears streaming and welling up in her puffy eyes.

Grieving that Sweden can't take in even more refugees while your own people suffer outrageous violence and crime waves, worsening economic conditions, and higher and higher taxes is bizarre and beyond strange.

But in Sweden it can always get stranger...

By late December 2015, Romson had composed herself, dried away her tears, and announced to Dagens Industri newspaper that, "50,000 to 100,000 immigrants per year to Sweden is way too low... we must have a system that can handle significantly more than that." Coincidentally, Dagens Industri also reported that based on a late December 2015 poll, Romson had scored the *lowest* confidence rating of all party leaders. *Surprised?*

Late-breaking stats prove wild imbalances
The latest stats from Sweden's official government site Migrationsverket revealed that by the end of November 2015, *males made up 71% of all asylum applicants* to Sweden. And *more than 90%* of those claiming to be "unaccompanied minors" were *young males*. All those new boys will tip the balance of population stats – so many more boys than girls... *Male dominance...* How's that going to work out for the locals?

Oh please, make the madness stop!
 http://www.thelocal.se/20151124/sweden-set-to-tighten-asylum-rules-for-refugees
 http://www.theguardian.com/world/video/2015/nov/24/asa-romson-sweden-deputy-prime-minister-cries-announcing-refugee-u-turn-video
 http://sverigesradio.se/sida/artikel.aspx?programid=159&artikel=3491113
 http://speisa.com/modules/articles/index.php/item.2311/vice-pm-of-sweden-wants-even-higher-immigration-than-today.html
 http://www.migrationsverket.se/Om-Migrationsverket/Statistik/Aktuell-statistik.html

(47) SWITZERLAND

Ah, wonderful Switzerland. Progressive and cutting edge. In 1971 they finally allowed women to take part in *and vote* in federal elections. They have the Alps. Chocolate. Financial powerhouses and banks. Traditional dancing and yodeling. Swiss watches, knives, and cheese. Zwickelbier and lagerbier. And a growing group of immigrants and second generation immigrants who are demanding all this be changed.

2014 census figures showed a 25% foreign population with Islam being the second largest religion and Muslims making up 5% of the population.

No minarets and other legal woes
In 2009, the Swiss passed an unprecedented *constitutional* ban on the building of minarets, those prayer-calling towers often found on Muslim mosques. The Swiss amendment has so far been upheld by the European Court of Human Rights against challenges by various groups.

For years, the Swiss courts have been inundated with all varieties of Islam-related cases, from headscarf and burqa ban issues and school clothes variations, to acquittals for jail sentences for Muslims involved in "honor crimes" usually against Muslim women not living modestly enough.

In 2010, immigrant group, SecondasPlus, which represents primarily second-generation Muslims in Switzerland ("secondas"), made statements that they found Switzerland was in the grips of "racist and xenophobic" trends, adding that "foreigners are basically undesirable and suspicious, they are tolerated but not respected." To this, SecondasPlus promised to "devote itself ...to the promotion and strengthening of the migrant population." The Swiss have been voting down all sorts of pro-migrant legislation and SecondasPlus does a good job of tracking these outcomes. The general theme is that while claiming to work out immigration issues, the Swiss are actually tightening regulations.

Beat her when necessary?
A Swiss TV documentary, *Behind the Veil,* aired on SF1 (now part of Swiss Broadcasting Corporation). It featured the secretary of the Basel Muslim Community on the Rhine River speaking about his beliefs regarding permissible spousal abuse and calling for Sharia law in Switzerland. The man said something along the lines that when a Muslim man "needs sex, that's why in extreme cases he is allowed to beat his wife if she refuses. If he did not do that, then the man would look for another partner, and this is not acceptable in Islam." This statement, along with some other comments about amputations and whippings as punishment for certain crimes, landed the man in hot water and he was put on trial for "public instigation to crime and violence." Released by the first court, he was next tried in a court of appeals. The judge said that "the declarations of the accused are clear instigations to violence. And as the secretary of a Muslim organization, he has a great capability of influencing others."

The court found that although "violence against women is strongly deserving of condemnation; these declarations are neither morally nor ethically right," yet since the man hadn't specifically called anyone to specifically behave in this way, he was free to go and practice his "freedom of expression."

Die infidel!
In 2012, a little boy in a Swiss school was reportedly bullied relentlessly until he suffered a nervous breakdown.

The school-loving and lively sixth grader suddenly became the focus of a Muslim classmate, the son of a Muslim cleric, who vowed to convert the infidel. Of the 19 students in the little boy's class, 14 were Muslim. The bully told the little boy that he needed to convert to Islam in order that they remain friends. The bully made fun of Christianity and during a class multicultural enrichment visit to a mosque, tried to force the little boy to worship Allah.

At some point the bully decided the boy must be demonically possessed and other students shunned the little boy as well. In a particularly troubling incident, several of the Muslim students restrained the little boy and the bully chanted "die, die, die" as he pelted him with ping pong balls. Not surprisingly, the Swiss child suffered increasingly from headaches and stomach aches and developed anxiety disorders. *Who wouldn't?*

A psychiatrist working with the young victim allegedly put it this way, "Because of the adaptation disorder with anxiety and depressive reactions, he is currently seriously impaired in his personal and educational development... In the last three years *similar reactions to school attendance* were seen based on conflicts that were mostly caused by the sociocultural differences in class."

Three years of related or similar incidents. Got that?

School authorities seemed surprised when contacted by journalists, and claimed this was an *isolated* case.

Surprised? Isolated?

The headmistress of the school played down the incidents, maintained that there were *no* conversation attempts, and claimed she had only *very recently* learned of any troubles.

Until, that is, her emails came to light. Damn those pesky emails!

When confronted by investigative reporters with emails proving she had been aware of the incidents at least one month prior, the headmistress refused to answer further questions.

The teacher that had contacted and spoken to the bully's mother after each incident also ducked questions. And the bully's father flat out denied the events, while trying to prevent the story from being reported. In the end, instead of removing the bully, the little Swiss boy was relocated to another school.

The news report ended with an example of another incident where a Muslim student began bullying and taunting Swiss female classmates because they chose to wear shorter skirts than he thought appropriate and, *gasp*, they liked tailored clothes.

Hey, it's just beginning.
http://www.tagesanzeiger.ch/zuerich/winterthur/Bekehrungsversuche-auf-dem-Pausenplatz/story/30846497

And get the "Switz" out of Switzerland

In 2013, SecondasPlus put together a campaign to get Switzerland to remove the white cross off its national flag. Yes, you read that right. As SecondasPlus stated, this Christian symbol "no longer corresponds to today's multicultural Switzerland."

How to recall billions of Swiss army knives and Swiss watches so they can be retrofitted with the new, non-offensive flag, was not included in the plan.

A SecondasPlus spokesperson added that a new flag, especially one with yellow, green and red colors, would be "similar to the current flags of Bolivia and Ghana and would represent a more progressive and open-minded Switzerland."

Also in 2013, SecondasPlus pushed for a new national anthem. It seems that they deemed the current Swiss national anthem too old fashioned. They want an anthem that "is based on what we are today... multicultural society. Switzerland needs a hymn in four national languages, but also in other unofficial but widely spoken languages in Switzerland (English, Spanish, Albanian, Portuguese, Turkish...). We need an anthem with which as many living in Switzerland people can identify, with or without a Swiss passport. This will only work, if not many are excluded because of their gender, origin or religion."

In 2014, SecondasPlus expressed outrage that Switzerland apparently seemed more interested in looking out for Swiss people, thereby alienating migrants.

The tireless fight to make Switzerland *less Swiss* goes on.
http://www.aargauerzeitung.ch/schweiz/weg-mit-dem-kreuz-secondos-fuer-neue-schweizer-fahne-113290242
http://www.secondos-plus.ch/
http://www.indexmundi.com/switzerland/demographics_profile.html
http://www.dofaz.net/weil-der-mann-sex-braucht-darf-er-seine-frau-schlagen_artikel_2826.html
https://worldradio.ch/wrs/news/wrsnews/muslim-secretary-acquited-of-inciting-violence.shtml

Where foreigners excel
As to crime statistics, they are very disproportionate. The Swiss even have a term for it: "Ausländerkriminalität" or "foreigner criminality." In 2008, almost 70% of the prison population was made up of foreigners. And foreign-committed crime has been growing for a long time.

In 1997, for the first time, Switzerland's penal system saw more foreign convicts than Swiss convicts. The Federal Department of Justice and Police put together a special report in 1998 to study what was going on. The report found that foreigners living in Switzerland were responsible for around 21% of all convictions, asylum seekers for 9%, and foreign tourists for an additional 21%. Arrests per 1,000 were made up of 2.3 Swiss citizens, 4.2 legal resident aliens, and 32 asylum seekers.

Asylum seekers were almost 1,400% more likely to be arrested for crimes than citizens.

The report detailed an alarming trend toward increasing and more deadly crimes as well. "Crime tourists" were most likely accused of money laundering (43%) and homicide (36%). And while the Swiss were most often convicted of non-rape sex offenses, foreigners were significantly more frequently convicted of a variety of violent and deadly offenses.

The highest rates of criminal activity came from foreign men 20-34 years old (isn't this demographically similar to the groups of refugees seen in today's endless videos from around Europe?) who were 970% more likely to commit crimes than Swiss residents. And that was way back in 1998.
https://www.vimentis.ch/d/publikation/154/Ausl%E4nderkriminalit%E4t+in+der+Schweiz.html

Statistics paint a sad picture
A 2010 published crime statistics by race report, which focused only on 18- to 34-year-old males in Switzerland in 2009, showed that African men from Angola, Nigeria, Algeria, and the Ivory Coast committed crimes about 600% more often than Swiss men. Immigrants from the Dominican Republic were the next highest criminal offenders. Columbian, Turkish, Serbian, and Brazilian immigrants fell in the 300% "more crimes" range.

The Swiss Federal Statistical Office also reported that certain nationalities were "less criminally minded" than Swiss nationals. For instance, immigrants from Austria, France, and Germany (with Germans being the least criminal of all nationalities) were up to about 80% *less likely* to commit crimes than even the native Swiss.

Reaction to the findings at the time ranged from surprise to blame. Some politicians called for limiting immigration to only EU countries. Others looked for ways to excuse the statistics as manifestations of integration failures and bureaucracy.

The *Federal Office for Migration* Chief stated that "the numbers are striking. Africans in Switzerland are still not well integrated." He added that 99 percent of Nigerian asylum seekers have no chance of getting asylum in Switzerland so "they do not come as refugees, but to do business" – engage in various crimes including drug trafficking.

These frank and honest statements angered Nigerian authorities that claimed the comments amounted to a "generalization that was undue." The chief of the *Federal Office for Migration* ended up in Geneva to informally discuss his comments with the Ambassador of Nigeria.

But Swiss law enforcement didn't seem surprised.

The president of the Swiss Association of Police Officials stated that, "For years we have watched certain populations that come with the intent of committing crimes in Switzerland." He added that he couldn't understand why these habitual criminals live freely in Switzerland without the threat of deportation.

Great question to investugate.
http://www.tagesanzeiger.ch/schweiz/standard/Neue-Statistik-Tamilen-sind-krimineller-als-ExJugoslawen/story/27784193
http://www.bernerzeitung.ch/schweiz/standard/Nigerianischer-Botschafter-verlangt-Aussprache-mit-Schweizer-Bundesamtschef/story/28664526

One event, many media spins
In Canton Bern, the media reported that a Turkish man, attempting to break up a protest, drove his car directly into a group of anti-Turkish Kurdish demonstrators resulting in at least a dozen injured immigrants.
https://www.youtube.com/watch?v=35oaNG19fgY

And that is exactly what the short edited video clip showed.

While the injuries were indisputable, the real story apparently was quite different. A longer video showed a more complete story. According to another version, apparently what "really" happened was that a violent group of Turks and Kurds had been fighting during protests in Switzerland. They were ready for war, and armed themselves with sticks, metal poles, wooden and steel bats, and other weapons of violence.

Yes, this happened in Switzerland.

Police officers were injured as the demonstrators attacked the police and fought with each other.

Reportedly, at some point, immigrants had surrounded an automobile, pulled a young Swiss woman and her child from that car, and were in the process of beating them both on the side of the road. The longer video showed one migrant thrusting a large wooden pole into one of the victim's heads. As the attack was in full gear, suddenly, a car swerved into the attackers and effectively broke up the brutal beating.

Now, how do you feel about the driver's actions? What if you and your child were being beaten senseless by a crazed mob, and someone sideswiped some of your assailants allowing you to flee? Feels a bit different than a "bad evil racist" trying to mow down peaceful innocent protesters. Everything is subject to spin. *All is not as it seems.* Welcome to the new Europe.
https://youtu.be/Kn-RBMGDozk

As this section was being written, more and more of the videos showing these migrants violently attacking people and attacking the police were being taken down or disappearing off the net.

Why is that?

At least the Swiss still have their Alps.

(48) TURKEY

Addressing the United Nations Security Council in April 2015, Hollywood superstar and Special Envoy Angelina Jolie prophetically stated that,

> "It is sickening to see thousands of refugees drowning on the doorstep of the world's wealthiest continent. No one risks the lives of their children in this way except out of utter desperation."

Remember that –
"No one risks the lives of their children in this way..."

And no one who saw the heart breaking picture, less than half a year later, in September 2015, of the little drowned migrant boy in the red t-shirt lying face down on the beach of Turkey will ever forget it.

"No one risks the lives of their children in this way except out of utter desperation."

The old-fashioned-controlled-media provided countless hours of in-depth coverage. Emotional and heart wrenching coverage that made the mere questioning of open-door reckless migration without accountability and security *anathema.*

How could you second guess migration in light of the tragic death of a little innocent immigrant boy fleeing war? You could only be a cold-hearted fascist animal.

The President of Turkey, Recep Tayyip Erdoğan, called the boy's father and reportedly said, "If only you had not put to sea, so that we could host you in our country."

The Independent ran a headline *"If these extraordinarily powerful images of a dead Syrian child washed up on a beach don't change Europe's attitude to refugees, what will?"* implying that anyone so heartless as to want to protect their families, homes, and country from migrants would now see the error of their ways and scramble to, instead, protect and empower the migrants. The Independent added that "The child, who is thought to be Syrian, has drowned in an apparent attempt to flee the war ravaging his country."

The Wall Street Journal noted, "He was 3 years old, from war-torn Syria. His final journey was supposed to end in sanctuary in Europe; instead it claimed his life and highlighted the plight of desperate people caught in the gravest refugee crisis since World War II."

The media was right about one thing. The boy had actually drowned. But that's where the "truth" ended.

Now we examine the curious story of one Abdullah Kurdi
We have all seen the heart wrenching sad photograph of the little dead Syrian boy on a beach in Turkey. Truly tragic. That was Abdullah Kurdi's son. We were told that Abdullah Kurdi and his wife and two little boys had been fleeing the horrors of the war in Syria. And that in desperation, the boy's father, Abdullah Kurdi, took his wife, the little boy, and the little boy's brother, on a boat to try and reach Greece from Turkey. Rough waves capsized the boat and Abdullah Kurdi's wife, and the two little boys drowned. Yet Kurdi himself somehow survived.

Here is what the old-fashioned-controlled-media apparently neglected to mention. Or maybe didn't explain. Or just stuck in the footnotes. Or forgot to examine. Or reported on page 351 of a 200 page report. Or neglected to fact-check. Or just left out.

While the old-fashioned-controlled-media would have you believe that Kurdi and his family were in the act of "fleeing immediate and grave danger," nothing could be further from the truth.

Nothing.

Far from being recent "fleeing refugees," Abdullah Kurdi and his family had actually lived happily and peacefully in a beautiful part of Turkey for about three years. Kurdi's sister in Canada was paying their monthly rent, and Kurdi had reportedly accumulated over $4,000 in cash.

Says who? Well, says Kurdi's sister, for one.

In fact, Kurdi's own sister in Canada, Teema Kurdi, clearly grieving and distraught, detailed, over the course of a heart-wrenching TV interview from Vancouver, that she had been working with her husband and neighbors and friends to get her brother Abdullah Kurdi and his family to Canada as a "private sponsorship" without any Canadian government funding.

Ms. Kurdi said she could only afford to sponsor one family into Canada at a time, so she had been working, unsuccessfully, on sponsoring the family of her older brother Mohammed and his five children. Once Mohammed was all settled, the plan was to sponsor Abdullah and his family.

Interestingly, when a reporter prompted Ms. Kurdi with the question, "Do you blame the Canadian government?" Ms. Kurdi answered, "Yes, they said 'missing document for your family.'"

In a later interview, Ms. Kurdi said she wanted to make it clear she "wasn't blaming the Canadian government," and that "every country has its rules."

Old-fashioned-controlled-media reporters seemingly kept framing questions to Ms. Kurdi in terms of "fleeing from Syria" and helping Abdullah Kurdi to "escape" and "blaming the Canadian government," and "do you think the Canadian government could have done more?"

But those were *their* words, not the words of Ms. Kurdi.

And none of the reporters seemed the least bit skeptical or probing as to *the facts.* It seemed that a meme had been set and there was a mad rush to get the best sound bites in support of that meme.

When asked by reporters, yet again to assign blame to the Canadian government, Ms. Kurdi said, "I don't want to just blame the Canadian government. I'm blaming the whole world for this, not helping enough, the refugee... the end of all this is to stop the war... *If nobody will fund the rebels, the war will stop."*

The part about blaming the Canadian government got a load of airplay. And some of the "blame the world" stuff got some interest, collective guilt and all. But complete silence and not one follow up question on the true gem, *"If nobody will fund the rebels, the war will stop."* Which rebels? Who is funding them? How? *Imagine what the answers might have revealed had follow-up questions been asked in the moment...* Nah, doesn't fit the meme, quick, let's see who else is to blame...

Back to why the boys and their mother were on that boat.

According to Ms. Kurdi, her brother Abdullah had a dental issue – he was missing his real teeth. She said she wanted to help him, but the price for implants, was projected to be

$14,000 and up. Dentists reportedly had to be paid "on the spot," and Ms. Kurdi couldn't get that much money to Abdullah Kurdi in one shot with Western Union limitations of $1,000 per wire. Another complication was that Ms. Kurdi said she couldn't send the money directly to her brother's name for some reason – which meant a third party would have to actually pick up the money and give it to Abdullah Kurdi.

In any case, Ms. Kurdi said she got money, $5,000, to Abdullah who was supposed to go to Europe alone. Then, Abdullah supposedly told his sister that because his wife was taking care of their two sons and wouldn't be able to work to support them at the same time, that they would all like to go to Europe together. According to Ms. Kurdi, she credited their father, who was living in Syria, with coming up with the idea to have Abdullah Kurdi and his family to "go to Europe for his kids and a better future... and then we'll see if we can fix his teeth." So, according to Kurdi's sister, that's why Abdullah Kurdi left the safety of their home in Turkey and set off for Europe in a smuggler's boat with his family.

Prophetically, prior to the trip, Abdullah Kurdi's wife and Ms. Kurdi allegedly spoke on the phone and the wife said she was terrified of going by boat since she couldn't swim.

"They were going for a better life," said Ms. Kurdi.

Think about that. *But there really is a lot more to think about.*

Within days of Kurdi's boat sinking, Turkish police rounded up and imprisoned four suspects, all of whom professed their innocence.

In mid-September, Turkish police arrested several people they also accused of migrant trafficking and being involved with the boat that Kurdi's family was on. But not a word about trials or evidence or anything. Completely confusing.

Abdullah Kurdi did reportedly say that he and his family had been living quite safely in democratic Turkey for years. According to him, they were not in a war zone, and he worked in construction.

Some speculated that Abdullah Kurdi may not have even been on the boat, claiming his "lack of injuries" from a reported "three hours drifting at sea" was unexplainable. Some also pointed to the fact that Kurdi had related *no less than* five different versions of what happened on the sinking boat. And worse, none of the stories meshed. Then he told some people that he "swam" to shore. And then he told others that he was "rescued by the coast guard."

Those are some pretty big basic details to screw up, right? Why all the disparities? Wait! What if he was actually the *smuggler* and not the *smugglee!*

No! Well.....

Australia's Network Ten Eyewitness News broke an exclusive story in which they interviewed a migrant woman who claimed to have been on the same boat with Abdullah Kurdi. The woman's two children also drowned when the boat sank. Except she said that Abdullah Kurdi was, in fact, "the smuggler," and "was the one who was driving the boat."

The eye witness claimed she was nervous to take the $10,000 trip, and was reassured by the arranger of the smuggling who said the "captain" of the dinghy would be bringing his wife and two children along for the trip.

The eye witness and her husband claimed that Abdullah Kurdi not only was the captain of the vessel, but that a) he overloaded the small boat, b) that there weren't enough life jackets for everyone, and that c) Kurdi's speeding caused the boat to capsize.

More eye witnesses finger Kurdi
News giant Reuters reported that other passengers also came forward and said Abdullah Kurdi was the boat's captain and that he begged them not to reveal him as the smuggler after he capsized the boat and about a dozen people drowned.

The Wall Street Journal reported that one set of witnesses, whose two children drowned as well, claimed that Kurdi told them, "I have lost my wife and my children also. Please do not tell the police." When the witnesses saw Kurdi at the hospital later, one said to Kurdi, "God get revenge on you, you did this."

Kurdi denied, and continues to deny all allegations.

What are we supposed to believe? Well, it's about to get ten times harder to figure out. *Hang on.*

Remember all the *fleeing Syria* and *running for your life from torture in Syria* and *escaping the horrors of the Syrian war* and all the rest of the old-fashioned-controlled-media's hypnotizing sound bites? Did you believe it all? Frankly, we did. Really. We hung on to the memes.

Until, that is, Abdullah Kurdi announced he was taking the bodies of his family back to Syria to bury them.

WHAT???

Now that's a *serious game-changer* !

Isn't a refugee or asylum seeker someone who *can't* return home? What just happened to *fleeing Syria* and *running for your life from torture in Syria* and *escaping the horrors of the Syrian war* and all the rest? How fast the mist vaporized.

Back home in Syria
So off Kurdi went, back home to Syria, for the funerals, and to hang out with relatives and friends. One major newspaper said,

"The grieving father of Aylan Kurdi has been photographed on his return to life among the ruins of the Syrian city his family had hoped to escape."

To the uninitiated (93.34% of America) it sure sounded like that is the place poor Kurdi and his family were fleeing. The photo showed a bombed out mess of rubble. Tragic. Inhuman. Unlivable. And "had hoped to escape" was a phrase constructed to make it sound like they were unsuccessful, assumptively due to the tragedy at sea.

But by now you have developed a knack for media spin, haven't you? You noticed what just happened. "Hoped to escape" was pure fakery – pure spin.

Remember, such crafted lie-phrases are designed to make you feel a certain way. The truth is, Kurdi was among the ruins of the Syrian city his family *did* escape! They *escaped* years ago, way before any of the bombings, and they lived freely and peacefully in democratic Turkey for three years *before* cooking up the *grass is greener* and *fix his teeth* schemes.

In another touching moment captured by a press photographer (professional "stagers"), Abdullah Kurdi was seen sitting next to a little boy identified as his nephew. As Abdullah glanced at the boy and patted his head with his left hand, he held a lit half-smoked cigarette in his right. *News flash, second hand smoke endangers children.*

> Hey photo dude – bad staging. *Hint, when going for the heart-tugging sympathy shot, at a minimum, remove all weapons, porn, and illegal and/or toxic substances from view, especially if a child is inches away from a lit cigarette.*

At some point Kurdi reportedly told a Turkish reporter that he now planned to take up arms and fight the Islamic State, explaining "I have nothing to live for. I will not go to Canada despite the invitation, nor to Europe. I'm not crazy about living in those places. *I was only hoping to provide a better life for my children."*

With all the weird inconsistencies and evidence, some have even called for Abdullah Kurdi to be arrested and face charges for endangering the lives of his little children, and wife, while trying to illegally enter a foreign country. They say he needs to be prosecuted for his carelessness. They say he needs to be held accountable for his reckless acts and decisions, that directly resulted in the deaths of his immediate family.

To put things in perspective, all over America, citizens are routinely arrested for leaving their dogs in hot cars. In many places you can get serious jail time. For instance, in liberal progressive marijuana-legal Denver, Colorado, leave your animal in a hot vehicle and it's animal cruelty carrying a fine up to $999 and AND/OR 1 year in jail.

Just imagine what you'd get for taking two tiny kids out on the ocean in a dinky boat without enough lifejackets while committing an illegal border crossing crime to get dental work done – during which they both drown.

Think about it.
http://www.wsj.com/articles/image-of-syrian-boy-washed-up-on-beach-hits-hard-1441282847
https://youtu.be/LnJ7Fs3SgrU
http://www.independent.co.uk/news/world/europe/if-these-extraordinarily-powerful-images-of-a-dead-syrian-child-washed-up-on-a-beach-don-t-change-10482757.html
https://youtu.be/QZUuoaq1MLM
https://youtu.be/3GJB-FH8U3s
https://youtu.be/ni3al6ONqds
http://www.hurriyetdailynews.com/if-only-you-had-stayed-in-turkey-erdogan-tells-drowned-syrian-toddlers-father.aspx?pageID=238&nID=88025&NewsCatID=359
https://youtu.be/EyY3XRJLA58
http://www.dailymail.co.uk/news/article-3230422/Abdullah-Kurdi-people-smuggler-migrant.html#ixzz3lVUxxi15
http://www.reuters.com/article/2015/09/11/us-europe-migrants-turkey-iraq-idUSKCN0RB2BE20150911#jySyuUBU3FXI3gcJ.97

http://www.dailymail.co.uk/news/article-3232251/Aylan-father-s-REAL-story-Abdullah-Kurdi-forced-deny-smuggler-new-questions-emerge-picture-shook-world.html
http://www.independent.co.uk/news/world/middle-east/aylan-kurdis-father-abdullah-returns-to-the-ruined-homes-of-kobani-after-burying-his-family-10489344.html
http://www.theglobeandmail.com/news/world/they-died-in-my-arms-father-of-drowned-migrant-boy-speaks-out/article26207543/
http://video.foxnews.com/v/4623178868001/dakota-meyer-why-potus-is-wrong-on-refugees/
https://www.denvergov.org/content/denvergov/en/denver-animal-shelter/shelter-programs/dogs-in-hot-cars.html

In the meanwhile, the immense power of the fictional tale lives on even though the truth is out there...

At the end of November 2015, NYC Mayor Bill de Blasio held up a photo of Abdullah Kurdi's deceased son being carried from the beach as *support for* why we need to help refugees!

Pulling at people's heartstrings is a pathetic and inappropriate use of that sad picture. Especially since it should be a crime scene photo in a child negligence case and not the poster child for refugees. But Bill is typical of so many ignorant people who trust the media to manufacture their opinions for them. And then perpetuate the fiction. Hook. Line. And sinker. So, Mayor de Blasio, unless you are trying to get attention for a program that prosecutes reckless parents for endangering the lives of their children, please shelf the photo.
http://www.thejakartapost.com/news/2015/11/28/drowned-syrian-boys-aunt-says-family-will-settle-canada.html

Super-strange on steroids

On Christmas Day 2015, Channel 4 News aired a message from Abdullah Kurdi to the world. Kurdi now said that he and his family had fled the war in Syria and, before their deadly boat ride, had gone to modern westernized and metropolitan Izmer, and then to sea-side Bodrum which had housed one of the ancient *Seven Wonders of the World*, both stunningly beautiful locations in Turkey. (Our details, not his.)

Likely weary of keeping track of the many different and varying versions he has told of what *actually* happened and his *true* role and involvement, Kurdi instead dismissed the tragedy at sea by saying "what happened, happened." Referring to his two young sons who drowned, he claimed "I'm happy I buried them at home" (in Syria).

Kurdi said his message was for "the whole world to open its doors to Syrians. If a person shuts the door in someone's face, this is very difficult. When a door is opened, they no longer feel humiliated... We ask just for a little bit of sympathy from you. I wish you a very Happy New Year. Hopefully the war will end in Syria next year and peace will reign all over the world."
https://youtu.be/hbJCNmuPsfc

We're guessing the media-manufactured sympathy points and "the photo" will shield Kurdi, even if he is found out to be the human smuggler that the witnesses identified him to be. And he'll probably be protected even if he is charged with child endangerment or depraved indifference for putting two little children's lives in mortal danger.

Unfortunately, the "facts" in this case are all over the place, and changing with the fluidity of a twisted river.

But there is one fact that is indisputable.

The death of those innocent children is not *your* fault. Not *my* fault. Not Europe's fault. Not Greece's fault. Not Canada's fault. Kurdi, and Kurdi alone chose to put them and his wife in harm's way. Nobody else.

As Ms. Jolie said, "No one risks the lives of their children in this way..." But, in fairness, she hadn't yet met Abdullah Kurdi.

The whole truth may never be known. But it should be.

Back to Turkey

In November 2015, in Istanbul, the Turkish and Greek national soccer teams were set to play each other. During a moment of silence for the victims of the recent Paris terrorist attacks, and with the Prime Ministers of Greece and Turkey present, the silence was disrupted apparently by Turkish soccer fans who hissed and booed and some chanted "Allahu Akbar."

What was that about?
http://www.cbsnews.com/news/turkish-soccer-fans-chant-allahu-akbar-paris-attacks-remembrance/

Who thinks this stuff up?

By December 2015, the EU had a new agreement in place with Turkey to try and limit the number of refugees still pouring in from Turkey. It sounded good, except one of the items the EU offered Turkey in exchange for sending along less migrants, besides a ton of cash, was *visa-free travel for Turks into Europe* as if they were part of the EU.

Plus there was some concern that more than half of the 700,000 Syrian children in Turkey were not enrolled in official schools. Further, since most Syrians can't speak Turkish, the fear was that the children would lose valuable education time. Add to all this the fact that an estimated 80+% of Syrian refugees in Turkey live outside of government shelters making it hard to keep track of them or service their needs.

Anyone who thinks this will end well, please speak up.
http://www.ft.com/intl/cms/s/0/a56fec72-975d-11e5-95c7-d47aa298f769.html
http://www.economist.com/news/europe/21679333-refugees-misery-still-drives-them-leave-europe-has-deal-turkey-migrants-will-keep

(49) UKRAINE

"Banking establishments are more dangerous than standing armies. And that the principle of spending money to be paid by posterity, under the name of funding, is but swindling futurity on a large scale."

—Thomas Jefferson
3rd President of the United States
Letter to John Taylor dated May 28, 1816

You probably heard all about the war in the Ukraine. And you probably heard *nothing* about the resulting refugees.

A simpleton's version of the situation
Since the breakup of the old Soviet Union, the Ukraine has desperately wanted to join the EU. After a load of alleged corruption, missteps, and bad breaks, the Ukrainians tried to cozy up to the EU and were told to make certain "reforms" in order to qualify for up to a staggering $17 billion bailout (loans) from the International Monetary Fund (IMF). *That's a load of cash!* And that was the bait...

To see how well other countries have done after taking enormous loans or bailouts from the IMF, check out Greece, Spain, Italy, Portugal, Ireland, Cyprus, and now the Ukraine. Are those financial and economic disasters just coincidences? Really?

By the way, things didn't seem to start to turn around for Iceland, or Ireland, or Hungary, until those countries divorced themselves from the IMF. Hungary actually got so fed up that it demanded that the IMF "get the hell out" of its country. But that's a whole other story.

Back to the Ukraine.

$17 billion being waved around by the banksters. A chance to get a few steps closer to the EU. And the President of the Ukraine got cold feet (was he afraid to get IMF-ed?) and refused to sign the cozy-up-with-the-EU agreement. Instead, he recommended a closer association with Russia and to borrow funds from Russia in order to cut out the IMF altogether.

Well, people went nuts. On *both* sides of the conflict.

In 2014, there was a revolution which ousted Ukraine's president and created a new interim government. Russia rolled into and took over Crimea, and declined to recognize the new Ukrainian revolutionary government. Pro-Russians and Pro-Ukrainians began fighting, especially in the areas of eastern Ukraine. "Separatists" carved out a large area of land on the Russian border an hoped to separate from the Ukraine. The often violent and deadly combat continues although everyone seems to be hoping for a resolution.

In the meanwhile, bloody conflicts beget refugees. Lots of them. So, did you know that over 2,000,000 people in the Ukraine were displaced or were refugees?

According to the UN, over 1,300,000 were displaced. Over 900,000 were refugees in neighboring areas. That's a huge number. By May 2015, the UN called the Ukrainian refugee crisis **"one of the worst humanitarian crises in the world today"** and getting worse with more than 2,000,000 refugees and displaced people. And thousands killed and thousands more wounded.

The UN reported that those refugees fleeing to Russia were greeted with good accommodations, food, medical services, and education. And the US Institute of Peace in October 2015 noted that the Ukraine had absorbed "its uprooted citizens with no significant social unrest – a tribute to the resilience of both the displaced people and the communities hosting them."

And all without tent cities and shelters.

But with so many Ukrainian refugees being "absorbed into cities and towns," even basic supplies were running out. Unicef was warning in 2015, that 700,000 children were at risk because of problems with heat, electricity, and water. The Red Cross was trying to keep up with supplying materials to repair bombed out houses. Many Ukrainians were reduced to eating solely buckwheat, if they were lucky, as they often had to decide between eating or heating their space. Shortages, especially of medicine and food, were rampant. It was estimated by the UN that at least 5,000,000 Ukrainians required humanitarian aid.

What a horrific humanitarian mess!

Probably the biggest story is in the Ukraine, *right now.*

And it was, and is, largely unreported or underreported or ignored by the old-fashioned-controlled-media which couldn't give enough attention and airtime to those economic opportunists arriving in Greece on a daily basis.

Why is that?

Think about it.
http://unhcr.org.ua/en/who-we-help/internally-displaced-people
http://www.usip.org/olivebranch/2015/10/19/europe-s-refugee-crisis-shows-ukraine-s-resilience
https://www.rt.com/news/262569-ukraine-refugees-crisis-russia/?

Oh, and remember the IMF and its $17 billion bailout carrot? Well, the Ukraine owes $3 billion to Russia, and if it defaults on any "official" "state" loans, by IMF rules, it won't be eligible for funding. So, the Ukraine called the loans "private" since IMF rules don't care about defaults on private loans. Russia said *nice try*, pay up.

Not so fast, comrade. The IMF said, *oh yeah?* well what if we change *our* rules to allow the Ukraine to default without jeopardizing the IMF funding. So *take that*, Russia!

Man, to what length will banksters go to secure those lucrative interest payments?

It's almost like, sensing a vulnerable future junkie, a greedy drug dealer bends cartel rules to get that first needle into that junkie's arm. Just... need... to... get... them... to... shoot up... once... for... a... lifetime... of... profits.... Ouch.

Not to worry, Russia threw the Ukraine a bone in November 2015 and offered not to demand the whole payment in one lump sum as originally agreed, but to take it in 3 payments over 3 years starting a year from now. Those are *better* terms than the *IMF* had asked for on Ukraine's behalf.

Talk about Slavs looking out for Slavs...

Unfortunately, we bet the Ukrainians will still cozy up to the IMF and end up a lot like Greece, Spain, Italy, Portugal, Ireland, and Cyprus. When it gets really bad, at least the Ukrainians will be able to hand over all of their natural resources, like their vast mineral deposits and coal, to the banksters. Free and clear.
https://www.rt.com/business/318630-putin-imf-ukraine-debt-russia/

(50) UNITED KINGDOM

In 2007, more than 20% of all of the crimes and about 30% of all sex crimes in London were committed by criminals of various foreign backgrounds. One police chief lamented "When they arrive they think they can do the same thing as in the country that they came from... their attitudes to drunk-driving are probably where we were 20 years ago." A leaked document from a Home Office minister revealed that "45,000 potential criminals from Romania and Bulgaria" were headed to the UK.

A half decade later, more statistics became available.

According to the Prison Population Statistics from the House of Commons, dated July 29, 2013, over 40% of prisoners were "young fighting-age," 15-29, and another almost 400 children aged 12-14 were in secure facilities. The amount of foreign nationals in prison has grown steadily over the years. More than 25% of prisoners were "ethnic minorities."

The report detailed that in 2013 while white English people made up 88.3% of the general population aged 15+, they accounted for 73.8% of prisoners and were underrepresented statistically. Chinese prisoners were also underrepresented based on their population statistics. Asians made up 5.8% of the population but 7.9% of the prison population, making them

136% overrepresented. Blacks made up 13.2% of prisoner population while only 2.8% of the general population, making them 470% overrepresented. Muslims, who made up 4% of the UK's general population aged 15+ made up just over 13% of the prison population for a total overrepresentation of 328%.
https://www.gov.uk/government/uploads/system/uploads/attachment_data/file/192317/prison-pop-tables-q4-2012.xls
https://www.gov.uk/government/uploads/system/uploads/attachment_data/file/192314/omsq-q4-oct-dec-2012__2_.pdf
http://www.telegraph.co.uk/news/uknews/1563890/Foreigners-commit-fifth-of-crime-in-London.html

The facts are the painful facts

By December 2015, the strange old-fashioned-controlled-media happily announced that there was no crime wave in the wake of the refugee influx to the UK. But with about 12.5% of the prison population made up of foreigners, it was a hard claim to make. Nonetheless, police in the UK also claimed crime rates had fallen. Who knows, but according to UK Crime Stats, from just September 2015 to October 2015, total crimes in England and Wales were up in each and every tracked category, with disturbingly large increases in violent crime, criminal damage, and arson. The latest figures available in January 2016 showed that October 2015 to November 2015 saw a 7% rollback in overall reported crimes yet with increases in burglaries, vehicle thefts, and muggings.
http://ukcrimestats.com/

England *owes* the world

In a fascinating insight into the immigrant mindset, a Muslim African immigrant to Britain, who grew up in England, told a television interviewer that he didn't "see himself as British, in any way, or English." He said that England destroyed his country in Africa and even though he and his family found safe refuge in England, that he was uncomfortable, *no*, downright revolted, with being identified as "British." He ended with, "this country (England) *owes* the rest of the world *anything it wants*, because of what it's done..."

Well, that pretty much sums up the entitlement mindset that can be seen exhibited by many people.
https://youtu.be/DHQ8ZQMUpaE

Convicts roam free as Britain is prisoner to her own laws
In 2014, the Express reported that some 4,000 migrants, convicted of a variety of crimes, were out roaming the streets of Britain. Unable to be legally deported since they had launched "human rights challenges," most were hiding behind the "right to a family life" clause in the Human Rights Act.

One English politician said in frustration, "It seems they protect the rights of rapists and murderers, rather than hard-working British people." Well, *yes.*

Certainly, only petty crooks were allowed to roam, right? Like red-light runners and pickpockets. Right? *Right??*

Nope. About 100 of the free-roaming convicts were found guilty of serious offences such as rape, murder, and child sex abuse. 10 were convicted pedophiles, 8 murdered people, and 48 were rapists, including 8 that raped children. *Roaming around...* Worse, official UK Government statistics showed that over 30 convicts were let loose into the community from jail every single week.

Brilliant. How's that working out for you?
http://www.express.co.uk/news/world/474234/Thousands-of-foreign-criminals-and-RAPISTS-roaming-Britain-and-dodging-deportation

Tower Hamlets
In the Tower Hamlets Borough of London, things ain't what they used to be. The Muslims are the majority. In fact, as of 2013, that borough had the largest number of Muslims per capita in all of England, outnumbering Christians 120%.

Tower Hamlets is also the scene of some very strange events.

On 11 November 1919, King George V started the tradition of observing "Two Minutes of Silence" at 11 am in honor of fallen comrades on the anniversary of Armistice Day, the end of World War I. The tradition continued annually and was named Remembrance Day, or Poppy Day, as bright red poppy flowers came to symbolize the red blood spilled during the war and were worn, woven into wreaths, and used to honor the dead.

Winston Churchill would have been proud
In November 2010, it was reported that a Muslim British citizen on welfare (free apartment in London's Tower Hamlets and a generous monthly allowance of various handouts including cash) decided that he would let his nation know exactly what he thought of Remembrance Day and the soldiers who sacrificed everything to keep him safe. So during the Two Minutes of Silence honoring the dead, he started dousing poppies with gasoline and setting them ablaze, chanting "Burn British soldiers, burn in hell."

At his trial, the judge noted that 'The two-minute chanting, when others were observing a silence, followed by a burning of the symbol of remembrance, was a calculated and deliberate insult to the dead and those who mourn or remember them."

Yet while the judge could have imposed a £1,000 fine, the man received a mere £50 fine.

After finding out his meager penalty, the poppy-burner laughed and made some wondrous statements including:
- "I don't have any respect for British soldiers, and if they lose a limb or two in Afghanistan then they deserve it."
- "I'm not being disrespectful for burning it, I'm being honorable. It's all about shock and awe, to get these soldiers out of Muslim lands."
- "It's my freedom of speech and I'm exercising that. I'm being persecuted for it. This fine, I will wear it as a badge on my shoulder. I did it for Allah."

- "You don't want another Afghanistan here do you? We want Sharia law in this country, and Inshallah (God willing) we will get it."

In the meanwhile, politicians and the old-fashioned-controlled-media were reporting that assimilation and integration was moving ahead swimmingly.

It's a long way to Tipperary. It's a long way to go...
http://www.dailymail.co.uk/news/article-1363772/Muslim-extremist-burned-poppies-Armistice-Day-fined-just-50.html

When in doubt, beat up the native Brits

English Defense League (EDL) members say on their website that they believe in "peacefully protesting against Islamist extremism." When a bus carrying 44 EDL supporters broke down in London's Tower Hamlets in September 2011, a group of 100 or so migrant teens took the opportunity to attack them with bricks and stones. Several hundred riot police quickly responded and arrested all of the EDL supporters.

Some said that it appears that these days, the police only protect the rights of migrants to protest, and view anyone with patriotic leanings or who supports "England" – as an enemy of the state.

As the arrested EDL supporters were being transported out in another bus, groups of migrant youths blocked the bus and refused to move, as a large group of migrant men began assembling. The police and migrants "scuffled" a bit and some migrants were also arrested as another group of migrants on a small bridge overlooking the scene heaved bricks and stones at the police. The bus was finally allowed to leave with police and their prisoners onboard.

Rule Britannia!
http://www.bbc.com/news/uk-england-london-14779772
https://youtu.be/H76Mf5q25sI

In the meanwhile, many people dismiss the EDL as being "skinheads" and "dangerous troublemakers." Police report that the left-wing anti-right group, Unite Against Fascism, particularly hates the EDL. When both groups are in the same vicinity, police go on high alert. At one gathering, 3,000 police officers were dispatched in anticipation of trouble.

In 2011, a long and peaceful protest outside a courthouse by EDL members was suddenly infiltrated by young Muslim men who began beating and punching English people by the dozens. In one instance, an English woman was so savagely attacked that she reportedly required a dozen stitches to her jaw and couldn't have solid food for 7 days. Video showed police who seemed completely unprepared, and really didn't seem able to protect the English people from the violent Muslim attack.

By the way, we don't know much about the EDL except from the videos and other recorded evidence we had watched. From what we saw, we never got the impression that they were anything more than a sometimes hot-headed and spirited group of pro-British people protesting against radicalization. Not until we watched old-fashioned-controlled-media "exposés" of the EDL did we learn that the old-fashioned-controlled-media has dubbed them a racist and Islamophobic hate group. *What is the truth? Whom do you believe?*

Brits better get with the new program
In 2011, the radical *Muslims Against Crusades* group announced their intention to mount a "forceful demonstration" to disrupt Prince William's Royal Wedding in order "to expose British English bigotry" and to highlight England's "quest to occupy Muslim land and wage war against the religion of God." On their website, they portrayed members of the Royal Family as Nazi sympathizers, imperialists, and brutal dictators. (Isn't that *hate speech* in some corner of this crazy universe? Or do migrants always get a pass?)

Muslims Against Crusades also called for Prince Harry and Prince William to quit the British Armed Forces and added that:

"We promise that should they (Princes Harry and William) refuse (to quit the military) then *the day which the nation has been dreaming of for so long will become a nightmare* and that it will Inshallah (God willing) eclipse the protests in Barking, Downing Street and the events of November 11."

"A nightmare that will eclipse November 11." *And that's ok? It isn't considered a threat or something? Goodness, the Brits really are a very tolerant lot.*

In the meanwhile, hundreds of members of the EDL volunteered to patrol all the subway stations near the wedding and to mount counter-demonstrations in support of their beloved Monarchy.
http://www.lutontoday.co.uk/news/local/royal-wedding-to-be-protected-by-edl-ring-of-steel-1-2608969

Who's in charge?

In 2014, an ex-EDL member accompanied by a reporter on the streets of Luton was attacked by angry Muslims asserting their new power. Suddenly, hundreds of Muslims swarmed onto the street in support of the attack. One Muslim, born in England, yelled, "We'll get out of *your* country when you get out of *our* country." Another young Muslim male said into the camera that "we're in a white man's world right now." And the old-fashioned-controlled-media reporter lamented that Muslims felt like the outsiders in England. Yet, the videotape showed *exactly* who was in charge. And it wasn't the Englishman nor the British police that responded.

America, you've been warned

The ex-EDL member prophetically stated, "America's going to see firsthand what's going to happen, how their freedoms are going to be attacked. This is what's happening. This is coming your way."

The reporter said she hoped "the voices of the many (as the audience was shown footage of radical Islamic protestors) drown out the screams of a few" (as the audience was shown video of British people protesting). Poor timing on the part of an editor? Or a not-so-subtle example of media spin. Think about it.

Unfortunately, as the accusations fly, the many snippets of truth likely spoken by both sides are buried in a media-created morass of non-coverage or mis-coverage.
https://www.youtube.com/watch?v=ctyyRgrRoM4
https://youtu.be/EDs6MRebb0U

Back to Tower Hamlets
During her June 2015 visit to England, the First Lady of the US, Mrs. Obama, chose to visit a school in Tower Hamlets, London. In case you missed it, in 2014 in Tower Hamlets, a Catholic nun made the news when she tore down a Muslim extremist flag that was being flown in support of Gaza and in protest of Israel.

The heavily Muslim Tower Hamlets area is very politically active with pro-Palestinian protests including people blocking traffic and tunnels, threatening journalists, and a mayor who flew the Palestinian flag over town hall to show solidarity with Gaza.

As far back as 2010, Islamic protesters were videotaped screaming fascinating tidbits such as – "if you dare touch a hijab on a Muslim woman's head or a hair on the beard of a Muslim man in Tower Hamlets, you will have to fight your way through 10,000 dead bodies first," and "it is *not* up to the police to decide when we march, where we march, and how we march."

Around the same time, the anti-British group *Muslims against Crusades* "disrupted" homecoming parades of UK soldiers returning from Afghanistan by calling the soldiers "cowards" and "butchers," waving anti-English banners, rioting, and eventually fighting the police as they caused all sorts of mayhem in the streets.

Of course, you're probably not surprised to learn that British police busied themselves protecting the Muslim demonstrators from some angry British citizens who were incensed at the complete lack of respect the UK veterans were shown.
https://youtu.be/oyZDVA2bG0w

This background setting makes Mrs. Obama's choice to stop over in Tower Hamlets an even more interesting choice.

Back to the visit.

With all the available choices in England, did Mrs. Obama choose a diverse school? A multi-cultural showcase? Where students of many ethnicities, religions, and backgrounds were working together in harmony?

Nope.

Mrs. Obama chose the Mulberry School for Girls, a single-sex establishment, which was almost entirely Bangladeshi, and according to a 2013 British Ofsted inspection report, had exceptional ratings but a "very small minority from other backgrounds, including White British, Pakistani and African" girls.

Mrs. Obama's speech to the girls was made under the "Let Girls Learn" banner. We guess the implication is that some bad people out there won't let girls learn, so Mrs. Obama wants to Let Girls Learn. Which reminds us of one of the worst cases we've heard of involving a girl not being allowed to learn by bad people – it was when 14-year-old student Malala was shot in the head by Islamic fundamentalists when she was open about pursuing her education and enjoying learning. The Islamic fundamentalists in the region had said that no girls could attend schools. Malala survived the shooting, toured the world speaking out for the right of girls to get an education, moved to the UK, won the Nobel Peace Prize, and donated part of her Nobel cash prize to rebuild 65 bombed-out schools for Palestinian children in Gaza. Curiously, all the Islamic fundamentalists imprisoned for her shooting were eventually set free due to a reported lack of evidence.

Back to the Mulberry School for Girls.

You and I are *so* alike
According to the White House website, Mrs. Obama said in her speech to the students that she chose to visit their school "because of you. I'm here because girls like you inspire me and impress me every single day... And I'm here because when I look out at all of these young women, I see myself."

The audience of primarily Bangladeshi girls in hijabs erupted often into enthusiastic applause. Mrs. Obama, who herself did not wear a headscarf, hijab, or burka, claimed she knew what "was inside girls like you and me."

Mrs. Obama told the girls "...maybe you read the news and hear what folks are saying about your religion, and you wonder if people will ever see beyond your headscarf to who you really are – instead of being blinded by the fears and misperceptions in their own minds. And I know how painful and how frustrating all of that can be. I know how angry and exhausted it can make you feel."

How exclusionary and painful these words must have been to hear for the handful of girls who weren't Muslim and didn't wear hijabs and realized that the message wasn't for them, but only for the hijab-clad Muslim girls. Was the intent to make those few girls in the minority at this school feel isolated? Hopefully they didn't follow Mrs. Obama's lead to get "angry" or "frustrated."

Mrs. Obama also said she was "so thrilled that today, our two countries are announcing a series of new partnerships that total nearly $200 million to help girls like you get the education they deserve. We're going to be working together to support young people – particularly adolescent girls – in areas affected by conflict and crisis, like the Democratic Republic of the Congo."

A wonderful and kind idea to send tons of millions of dollars out of the United States to benefit foreign teens while American schools continue to decay. No. Wait. It's worse. Imagine the reaction if a parent were caught going to distant neighborhoods to teach and support strangers while their own children languished at home. The outrage would be deafening. And this is different how?

As to the "Democratic" (elections are fraught with fraud, stuffed ballot boxes, and murdered voters) Republic of the Congo, a senior United Nations official called it "the rape capital of the world." Doctors Without Borders healthcare professionals recently reported treating slaves and sex slaves for a variety of injuries. Add in female genital mutilation (FGM) practices, open violence against females, child labor, child soldiers, and rampant plundering of the treasury by corrupt officials, and you might guess any money sent there will probably go to pay for liquor and dancing at elitist government parties.

In the meanwhile, the Mulberry School for Girls is now running fundraisers since the Obamas extended an invitation to come by and visit them at the White House in 2016. And to think we had to write to our Congressman three months ahead of time just to see the general tour.

The rosy future truly belongs to migrants.
http://www.theguardian.com/us-news/2015/jun/16/michelle-obama-london-schoolgirls-education-first-lady
https://www.whitehouse.gov/the-press-office/2015/06/16/remarks-first-lady-let-girls-learn-event-london-uk
http://www.msf.org.uk/
http://www.ibtimes.co.uk/malala-yousafzai-nobel-laureate-donate-50000-prize-money-gaza-un-schools-damaged-by-israel-1472352

FGM

In February 2015, London's Tower Hamlets Council issued a press release that they would be participating in "Zero Tolerance on FGM Day." FGM is petrifying, and the Tower Hamlets Council would know. After all, of the 1,300+ incidents of female genital mutilation (FGM) in England last year, about half were committed in London.

As the ticket for the event noted, "The Somali community is one of the foremost communities practicing FGM..."

Joined by London's Ocean Somali Community Association, all of the groups came together to discuss how best to "help prevent FGM and all other forms of violence against women and girls."
http://www.towerhamlets.gov.uk/news_events/news/february_2015/fgm_conference.aspx

Peaceful coexistence

In September 2015, a group of about a dozen Muslim men was videotaped beating a white Englishman with fists and a heavy road sign. Although at one point the Englishman was beaten to the ground, he managed to stand, stumble away, and escape.

Also in September 2015, a large group of possibly three dozen Muslim men was videotaped beating a white Englishman on a sidewalk in front of some stores. The Englishman who was missing his shirt was beaten to the ground. As he collapsed to the street, the group kicked and pummeled and punched and beat him. As he lay motionless, Muslim men were seen casually strolling over to get a better look at his body.
https://youtu.be/Yo8oJIyrXMY

Remember Rotherham?

Do you remember back in the summer of 2014, when it was revealed that there was systematic horrific child abuse being perpetrated by gangs of migrant men? No? *Missed that one?* One child would have been bad enough, but it was thousands...

A few minutes from Sheffield, the town of Rotherham has about a quarter million residents. It sports a castle, some ancient churches, many old ruins, a glassworks cone, and an active town center. According to a government report "around 8% of residents are from black and minority ethnic groups."

In the South Yorkshire town of Rotherham, investigators found that young children, as young as 11, were systematically sexually abused, often violently, by gangs of male Pakistani migrants.

The official government report noted that while the actual scale of the child sexual exploitation in Rotherham may never be known, that their "conservative estimate was that approximately 1,400 children were sexually exploited over the full inquiry period, from 1997 to 2013." The report stated that the abuse continues.

1,400 exploited children in just *one* English town. *Sickening!*

I dare not get involved, lest I be branded a racist
The report further stated that child victims were "raped by multiple perpetrators, trafficked to other towns and cities in the north of England, abducted, beaten, and intimidated. There were examples of children who had been doused in petrol and threatened with being set alight, threatened with guns, made to witness brutally violent rapes and threatened they would be next if they told anyone. Girls as young as 11 were raped by large numbers of male perpetrators."

Why was nothing done? According to the government report, while the sexual abuse was a well-known problem, since virtually all the perpetrators were Pakistani, social care workers "described their nervousness about identifying the ethnic origins of perpetrators *for fear of being thought racist*; others remembered clear direction from their managers not to do so."

According to the government investigators, "children would be reluctant to seek help because they would be ashamed and also afraid that they would be placed out of the area far away from their families and friends. One young person told us that 'gang rape' was a usual part of growing up in the area of Rotherham in which she lived." About half the children had been plied with alcohol as part of the "grooming process" used by the degenerate Pakistani migrants.

Most of the 1,400+ victims were young girls but males were at risk as well. A 2007 police operation resulted in the criminal conviction "of an offender who abused over 80 boys and young men." Social services didn't feel all of the victims needed post-rape services and "one of the children who failed to meet the threshold for social care went on to become a serious sex offender, convicted of the abduction and rape of young girls."

Blaming the victims, protecting the migrants
One police officer said that "the girls were blamed for a lot of what happened. It's unbelievable and key to why it wasn't taken seriously as an issue." A social worker said, "If we mentioned Asian (Pakistani) taxi drivers we were told we were racist and the young people were seen as prostitutes."

"The number one priority was to preserve and enhance the (Pakistani) community – which wasn't an unworthy goal but it wasn't right at the time."

Frankly, it was hard to get through the detailed government report without feeling sick. It *really* was that bad.

What was worse was that people didn't come forward and expose the migrant rapists because they were scared to be called "racists."

Is the price of "political correctness" worth it?
http://www.rotherham.gov.uk/downloads/file/1407/independent_inquiry_cse_in_rotherham

But it wasn't just Rotherham. According to England's Children's Commissioner, over the course of a year, a minimum of 16,500 children were considered to be at high risk for child sex exploitation.

Rochdale
It is thought that at least 50 young white girls were systematically sexually abused repeatedly by a gang of rapists operating out of Rochdale. Typical of their brutality and disinterest in their victims, they allowed one of their underage victims to be gang raped by 20 Muslim men in one night alone. According to court records, one of the sex gang's leaders taught religious studies at his local mosque.

When the 9 Muslim men were found guilty, in 2012, of raping and trafficking young white girls aged 13-15, one brave journalist stated that "turning a blind eye to appalling, illegal practices because 'it's their culture' is what has brought our country to this obscene pass."

Writing in the Telegraph, Allison Pearson also made the point that had 9 white men been found guilty of raping and pimping 13- to 15-year-old minority girls, media coverage and public outrage would have been far greater. Ms. Pearson also stated that "social workers and the police turned away for fear of being seen as racist." The chief prosecutor admitted that "imported cultural baggage" played a role in the crimes.

Ms. Pearson noted, "That's the same baggage that brought quaint customs like forced marriages, honour killing and female genital mutilation to these isles."

It's not the migrants
Lest you were starting to think that maybe race had something to do with this crime wave, Commons Home Affairs Committee Chairman, Keith Vaz, told the BBC in 2012 "not to condemn a whole community... I don't think this is about white girls... I do not believe it is a race issue... I think we do need to look into

this but I think it is quite wrong to stigmatize a whole community."

What about the victims?

It's never about the victims...
http://www.telegraph.co.uk/comment/columnists/allison-pearson/9254651/Asian-sex-gang-young-girls-betrayed-by-our-fear-of-racism.html
http://www.telegraph.co.uk/news/uknews/crime/9253978/Keith-Vaz-says-child-sex-ring-case-not-race-issue.html

Oxford
In Oxford, in 2013, seven Muslim (5 Pakistanis, and 2 Africans) rapists of pre-teen and underage white teen girls received prison sentences ranging from 7 years to 20 years for the rape and trafficking of 6 white girls aged 11-15. In 2014, police said they found that the actual number of victims was 50-60 young girls. In 2015, a review of the case found that the actual number of children sexually abused and exploited by the 7 Muslim men was closer to 373 children, including about 50 boys.

The details are as bad as you can imagine. Suffice it to say, violence, torture, beatings, abortions, prostitution, and frequent multiple gang rapes, often over the course of days, all came out in the court trial.

Brave Muslim lays it out
Reacting to the Oxford case, the imam of the Oxford Islamic Congregation, Dr Taj Hargey, authored a piece for the UK Daily Mail entitled "The Oxford sex ring and the preachers who teach young Muslim men that white girls are cheap." Some highlights from the article Hargey wrote include:

> "The fact is that the vicious activities of the Oxford ring are bound up with religion and race: religion, because all the perpetrators... were Muslim; and race, because they deliberately targeted vulnerable white girls, whom they

appeared to regard as 'easy meat', to use one of their revealing, racist phrases."

Hargey got that exactly right. Yet the old-fashioned-controlled-media saw the same events unfolding, heard the same testimonies, and could have easily found out the same facts, but didn't go there. Why?

Hargey went further, accusing the politically correct of not telling it like it is.

> "Indeed, one of the victims who bravely gave evidence in court told a newspaper afterwards that 'the men exclusively wanted white girls to abuse'. But as so often in fearful, politically correct modern Britain, there is a craven unwillingness to face up to this reality. Commentators and politicians tip-toe around it, hiding behind weasel words... While it is, of course, true that abuse happens in all communities, no amount of obfuscation can hide the pattern that has been exposed... the abusers were Muslim men, and their targets were under-age white girls."

Again, Hargey made perfectly sound observations which no one in the old-fashioned-controlled-media would dare to explore. He continued by firmly blaming part of the tragedy on "politically correct thinking." He observed that he thought authorities were "terrified of accusations of racism, desperate not to undermine the official creed of cultural diversity, they took no action against obvious abuse..." And because they were scared to be labeled, they helped not.

Most telling may have been his comments about the views about women held by some Muslim men. Hargey didn't sugar-coat a thing.

> "The view of some Islamic preachers towards white women can be appalling. They encourage their followers to believe that these women are habitually promiscuous,

decadent and sleazy — sins which are made all the worse by the fact that they are kaffurs or non-believers. Their dress code, from mini-skirts to sleeveless tops, is deemed to reflect their impure and immoral outlook. According to this mentality, these white women deserve to be punished for their behaviour by being exploited and degraded."

A brave lone voice in the wilderness.
http://www.childrenscommissioner.gov.uk/news
http://www.cps.gov.uk/news/latest_news/seven_men_jailed_over_oxford_child_sexual_exploitation_case/
http://www.telegraph.co.uk/news/uknews/crime/10061217/Imams-promote-grooming-rings-Muslim-leader-claims.html
http://www.dailymail.co.uk/debate/article-2325185/The-Oxford-sex-ring-preachers-teach-young-Muslim-men-white-girls-cheap.html

Telford
Similar story, different town.

This time, 7 Pakistani men, identified by the media as "Asian," were imprisoned in 2013 for targeting and sexually abusing and exploiting what police said may have been more than 100 young white girls, aged 13-16. This child prostitution ring operated for years as police tried to build their case so as not to appear to be racists. As one of the Deputy Chief Inspectors said on a television program, "How do you deal with that (making arrests), without being accused of being racist?"

That's right. Scores of young girls are being raped and it's important to consider how it will look to lock up the rapists because they're not Europeans.

Think about that.

One journalist who interviewed many people close to the case reported that investigators heard horrific accounts of deviant sexual abuse and torture of children "violating them in every orifice, as well as gang-rape by queues of men while girls were held hostage for hours, sometimes days – all the while being forced to listen to the screams of girls in other rooms with other men. Inhumane doesn't get close to describing it; it's the stuff that parental nightmares are made of."

On the other hand, a children's services worker told a reporter that "We have been clear from the start that this is purely about criminal behavior by a few individuals."

What about the victims? It's never about the victims...
http://www.shropshirestar.com/news/2013/05/19/tv-special-to-expose-sex-ring-investigation-in-shropshire/
www.channel4.com/programmes/dispatches/articles/britains-sex-gangs-tazeen-ahmad-feature

Derby
If the cases all start to sound way too similar, they are.

This time it's 2010 and we're in Derby. 13 men were accused of 75 offences with 27 girls. 9 were convicted. The gang had been targeting, raping, and imprisoning young white girls between the ages of 12 and 18. Violent gang rapes involving up to 8 men, gang rapes filmed on cell phones to the sounds of cheering, prolonged abuse and torture. One of the police investigators categorized the systematic assaults as "a campaign of rape against children."

Well, to be totally accurate, *white* British children.
http://www.bbc.com/news/uk-england-derbyshire-11799797

The Telegraph reported in 2011 that "50 out of 56 men convicted in English courts of on-street grooming of girls were Muslims, the majority of whom were from the British Pakistani community. Most of the victims in the 17 separate cases, which spanned 13 years, were white.

Damned if you do, damned if you don't
Member of Parliament Jack Straw said "There is a specific problem which involves Pakistani heritage men... who target vulnerable young white girls." To which another Member of

Parliament, Khalid Mahmood, shot back "To generalize in this stereotypical manner and castigate a whole community is not becoming of him."

In the same article, a social cohesion think tank director said about young Muslim males that "their views about women would horrify many people. They often regard women as second-class citizens, and white girls are regarded differently as acceptable prey in a way Muslim girls aren't... Of course this problem only relates to a minority of Pakistani men, but it is an issue that needs addressing..."

What do you think about that?
http://www.telegraph.co.uk/news/politics/8248189/Jack-Straw-sparks-row-with-Pakistan-easy-meat-remark.html

Bristol
Near the end of 2014, a gang of 13 Africans from Somalia were sentenced for a variety of sex crimes including rape, child prostitution, child pornography, sexual activity with a child, and drugs. Most of the perpetrators were said to be in their early 20s and their arrests shocked members of their Muslim community. Their victims were all mostly white underage British girls aged 13-17.

The investigation into this gang started after the gang rape of a 13-year-old white British girl by three rapists. It would later be revealed that one of the Somalis had previously raped this same girl when she was only 11 years old, telling her "this was his culture."

The *Evening Standard* reported in 2015 that "many of the girls were groomed to view the abuse as a normal part of being the 'girlfriend' of a Somali man, as it was said to be 'culture and tradition' to be raped by their 'boyfriend's' friends."

Purely sickening.

The perpetrators got sentences ranging from 2 years to 13 years 8 months. At one point, the judge minced no words as he told one perpetrator, "The repeated humiliation of a small 13-year-old girl was completed in a rough, callous and very nasty manner... You behaved without humanity and simply took what you wanted, leaving your victim totally humiliated and bleeding."

In the meanwhile, Bristol Police reportedly were busy looking into "49 other suspects" involved in similar cases of child sex assaults.

Most worrisome was a comment from the director of a victim support group who said this was just the "tip of the iceberg" and that "such abuse was going on across the UK."

That was 2014. Think about it.
http://www.theguardian.com/uk-news/2014/nov/27/guilty-prostitution-bristol-rape-girls-sex-abuse-somali
http://www.standard.co.uk/news/crime/gang-who-were-part-of-inner-city-sex-ring-which-preyed-on-british-girls-are-jailed-for-40-years-9890675.html

Middlesbrough

In the early part of 2014, two Muslim men (ages 32 and 19) and their 17-year-old accomplice stood trial in Middlesbrough for their roles in child exploitation in a case involving many underage schoolgirls (ages 13-15). One man pled guilty to 5 counts of sexual activity with a child, the second was found guilty of 4 counts of sexual activity with a child (plus one child abduction – he abducted and raped a young girl in his taxicab), and the migrant teen was found guilty twice of having arranged or facilitated child sex offences. The migrant men each received 8 years in prison and the teen received 3 years in a juvenile institution.

In sentencing the sexual predators, the judge said, "The fact that the girls have been condemned, and not you, reveals a profoundly worrying attitude to what has gone on here; an attitude which, if not challenged, will lead to further cases like this in the future, just as it has in the past."

What of the victims?

The migrants and their comrades continued to make the lives of their prey miserable. The underage victims had already been subjected to the unthinkable – and now, according to the prosecutor in the case, were subsequently harassed by *friends and family* of the defendants who called the girls "sluts" and "white trash" and accused them of being "racist" for turning in their migrant attackers.

From the name calling to online threats, from filthy messages to cruel rumors, from intimidation (one girl's family had been forced to move) to vandalism, the prosecutor called it additional "horrifying abuse" after the sexual abuse.

But there's more.
http://www.gazettelive.co.uk/news/teesside-news/grooming-trial-judge-condemns-middlesbrough-6707567
http://www.gazettelive.co.uk/news/teesside-news/grooming-trial-mum-victim-tells-6379358
http://www.darlingtonandstocktontimes.co.uk/news/11009663.Three_Middlesbrough_men_jailed_for_grooming_underage_girls_for_sex/

Banbury
Yet another similar sounding story. How very profoundly sad.

This time we're in Banbury where five young African migrant men and a 17-year-old male teen were found guilty of various child sexual exploitation charges, from sexual activity with a child to rape.

The perpetrators attacked seven young white girls aged 13-15 after luring them via social media to "parties." The young girls were abused in automobiles, in the woods, and in the homes of the perpetrators.

The senior police investigator said the young girls were "subjected to horrific sexual offences at the hands of these men which will have a lasting impact upon their lives. No one should have to experience this. The offenders maintained they were not guilty of the crimes of which they were accused which resulted in the victims having to relive their experiences by giving evidence in court... I also want to make it clear that this case is about the victims. They have shown exceptional courage and resolve and we should not underestimate just how difficult it has been for them throughout..."

Yes. It is the victims that should be the focus.

Sadly, there are so many more cases in the "new "England. But let's turn our attention for a moment to English schools. Surely English schools are teaching English children to respect themselves and each other without exceptions, right?
http://www.banburyguardian.co.uk/news/local-news/banbury-sex-exploitation-trial-offenders-subjected-girls-to-horrific-offences-1-6619377

The Trojan Horse Scandal
From 2013-2015, a multitude of reports including detailed features in the UK's *Mirror* revealed that Muslim extremists had allegedly implemented a secret plan to hijack British schools, specifically in Birmingham.

Non-Muslim teachers were bullied and intimidated out of their jobs as schools became "Islamified." Girls and boys were segregated, music was banned, and raffles were eliminated for being anti-Islamic.
http://www.mirror.co.uk/news/uk-news/trojan-horse-school-chief-exposed-3893455
http://www.mirror.co.uk/news/uk-news/trojan-horse-scandal-schools-employed-6686781
http://www.mirror.co.uk/news/uk-news/struggling-pupil-trojan-horse-linked-6903549

The imposition of Islam on British school children was nicknamed *Trojan Horse* and had many outrageous alleged manifestations including:
- Employment decisions in favor of Muslim teachers over all others
- Infusing Muslim beliefs into the secular curriculum
- "Collective worship" time was exclusively Muslim
- Muslim students received special prayer privileges
- Students weren't allowed to develop as regular British citizens
- Girls not wearing hijabs were denied extra help
- An elimination of all art showing the human form
- No instruments to be found in music departments
- Students at assemblies were led in chants of "We don't believe in Christmas, do we?" and "Jesus wasn't born in Bethlehem, was he?" and "Do we send Christmas cards? No!" and "Do we celebrate Christmas? No!"
- Some school signage and notifications were only in Arabic to exclude non-Muslim teachers and staff
- A Saudi Arabia school trip was only available to certain Muslim male students
- Weekly school time was missed to accommodate Muslim prayers
- Traditional annual Christmas celebrations were cancelled allegedly because students couldn't afford to lose time studying
- Classrooms were segregated so girls sat in the back
- Singing and musical instruments were banned
- The drawing of eyes or trees was forbidden
- Students were punished by being made to stand in the rain
- Taxpayer funded school trips that excluded Christian students
- Calls to Muslim prayer broadcast over school loudspeakers
- Children were taught that boys had empowerment over girls in sexual situations

- Children were taught that "women would be smited if they refused to have sex with their husbands" and "forced into an eternity in hell"
- Girls were forbidden from taking part in sports when males were present as it made the males uncomfortable
- Students were addressed by invited speakers who spoke of God destroying the enemies of Islam

Think about it.
http://www.mirror.co.uk/news/uk-news/teachers-become-first-uk-face-6843971
http://www.mirror.co.uk/news/uk-news/pupils-allegedly-chanted-we-dont-6802761
http://www.birminghammail.co.uk/news/midlands-news/trojan-horse-style-concerns-raised-birmingham-8461875
http://www.mirror.co.uk/news/uk-news/pupils-trojan-horse-school-told-6663107

In 2014, the Muslim *Chairman of Governors* at a British school in Birmingham was videotaped stating that
- "The colonial blood they have within them, these white people, it's very difficult to get rid of that very quickly."
- "White British English children are lazy"
- "Our (Muslim) women are much much better consciously in the heart than any white women"
- "If an English Jew goes to Israel and kills people he is welcomed back to England with open arms... if a Muslim or any other person goes and fights for their people and comes back, they're classed as terrorists."
- "White women have the *least* amount of morals."
- "Emotionally, women are much weaker... they are not on the same level."
- Imprisoning homosexuals and adulterers under Sharia Law is a "moral position to hold."

Really think about *all* of that.
http://www.mirror.co.uk/news/uk-news/trojan-horse-school-chief-exposed-3893455

Red flags and warnings ignored
In 2013, an anonymous letter tipped off authorities to the seriousness of the Islamification agenda. But none of this should have been much of a surprise. It had been going on a long time. And so had the warnings.

In 1994, senior officials in schools had raised alarms about the Islamification of British schools and even copied the Prime Minister in on their correspondence. Since then, many red flags were waved over the years *but not much had been done* by officials, possibly for fear of being labeled racists or xenophobes. *Pathetic.*

Let's rename Christmas not to offend anyone
In 1998, the spineless politically correct Birmingham City Council unsuccessfully tried to "rebrand" Christmas as "Winterval" in a lame attempt to be "inclusive" and not offend local Muslims. Community outrage and media attention put an end to the exercise by 1999.

Banned for life
In the summer of 2015, a teacher at the Knowsley Junior School in Oldham was "banned for life from the classroom" after she started tweeting, in October 2014, her support of the jihadi murder and beheading of British aid worker Alan Henning.

The Muslim teacher's vile rants included, "A beheading deserved... Best thing for the Kafir (nonbelievers) is to **** off out of Muslim countries... Well done IS...don't blow the shrines up... kill kafir for wat they've done... (that) many have sympathy for Alan is the scale of bitchiness of white women."

The teacher had been previously fired "from the school in December 2010 and was subject to an interim prohibition order for being abusive towards staff, including the head teacher." She had been trying to work her way back into the education system but her inability to control her "racist hate

speech" and encouraging "the murder of non-Muslims by ISIS" sealed her fate.
http://www.dailymail.co.uk/news/article-3147288/Junior-school-teacher-banned-LIFE-spewing-racist-bile-Twitter-including-praising-beheading-Alan-Henning-urging-murder-non-Muslims.html

More teachers banned for life
In mid-November 2015, several Muslim teachers were *banned for life* from British classrooms for over-imposing Islam on students.

The *Mirror* reported that "both teachers were found guilty of reforming... curriculum to exclude proper sex education. Pupils were not taught about homosexuality, AIDS, HIV or contraception, while boys were told good Muslim wives should always obey their sexual demands. Pupils were needlessly segregated, while Islamic prayer sessions became more frequent."

Maybe there is hope for Britain. Unless the new Muslim majority votes the Brits out of office...
http://www.mirror.co.uk/news/uk-news/pictured-muslim-teacher-dubbed-general-6642085
http://www.mirror.co.uk/news/uk-news/muslim-schoolgirls-told-women-would-6636342

Helpful civilians patrol the streets
Street patrols by volunteers were a time honored tradition in England during World War II. The streets of English towns and cities, especially London, were diligently patrolled by brave civilians who performed many important tasks while keeping an eye out for Nazi agents. They relayed the locations of bombings, looked for and helped extinguish fires, decontaminated buildings from gas attacks, searched for victims of bombings, rescued people trapped in rubble, performed first aid, and helped clothe, house and feed survivors of bombings.

Truly selfless giving at its British-best.

A new more helpful patrol for a new England
In the spirit of selfless giving, young Muslim men have revived the English street patrol tradition, except with a *new* twist. They have formed Sharia Patrols, donned Sharia Police vests, and hit the streets seeking out English people to help them better understand the error of their evil British ways.

From yelling "slut" and "whore" at British women not wearing burkas or hijabs, to surrounding and intimidating young British men drinking alcohol, to harassing young women out on the town, Sharia Patrols regularly volunteer their time to weed out infidels and infidel practices.

During a recorded tour of a town near Tower Hamlets in 2011, a videographer captured an aggressive Muslim defending Islamic law and calling British people opposing Sharia law "racists." As the British man tried to drive away, the Muslim punched the British driver in the face.
https://youtu.be/rP6U6Hhy_2M

Not so "Great" Britain anymore
In another video, Sharia Patrols hunted down English people on the streets of London and harassed them for
- *drinking alcohol* warning them that they were in a "Muslim area" and that "alcohol bad"
- *being homosexual* with warnings of "you're a gay mate, get out of here mate, get out of here you f*g"
- *being women wearing skirts above the knee* with the admonishment "to not dress like that in Muslim area"

The Sharia Patrol leader admonished British people that
"it's not so 'Great' Britain" anymore, saying ultimately he wants to see "every single women in this country covered head to toe, I want to see the hand of the thief cut (off), I want to see adulterers stoned to death, I want to see Sharia Law in Europe, and I want to see it in America as well. And I believe our (Sharia) Patrols are a means to an end."

A number of members of Muslim Patrols or Sharia Law Patrols had been arrested on various charges, but patrols persisted.
https://youtu.be/ra45nX9JmW4?list=PLA1N-cMYpjPZOPQMH9mVbok3JRTevjJdd

Law of the land *go to hell*
In 2013, a report on Muslim Patrols highlighted them making statements such as "we are Muslim Patrol, we are in North London, we are in South London, East London, and West, London... we forbid evil, Islam is here in London, Mr. David Cameron (British Prime Minister), Mr. Police Officer, whether you like it or not..." and "the law of the land go to hell... no respect for the British law whatsoever..."

By 2014, an English group, *Britain First*, formed "Christian Patrols" to counter the Muslim and Sharia Law Patrols, and took to the streets of East London in a bullet-proof truck handing out Christian literature.

Muslims felt threatened
A spokesperson for the local Muslim community said they felt "threatened" by Christian patrols. Some local residents felt the Christian patrols were unnecessary and some felt Christian patrols shouldn't be allowed. Interestingly, no one commented on whether Sharia patrols were necessary or should be banned as well. The old-fashioned-controlled-media did seem to condemn the Christian Patrols and likened them to vigilantes.

In the meanwhile, Muslim Patrol activity reportedly had lessened but it wasn't clear if the recent arrests of aggressive Muslims trying to impose Sharia law had toned down the activity.

Luckily, no Brits had come forward to say that the Muslim Patrols had made them feel threatened. It's all good.
https://youtu.be/cYFzrEIzoHE
https://youtu.be/7lixGYdDQ_A

Attempted beheading goes beyond insanity
In Woolwich in May of 2013, two African Muslims targeted, attacked, and murdered an off duty British soldier in a revenge murder.

As one of the smiling African killers excitedly explained on video from the scene of the murder, *before the police arrived and as the body of his victim still lay in the street*, "the only reason we have killed this man today is because Muslims are dying daily by British soldiers. And this British soldier is one, is an eye for an eye, a tooth for a tooth, by Allah, we swear by the Almighty Allah we will never stop fighting you until you leave us alone."

That someone would stand there and film this guy as he made these statements, blood literally still dripping from his hands, is a whole other story we won't even get into.

Apparently, the two African Muslims, one who told an eye witness that they "want to start a war," first ran the British soldier over with their car. Next, the pair began violently stabbing and hacking away at the British soldier's crumpled body with knives and meat cleavers to kill him and in an attempt to also behead him. Then the pair proudly announced to anyone who would listen the great deed they had done for the glory of Allah. They chatted away with strangers on the street and milled about until the police arrived, at which point they charged the police with knives raised, in an attempt to get killed and become "martyrs for Islam."

Both were shot. Both lived. Both were tried. Eventually, both were sentenced to life in prison. The brother of one of the killers said in a televised interview that he was proud of his brother "in that he is a Muslim and that he sought to please Allah by fighting in His cause and dying in His cause, then, to this extent yes... I love (my brother) more (now, than before)."
http://www.theguardian.com/uk-news/2014/dec/03/lee-rigby-killer-michael-adebolajo-loses-bid-conviction-quashed

What about the victim? And his family? And the surrounding community? Was anyone else targeted? Were British soldiers and their families afforded special protection?

Well, not much. Base security was increased. And the Ministry of Defense did warn English soldiers to hide their British uniforms when in public lest they *provoke* attacks.

Wearing British uniforms might PROVOKE attacks? Is this the same mighty Empire upon whose shores the sun never set?
http://www.bbc.com/news/uk-22642441

Yet there was *swift action* from 2 groups
Right after the attack, the Islamic Society of Britain quickly raised concerns and alarms for the safety of Muslims in England. *Apparently all Muslims in London were suddenly in harm's way now that several Muslims had butchered a British soldier.*

Which led to a speedy reaction from authorities.

London police flooded the streets with over 1,200 additional police officers to reassure and prove to the Muslim and minority communities that they would be safe in London, and to safeguard and protect London's Muslims from potential attacks from "racist" Brits.

As England's Queen Elizabeth II called for "calm," Prime Minister David Cameron stated that the cold blooded murder of the innocent British soldier "was a betrayal of Islam and the Muslim communities that give so much to our country."

Interestingly, when the judge sentencing the murderous pair said the same thing, that their actions had been a "betrayal of Islam," the killers completely disagreed as the judge had *gotten it all wrong* – and went berserk, screamed filth at the judge and court, yelled "Allahu Akbar," swore that "Britain and America would never be safe," and fought and wrestled with court officers before being dragged out of the courtroom.

The murderous duo made it crystal clear that they had intended to become Muslim martyrs, they hadn't "betrayed Islam," and no British judge was going to label them with *that* anathema.

Think about it.

In the meanwhile, the murdered British soldier, Lee Rigby, was a young 25-year-old proud member of the Royal Regiment of Fusiliers, an infantry regiment where he was also a member of the Corps of Drums. He left behind an ex-wife, a fiancée, and a 2-year-old son. His family was heartbroken, grieved, and frequently cried over his senseless and tragic loss.

However, as seems to be the new trend, a tremendous amount of coverage. conjecture, and analysis was devoted to the two heartless murderers.

Terms used to try and explain away their rage included: Traumatized. Mistreated. Narcissistic. Victim. Misguided. Suffering. Lost. Troubled. Young. The whole *radical crazed animalistic killer* thing really wasn't too popular among the old-fashioned-controlled-media.

But it's never about the victim. Not these days.
https://youtu.be/UIO3f1Vz0Pw
http://www.independent.co.uk/news/uk/crime/lee-rigby-murder-michael-adebolajo-and-michael-adebowale-sentenced-to-life-in-prison-9155196.html

Party at my house
In February 2013, a 19-year-old British woman got a text from a 20-*something* migrant man she had met during New Year's with an invitation to come over and hang out at his house.

This can't end well...

Upon arriving at the house, the woman found the friendly gathering had grown to two migrant men. She made the fateful decision to stay and was treated to way too much vodka by her charming hosts. When she said she was "tired," the men took her to a bedroom and locked her in it with one of the migrants. The migrant proceeded to rape the woman as she protested.

Confused and scared, when her captor allowed her to use the bathroom, she called the police. By the time officers arrived, the two migrants had fled. The rapist was arrested about a half year later when he showed up at an immigration office. After trial, he was sentenced to 4 ½ years prison time after which time he may be deported.

The convicted rapist's lawyer argued that the rapist was concerned the Taliban might kill him if he is deported so maybe he should be allowed to stay in the UK.

What about the victim?

The judge stated that "She has suffered depression and has spent time in a hospital as a result. What you (the rapist) did has affected her badly."
http://www.theboltonnews.co.uk/news/11031932.Refugee_raped_19_year_old_in_locked_bedroom/

After alcohol, a cab is a smart choice, except when it's not
At 2 am what's safer than a cab after you've been out drinking?

That's what the victim of a sexual assault thought as she got into a private taxi cab to get to Bristol Temple Meads station in mid-January 2015. Unfortunately, the sexed-up migrant driver had some very different ideas.

As the migrant drove and suggested they "go back to his place," the woman refused and the driver groped her. Next, he drove past the station, stopped his cab, and proceeded to sexually assault the woman. The woman was able to escape and take a photograph of the migrant's license plate before he sped off – allowing police to eventually track him down.

Cut and dry, right? Throw the book at him, right? Well... he is a hard-working migrant...

Turns out the sexual assailant was also the "hard-working" father of four children who fled Somalia, Africa, and sought asylum in the UK. His lawyer claimed that the man had not only been the *victim of persecution* in Somalia, but now he had *lost* his job and good name *as a result* of these charges.

Read it again. Aren't there a ton of built-in excuses and explanations in one sentence? The sexual attacker had been a *victim* of persecution. He had been taken in by England, offered refuge and safety, and probably free healthcare, free education, and a decent residence. Now, *because of the attack*, he had no more job and his reputation had been sullied. *What? Seriously?* Frankly, who cares about all that other junk. Stay on point... he *sexually assaulted* a woman.

In April 2015, a jury found the man guilty of "sexual assault and causing a person to engage in sexual activity without her consent."

The Brits have regained their senses, right? Throw the book and the bookshelf at him, right? Well... this is the new UK...

The court sentenced the sexual assailant to a suspended two year sentence – *zero* jail time. Instead, he'll have to do 100 hours of volunteer work, be supervised for two years, and be the subject of a sexual harm prevention order (which restricts him from certain activities, *if* he decides to follow the order).

Again, no jail time whatsoever for a sexual assault.

And what of the victim? *It's really never about the victim.*
http://www.express.co.uk/news/uk/569551/Asylum-seeker-taxi-driver-free-sex-assault-cab

Christian is almost martyred, again
In November 2015, a CCTV camera recorded a Christian man being viciously beaten with a pickaxe handle by a group of young males in what police are calling a "religious hate crime."

The victim, a real estate entrepreneur, had previously been forced out of his last home by militant Muslims and was attacked by Muslims over the past, but claimed that the police failed to protect him or help him until now.

Apparently the young Muslim male attackers were exacting some version of Sharia law since the victim was a former Muslim who converted to Christianity years ago and was regarded as a "blasphemer."
https://youtu.be/tw-t7u7QQtU

Die in Your Rage
In November 2015 England's Channel 4 aired a chilling documentary, *ISIS British Women Supporters Unveiled*, exposing a growing anti-democratic anti-Western movement in England in support of Sharia law, and the Islamic fundamentalist and ISIS recruitment activities in the UK by radical Muslim British women.

A British Muslim burka-clad reporter went undercover for a year. She discovered a network of women-only educational sessions, the distribution of extremist ideologies complete with anti-Semitism, and the enticement and recruitment of young women to join ISIS and fight to spread Islam. Young girls (as young as 15) and women recruits were told that it is their duty to go to Syria and live under ISIS, and were encouraged never to vote in UK elections and to reject England's laws and values.

The beliefs are spreading. During the frequent Muslim demonstrations in London, one Muslim protester explained "We will never stop rejecting democracy and British values."

"Die in your rage" is a popular extremist slogan, used frequently by ISIS, and repeated endlessly around recent events such as the Paris massacres and heard on the video of the shooting down, and subsequent murder, of the parachuting Russian fighter pilot over Turkey in November 2015. And "Die in your rage" is used by one of the British women supporters of ISIS on her social media pages.

The undercover footage revealed protests and messaging on the streets of Britain along the lines of "Islam is superior." And "NO to democracy – YES to Islam." And "Sharia law is the best for mankind." The radical women told the reporter that they had a regular meeting for women in Walthamstow.

> *Walthamstow? How great. It's less than 7 miles from Tower Hamlets. Maybe they'll invite Mrs. Obama next time she swings by. How cool would that be?*

At one of the Muslim women's meetings, ironically held at a local north London community center *supported by the funds of clueless British taxpayers*, the reporter infiltrated and filmed the goings-on. Radical Muslim women, teenage girls, and children all occupied a meeting room as one woman preached for an hour about her love and devotion to Islam, her admiration for jihadists, and the like.

The reporter was invited back to another secret meeting, this time in east London. Larger group, but same deal – women, teenagers, and children. Again, the theme was anti-England and anti-British values and anti-democracy, including a rant about the "filthy Jews." Eventually, the extremist women grew suspicious of the undercover reporter and the story ended as her "cover was blown."
https://youtu.be/qA_n84Hz15g

Surgery can be dangerous

In November 2010, a 21-year-old Muslim woman attempted to murder a British Member of Parliament by stabbing him at a "constituency surgery."

No – it isn't at all medical related. In England, constituents of a Member of Parliament can meet with them in person to discuss issues of concern – kind of an open house to meet your legislator called a constituency surgery. No appointment necessary, walk-ins welcome... unless of course, you're carrying two knives... Two? Well, of course, in case one breaks... or so that was the testimony the court eventually heard.

The Member of Parliament was listening to the needs and concerns of his constituents when this would-be killer came in and stabbed him several times in the stomach before being restrained. Apparently she told officers she intended to kill him to exact "revenge for the people of Iraq" since this Member of Parliament had voted for the Iraq war.

The judge who sentenced the stabber to "life" (technically a 15 year minimum sentence) for attempted murder said, "You said you ruined the rest of your life. You said it was worth it. You said you wanted to be a martyr. You intended to kill in a political cause and to strike at those in government by doing so. You did so as a matter of deliberate decision making, however skewed your reasons, from listening to those Muslims who incite such action on the internet. I also hope that you will come to understand the distorted nature of your thinking, the evil that you have done and planned to do, and repent of it. You do not suffer from any mental disease. You have simply committed evil acts coolly and deliberately."

Interestingly, the old-fashioned-controlled-media didn't label the stabber as a racist or hater or xenophobe or Britophobe.

Guess the shoe was on the other foot that day.
http://www.bbc.com/news/uk-england-london-11682732

A good boy

On Saturday December 5, 2015, a crazed knife-wielding African migrant from Somalia reportedly shouting "this is for Syria" and "all your blood will be spilled" attacked people at London's Leytonstone tube (subway) station. Before being subdued by police, the attacker reportedly had lunged at people's throats, seriously injured one random innocent man and injured several other innocent bystanders. The attacker was charged with attempted murder. Police said they were treating the attack as a "terrorist" incident.

The old-fashioned-controlled-media initially did their best to hide the migrant background of the assailant as well as to downplay the attack by announcing that "the most seriously-hurt victim's injuries were not believed to be life-threatening."

Well, if the worst-hurt victim's wounds weren't life-threatening, then it was probably no big deal, right? Phew, and I was going to get all upset. Thank goodness it was nothing... nothing but media spin, that is.

Of course as the story unfolded, much of it on the internet, all was soon to be revealed.

Focus 100% on the perp

The old-fashioned-controlled-media then spent an inordinate amount of time studying the attacker trying to figure out why he had attacked innocent people.

They found and interviewed his brother, Mohamed, who said that the attacker "was good boy" who came to England from Somalia at age 12, had a passion for marijuana (which his brother said gave him his mental problems), liked football, hung out with a bad crowd, had been treated for paranoia, saw "people floating around" as well as "demons," and was working as a cab driver.

Unfortunately, the brother said although his family tried to get help for the attacker long before the attack, the local authorities apparently failed to act, saying there was nothing they could do since he presented no threat to others or himself. Leaders of the Somali community in London were very vocal about their fears and worries, especially on behalf of Somali cab drivers, that now "everyone else will look at us with suspicious eye... and highlighting the man's mental condition would help the population here to understand that there is something behind it (the attack)."

The Chair of the Somali Youth Forum added that he prayed for the victims and that the attacker was a young man with mental problems about which the attacker's family had alerted authorities.

Oh, and a local MP (Member of Parliament) cautioned a nervous public that to connect the attack to Britain's military operations against ISIS in Syria would be "dangerous." Maybe as "dangerous" as going to use the subway and getting cut up by someone yelling "this is for Syria." But, relax, an MP thinks there is no connection.

Inconveniently, though, the attacker's pesky cell phone allegedly was full of ISIS slogans, images of Islamic State flags and other images related to Islam and the like. Like the Paris terrorist attacks by Muslims. The San Bernardino, California massacre by Muslims. And even a "recent UK police training exercise on how to deal with a potential active shooter." But, obviously there's no connection. Keep your eye on the watch as it swings back and forth, you're getting sleepy now, very sleepy, repeat after me, there is no connection... Damn those cell phones.

Oh, and how about the victim?

Well, thank goodness, as the old-fashioned-controlled-media endlessly reported, his injuries "weren't life threatening." Even so, the victim spent 5 hours in surgery. *Wait.* What was that? FIVE hours? Not "life-threatening"? Judge for yourselves...

According to prosecutors, the Somali migrant was accused of attacking this main victim from behind, ambushing him, beating him to the ground, then kicking him repeatedly, stabbing at him and finally grabbing his head while slicing his neck wide open.

Not "life-threatening"?

Another attempted beheading?
Prosecutors further alleged that based on evidence, the Somali attacker then "took hold of the victim's head and used a sawing motion at his neck with a knife." As social media was flooded with photos of the slumped hapless victim in a large pool of his own blood, one media outlet reported that the attacker was "accused of attempting to behead" his victim. Prosecutors also reported that "he was arrested and said he was doing this for his brothers in Syria which he repeated whilst in custody."

Suddenly all that initial media spin makes so much more sense.

After all, the facts are just so *damn inconvenient* when you've got a fairytale to protect.
http://www.bbc.com/news/uk-35018789
http://www.independent.co.uk/news/uk/crime/leytonstone-tube-stabbing-accused-muhaydin-mires-family-contacted-police-three-weeks-before-attack-a6764276.html
http://www.independent.co.uk/news/uk/crime/leytonstone-tube-stabbing-accused-muhaydin-mires-family-contacted-police-three-weeks-before-attack-a6764276.html#gallery
http://www.independent.co.uk/news/uk/crime/leytonstone-attack-suspect-muhaydin-mire-appears-in-court-on-attempted-murder-charge-a6763236.html
http://www.independent.co.uk/news/uk/crime/leytonstone-attack-local-mp-says-it-would-be-dangerous-to-link-stabbing-to-vote-on-syria-air-strikes-a6762251.html
http://www.dailymail.co.uk/news/article-3350045/Family-attempted-murder-suspect-called-police-tube-attack.html

Sadly, we could stay in the UK for literally thousands of pages more, but it is time to move on.

Here's one final thought.

Honestly, is this the same nation that gave us the Magna Carta, the steam locomotive, Lord Nelson, the telephone, inflated rubber tires, the Beatles, the television, penicillin, Shakespeare, hovercrafts, warm beer, and CAT Scans? That brought civilization and advancement to so much of the world?

What happened? Think about it.

Cheerio.

(51) VATICAN CITY / HOLY SEE

In September 2014, after warnings from intelligence agencies across the globe, as well as a personal heads-up warning from Iraq's ambassador to the Vatican, about Muslim jihadist threats against the Pope, security around the Pope and the Holy See ratcheted up big time.

In April 2015, as ISIS militants in Libya were beheading dozens of Christians and vowing "to march on Rome," Italian police arrested a bunch of Pakistani and Afghan immigrants who had planned a "big jihad" of the Vatican.

In September 2015, Catholic Church leader Pope Francis called for all religious groups in Europe to help out with the refugee crisis. He called upon every religious community and parish to house at least one refugee family.

During the same month, addressing the US Congress, the Pope said, "Three sons and a daughter of this land, four individuals and four dreams: Lincoln, liberty; Martin Luther King, liberty in plurality and nonexclusion; Dorothy Day, social justice and the rights of persons; and Thomas Merton, the capacity for dialogue and openness to God. Four representatives of the American people."

Pope Francis urged compassion and love for refugees and illegal aliens alike, adding "we must not be taken aback by their numbers, but rather view them as persons, seeing their faces and listening to their stories, trying to respond as best we can to their situation."

"We need to avoid a common temptation nowadays: to discard whatever proves troublesome. Let us remember the Golden Rule: 'Do unto others as you would have them do unto you'" added the Pope.

In September 2015, Pope Francis's Vatican took in *one Melkite Greek Catholic* refugee family from Syria. Considering 70-80% of the refugees are young males, and 80% or more of refugees are estimated to be Muslim, for the Pope to find a family, let alone a Catholic family, to help out is rather remarkable.

In the meanwhile, the Vatican does sit on top of a literal treasure trove of riches – that's beyond its gold, real estate, stocks, property, and other holdings worldwide – leading experts to claim that the estimated worth of the Vatican is literally "immeasurable."

Immeasurable wealth. *One family.* Immeasurable. *One.*

So exactly what does the Pope know that keeps him from flinging his own doors wide open and taking in a whole lot more refugees?

Think about it.
http://www.telegraph.co.uk/news/worldnews/the-pope/11110644/Security-stepped-up-at-Vatican-over-fears-of-terror-attack.html
http://www.foxnews.com/world/2015/04/24/italian-police-make-several-arrests-in-anti-terror-sweep/
http://www.thestreet.com/story/13295788/1/how-rich-is-the-catholic-church-it-s-impossible-to-tell.html

THE GULF COUNTRIES

That concludes our brief look at each of the 51 countries and independent states that make up Europe today. Here are a few words about the Gulf countries.

According to Amnesty International in a September 2015 report, "Gulf countries including Qatar, United Arab Emirates (UAE), Saudi Arabia, Kuwait, and Bahrain have offered zero resettlement places to Syrian refugees" with the bulk of refugees in Lebanon, Jordan, Turkey, Iraq, and Egypt.

Gulf countries could be a natural fit, since, like most Syrians, they speak Arabic and they are Muslim. Far less culture shock. And they have much warmer climates than much of Europe.

According to US News and World Report, in reality about 250,000 Syrian refugees had already moved to the UAE since the start of the Syrian civil war in 2011. The UN said the number was closer to 500,000. Further, Saudi Arabia has likely taken in hundreds of thousands of Syrians. Yet the magazine concluded that the Gulf countries certainly could do a better job of helping Syrian refugees.

In the meanwhile, the Gulf countries reportedly have taken in hundreds of thousands of Syrians and have given hundreds of millions of dollars to relief efforts. Further, in an all too familiar scenario, many of the Gulf countries are also too expensive for migrants to settle in permanently. Seriously, how many migrants could afford rent in Dubai, or meals in Kuwait?

For now, what the role of Gulf countries has been, will be, or should be remains to be seen.
https://www.amnesty.org/en/latest/news/2015/09/syrias-refugee-crisis-in-numbers/

HOW WILL THIS "CRISIS" AFFECT THE UNITED STATES?

With Europe currently taking in over a million refugees, and the United States of America estimating that it will be taking in upwards of several hundred thousand refugees over the next few years, *many, if not most, from Syria*, things will be changing on a global scale never before seen in recorded history. To get a better feel for what tomorrow may hold, let's take a look at how things have gone so far.

While this book deals with what we've uncovered to date in Europe, we wanted to devote a few pages to the United States. As you have read in the rest of this book, you may find yourself thinking that although the names and places have changed, the narratives are very similar...

US President Barack Hussein Obama said that at least 10,000 Syrians would be welcomed into the US in 2015. Another 85,000 would be able to come in 2016 when the limit on refugee admissions numbers are changed to accommodate more refugees. John Kerry, US Secretary of State, said he will raise the quota cap to allow another 100,000+ refugees into the USA in 2017.

The State Department says it has plans to settle the refugees across the US in special "resettlement" centers where "workers" will help refugees get acclimated and find work (with *so* many unemployed US citizens and *so* many US students graduating college and not being able to find suitable employment, these "workers" will have to be magicians!). After 90 days, the State Department sets the refugees loose to go and do whatever they want. Many think that the refugees will likely end up on government subsidized programs and welfare rolls.

In fact, a majority of the governors of the 50 US states disagreed with the resettlement plans and said that their states *wouldn't* be taking in Syrian refugees. By late November 2015, the US House of Representatives suspended the plan to accept refugees, and was considering a tighter screening process while the FBI Director testified that the US doesn't have the means to screen Syrian refugees effectively. At the same time, the US Homeland Security Secretary claimed Syrian refugees would be going through "extensive thorough background checks."

So which version of security screening was more accurate?
http://www.bloomberg.com/politics/graphics/2015-syria-refugees/?=2
http://www.cnn.com/2015/11/16/world/paris-attacks-syrian-refugees-backlash/

First, how has that worked out in the past?
Security breaches have been happening for a long time. In November 2013 the FBI admitted that dozens of suspected "terrorist bomb makers" had been mistakenly allowed to immigrate to the US as "war refugees." In fact, several al Qaeda insurgents who claimed to be Iraqi war refugees (but who actually had attacked many American soldiers) were discovered living happily *on welfare* and in *public housing* in Bowling Green, Kentucky, where they were arrested in 2009 while they were busily compiling weapons and money to send to their militant buddies in Iraq.

As the FBI press release stated in 2013, "These two former Iraqi insurgents participated in terrorist activities overseas and attempted to continue providing material support to terrorists while they lived here in the United States."
http://abcnews.go.com/Blotter/al-qaeda-kentucky-us-dozens-terrorists-country-refugees/story?id=20931131

Played the fool. Big time.
How does a murderous wretch "sneak" into the US and get welfare, subsidized public housing and medical care? All the terrorist bomber had to do was claim he "faced persecution

back home" in Iraq and the US took care of everything else. The US Department of Justice's "Known Iraqi Troublemakers" database didn't list the men, so they were good to go. *Welcome to America boys!*

To add to the sheer terror of the situation unfolding, in October 2015, the Director of the FBI testified that the database they have for Iraq is *much more extensive* than anything they have for Syria. Read that again.

When "challenging" really means "impossible"
In October 2015, US Congressman Gohmert from Texas asked the FBI Director the following question about the Syrian database,
 "Well without a good fingerprint database, without good identification, how can you be sure that anyone is who they say they are if they don't have fingerprints to go against…?"

FBI Director Comey answered,
 "The only thing we can query is information that we have. So, if we have no information on someone, they've never crossed our radar screen, they've never been a ripple in the pond, there will be no record of them there and so it will be *challenging*."

What a mess!

So, dozens of terrorists slipped through a far more robust database (Iraq) and now we're swinging our doors open based on a weak and meaningless database (Syria)?

Great plan.

Forward my mail to the cabin in Belize.
http://gohmert.house.gov/news/documentsingle.aspx?DocumentID=398267

Hasta la Vista EUROPE!

The terrorists next door
In December 2015, two Muslims living in California shot up a holiday party and killed 14 people, injuring many more. It is thought that they partly financed their death spree as well as their activities – complete with ammo, pipe-bombs, and target practice – with a $28,500 on-line loan.

The husband and wife killers easily sidestepped California's strict gun control laws by using rifles supplied to them by an accomplice, a former Wal-Mart security guard.

Law enforcement officials agreed that it would have been hard to prevent this terrorist attack. Unlike you and me, bad guys *can always find* the weapons they need.
http://www.latimes.com/local/california/la-me-san-bernardino-shooting-terror-investigation-htmlstory.html

Open door Toronto!
In stark contrast to the September 2015 ads that Denmark's Ministry of Immigration, Integration and Housing placed in four Lebanese newspapers telling migrants why settling in Denmark was a really really bad idea, Toronto said *come on in!*

On December 10, 2015, a major Canadian newspaper, the *Toronto Star,* welcomed the first of 25,000 Syrians due to be settled in Canada with a front page greeting. The *Toronto Star* went on to say that "Ahlan wa sahlan. You're with family now. And your presence among us makes our Christmas season of peace and joy just that much brighter... You'll find the place a little bigger than Damascus or Aleppo, and a whole lot chillier. But friendly for all that. We're a city that cherishes its diversity; it's our strength. Canadians have been watching your country being torn apart, and know that you've been through a terrifying, heartbreaking nightmare. But that is behind you now. And we're eager to help you get a fresh start."
http://www.thestar.com/news/world/2015/09/07/denmark-tells-migrants-dont-come-here.html
http://www.thestar.com/opinion/editorials/2015/12/10/to-the-newcomers-from-syria-welcome-to-canada-editorial.html

Everything is bigger in Texas

In March 2015, in Irving, Texas (Dallas County), legislators narrowly endorsed Texas House Bill 562 (5-4) which codifies that United States laws and State laws supersede foreign laws.

Obviously... Well, not to the thousands of Muslims in Texas who had created their own Sharia law courts complete with judges that handle all sort of civil disputes outside of the US legal system. Numbering around 40,000 strong, Muslims make up about 20% of Irving, Texas.

The mayor of Irving, Beth Van Duyne, explained during an interview that "Equal treatment under the law doesn't seem to exist. I think you need to put your foot down and say, 'This is America, we have laws here already. If you want to consult, if you want to arbitrate, that is well within our law.' ... I've got no problem with it. But setting up a separate court, setting up separate law, is not..."

The mayor reiterated that the bill made no mention of Islam or religion. The bill simply stated that it "would forbid judges from using foreign law in their rulings."

Well, duh. We are in America, right? Why would we have to make sure judges stuck to American laws? What's going on?

That dog don't hunt

Surprisingly, simply for standing up for American laws, the mayor was labeled an Islamophobe, and was smeared by Muslim leaders as having chosen "hatred, fear and bigotry" over "diversity."

Sorry, we don't see the connection except maybe the time-honored tradition of smearing people with baseless labels rather than engaging in proper debate.
http://www.dallasnews.com/news/metro/20150319-dispute-on-islam-roils-irving.ece.5
https://youtu.be/BVK0DsXNA84

Clock Boy and the death of common sense
Fast forward to September 2015. We're still in Mayor Beth Van Duyne's Irving, Texas.

You must have all heard about the poor little innocent boy who hand-built a "clock" to impress his teachers and friends and innocently brought it in to school only to be arrested, right?

And the resulting cries of Islamophobia? And that this proved what haters and racists and bigots the authorities, and Americans in general, are?

Then, once the police decided not to press charges for bringing a "hoax bomb" into school, the little innocent boy was invited to the White House by President Barrack Hussein Obama to be lauded for his "inventiveness."

The President tweeted,
"Cool clock... Want to bring it to the White House? We should inspire more kids like you to like science. It's what makes America great."

The President's press secretary added that this
"is a good illustration of how pernicious (*causing great harm or injury*) stereotypes can prevent even goodhearted people who have dedicated their lives to educating young people from doing the good work they set out to do... The president, like many of us, was struck by the news reports of this particular incident. The fact is, America's best teachers and our schools and our best schools, at least, nurture the intellectual curiosity of all of our students. And this instance, it's clear that at least some of Ahmed's teachers failed him. That's too bad. But it's not too late for all of us to use this as a teachable moment and to search our own conscience for biases in whatever form they take."
http://www.cnn.com/2015/09/16/politics/barack-obama-ahmed-texas/

Wait! So maybe nothing *should have been done? Seriously?* What a stupid notion! *Had this "homemade clock" been spotted in a car, it would have shut down major tunnel crossings in NYC. The NYC Transit Department has a whole program to raise awareness of "suspicious packages" – "if you see something, say something." And we've personally experienced many long delays while robots and dogs checked out "packages" far less dangerous looking than this "homemade clock."*

And don't even think about what the "clock" would have done if it were discovered at any major airport! Hours of delays. Frantic passengers. Bomb sniffing dogs. Crying babies. SWAT. Think about it! *Is the implication that if anyone asks questions, they are somehow overreacting? Stifling creativity? Bigots? Anti-kids?* How utterly moronic! *With all the craziness in the world, what happened to "better safe than sorry?"*

Further, imagine how *you* would feel if *nothing was done* at your school, your kid's school, or at your office, or workplace, or the White House, or *just about anywhere* after someone *(age is irrelevant – as evidenced by the Khmer Rouge, Viet Nam, and Gaza)* brought in a small briefcase with a jumble of wires and electronics and an active timing mechanism.

Let's ignore the fact that the "clock" was "built" inside a briefcase so you couldn't see the clock or tell what time it was without opening the briefcase – planning is everything...

> By the way, electronics experts who studied the photos of the clock "invention" claimed it was simply a disassembled digital clock, pulled out of its factory case, and the contents placed in a metal briefcase... No "ingenuity"... No "invention"... zero... zippo... squat...

It would seem there was far more crafting and fabrication put into this "stunt" than into the so called clock invention...

Think about it.

Yet there is so much more to the story. But you already know it, right? *What?* You don't recall the "rest" of the story? Let's catch up...
- The innocent boy's father is a Sudanese immigrant, a citizen of the Sudan and the USA
- The US has long-standing sanctions in place against the Sudan for suspected sponsorship of terrorism
- The innocent boy's father refers to himself as a "sheik" and is a self-proclaimed Muslim "religious leader" although the imam who heads the Irving Islamic Center said "This so-called leader, we have never heard of this person... I believe the whole thing is made up."
- The innocent boy's father has been a presidential candidate (2010, 2015) for the office of the President of Sudan where the legal system is based upon *Sharia Law*
- According to Sharia law, death can be called for in murder cases, adultery, homosexuality, or converting to another religion from Islam
- Several women were officially sentenced to be stoned to death in Sudan for adultery in recent years
- UNICEF reported in 2013 that almost 90% of Sudanese women had undergone female genital mutilation (FGM)
- Years before, the innocent boy's father had agreed to travel to Florida to be the "defense attorney" in the infamous 2011 Rev. Terry Jones "Quran Trial" but admitted to the Seattle Times that he also was there to "kill two birds with one stone" – to take his 5 kids and wife to Disney World (tax write-offs are great, right?)
- The innocent boy's father reportedly posted a theory on a social media site claiming that the attacks on the Twin Towers were a US-sponsored hoax to launch a war against Islam and Muslims
- The photo of the allegedly "homemade clock" shows what appears to be a "terrorist bomb" that could be featured in any variety of Hollywood movies and certainly doesn't resemble a benign science kit

- The first teacher the clock was shown to, the one the boy said he had hoped to "impress" with his ingenuity and engineering skill, reportedly praised his work, but suggested it not be shown around (possibly because it looked so suspicious)
- The innocent boy would later claim that this first teacher "thought it was a threat to her"
- The innocent boy then allegedly took the "clock," complete with wires mysteriously hanging off the case, to his English class where no one bothered him until the clock alarm suddenly started to sound (why had the innocent boy set his alarm to go off right in the middle of an English class??), and then, *and only then*, after the innocent boy had revealed the briefcase of wires and circuit boards and active alarm to the teacher, were officials finally notified
- During a Dallas Morning News interview, the innocent boy, who frankly seemed rehearsed and used carefully prepared specific buzz words and phrases ("hobby to invent stuff... interrogated me... took my invention... made me feel like a criminal... charging me... made me feel like I wasn't human... couldn't call my parents during the interrogation..." etc.), admitted that instead of simply closing the case with the latches, he used a dangling wire "cable" to secure the briefcase saying that he "didn't want to lock it to make it seem like a threat so I just used a simple cable so it won't look that much suspicious (sic)..."
- Why the innocent boy would be concerned, *before* bringing his "clock" into school, about the case looking like a threat or "suspicious," is anyone's guess...
- Instead of telling nervous police officers more information, all the innocent boy kept allegedly repeating was that it was a clock, and reportedly not cooperating with the police, predictably causing police to get really concerned

Sibling rivalry
The New York Post said that the innocent boy's "sister once may have also been suspended for a bomb threat." The Daily Beast quoted the innocent boy's sister telling a reporter that "I got suspended from school for three days from this stupid same district, from this girl saying I wanted to blow up the school, something I had nothing to do with." *Fascinating!*

The school district apparently wanted to fill in *lots* of similar details but couldn't since the innocent boy's parents wouldn't sign the *Family Educational Rights and Privacy Act* waiver that would have provided access to all the information.
https://youtu.be/3mW4w0Y1OXE
http://www.ndtv.com/world-news/woman-faces-death-by-stoning-in-sudan-495250
http://www.okayafrica.com/news/istandwithahmed-mohamed-elhassan-mohamed-sudanese-father-backstory/
http://www.seattletimes.com/nation-world/muslim-at-quran-trial-says-he-didnt-know-book-would-be-burned/
https://web.archive.org/web/20110903180626/http://www.alislahalwatani.com/index.php/home
http://nypost.com/2015/11/24/whats-the-real-story-behind-clock-boys-15m-lawsuit/

How extraordinarily suspicious everything is turning out to be... especially with all the other strange anomalies... nothing seems to be as straightforward as it should be... Why is that?

In the end, you are certainly aware of the fact that the innocent boy and his family moved to the Middle East, to Qatar, right?
http://universalmediagroup.newswire.com/press-release/ahmed-mohamed-accepts-scholarship-to-qatar-foundation-embracing

Let's pack the bags and move to the Middle East
Well, only a few hours after hanging out with President Barrack Hussein Obama at the White House and chatting about his great inventiveness, the innocent boy's family announced that they were all moving to the Middle East after the Qatar Foundation offered the innocent boy a scholarship and according to his family's press release, "we, as a family, will

relocate to Qatar where (innocent boy) will receive a full scholarship for secondary and undergraduate education."

Scary hugs
The innocent boy was also "honored" and hugged by the President of Sudan, Omar al-Bashir, a war criminal condemned in 2008 by the International Criminal Court and *still wanted for* taking part in the genocide of 300,000 victims, crimes against humanity, and war crimes in Darfur. Interesting company to keep, right? Just the guy you want hugging you, right?

Oh, but we're sooo not done yet.

The latest is that the innocent boy is now looking to strike it rich to the tune of $15 million. Is he licensing his "clock" invention? Is he selling *Do It Yourself* plans for the clock so other little children can break apart clocks and make their own versions? Is he going to be starring in his own reality TV show where he scours the globe for inventive children to interview?

No, no, and no. The plan is far simpler...

First, he demanded $5 million from Irving, Texas, and quickly ratcheted it up another $10 million... Yep, the innocent boy wants an apology and $15 million cold hard cash simply to go away and not file a civil rights lawsuit...

If he wins, imagine how many children will be empowered to march into their schools with cases filled with beeping and glowing electronics. Why would kids stop there? *Why not demand their right to board planes laden with homemade clocks? And why not have hundreds of children visit the White House with hundreds of homemade clocks, glowing, ticking, beeping, with hanging wires and all?*

Imagine the lunacy...
http://irvingblog.dallasnews.com/2015/11/letter-demands-5-million-and-an-apology-for-ahmeds-treatment-over-clock.html/

Other US kids not as privileged or lucky as Clock Boy

All this forgiveness for Clock Boy and his "hoax bomb" happened in the USA where less-privileged children are routinely suspended or expelled from school or arrested or villainized for *far lesser incidents* such as

- the 6-year-old who made a pretend gun out of his finger
  http://www.krdo.com/news/6yearold-suspended-after-pointing-at-classmate-in-shape-of-gun/31597538
- a 7-year-old who chewed his snack into the shape of a gun
  https://www.washingtonpost.com/local/education/boy-suspended-for-chewing-breakfast-pastry-into-a-gun-shape-will-get-hearing/2013/09/13/8326c878-1bf6-11e3-8685-5021e0c41964_story.html
- the 10-year-old who brought a dinner knife to school to cut and eat her steak lunch
  http://www.foxnews.com/story/2007/12/18/girl-10-arrested-for-using-knife-to-cut-food-at-school.html
- an 8-year-old who drew a stick-figure picture of Jesus on the cross
  http://www.tauntongazette.com/x1903566059/Taunton-second-grader-suspended-over-drawing-of-Jesus
- a 13-year-old for burping
  http://www.cbsnews.com/news/student-arrested-for-burping-lawsuit-claims/
- the 12-year-old for doodling on a desk
  http://www.upi.com/Odd_News/2010/02/05/Girl-12-arrested-over-desk-doodle/UPI-84371265405376/
- the 9-year-old who talked about the Lord of the Rings movie
  http://www.nydailynews.com/news/national/texas-boy-suspended-bringing-ring-power-school-article-1.2099103
- a 13-year-old who twirled a pencil in what another student felt was a "gun-like" manner
  http://newjersey.news12.com/news/vernon-teen-cthan-chaplin-suspended-from-school-for-pencil-gesture-1.7613736
- the 6-year-old who had a tiny little plastic toy gun the size of a quarter, or
  http://legalinsurrection.com/2013/05/6-year-old-brings-quarter-sized-toy-gun-on-bus-threatened-with-detention-and-suspension/

- the California high school students sent home for wearing American flag t-shirts to school on Cinco de Mayo, lest they offend other students with their display of the American flag.
  http://www.latimes.com/nation/la-na-supreme-court-american-flag-20150330-story.html

If Clock Boy is suing, why can't these kids sue as well?

Henry Ford's town

Dearborn, Michigan, home of Henry Ford's motor company, is also home to about 40,000 Arab Americans who now make up more than 40% of the population. With a Muslim Police Chief, a Muslim Sheriff's Office Deputy Chief, and many Muslims in bureaucratic positions, some critics have detailed what they call a serious decline in the tried and true American tradition and right to free speech.

Seriously?

A 2010 video shows three apparently peaceful young Christian men standing quietly on a sidewalk outside an Arab festival handing out free copies of the Gospel of John, in English and Arabic, for just a few minutes. Suddenly, they are surrounded by 8 police officers. The man who is videotaping the incident on a public street, across the street from where the other men are, is ordered to cease videotaping the police and has his camera confiscated. Then all four men are taken into custody. They apparently were photographed, had their ID processed, and cameras reviewed. Then as they were released police allegedly told them that they weren't free to hand out copies of the Gospel of John inside the festival, or anywhere near the festival, and that they would have to stay at least 5 blocks away if they wanted to distribute anything.

One of the young Christian men, a former Muslim, is seen in another video having conversations with various people at the Arab festival. A few Muslims approach the young Christian man and mock him for his faith, especially when they find out he used to be a Muslim. He finally ends up speaking with a group of young Muslim teens about various aspects of their respective faiths, when suddenly police surround and arrest him. He was later taken to the Dearborn City Jail and charged with "Breach of Peace."

The way the police allegedly wrote up their police report it made it clear that the young Christian man was "screaming into the crowd" of Muslims, that he was "yelling into the crowd, further inciting the crowd," and that the Christians were handcuffed "in an attempt to gain control of the situation and a possible riotous crowd." It all *reads* well, save for one small little detail.

The Christians had videotape of the whole thing...

There was no "yelling" into the crowd. There was no "inciting the crowd." And there was no "screaming into the crowd."
https://youtu.be/Smw9QuH1xkA
https://youtu.be/0relDfMQ4xQ

According to the ACLU, in 2011 Dearborn purportedly tried to silence some Christian evangelists and demonstrators by charging huge "demonstration fees," and tried to make Christian protestors pay for the costs of law enforcement handling the *anticipated reaction* of crowds to their messages.

Seriously? How far would Black Christian activist, the Rev. Martin Luther King Jr., have gotten if he had to pay not only huge demonstration fees, but also was held liable for the costs of "handling the anticipated reaction of crowds" to his message. *How preposterous and discriminatory!*

The ACLU made the point and cited that "speech cannot be financially burdened, any more than it can be punished or banned, simply because it might offend a hostile mob."
http://www.aclumich.org/sites/default/files/TerryJonesACLUAmicus.pdf

Proselytizers get processed
Some years later, in 2014, the American Freedom Law Center filed a federal civil rights complaint on behalf of a Christian group, with the US District Court, and named officials from the sheriff's department, among other defendants, who in 2012 allegedly "sided with a Muslim mob intent on suppressing the Christians' speech."

Based on the opinions of two out of three district court judges, the court held that the First Amendment free-speech and free-exercise rights of the Christian group had *not* been violated by the sheriff's department and the others named as defendants, stating that the Christian group's "words induced a violent reaction in short order; the crowd (at the Arab International Festival) soon began to throw bottles, garbage, and eventually rocks and chunks of concrete. Moreover, members of the crowd can be heard to shout "get them" and "beat the s*** out of them"; one (Christian) was pushed to the ground. Another's (Christian's) face was cut open and was bleeding from where he had been struck by debris. And the crowd itself continued to swell and swarm, undeterred by the sheriff's office attempts to contain it."

Therefore, the court reasoned, law enforcement was justified in forcing the Christians to stop proselytizing, ordering them to leave, and threatening to cite the Christians for disorderly conduct if they refused to leave – and that such conduct was necessary to keep the peace under the circumstances and did not violate anyone's free-speech rights. *And no outcry?*
https://youtu.be/KD3Bf4IrgHQ
https://youtu.be/m_8MO7IllCw

Not everyone agreed with this view, particularly not the other district court judge who dissented and wrote that "In my view, the video tape shows that Defendants (including the Sherriff's Department) did just about nothing to control the crowd as it grew and became agitated. Defendants only stepped in to inform Plaintiffs (the Christian group) that the police were

powerless and that Plaintiffs needed to leave under threat of arrest. **This is not good faith—it is manufacturing a crisis as an excuse to crack down on those exercising their First Amendment rights.** Jurors, not judges, should decide this issue... Regrettably, law enforcement officers have a track record of chilling the free speech rights of (Christian) proselytizers (evangelists) at the Festival."
http://www.ca6.uscourts.gov/opinions.pdf/14a0208p-06.pdf

Discussions not concussions
Whatever side you find yourself on, the issues involved are downright polarizing, especially when people think it is fine to resort to throwing rocks and chunks of concrete at the people they don't agree with. Just like we've seen in Europe...

Debates and discussions don't mean *absolutes and concussions.*

Well, at least not in the America we thought we knew...
http://www.wnd.com/2012/09/cops-to-answer-in-court-for-stoning-of-christians/
http://conservativetribune.com/video-shariah-law-arrests-christians/
http://insider.foxnews.com/2015/10/06/watters-world-talks-muslims-dearborn-michigan-about-sharia-law

The city of unbrotherly love
Unfortunately, radicalized violence is up. On January 7, 2016, a troubled black man with a prison record ambushed a police officer in Philadelphia, firing more than a dozen rounds at the cop. Amazingly, the heroic police officer, *before being hospitalized with serious injuries*, managed to chase down the attacker and shoot him in the butt.

After being captured, the shooter identified himself as a Muslim loyal to ISIS and told investigators, "I follow Allah. I pledge my allegiance to the Islamic State and that's why I did what I did." The shooter's mother called her son a devout Muslim who felt targeted by the police.
http://www.cbsnews.com/news/philadelphia-shooting-suspect-ambush-police-officer-islam/

2016. NEW YEAR. SAME OLD STORY

About that 2016 "New" Year message from Angela Merkel
First, some background concerns about Angela Merkel, the seemingly single-handed architect of the re-creation of Europe.

The old-fashioned-controlled-media is fond of transmitting some version of the "Merkel grew up under communism in East Germany" fairytale. Well, technically it is quite true. But Merkel didn't apparently just grow up *under* Communism. If a variety of journalists, historians, and eye-witnesses are to be believed, Merkel was actually immersed and very active *in* Communism.

Let's take a quick look at what's out there in plain sight.
http://time.com/time-person-of-the-year-2015-angela-merkel/
http://www.spiegel.de/international/germany/how-chancellor-angela-merkel-has-paralyzed-german-politics-a-900330.html

In an interview published in Spiegel Online in May 2009, in response to the statement :
> "German Chancellor Angela Merkel wants to continue to measure the Left Party by its attitude toward East Germany's past."

German Left Party Chairman Oskar Lafontaine was quoted as noting:
> "An interesting psychological case. People tend to accuse other people of their own mistakes. Ms. Merkel needs to deal with her own past in East Germany and that of her own party. She was an FDJ functionary for agitation and propaganda (ed's note: The FDJ was an official youth movement in communist East Germany). As such she belonged to the fighting reserve of the party (ed's note: the Communist Socialist Unity Party (SED)).

http://www.spiegel.de/international/germany/interview-with-left-party-leader-oskar-lafontaine-we-want-to-overthrow-capitalism-a-624880.html

In their 2013 book "The First Life of Angela M.," journalists Günther Lachmann and Ralf Georg Reuth made the case for Merkel being far more involved in the Communist Party and Communist movement than she lets on. The authors quoted an ex-colleague of Merkel when she was at East Berlin's Academy of Sciences, Gunter Walther, saying Merkel had served in the FDJ youth organization as the "Agitation and Propaganda" secretary.

And according to former German Transport Minister Günther Krause, Merkel actively spread Marxism-Leninism. In "The First Life of Angela M." he is quoted as saying,
"With Agitation and Propaganda you're responsible for brainwashing in the sense of Marxism... That was her task and that wasn't cultural work. Agitation and Propaganda, that was the group that was meant to fill people's brains with everything you were supposed to believe in the GDR, with all the ideological tricks. And what annoys me about this woman (Angela Merkel) is simply the fact that she doesn't admit to a closeness to the system in the GDR. From a scientific standpoint she wasn't indispensable at the Academy of Sciences. But she was useful as a pastor's daughter in terms of Marxism-Leninism. And she's denying that. But it's the truth."

Wow! A possible student of, and potentially an expert in agitation, propaganda, brainwashing, and ideological tricks.

Of course, Merkel predictably claimed she was simply a "cultural secretary" and had a very different, watered-down, *can-only-rely-on-my-memory* version of her involvement with the Communist movement. Curiously, though, Merkel is quite fluent in reading and speaking Russian. Hmmm...

Seeing is believing
Oh, yes, also in 2013, one of Angela Merkel's former classmates gave German newspaper giant Bild an old snapshot of a young smiling Angela Merkel marching happily around the forest in

her Communist uniform alongside a Communist East German officer and her many other uniformed Communist comrades, which Bild happily published for all to see.

Damn those embarrassing old photos.
http://www.bild.de/politik/inland/angela-merkel/merkel-bei-ddr-zivilschutzuebung-30471902.bild.html

So imagine Merkel's immense influence and power when she was recently crowned Time Magazine's *Person of the Year* in 2015, and the whole thing about being a *former-uniform-wearing-active-Communist* was nowhere to be seen.

How cool is that? A complete suppression of an inconvenient past. Poof. It's gone.

It almost parallels the EU experience with migrants who are showing up and reinventing themselves based on their claims that they have "no identification." They are students and doctors and lawyers and engineers. Maybe they're 14 years-old, or maybe they're 34 years-old. Whatever they claim, say amen! You must take them at their word. Their version is the new version...

Hey, wait just one minute! Could this have anything to do with why Merkel seems to have such a soft spot for migrants trying to reinvent themselves and claiming amnesia about their real past lives which may have been plagued with some uncomfortable facts? Does Merkel, per chance, see herself in their plight of reinvention and economic opportunism?

Give that one some thought.
http://www.spiegel.de/international/germany/new-book-suggests-angela-merkel-was-closer-to-communism-than-thought-a-899768.html

2016 New Year message decoded

Now that all of this information has had a chance to sink in, and remembering what we learned in the Hungary chapter about media spin, let's look at Chancellor Merkel's New Year 2016 message.

Here's how that message might look after decoding...

Former-bonafide-uniform-wearing-Communist-Party-Member, *possible* agitation, propaganda, brainwashing, and ideological tricks expert, and now German Chancellor, Angela Merkel looked like a tired and hardly sincere politician as she listlessly and somewhat robotically delivered her carefully worded 2016 New Year address.

Always calculating, she arranged for her words to be broadcast in German *with* Arabic subtitles.

> *Propaganda alert*
> Arabic subtitles were a peculiar choice since as we have previously learned, the German Federal Employment Agency noted in late-October 2015 that of the recently arrived refugees and migrants, a high number were uneducated and quite literally *illiterate*. So the Arabic subtitles were likely more of a message to the world that Merkel was "embracing" the newly arrived migrants, and including them in her plans. Hopefully the handful of literate migrants will tell the others what she was saying. And hopefully, Merkel won't upset the devote men by trying to shake their hands.

Merkel began her address by referring back to her 2014 address stating that "we had to look back on a year which had too many wars and crises. Some of them, like the Ebola catastrophe in Africa, have disappeared from the headlines. But other issues that touched us last year haven't lost any of their relevance in 2015. Unfortunately. That includes the war in Syria and the brutal murders by the terror organization 'Islamic State.'"

> *Psychological manipulation*
> Merkel used a tried and true technique of recapping events in an attempt to make the listeners feel comradery with her as she implied that they had lived through those same

experiences together. Except they hadn't. The war and the rest of it wasn't on anyone's plate but Merkel's plate.

Interesting sidebar: Official European Union statistics agency *Eurostat* revealed that in the first quarter of 2015, of the 185,000 first time asylum seekers seeking refuge in the EU, only about 16% were Syrians. During the second quarter of 2015, of the 213,200 asylum seekers, only about 20% were Syrians. During the third quarter of 2015, of the 413,800 first time asylum seekers, only about a third were Syrians. Think about it. Merkel specifically called out the war in Syria and yet the actual stats seem to say that, while the trend for Syrians (or alleged "Syrians" – since as we've seen, many migrants pretend to be Syrians to get better benefits) is "up," the vast majority of refugees during the available periods were not even Syrian.

On December 22, 2015, the UN issued a recap that showed that of the 1 million people that had arrived in the EU in 2015, only about half were "Syrian."

As the Washington Post reported in late September 2015, "Moving among the tens of thousands of Syrian war refugees passing through the train stations of Europe are *many* who are neither Syrian nor refugees, but hoping to blend into the mass migration and find a back door to the West... The prize, after all, is the possibility of benefits, residency and work in Europe."

Prize?

More like a jackpot!
http://ec.europa.eu/eurostat/web/products-press-releases/-/3-18092015-BP
http://ec.europa.eu/eurostat/en/web/products-press-releases/-/3-10122015-AP
https://www.washingtonpost.com/world/europe/migrants-are-disguising-themselves-as-syrians-to-gain-entry-to-europe/2015/09/22/827c6026-5bd8-11e5-8475-781cc9851652_story.html
http://data.unhcr.org/mediterranean/regional.php

Merkel next said that "last New Year's Eve, I said that one consequence of these wars and crises is more refugees worldwide than we've seen since World War II."

> *Psychological manipulation*
> Beyond a simple "I told you so," Merkel laid claim to having foretold upcoming events. Like a carnival fortune teller, Merkel attempted to establish trust and authority with her audience by saying she correctly predicted the future. A keen observer would instantly counter with *yes, but then again, you also helped to cause it all to happen so we're not impressed.* And others may quip, *if you claim you saw this disaster coming, why in the world didn't you do everything you could to prevent it?*

Shamelessly, Merkel continued and said, regarding the refugees, "many have literally escaped death."

> *Propaganda alert*
> This wording is particularly clever! While *many* migrants "may have literally escaped death," according to more than a few EU leaders, *most* are economic opportunists. Thus their brushes with death are for reasons of *monetary* gain, not to "save their lives" as is implied. But a casual, *or brainwashed* listener would never pick up the subtleties. Well crafted, Comrade Merkel!

Merkel then "thanked" Germans for their generosity.

> *Agitation alert*
> Actually, Germans had no choice since Merkel pushed her grossly unpopular migrant policies through on her own without input and *while silencing opposition.* Remember that in September 2015, Die Welt reported that Merkel was caught on an open mike pressuring the Facebook CEO to *monitor* "hate speech posts." And exactly what was "that" all about? If you *hate* her crazy policies and *hate* her stupid decisions and *hate* the destructive direction in

which Merkel is taking Germany, is that *hate* speech? At this point, who knows what that former Communist party member is thinking.

Then Merkel continued claiming that "so many people embarked on often life-threatening journeys to seek refuge here."

Propaganda alert
Merkel was using repetition to push the "death" and "life-threatening" angle. Obviously any journey can be life threatening. As we've seen, a boat trip to get dental work done can have devastating consequences. A walk around the block can be deadly. And many of the most dangerous accidents often happen in your own bathroom – but the real clincher here is the *to seek refuge here* which Merkel knows is complete garbage since it really is *to seek welfare here*. Merkel is counting on the intoxicated masses to quickly swallow the "deadly" and "refuge" misdirection.

Throwing a bone to long-suffering German volunteers, Merkel commended them for their "warmth of heart" and "readiness of action."

Ideological tricks
These empty words are designed to make it seem that if you volunteered to serve migrants you were *good*, and if you didn't you must have had a cold heart and didn't act. Complete rubbish. While some might question why one would, in their right mind, volunteer to help destroy their own country, Merkel was using the technique of moving fast so her legerdemain would be less noticeable. The faster you spin, the less people analyze and the more they hang on to sound bites. Something a person skilled in propaganda and agitation might count on.

Merkel thanked all sorts of municipal employees (police, soldiers, others) who she said "do far, far more than their call of duty."

> *Propaganda alert*
> Yes, everyone knows that Germans are straining under the weight of this new and orchestrated crisis. The employees have told us they are strained and overwhelmed and some are at their breaking points. The real message is, why are they being forced to do so much more? Why are they overwhelmed and strained? *Who* decided to open the floodgates and cause this excessive environment?

Merkel then tried to make believe that all the efforts of the volunteers and paid professionals were really part of some greater good when she mystically referred to having "achieved something outstanding together."

> *Ideological tricks*
> "Something outstanding" sounds like a description of a knife sticking out of someone's back. It *is* something, and it *is* outstanding.
>
> But none of this has been proven good, nor is it "something" to be proud of yet. Only time will tell, but we suspect that there will be far more shame than pride once the dust settles. But Merkel designed the words to make people feel either justified in having followed orders blindly, or to feel left out and to want to join the "something outstanding" movement. Basic Marxist stuff.

Merkel then stated that the "arrival of so many will demand a great deal from us."

> *Stick in the eye alert*
> She could have at least been honest and said, "My nutty decision to fill this country with mostly young male economic migrants with virtually no identification is now

on your heads." Slyly, Merkel just ripped the monkey off her back and affixed it squarely to the backs of average Germans who will now pay the price. Look to Sweden for a rough idea of what the future may look like.

Then Merkel said that "it will require time, strength and money especially in regard to the important task of integrating those who remain here permanently."

Propaganda alert and ideological tricks
Money? That will be taken straight from the pockets of German citizens. *Integration?* Seriously? How Merkel feels she will succeed where every other European nation has miserably failed is anyone's guess. *Those who remain permanently?* Merkel's attempt to make people think that she may yet be planning to send a meaningful number of migrants back is laughable.

Merkel went on about German values, traditions, justice, language, laws and rules saying "they underpin our society. They're the fundamental requirement for everyone in our country to live together with mutual respect. That applies to everyone who wants to live here."

Propaganda alert
What a complete joke. Merkel must know what the experiences in Sweden and elsewhere have been. To think her comments will mold migrants *into* Germans is insane! And all Germans know, or will soon find out, mutual respect and the rest of it is *only* for migrants to benefit from. Native Germans will more likely be bent to the fancies of migrants, not the other way around.

Then Merkel stated "Successful immigration, however, benefits a country—economically as well as socially."

Propaganda alert
Sure, successful immigration is great, but this isn't successful immigration, Comrade Merkel. Is it? It is something else. But what? Cat got your tongue?

The former-uniform-wearing-Communist then stated that it's wonderful Germany was now reunified and added, "Isn't it wonderful to see where we are today, after 25 years? We've grown together as a nation. We have lower unemployment and more people working than ever before in a unified Germany. For the second year in a row the federal government has accrued no new debt. Real wages are increasing and the economy is robust and innovative. If we handle things right, I'm convinced that today's challenge of accepting and integrating so many migrants is an opportunity for tomorrow."

Propaganda alert and ideological tricks
Where to start? As a uniform-wearing youth member of the Communist Party in Communist East Germany, Merkel certainly wasn't fighting for reunification. Now she says it's wonderful. How convenient. Next, Merkel pointed at a robust economy as the vehicle for "integrating" more than a million migrants. Seriously? That is like saying "My business is making a nice profit so now I will give away goods for free and hope my bottom line grows." Crazy talk, unless you intend to use the *opportunity* to take the necessary funds *tomorrow* out of the pockets of German citizens to fund this population shift.

Merkel droned on, "We are working nationally, in Europe and internationally to improve the protection of European external borders, to turn illegal migration into legal migration and to combat the causes of flight and thereby noticeably reduce the number of refugees – sustainably and permanently. Germany is also making a major contribution to the fight against IS terrorism. Our soldiers are risking life and limb to defend our values, our security and our freedom. For this I say to them: I thank you with all my heart."

Propaganda alert
Nice words. Let us know how those "efforts" turn out. History will judge Merkel in the end. Our guess is that just as Nero set Rome ablaze and fiddled, history may very well footnote Merkel as the Nero of the 21st century. In fact, we predict that the term "merkeled" will be widely used to describe aspects of self-harm or reckless self-genocide, as in "Knowing the dangers, he smoked anyway and merkeled himself," or "The entire family was merkeled one night after they made the irresponsible decision to sleep with their doors open and piles of cash strewn all over."

Here comes the real crafty spin...

Merkel turned up the Marxist-Leninist heat with "Next year... one thing will be especially crucial: our cohesion. It is important for us always to listen to others' arguments even if those people weigh concerns and opportunities differently than we do ourselves. It is important for us not to let ourselves be divided. Not by generation, and also not socially or into the categories of long-time residents and new residents. It is important for us not to follow those with coldness or hatred in their hearts who seek to claim German identity for themselves alone and to exclude others. It is important for us to keep wanting to be a country where we are self-assured and free, compassionate and open-minded – with the joy of success and the joy of giving our best."

Ideological tricks
Merkel has the nerve to claim she thinks it is important to listen to others' arguments, but we now know that is complete bunkum as she tried to cajole the CEO of Facebook to monitor "hate speech posts" on her behalf.

Your avowed dedication to differences in opinion and free speech really isn't free if you monitor it and try to censor it, isn't that correct former-Communist Comrade Merkel? Bet whenever you don't like that someone "hates" one of your stupid ideas, you label it "hate" speech... sound familiar Commissar? How Marxist *and* Leninist of you.

Next, the former Communist warned people not to be divided... nice try. We suppose that means that there is only one party, and one opinion, and one way. Right? Again, how very Marxist and Leninist of you.

> Which reminds us of the Soviet era joke (around the time Merkel was marching around the forests in her Communist uniform)...

> *At the election booth in Moscow, the ballot read "Vote yes for Brezhnev, or vote yes for Brezhnev." After all the ballots were counted, Brezhnev won in an uncontested and unanimous vote of confidence from those grateful countrymen that lived through the election...*

Then Merkel laid bare her treachery by the don't "follow those with coldness or hatred in their hearts who seek to claim German identity for themselves alone and to exclude others." Does Merkel want people to believe those that are proud to be German have coldness or hatred in their hearts? What in the world is she implying? If you're German, you're German – you're not claiming anything for yourself. And someone who isn't German isn't being *excluded* from being German just because they are ethnically Syrian or Somali or whatever. They simply grew up with a completely different identity. And if they are accepted for asylum and work hard at assimilating and integrating, they, too, can become German citizens. So what this former uniform-wearing Communist really means by her asinine pronouncement is up for grabs.

Merkel followed with "It is important for us to keep wanting to be a country where we are self-assured and free, compassionate and open-minded – with the joy of success and the joy of giving our best."

> *Propaganda alert*
> Merkel's implication that if you don't drop everything to help migrants is positively criminal. Further, if you question her lunacy, if you are uncomfortable with more than a million unidentified foreigners added to the country overnight, Merkel is labelling you uncompassionate, close-minded, unsuccessful, and worse. *Wow*. Patriotism is a dangerous pursuit these days in much of the EU.

Merkel then added gibberish about businesses, workers and employers giving their best, developing science, art and culture, and even mentioned sports. Meaningless drivel designed to make her seem like one of the common folks – just like all the other former Communists out there.

Merkel ended with "It is true that we are living in unusually challenging times. But it is also true that we can make it through these challenges because Germany is a strong country. On that note, I wish for us all to share good health, strength, confidence and God's blessings in the New Year 2016."

> *Propaganda alert*
> Merkel used the tried and true Soviet-era technique of admitting a problem and making it go away with "we the proletariat can get through it!" Following the formula, Merkel admitted that times are "unusually challenging" but concluded all will be well because "Germany is a strong country." Comrade, so *was* Sweden. *Was*.

And that, Comrades, is how the Merkel subterfuge is decoded, sentence by sentence. Think about it.
https://presseportal.zdf.de/pressemitteilung/mitteilung/zdf-zeigt-neujahrsansprache-der-bundeskanzlerin-online-mit-arabischen-untertiteln-untertitelte/772/

Putting it all together
It seems that quite a few Germans heard Chancellor Merkel's message and were already one step ahead of her in throwing

away their centuries-old traditions. Quite a number of towns and municipalities had previously curtailed, cancelled, or banned the use of fireworks for the 2016 New Year's celebrations *for fear of upsetting migrants* who they felt might link the fireworks with memories of war or trauma.

It was also feared that inexperienced migrants might hurt themselves or even set their shelters on fire if they were to improperly blow off fireworks.

North Rhine-Westphalia banned fireworks at all migrant shelters. Arnsberg's fire department asked everyone to refrain from fireworks out of deference to migrants who fled war. Saxony similarly issued warnings. And on and on it went.

One extremely sensitive example was from Reichenberg, Bavaria, where a migrant workshop, complete with multi-lingual flyers and sample fireworks displays, was held to help acclimate migrants to the sounds and sights of European New Year's celebrations.

We dare not frighten anyone.

Since statistics have shown that the vast majority of migrants are young fighting-age males, we're guessing all the sensitivity training was a bit overdone.

Which brings us to New Year's Eve in Cologne.
http://www.sueddeutsche.de/bayern/reichenberg-probefeuerwerk-fuer-fluechtlinge-1.2799117
http://www.cnn.com/2015/12/30/europe/germany-fireworks-refugees/
http://www.feuerwehr-arnsberg.de/

Cohesion – sticking together – flash mob violence
At least 1,000 people in and around Cologne must have heard Chancellor Merkel's message since they took it to heart. Well, at least the part about "cohesion." Merkel had said "one thing will be especially crucial – our cohesion... It is important for us

not to let ourselves be divided." And that's literally what the police said happened. Cohesive gangs operating in groups of 30-40 young foreign males (15-35 years-of-age) "tightly surrounded" their victims, mostly younger German females, and groped and assaulted and robbed them with impunity.

Cologne

In Cologne, Germany, on New Year's Eve and early New Year's Day (2016), reportedly a very cohesive group of young men of North African and Arabic backgrounds created havoc never before experienced in Cologne. Or anywhere else in Germany. Until now.

Initially, police said that the Cologne New Year's Eve celebration had been "largely peaceful." Even *they* couldn't keep a straight face. Because the police knew it was a BIG lie.

And many members of the old-fashioned-controlled-media, too, tried desperately to completely ignore the story by *ignoring it* – a complete media blackout. As if it didn't happen. And when they finally had to acknowledge the record-setting catastrophe, they hid the identity of the attackers with the words "youth" and "young men."

> Until it *leaked* out all over the internet. Like an unplanned flood in the basement while you're away on a long vacation with no one around to shut off your water main...

Eventually, even federal state-owned news giant ZDF was forced to apologize, stating that "The news situation was clear enough. It was a failure that the (January 4, 2016) 7 P.M. broadcast didn't report the events. The ... editors decided to delay the report... to get more time for interviews to be completed. That was clearly a judgment error."

When the truth began to emerge, calling New Year's Eve in Cologne "largely peaceful" was like calling the Titanic an uneventful boat ride.

When they finally had to reveal the truth about what really happened, the police held a news conference and the Police Chief reported that a group of 1,000 or more young males, mostly between 18 and 35 years of age (*aren't they all?*), described by police officers as having "Arab or North African region" backgrounds, sexually assaulted, raped, threatened, and/or robbed women in the vicinity of the historic Cologne cathedral and the main train terminal.

A new dimension in crime
Heiko Maas, Germany's Justice Minister warned this was a "new scale of organized crime." The Cologne Police Chief called what happened "an intolerable situation that such crimes are committed in the middle of the city," "sexual crimes took place on a huge scale," and that this was a "crime of a whole new dimension." Within days the Police Chief would be removed.

821 attacks and counting
Possibly initially scared to say anything about the assaults for fear of being labeled racist or xenophobic, reportedly over 821 women filed criminal complaints within the first few weeks or so after the terrifying mass assault. Reportedly, over 359 women reported sexual assaults including 126 claims of "rape by a group" and 47 allegations of "sexual assault by a group." Commenting on the mass attacks, the police admitted that they were also "investigating crimes that amount to rape." Police were asking victims to come forward and said they expected the total figure "to be extremely high."

Asylum seekers were perpetrators
"Those in focus of criminal police investigations are mostly people from North African countries. The majority of them are asylum seekers and people who are in Germany illegally," police said.
http://abcnews.go.com/International/wireStory/minister-punish-cologne-offenders-origin-36112668
http://www.dailymail.co.uk/news/article-3391288/Cologne-police-chief-sacked-string-sex-attacks-migrant-workers-New-Year-s-Eve.html

http://www.dw.com/en/cologne-new-year-assault-reports-more-than-double-in-number/a-18969345
http://www.dailymail.co.uk/news/article-3393228/Cologne-sex-attacks-planned-gangs.html
http://www.express.co.uk/news/world/636944/Cologne-sex-attacks-list-crimes

What happened?

As Germans have done for decades, New Year's Eve celebrants gathered in the square between Cologne's Cathedral and train terminal to enjoy a beautiful night full of promise and an exciting future. At some point, migrant miscreants allegedly began shooting rockets into the crowds and throwing fireworks at people. They also began shooting rockets at the dome of the historic Cathedral and other buildings. They also were seen shooting fireworks and rockets at the responding police officers. The young men involved in the fireworks "attacks" certainly didn't seem "traumatized" by any previous war experiences as they shot exploding pyrotechnics at the crowds of frightened people and nearby buildings. Witnesses reported that terrified people trying to escape the attacks were blocked in by gangs of young men and restricted from moving.
https://youtu.be/IzjoNT7-ToE

Police unprepared for the sheer volume of assaults

One police officer reported that his squad got a call to respond to a brawl between 400 foreigners at the train terminal. He explained, "But it was not like that. In fact, there were nearly 2,000 people who threw firecrackers... and New Year's Eve rockets. "

Allegedly the foreigners were congregating around the train station to better target victims, specifically younger females, to attempt to rob or assault or rape as they arrived by train to enjoy the festivities in Cologne. When police moved in to stop the madness, officers reported that the young men didn't seem to understand German so they had to be physically prodded.
http://www.express.de/koeln/sexuelle-uebergriffe-polizist--so-brutal-war-das-chaos-am-koelner-hbf-an-silvester-23252866

Spiraling out of control

As officers tried to restore order, a crowd of 1,000 young men (police said most appeared to be from Morocco, Algeria and Tunisia) split up into groups of large roving gangs. They had none of the "warm-hearts," "compassion," or "open-mindedness," that Angela Merkel had spoken about in her New Year's address. In fact, they were hell bent on getting, by force, anything they wanted. And they wanted plenty.

Casualties were already mounting as people sought medical treatment for injuries and burns, some serious, sustained by the "high-risk" exploding fireworks and rockets that were shot at them. But the night hadn't really started yet.

Police reported that many people innocently trying to enjoy New Year's Eve in Cologne were now being surrounded by these huge gangs of young foreign men and were being sexually assaulted, robbed, stripped, pickpocketed, physically assaulted, groped, and sometimes even raped.

No matter what the old-fashioned-controlled-media tried to do to sanitize, excuse, downplay, analyze, explain, and ignore the scene, it was *bad*.

A police officer said that "shortly after midnight, the first women came towards us. Weeping and shocked they described how they had been sexually harassed by a massive group." So the police started to look for women to protect. The police were able to save one young 20-year-old German girl visiting from Stuttgart. The police reported that the poor girl "screamed and cried. She had her panties torn off her body." Officers added that she had been "also touched inappropriately in her private parts." Sadly, her three girlfriends who were likewise being assaulted by the throng were left to fend for themselves as would-be rescuers were repelled with fireworks.
http://www.express.de/koeln/sexuelle-uebergriffe-polizist--so-brutal-war-das-chaos-am-koelner-hbf-an-silvester-23252866

Some migrants show more of their true colors

Speaking with the BBC, a man told how he, "his partner and 15-year-old daughter were surrounded by an enormous crowd outside the station and he was unable to help. 'The attackers grabbed her and my partner's breasts and groped them between their legs.'"
http://www.bbc.com/news/world-europe-35231046

One young German woman, a native of Cologne, met up with her two girlfriends and their male friend at the train terminal shortly after midnight. As they walked to the waiting room, they were surrounded by a group of "young foreign men." The German woman said that the foreign men formed a human barrier, surrounded her and her friends, and "suddenly I felt a hand on my buttocks, then on my breasts... I was groped everywhere. It was a nightmare. Although we shouted and hit them, the guys did not stop. I was desperate and think I was touched around 100 times in the 200 meters" as the foreign men yelled "f*cky," called them "sluts," and far worse.

The terrified German woman added she was glad she wore trousers since they would have probably "torn off my skirt if I was wearing one."

Although police responded quickly, the German woman said "we could not tell which man had now touched us exactly where in the body." Under these circumstances it will be nearly impossible to arrest and prosecute criminals that operate in the relative safety of gangs of so many assailants.
http://www.express.de/koeln/koeln-sexuelle-uebergriffe--opfer-erzaehlt-vom-horror-am-hauptbahnhof-23252186

Euronews reported that another young German female victim said "We were fondled, I was groped between my legs. My friends were also fondled. My boyfriend tried to pull me away. There was quite a big group of people, maybe thirty or forty."
http://www.euronews.com/2016/01/05/victims-speak-out-after-nightmare-new-year-in-cologne/

Using fireworks as weapons, again

One young German woman suffered serious burns and permanent scarring after having fireworks shoved into her hoodie. Another young German teen told how she was surrounded by "dozens of 'angry men' who groped her and her female friends then stole their belongings as they fled."

Another young German, part of a group of about a dozen German teenage girls celebrating New Year's Eve, was assaulted by a large group of foreign men she said were "full of anger." The horrified teen said, "we had to make sure that none of us were pulled away by them. They were groping us and we were trying to get away as quickly as possible." As the girls ran, the men stole whatever they could including cell phones.
http://www.dailymail.co.uk/news/article-3386673/Women-Cologne-lockdown-council-admits-no-longer-safe-wake-African-Arab-mob-s-rapes-declares-upcoming-carnival-no-area-females.html

A British tourist told BBC she was shot at with fireworks, attempted to be kissed and touched, her friend had a bag stolen, and then "another (male) tried to get us into his 'private taxi'. I've been in scary and even life-threatening situations and I've never experienced anything like that."
http://www.bbc.com/news/world-europe-35231046

One man posted a video in which he described what he saw that violent night. The man said he was working at a hotel nearby and witnessed police round up many suspects. But after more than an hour, when no prisoner transports had come, the police let many of the suspects go. The freed suspects then stood around the police cars and shouted "F*ck police" as they spit on windshields. The man said that seasoned police officers confided in him that they'd never seen anything like this in their lives and called it like "a civil war."
https://youtu.be/nsHqW0ctKI4

A sea of weeping women
A German woman was quoted in Sueddeutsche Zeitung as saying that when she arrived at the Cologne train station after midnight, she felt "like I was in a foreign country. It was so crowded and so loud." At first she just wrote off the weird feeling as "New Year's Eve" madness.

Then she said she noticed something profoundly disturbing, *countless distraught and weeping women.*

Suddenly the horror of the situation became real.

The woman reported being in a crowd of "Arab or North African-looking men" who laughed and mocked and spoke in languages she couldn't understand except for the filthy sexist epithets that they yelled at her including, according to her, the "c-word," the "b-word," and "stupid whore."

At one point, the woman said "I saw a young girl. I remember that she had long blond hair. She was totally crying, had torn pantyhose, her skirt was askew, and she was exhausted." She quickly lost sight of her in the mayhem. As she made her way through the crowd, the woman noted "I've never seen so many weeping women – women who were so full of fear."

The woman ended her interview by mentioning that she had been physically assaulted and robbed only a week earlier on Christmas Eve by refugee men who she said looked very similar to the men she witnessed rampaging through Cologne on New Year's Eve.
www.sueddeutsche.de/panorama/koeln-ich-habe-noch-nie-so-viele-heulende-maedchen-gesehen-1.2806316

Clothes-tearing animals
Another terrified young German woman told police of an assault by an aggressive group of 40-100 foreign men who

swarmed her and reportedly tried to claw at and rip off her clothes leaving "her pantyhose and panties almost completely torn from her body."
http://www.express.de/koeln/koeln-sexuelle-uebergriffe--opfer-erzaehlt-vom-horror-am-hauptbahnhof-23252186

Over and over and over again
This scenario apparently repeated itself *dozens and dozens and dozens and dozens* of times throughout the night. Even a policewoman was reportedly sexually molested. Kölner Express quoted one investigator as saying that "the female victims were so badly pushed about, they had heavy bruises on their breasts and behinds."

Hamburg too
And don't think it was an isolated event. The BBC reported that "In Hamburg several women told police that gangs of foreign men had molested and robbed them on New Year's Eve on the Reeperbahn - a street known for its boisterous night life." The Wall Street Journal reported that "In Hamburg, where similar assaults took place on the same night, police said they had received 53 complaints by January 6, 2016 of which 39 included women reporting being sexually assaulted." Three days later, the number of crime reports filed by women coming forward had more than doubled to 108. Days later, they would top 133 reported criminal attacks.
http://www.bbc.com/news/world-europe-35231046http://www.wsj.com/articles/german-authorities-investigating-three-in-connection-with-new-years-eve-assaults-1452091543
http://www.rp-online.de/panorama/deutschland/sexuelle-uebergriffe-an-silvester-in-hamburg-zahl-der-anzeigen-springt-auf-ueber-100-aid-1.5678508

***Women-hunting* sex packs**
In their article "Sex-pack went women-hunting in Hamburg," news giant Bild reported that after midnight groups of 5-15 mostly young North African men hunted down German girls to assault and rob. One terrified teenage girl said "girls were chased like cattle. That such a thing is possible in Hamburg,

makes me stunned. You are afraid to go out and celebrate in your own neighborhood."

At a Hamburg New Year's market, two young schoolgirls (ages 16 and 17) found themselves in a world of trouble as they described "being hunted" by young Arabic-looking foreign men who first tripped them and then grabbed at them. "We were completely in panic, hands were touching us all over. When you pushed one hand away, there was another one suddenly back on the same place. They were grabbing us on our breasts, crotch and backsides."

The mobs of young men prowling through Hamburg first called the girls sexist slurs, then "rounded them up, robbed them and assaulted their breasts and groins."

Police reported writing up reports from girls 18-24 years of age. More reports were expected although it was noted that some women may never come forward from "shame."
http://www.bild.de/regional/hamburg/sexuelle-belaestigung/auf-der-reeperbahn-44017940.bild.html

Wonderful night turns horrific
Spiegel Online detailed the experiences of a 19-year-old German girl who was out celebrating New Year's Eve in Hamburg in a chic club dress and high heels.

The nicely dressed teenager and her girlfriends were walking on a street when a group of 20-30 "foreign men" surrounded them, blocked them, separated them, and began sexually assaulting them.

The girl said she screamed and cried, and "felt helpless" as many men reached under her dress, groped her, pulled her around by the hair, and eventually threw her to the ground. She escaped and met up with her distraught and disheveled girlfriends who all reported having been similarly assaulted.

The girls filed police reports but couldn't provide exact descriptions of the mob attackers.

Another witness said that he observed an attack on three blonde women by a gang, and then, within minutes, he saw multiple additional sexual attacks of women by groups of men who groped them and grabbed at their breasts.

Several 23-year-old German girls out at the Jungfernstieg, Hamburg's foremost promenade and boulevard, reported being sexually groped a half dozen times *each* by large groups of foreign men while making their way to the subway station. As they screamed, the men allegedly yelled "You bitch, shut up!" The girl said she'd never experienced anything so horrifying in her life.
http://www.spiegel.de/panorama/justiz/silvester-in-hamburg-betroffene-und-augenzeugen-berichten-a-1070590.html

Düsseldorf too
Police in Düsseldorf reported some attacks on women but they thought more women may come forward. In one case, two women (25 and 26) were near the train station where 300 migrants had assembled. The women were quickly surrounded by several men from the larger group who groped their bodies and then tried to rob them. The young men were described as "dark-skinned and speaking broken German." In another incident involving members of a 20-man gang, two women were allegedly harassed and groped before they ran away from their attackers who reportedly spoke broken German.

Stuttgart too
In Stuttgart things were no better, if only on a bit smaller scale. Less than a week after New Year's Eve, news source FTF1 reported that Stuttgart police had received at least a dozen reports of assault from women ranging in age from 16-25 perpetrated by "Arab-looking young men." One suspect was under arrest, an Iraqi asylum seeker. Police reported that they had arrested, based on witness statements, a "20-year-old man

who is said to have sexually molested two young girls aged 15 to 18 years."

According to police, "Arab-looking young men" would surround women, prevent them from moving, harass them, sexually assault them, and rob them mostly of cell phones and purses.

German news agency Bild reported that a group of about 15 Arabic-looking men met up at the Stuttgart square and "despite the fact that thousands of people were around, had grabbed a group of 18-year-old girls who they groped on their crotches."

Who would punch a young girl in the face?
UnserTirol24 covered another attack in their article "Young Girl Badly Beaten." A 24-year-old German girl was celebrating New Year's Eve with friends when some foreign young men ("immigrants" according to the victim's father) apparently approached the young woman and her girlfriend, made aggressive sexual advances, verbally abused them, and then allegedly threatened them. *Par for the course, as we've seen.*

The young German fellas with the girls were outnumbered and when they tried to defend the honor of the girls, were attacked by the foreigners. One of the Germans was beaten and smashed so hard in the head with a glass, that he required stitches.

As the German women tried to leave, the young foreign men followed them and beat one girl to the ground, leaving her in the street bloodied with a "broken and cracked" nose and bruises.

The girl's father reported that her "broken and cracked" nose also required stitches, that her eyes were swollen almost completely closed, but that the rest of her face and head luckily didn't require surgery and, "She was alive."
http://www.rtf1.de/news.php?id=12054
http://www.unsertirol24.com/2016/01/04/junge-frau-arg-zugerichtet/

Berlin too

Berliner Morgenpost reported that while not on the scale of Hamburg, Berlin did have a rash of sexual assaults on women on New Year's Eve.

At least three "sexual harassments" occurred near Berlin's world famous Brandenburg Gate. Police confirmed that they arrested "two men from Iraq and Pakistan. Both are reported in a refugee camp." Police noted that another woman, a tourist, had been sexually assaulted by 3-5 foreign men. Another woman reported being groped and molested by a group of men "in front of a music stage on the festival mile." And several more women came forward to report sexual assaults that police were still in the process of investigating.
http://www.morgenpost.de/berlin/article206892155/Sexuelle-Uebergriffe-zu-Silvester-auch-in-Berlin.html

Asylum-seeker evidence abounds

In the attack *in* Cologne on a German girl *from* Stuttgart, police reported making arrests of a group of about 8 young men who "were carrying residence certificates for asylum procedures."
http://www.express.de/koeln/sexuelle-uebergriffe-polizist--so-brutal-war-das-chaos-am-koelner-hbf-an-silvester-23252866

Sweden, Finland, Switzerland, and Austria too

Of course, it won't surprise you to learn that the New Year's Eve sexual assaults were not isolated to Germany.

Calling it unprecedented, police in **Finland** reported a *never-before-seen sexual assault spree* on New Year's Eve carried out by asylum seekers. Helsinki's deputy police chief reported that "there hasn't been this kind of harassment on previous New Year's Eves or other occasions for that matter... This is a **completely new phenomenon of sex crimes** in Helsinki." Apparently about 1,000 primarily Iraqi asylum seekers converged on the Helsinki train station and sexually assaulted and harassed women.
http://www.afp.com/en/news/unprecedented-sex-harassment-helsinki-new-year-police

Six women reported being "sexually molested and robbed while celebrating the New Year in Zurich" **Switzerland** by "dark-skinned men." Police said the women had been groped and robbed by "groups of men."
http://www.swissinfo.ch/eng/new-year-crime_zurich-women-report-cologne-style-sex-attacks/41880556

In Kalmar, **Sweden**, on New Year's Eve, more than a dozen young women, ages 17-21, were reportedly sexually molested. Some were reportedly assaulted by a group of young foreign males who spoke no Swedish. A 15-year-old and a 20-year-old suspect had been arrested. Of course, Swedish authorities seemed to make light of the attacks in relation to the attacks in Germany. *Never blame the migrants!*
http://www.aftonbladet.se/nyheter/article22054659.ab
http://www.thelocal.se/20160108/swedish-police-probe-new-year-sex-assaults

In **Austria**, police reportedly tried to "protect" migrants from revenge attacks by initially **covering up** many migrant-perpetrated sex assaults that occurred on New Year's Eve. Groups of young foreign men would surround and trap girls, grope, assault, and rob them. One incident seemed to be rather representative. A group of girls reported being sexually assaulted by a group of 10-15 foreign men near Salzberg. Without warning, the gang of men screamed as they ran the girls down, surrounding them and grabbing them. One witness stated that "one of (the foreigners) put my girlfriend in a headlock. He... licked her face. She said that she had no strength to free herself, she was completely at his mercy." When the women posted their experiences on social media, they learned that the problem was widespread. Other women reported being sexually harassed by Afghan and Syrian migrants at various locations. Many incidents also involved robberies of purses and cell phones. One terrified girl reported almost being abducted by a group of foreign men save for the intervention of a passerby.
http://www.oe24.at/oesterreich/chronik/Sex-Mob-wuetet-auch-in-Oesterreich/218780106

Geez. What is the common thread? I can't figure it out...

Now don't you go jumping to conclusions about the attackers being asylum seekers or refugees or migrants. That would make you a racist xenophobe psycho!

It's not refugees who were the problem according to bureaucrats. The politicos, who held the doors open for migrants, instantly blamed the police for their inability to control the rampaging foreigners.

Oh, it wasn't the fault of rampaging foreigners, it was the fault of the overwhelmed police. Hmmm. How fair is that?

Amateur denial
Germany's Interior Minister, Thomas de Maiziere, was quoted as saying "you cannot draw a general suspicion against refugees from the indications that they were perhaps people who looked North African."

Expert denial
Henriette Reker, the mayor of Cologne (who had been reportedly stabbed in the neck several months prior by a mysterious unemployed Cologne painter living on welfare in what police called a "racist" and "political" attack), said there was *no* reason to believe refugees had anything to do with the unprecedented violence, mayhem, crime, attacks, and assaults in Cologne on New Year's Eve. Reker added that "We need to prevent confusion here, about what constitutes happy behavior and what is utterly separate from openness, especially in sexual behavior." We can't even begin to guess what Riker meant by that – maybe the assaulted women were at fault for confusing the foreign young men? Riker wouldn't try and blame the victims, would she? *Next paragraph.*

Reker the perpetual excuse-maker
For those who thought there may be some redeeming qualities to Reker, all hope was dashed when, several days after the

mass attacks, Reker responded to a question about *what women can do to better protect themselves* by posting this gem on social media – "There is always the possibility of keeping a certain distance, more than an arm's length, from strangers."

Oh, so it was the *victims'* faults. They just let the criminals get too close. Silly girls. Now *that* makes sense. So when a gang of 30-40 men surround you, rob you, and sexually assault you, all you need to do is stay more than an arm's length away from them... *Seriously? Yeah, whatever. A dope is a dope. Up is down. Red is green. There were no "refugees" involved, just refugees...*
At a certain point, you either wake up, take responsibility for the shape you're in, and fix things, or you continue to make up lies and excuses as you justify watching yourself keel over.

As this book went to print, German police were admitting that the "majority" of sex attackers were refugees. Other groups denied that refugees were responsible. But after reading this book, you probably guessed this already.

Rape-fugees not welcome
One last media propaganda spin example.

The old-fashioned-controlled-media was out in full force desperately attempting to spin the "attacks." When thousands of German people took to the streets on January 10, 2016, to protest the barbaric assaults on their women, the old-fashioned-controlled-media saw its chance.

Reporting from Cologne, Germany, CNN seemed to frame the anti-assault protest story in such a way as to make the Germans protesting against the sexual assaults of their women look like angry, unruly, criminal xenophobes.

Here is what CNN reported: "There's a lot of anger... this is what this is, a lot of anger... These assaults have... fed into the fears of people and it's given them an excuse, an opportunity to... vent their frustrations, their fears and their angers."

Three uses of the word "anger" within seconds. Pummeling a derogatory label. That's classic Soviet-era propaganda!

Let's see what else we can find.

"These assaults have...fed into the fears" implies that the assaults were 'no big deal' but they were being used to fuel people already filled with fear (usually a propaganda code phrase to describe ignorant, less advanced people – 'full of fear' of technology, fire, the unknown, strangers, whatever – and the implication is always that the 'fear' is some sort of 'irrational' fear born of something along the lines of hatred or ignorance or racism) and "it's given them an excuse, an opportunity to... vent their frustrations, their fears and their angers" implies that something negative is happening therefore the "excuse" comment (for example, the media went along with the WMD Weapons of Mass Destruction lie which gave countries the 'excuse' to invade other countries) and the "opportunity" comment (used in a negative sense such as the criminal saw an 'opportunity' to assault his victim) leading to the "frustrations, fears, angers" trifecta, labelling the protesters as bad.

CNN continued: "Using beer bottles that are being thrown, using fireworks, using slogans and big signs that say 'Refugees not welcome' ... one of them said 'Rape-fugees not welcome...'"

Were actual 'beer' bottles being thrown, or just bottles? In either case, was that a smear tactic to imply both violence (throwing bottles) and that the protesters were just "drunken" Germans who should be shunned?

Amazingly, CNN didn't bother to speak to any of the protesters for this segment to find out what they were upset about... Everything was interpreted for us against the backdrop of a police water cannon vehicle spraying people.

The mention of 'fireworks' sounds suspiciously like an attempt to paint a parallel between the migrants who shot fireworks at innocent civilians, police, and property, and these demonstrators. Are viewers being conditioned to see these demonstrators in the same way as the migrants?

CNN went on: "So there is that boiling anger that's now surfacing... this... is a small segment of German society but it is a very vocal one..."

Boiling anger? What boiling anger? Says who? CNN? And the implication is what? That these protesters are 'unjustified' at being upset that hundreds of their women were sexually assaulted by gangs of foreign men? That if migrants commit horrific assaults, that you have no right to be upset? And if you are upset, then you are just as bad as the assaulters?

Seriously?

CNN continued: "On the other side of the station we see 1,700 protesters in *support* of those victims of the assaults, in support of continuing to open the doors to refugees, but what this kind of tension shows is that deep divide in society..."

First of all, the video-report showed no other protesters even though CNN said "on the other side... we see 1,700 protesters." Guess we'll just take their word for it.

In a classic Soviet-era propaganda technique...'if one side is Pro the other must be Anti'... CNN claims the 'other' protesters are protesting in support of *the assault victims. So do they expect us to draw the conclusion that the current protesters must be anti-assault victims? What hogwash!*

CNN then claims this 'tension' reveals a 'deep divide in society.' Well, yeah, if a deep divide means certain migrants have no respect for European women, European laws, and European values. And that before the migrants were welcomed into the country, sexual assault crimes on this scale NEVER EVER happened. Then, yes, a huge divide exists.

As the police used water cannons on German protesters, CNN added, "This is their (police) way of saying, stop this protest, we will disperse (you) if this behavior is continuing..."

Where were the police with their tear gas and water cannons when hundreds of German women were being assaulted? Is it now permissible to attack and harass your own concerned and outraged residents while treating foreign migrants with kid gloves? Where was all the detailed CNN coverage when this New Year's Eve unprecedented mass sexual assault was developing?

"Refugees Welcome Event" cover-up
Here's a story that came to light *only* after the massive New Year's Eve sex attacks. It had been intentionally hidden from the public until one of the victims finally broke her silence...

What better way to welcome the refugees, those poor beleaguered victims of horrible events, than a friendly welcome event? And why not go all out and hold it on a yacht with a load of friendly welcoming German coeds?

You just know this won't end well.

On November 7, 2015, young German coeds were among those that hosted a "Welcome Refugees" event held on a boat. An attendee estimated that there were 100-150 "asylum seekers" at the event.

Things turned bad almost immediately.

One of the young victims reported, "I'd only been there a few minutes, and I got the first hand on my breast." Things got seriously dangerous in seconds as sexual groping escalated to the point where the victim reported that "up to four men were pressing themselves on me and my friend at the same time."

Young women guests fled the event in terror as gangs of migrants sexually assaulted girls without shame. Police reported that it was so bad that the people running the event kept stopping the music to make announcements in Arabic to tell the migrants to stop sexually assaulting women. *And yet event organizers never called the police for help!* Ignoring the victims, were the organizers scared of being labeled racists? Or were they terrified of going against the official fairytale?

Don't make a fuss
The German official in charge of migrant integration in the area "admitted organizers knew about the sex attacks at the event but did not want to make a fuss." Nauseatingly, she reportedly couldn't remember if she had advised the women that had been sexually attacked to make police reports or not. She did, however, say that she felt the "event's student organizers 'had learned from the situation.'"

Learned what? That you are a complete reckless moron?

There is no hope...
http://www.express.co.uk/news/world/634815/Cologne-attacks-fury-migrant-sex-cover-up-refugee-event-groping-Germany

It's just taharrush
More and more people were hearing about "taharrush." It refers to a group sexual attack where a crowd of males surround a woman and then sexually assault and violate her. In 2011, CBS reporter Lara Logan went public when she was a victim of taharrush while covering a news story in Egypt. Horrifically, Logan said 200-300 Egyptian men surrounded her and brutally sexually assaulted her for about a half hour, even snapping shots with their cellphones, before she was rescued.

More and more instances of taharrush assaults are being seen in Europe as migrants from North Africa, where taharrush is "common," move in. Of course, New Year's Eve in Cologne was the worst multiple taharrush attacks in Europe so far. *So far.*
http://www.cbsnews.com/videos/lara-logan-breaks-her-silence/

Muslim imam in Cologne explains everything

In an exclusive Russian media interview, an imam from Cologne told RENTV that people "need to react to the events properly" and shouldn't add "fuel to the fire." According to the reporter, the imam recapped main points from one of his recent sermons on the topic. In the segment, it was made clear that the essence of the message was that the "European girls were at fault," "they had brought the attacks on themselves," and the imam specifically said that one of the reasons for the New Year's Eve attacks was that German girls "weren't sufficiently clothed, wore perfume, and so things happened."
http://ren.tv/novosti/2016-01-17/imam-mecheti-v-kyolne-poyasnil-chto-bezhency-nasiluyut-nemok-iz-za-ih-priyatnogo

Is Merkel suffering from amnesia? Or mental incapacity?

Way back in June 2011, before she threw her gates wide open, Angela Merkel was featured in a video message addressing integration, youth crime, and violence in Germany saying that,

> "We have to accept that criminal activity for young immigrants is particularly high."

Particularly high?? And Merkel knew this *before* she opened the floodgates?? *Recklessness has met its match...*

So why Merkel did, *and is doing what she's doing*, without proper planning and protection, is the enigma of the decade. But just like with nuclear fallout, the lingering consequences of her actions have the real potential to live on for centuries, and to affect people that haven't yet been born. Maybe they should get Elba cleaned up and ready for a new despot-in-exile. Be sure and paint the walls of her room red. It will probably be of comfort to the former uniform-wearing-Communist...
http://www.welt.de/politik/deutschland/article13437128/Merkel-beklagt-hohe-Zahl-von-Migranten-Straftaten.html

600,000 missing

Fortunately, in mid-January 2016 the Interior Ministry of Germany admitted that it had lost track of 600,000 asylum seekers. The UK Express reported that "The German government has admitted it cannot locate more than half of the one million asylum seekers allowed into the country."

"Terrifying" doesn't do this justice.

Merkel's crazy drive to quickly scoop up over 1.1 million migrants has yielded only about 476,649 who have actually registered for asylum. More than 600,000 people are unaccounted for according to the German government. No matter what clever excuses and explanations Merkel and her comrades concoct using propaganda and agitation skills, that's simply *uber* bad!
http://www.express.co.uk/news/world/636997/Germany-where-asylum-seekers

More serious problems unearthed
In January 2016, police in Cologne investigating the New Year's Eve mass sex attacks raided some migrant shelters, and they discovered that
 a) most migrants they questioned claimed to be Syrian, but were in fact African
 b) 50% had registered *twice* on the refugee quota list
 c) some migrants had upwards of 4 or 5 fake identities

And that is from just one tiny sample of the multitudes of Merkel's "Syrian refugees." *Most of whom may not even be Syrian! When will everyone realize just how badly the people of Germany and Europe have been merkeled?*
http://www.express.co.uk/news/world/636997/Germany-where-asylum-seekers

Migrants seem to assimilate well with lawyers
In the meanwhile, on January 21, 2016, the UK Express reported that "More than 200 migrants in (Germany) have launched a lawsuit against the Federal Office for Migration and Refugees because they have been waiting over a year for a decision on whether they can stay in the country." Expect far

more of the same as these economic opportunists start to flex their muscles with the help of their eager attorneys.
http://www.express.co.uk/news/world/636690/migrants-SUING-German-government-asylum-process

American presidential candidate captures the moment
Billionaire and real estate mogul Donald Trump may have said it best when he remarked,

> "I used to think that Merkel was some sort of strong leader. What Merkel has done in Europe is insane."

> "Do you see what she's (Merkel) done to Germany? ... the rapes, the riots, what's happening is unbelievable. It's unbelievable. Unthinkable!... Hundreds and hundreds of rapes on New Year's Eve... Germany?!! They have a problem. She (Merkel) went off the reservation... I don't know what happened to her... the crime is astronomical... it's not working... they're having riots now in the streets and the German people are saying *'We've had it! We've had it!'*"

That's exactly right.

The German people "have had it." And the European people "have had it." *Everyone* has had it!

Now, what exactly needs to be done to make it right again?

In the meanwhile, *Hasta la Vista, Europe!* Good luck.

It's been real.

http://www.dw.com/en/attack-on-cologne-mayoral-candidate-motivated-by-xenophobia/a-18788902
http://www.stuttgartdailyleader.com/article/ZZ/20160106/NEWS/301069955
http://www.zerohedge.com/news/2016-01-13/rapes-riots-trump-blasts-merkels-immigration-policy

Printed in Great Britain
by Amazon